D0397107

The Analytic Attitude

THE ANALYTIC ATTITUDE

Roy Schafer

Basic Books, Inc., Publishers

NEW YORK

Library of Congress Cataloging in Publication Data

Schafer, Roy.
  The analytic attitude.

  Bibliography: p. 297
  Includes index.
  1. Psychoanalysis—Addresses, essays, lectures.
I. Title. [DNLM: 1. Psychoanalysis. 2. Psychoanalytic
therapy. 3. Psychoanalytic interpretation. WM 460
S296ac]
RC509.S347 1982   616.89′17   82-16245
ISBN 0-465-00267-6

To Helen

Contents

Preface

It is my aim in this book to clarify the intellectual and emotional attitude adopted by the analyst at work. I take up neutrality, discipline, empathy, authenticity, fidelity to a system of psychoanalytic thought and practice, and the tensions inherent in the analyst's professional development and daily work. I also look as deeply as I now can into the nature of psychoanalytic interpretation. I focus not so much on the content of interpretation of the sort one finds in textbooks that deal narrowly with technique or with specific theories of psychical development or psychopathology; much more, I focus on the presuppositions of making any interpretation at all, the structure and logical justification of interpretation, the ways in which interpretation is a form of narration through creating life histories and treatment histories, and the ways in which it is circular and self-confirming but not on *cf Heidegger* that account foolish, false, or unhelpful. Much neglected by analytic *on truth* theorists and teachers of technique, the theory of interpretation makes clear just what kind of work one does in doing analysis. So long as the theory of interpretation continues to be neglected, our understanding of the major cognitive aspect of the analytic attitude will remain in a primitive state, and the further result will be the needless controversy, dogmatism, and self-misunderstanding that, in my view, characterize a good deal of psychoanalytic discussion.

In order to arrive at an understanding of the analytic attitude, however, one must consider it in relation to the ways in which analysands continuously and necessarily challenge it. Analysands mount these challenges in the form of their transferences, their resistances, and their rigid adherence to disruptive character traits owing to their unconsciously maintaining certain infantile fantasies, theories, and convictions about themselves and others. Upon being analyzed rather than responded to in their own terms, all of these challenges are shown to be ways in which analysands provide the essential material for their analyses; thereby they also establish a basis for significant beneficial personal change. In order to show how this is so, I include in this book on the analytic attitude discussions of transference, resistance, character, fantasy, and the Unconscious or what (in later chapters) I call the second reality of psychoanalysis. Constructed in the analytic dialogue rather than simply uncovered or encountered by the analyst, this second reality is concrete, fluid, timeless, magical, passionately wishful, desperately frightened, and replete with subtle compromises. In maintaining the analytic attitude, the analyst is prepared for the arduous and exciting job of participating in the construction and reconstruction of this second reality, and through that, helping the analysand grow beyond the narrow and painful confines of his or her disturbed life.

The chapters that make up this book are grounded in practice. They all include examples of clinical phenomena, problems, and interpretive activity. And all of them are cast essentially in the language of action. This is the language I worked out in previous books and papers and that here I review and apply to such basic concepts as conflict, anxiety, danger situation, and defense; also, mental structure, character, and the self; additionally, free association, transference, and resistance; and further, fantasy, psychical reality, and reality testing. Taken together, these chapters, though they do not add up to a set of instructions on how to do analysis, should be useful in developing further the foundations of all psychoanalytic clinical work. They should be useful as well in developing the foundations of a modern epistemology for psychoanalysis and, in tandem with that, developing a much needed discipline of comparative psychoanalysis.

Roughly half the material in this book has never before been published. What has been published is scattered in a number of journals, only some of which are readily accessible to most readers. This published material has been revised: in some instances slightly, in others extensively. A section on technique has been added to the chapter on character. A few of the titles have been altered. Useless repetition has been eliminated along with comments specific to the special occasions on which some of this material was first presented. In some places the wording has been changed to achieve greater clarity and consistency of exposition. In some places misleading or confusing statements or turns in the argument have been changed or deleted. One paper has been divided in two. Some footnotes have been eliminated and others moved into the text. Some transitional material has been introduced in order to unify the book. But in no case has the basic argument of a previously published essay been significantly altered.

I want to mention with pride and gratitude that portions of this book were written in response to special invitations: chapter 5, as the inaugural Bernard Thomson Memorial Lecture at North Shore Memorial Hospital; chapter 7, as a featured address at the fiftieth anniversary celebration of the Menninger Clinic (where I began my clinical career); chapter 8, as the twenty-first Rado Lecture before the Association for Psychoanalytic Medicine in association with the Columbia University Center for Psychoanalytic Training and Research (where I am now a member of the faculty); chapter 10, as part of the program of the fiftieth anniversary celebration of the founding of the Chicago Institute for Psychoanalysis; and the greater part of chapter 16, as the thirty-second Freud Anniversary Lecture before the New York Psychoanalytic Institute. I have earned these honors by continuing in the tradition of my principal teacher during the early years of my professional career, the late Dr. David Rapaport, one of the great psychoanalytic theorists. Often he referred to his work as thinking about thinking; he could envision nothing more worthwhile. Although I have not maintained his specific and intense commitment to the systematization of psychoanalytic metapsychology, I have, with his unflagging encouragement in my psychical reality, continued to do what he did: think about thinking, now, however, in connection with the clinical analyst at work.

ROY SCHAFER
New York City, 1982

Acknowledgments

I thank a number of editors for permission to print articles that appeared first in their journals:

1. Chapter 4, "Appreciation in the Analytic Attitude," is the first part and chapter 13, "The Construction of Multiple Histories," is the latter part of an article entitled "The Appreciative Analytic Attitude and the Construction of Multiple Histories," which appeared in *Psychoanalysis and Contemporary Thought* 2: 3–24, 1979.

2. Chapter 6, "Conflict as Paradoxical Actions," appeared in *Psychoanalysis and Contemporary Thought* 1: 3–19, 1978.

3. Chapter 7, "Danger Situations," is reprinted with permission from the *Bulletin of the Menninger Clinic* 40 (5): 459–478, copyright © 1976, The Menninger Foundation.

4. Chapters 8 and 9 appeared in the *Journal of the American Psychoanalytic Association:* chapter 8, "The Interpretation of Transference and the Conditions for Loving," in 25: 335–362, 1977, and chapter 9, "The Analysis of Character," under the title of "Character, Ego-Syntonicity, and Character Change," in 27: 867–891, 1979.

5. The section on technique in chapter 9 appeared in the *Bulletin of the Association for Psychoanalytic Medicine* (March 1982) 21: 91–99, under the title "Problems of Technique in Character Analysis."

6. Chapter 12, entitled "Psychoanalytic Reconstruction," appeared under the title "The Relevance of the 'Here and Now' Transference Interpretation to the Reconstruction of Early Development," in *The International Journal of Psycho-Analysis* 63: 77–83, 1982.

7. Chapter 14, "Narration in the Psychoanalytic Dialogue," appeared in *Critical Inquiry* 7: 29–53, 1980.

8. Chapter 15, "Action and Narration in Psychoanalysis," appeared in *New Literary History* 12: 61–85, 1980–81.

9. Chapter 17, "On Becoming a Psychoanalyst of One Persuasion or Another," appeared in *Contemporary Psychoanalysis* 15: 354–360, 1979.

I wish to thank Jane Isay, co-publisher of Basic Books and editor of my two previous books, *A New Language for Psychoanalysis* and *Language and Insight*, who encouraged and counseled me in her usual kind, appreciative, and helpful manner. My thanks go, too, to Linda Carbone, project editor of this book.

The Analytic Attitude

1
The Analytic Attitude: An Introduction

The analytic attitude ranks as one of Freud's greatest creations. If the analyst is to provide the analysand with the best chance for a searching and beneficial analysis, then he or she must maintain this attitude with a high degree of consistency. Both the findings of psychoanalysis as a method of investigation and its results as a method of treatment depend on this consistency. But what is the analytic attitude? Something so important should be formulated in a relatively concise, complex, and generally acceptable way, yet we have no such formulation. None was offered by Freud, though a version of his ideas on the analytic attitude can be derived from his papers on technique (see chapter 2), especially when these papers are considered in the context of all his works.

Over the years, many other analysts have published significant contributions to this topic. Typically they have done so in connection with their discussions of analytic technique. From a very long list of notable contributions of this sort, I wish to mention those made by Sandor Ferenczi, Karl Abraham, Anna Freud, Melanie Klein, Wilhelm Reich, Otto Fenichel, Edward Glover, John Strachey, Ella Freeman Sharpe, Theodor Reik, Ernst Kris, Rudolph Loewenstein, Annie Reich, Edith Jacobson, Kurt Eissler, Ralph Greenson, Leo Stone, Jacob Arlow, Charles Brenner, Merton Gill, and Heinz Kohut. But it must be noted that this rich literature presents difficulties. For one thing, the chief emphases in these contributions are not always the same, there being variation, for example, with respect to the desirability of the analyst's maintaining emotional detachment, making early, deep interpretations, and focusing intensively on transference. Emphases also vary on manifesting a caretaking and self-expressive humanness, engaging in forceful and dramatic confrontations, and centering attention on the uses and significance of empathy. For another thing, in many instances the relevance of these discussions to the analytic attitude, being only implicit, must be teased out, and so may be construed differently by different readers. And finally, some of these technical contributions are more controversial than others, or at least are more difficult to include in a general synthesis.

But it is not only in writings on technique that one may find contributions to a formulation of the analytic attitude, for this attitude is often beautifully exemplified in analytic writings on psychological development, psychopathology, general theory, the theory of the analytic process, and applications to the humanities. Here, the names of Erik Erikson, D. W. Winnicott, Heinz Hartmann, and Hans Loewald, to name now only a few of many, may be added to those already mentioned. In these writings the analytic attitude is exemplified in the kinds of questions that are raised, the evidence that is selected, the clear-sighted and balanced way in which it is interpreted and integrated, and the individualized evocative mode of expression ("the voice") that has been cultivated. Thus the psychoanalytic literature as a whole may be read from the point of view of what it can teach about the analytic attitude. Again, however, there are difficulties. One finds variation with respect to what should be taken as the major features of the analytic attitude, in addition to which some of these exemplifications are more open to theoretical controversy than others or present more obstacles to a general synthesis.

Could it be that what stands in the way of a satisfactory formulation of the analytic attitude is a problem that is more fundamental than anything that has yet been mentioned? Analytic pedagogy suggests that there is such a problem. It has become a pedagogical commonplace to acknowledge that, as a rule, students learn more about the analytic attitude from undergoing their own personal analyses and the supervision of their clinical work than they do from case seminars, more from case seminars than from didactic courses on technique and the theory of the analytic process, and more from these didactic courses than from independent reading. This commonplace recognizes how much always depends on context, most of all on the concrete context made up by the individual analyst and analysand, the nature of the problems being analyzed, and the phase of the analysis under discussion. Consequently, the project of presenting a definitive set of generalizations about the analytic attitude cannot be undertaken very hopefully, for these generalizations will serve only as the roughest of guidelines for sorting out, one from the other, the full, the compromised, and the failed analytic attitude. Moreover, a set of such gener-

4

alizations cannot fail to sound like an overblown admonition to be a good analyst.

Now, it need not be argued that doing analysis is taxing intellectually and emotionally and that, as this work is done by human beings who, fortunately, are neither machines, saints, nor romantic heroes, it is not to be expected that in each and every case the analyst will function impeccably from beginning to end. But to recognize human limitation and variability is not to conclude that it is useless or foolish to attempt to set forth standards of excellence for analytic work. Nor is it to come to the conclusion that formulating the ideal analytic attitude is equivalent to idealizing, platitudinizing, or being oppressively perfectionistic. For it is on the individual analyst's efforts to approximate this ideal that the beneficial effects of analyzing largely depend, and in the final analysis it is these individual efforts which must concern us. Therefore it seems to me that it will be worth the effort and the risk to introduce the chapters that make up this book with a brief outline of my conception of the analytic attitude. The chapters themselves will have to bear most of the burden of exemplifying this conception. Ultimately, it is concrete exemplification that counts.

The Analyst Maintains an Attitude of Neutrality

The analyst remains neutral in relation to every aspect of the material being presented by the analysand. This is material that is presented not only verbally but nonverbally, not only consciously but preconsciously and unconsciously, and not only in great distress but some times blithely or blandly. In his or her neutrality, the analyst does not crusade for or against the so-called id, superego, or defensive ego. The analyst has no favorites and so is not judgmental. The analyst's position is, as Anna Freud (1936) put it, "equidistant" from the various forces at war with one another.

The simplistic, partisan analyst, working in terms of saints and sinners, victims and victimizers, or good and bad ways to live, is failing to maintain the analytic attitude. In this failure, he or she can only be encouraging the analysand to fixate on some pattern of paranoid and depressive orientations, to persevere in sado-masochistic fantasizing and acting out, or to engage in wholesale repression of disturbing factors.

In contrast, the analyst who remains neutral is attempting to allow all of the conflictual material to be fully represented, interpreted, and worked through. The neutral analyst is also attempting to avoid both the imposition of his or her own personal values on the analysand and the unquestioning acceptance of the analysand's initial value judgments. In addition, the neutral analyst is being unpresumptuous, for it is a plain fact that for a very long time very little is known or understood well enough to warrant the analyst's forming any opinion at all on the desirability or undesirability of one or another course of action or mode of experience. (The exception being only that there are rough guidelines for what may seriously disrupt the continuity or effectiveness of the analysis or threaten the basic welfare of the analysand. These factors include the analysand's constant precipitation of life crises, prolonged absences, nonpayment of fees, acts of gross delinquency, physical illness, toxicity, suicidal depression, schizophrenic regression, etc.)

Owing to his or her recognition that over the course of an analysis the analysand will present highly selective and changing pictures of other people, the neutral analyst remains nonjudgmental about these others, too. It is particularly important to maintain this neutrality in relation to parental figures and spouses, for to some extent the analysand is identified with them and is vulnerable to the same value judgments that may be passed on them. Also, the analysand may be referring to other people in order to represent indirectly, as in a dream, some disturbing feature of his or her own self. For this reason, too, the analyst must take care to regard these others neutrally. But the effort to remain neutral toward all parties concerned should not lead the analyst to avoid looking at things honestly and, when appropriate, taking them up forthrightly with the analysand. It is not a departure from neutrality to call a spade a spade.

To achieve neutrality requires a high degree of subordination of the analyst's personality to the analytic task at hand. Subordination of personality is not to be understood as making misguided, futile, and phobically aseptic efforts at elimination of personality, as in total nonexpressiveness. It is to be understood in terms of the analyst's appropriate moderation, regulation, and often simply curtailment of any show of activity of a predominantly narcissistic sort. Narcissistic activity both implies and readily makes for disruptive countertransference reactions. It is the sort of activity through which the analyst tries to cure by "force of personality," or to "win at analysis" (as though at war), or to demonstrate analytic "genius" conclusively. Such vanity

6

and impatience obviously preclude maintaining the analytic attitude through appropriate subordination of personality. Another such interference lies in the analyst's adopting a condemning attitude toward that which is different, not readily understandable, or difficult. In this case the analyst too easily feels frustrated because the analysis is not developing in the wished-for or expected way, and so he or she is all too ready to become self-righteous and punitive. Additional problems of this sort stem from the analyst's insisting, in a blunt, rigid, and disrespectful way, on a few familiar lines of interpretation. For in being thus insistent the analyst is being a bully and is not allowing the analysand to explore freely and experience fully the complex network of derivatives of unresolved, unconsciously perpetuated, infantile issues. Because these are the issues in terms of which the analysand has been living his or her painful and limited existence, they must be helped to emerge into the light of analysis in their individualized forms.

A desirable degree of subordination of personality will be evident in the analyst's remaining curious, eager to find out, and open to surprise. It will be evident also in the analyst's taking nothing for granted (without being cynical about it), and remaining ready to revise conjectures or conclusions already arrived at, tolerate ambiguity or incomplete closure over extended periods of time, accept alternative points of view of the world, and bear and contain the experiences of helplessness, confusion, and aloneness that not infrequently mark periods of analytic work with each analysand.

The Analyst Avoids Either-Or Thinking

The analytic attitude is evident in the analyst's taking great care to avoid viewing significant problems and figures in either-or terms. For if there is anything that consistently characterizes psychoanalytic interpretation it is the analyst's recognition that multiple and often contradictory meanings and consequences may be usefully ascribed to one phenomenon, and that common meanings and consequences may be ascribed to apparently diverse phenomena. Much time in analysis is spent interpreting the analysand's need to see things as either black or white.

But progressive movement in analytic interpretation is not only toward increased complexity and tolerance of contradiction, it is also toward the greatest degree of particularity of that which is being explained. Freud (1909b) presented a model (one of many) of this blend of complexity and particularity in his account of the overdetermination of the Rat Man's rat complex. There, he returned again and again to the explanation of the choice of rats, striving to reach a point where he would be convinced that nothing else but rats would do for the cross-purposes of this man's obsessional neurosis. It is breathtaking to realize how long and how fruitfully he persevered.

The avoidance of either-or has been formalized in the principles of overdetermination (multiple meaningfulness of psychical phenomena) and multiple function (the interpretive focus on conflict and compromise formation within and among the so-called psychic structures—the id, the ego, and the superego). In another respect, the avoidance of either-or is based on the assumption that some degree of love-hate ambivalence characterizes every important activity and relationship.

If one takes seriously these principles of overdetermination, multiple function, and ambivalence, one can only judge it to be a failure of the analytic attitude to encounter an analyst speaking of what something "really" means. For to speak of the "real" meaning disregards these principles. The fact that one has discerned *further* meaning, *weightier* meaning, *more disturbing* meaning, *more archaic* meaning, or *more carefully disguised* meaning than that which first met the eye or the ear does not justify the claim that one has discovered the ultimate truth that lies behind the world of appearances—the "real" world. To make this claim is to engage in either-or thinking, and it is unanalytic in that no one feature of reality is any more real than another. The analytic attitude will be evident in the analyst's making a more modest as well as sounder claim, namely, that a point has now been reached in the analytic dialogue where reality must be formulated in a more subtle and complex manner than it has been before. At this point it is likely to be useful, even if difficult, for the analysand to give some sustained thought to this new development in the analytic material and not to be bound by versions of experience previously emphasized.

The Analyst Analyzes

The analyst's focus is on the interpretation of psychical reality. With this focus the analyst is not obliged to respond in kind to the analysand's emotional overtures. These overtures usually condense sexual and hostile as well as defensive and self-punitive features. They may take the form of rebellion or submission, control or helplessness, flattery or insult, excitement or lassitude, seductiveness or rejection, etc. The analyst's obligation is to analyze these overtures, particularly by interpreting their resistant and transferential origins, functions, and significance.

By not responding in kind I mean, for example, not meeting love with love or rejection or exploitation; not meeting anger with retaliation or self-justification or appeasement; and not meeting confidences with thanks or with self-revelations of one's own. As a rule, responding in kind impedes the work of analysis. Sometimes the analyst is in a position to interpret these overtures immediately; sometimes only after preparatory confrontation of the fact of emotional pressure on the analyst and after clarification of its occasion and its connections. Most often he or she can only do so by deferring any response at all until the pressure has taken definite form, reached noteworthy intensity, and led to its own clarification, through the delivery of further associations by the analysand, which is to say only after a period of careful listening by the analyst.

The analyst's ideal is to rely so far as possible on interpretation and careful preparation for interpretation through confrontation and clarification. This ideal will appear to be inhumanly rigid, exploitative, authoritarian, or unsupportive only to those who reject the general guidelines of psychoanalytic understanding and so do not appreciate the benefits ultimately to be derived from the analyst's consistently maintaining the analytic attitude. There does exist a stereotype of the Freudian analyst as one who maintains an arid, stiff, utterly impersonal atmosphere in the analytic session. But in fact there is always room in analytic work for courtesy, cordiality, gentleness, sincere empathic participation and comment, and other such personal, though not socially intimate, modes of relationship. These modes of relationship are recognized to be part of the preparation for interpretation in that they help develop an atmosphere of safety within which the analysand may begin to communicate that which is most distressing, exciting, secret, or conceptually unformed. In addition, these modes of relationship help the analyst to work in as relaxed and poised a fashion as possible.

Because it would fall within the province of technique to discuss fully how far one may go, and in which direction in order to prepare the way for interpretation, nothing of that sort will be developed here. But emphasizing the importance of careful preparation does belong to a formulation of the analytic attitude, and it is this consideration which warrants my saying that the analysis should take place in a context of unabashed, unfussy, untheatrical, and unhectoring human relatedness. This requirement holds even if most of that relatedness is shaped and limited by a radical division of labor between analyst and analysand. (As I said, the analyst is not obliged to respond in kind.) And this requirement holds even if at one time or another most of that specialized relatedness will itself be examined analytically as to what it implies for the analysand in the way of gratification, deprivation, and compromise.

In this respect, there is a tension in analytic work that can never be dispelled, nor should one try to dispel it. The question of preparation for interpretation introduces just one aspect of this general tension which may be summed up in the following way. Except with respect to relatively clearcut extremes, the analyst cannot know *exactly* just when, what, how, and how long to interpret, or, as the case may be, not to interpret but instead to listen or introduce some other type of intervention. As a rule, the meanings and effects of the analyst's interventions and silences may be adequately formulated only after the fact, if then. Will it be or was it "correct" to smile when saying hello or goodbye, to laugh at the analysand's joke, to ask or answer a particular question? Has the analyst persevered adequately in working through an issue interpretively before concluding that interpretation has reached its limits and that perhaps what Eissler (1953) called a parameter is now in order? Can the analyst be sure in advance what will be the "cost to the ego" (as Eissler called it) of each intervention or, I would add, nonintervention?

In these respects, it is not necessary that the analyst get obsessionally bogged down in doubt about what to do or how to be. For I do believe that much is already known about how to prepare the way for, and to arrive at, timely and plausible if not probably correct interpretations, and I also believe that what is known can be taught to students and consolidated and extended by them as they gain clinical experience. The fact remains, however, that analysts cannot avoid experiencing the tension of being required to act under conditions of incomplete understanding. They must be prepared to intervene interpretively and expressively (or to refrain from that) just in order to develop further whatever understanding they already believe has been achieved. The analyst who tries to avoid this tension rather than recognize and accept it as being one of the inherent features of analyt-

An Introduction

ic work is the analyst who is seriously involved in his or her illusions of omniscience, in either-or thinking, and in artificial impersonality.

A final word on the analyst as analyzer. Analyzing is not giving didactic instructions on how to be a "good" or comfortable analysand, nor is it teaching psychoanalytic generalizations about individual development or the way of the world. Certainly it is not giving advice and reassurance or issuing commands or prohibitions. As a rule, acting in any of these ways is neither analyzing nor preparing the way for interpretation. Most likely it is setting limits on what can be worked through later in the analysis. Consequently, such departures from the analytic attitude should be carefully limited. They may only be expressions of the analyst's narcissistically wishing to play guru. And the more the analyst plays guru, the more he or she reinforces the resistance to one important aspect of what remains to be analyzed more fully, namely, the analysand's presentation of a weak, empty, fragmented, "castrated," ego to the analyst in hopes of receiving his or her good ministrations (which, for the analysand, may be sadistic, rapacious, depriving, etc.). Freud (1919) noted long ago that one should never underestimate the human being's irresolution and craving for authority. One of the analyst's temptations, much played on by the irresolute analysand, is to purvey wisdom when it would be more appropriate to the job at hand to analyze wisely.

The Analyst Aims to Be Helpful

As has been mentioned, analytic help is offered not through advice, reassurance, exhortation, or other such measures, but so far as possible through careful listening and judicious and well-prepared interpretation. The help that is offered is help in understanding one's past and present life more fully in order to be able to change oneself for the better (however that may be individually worked out over the course of analysis).

Analysts do not view their role as one of offering or promising remedies, cures, complete mental health, philosophies of life, rescue, emergency-room intervention, emotional Band-Aids, or self-sacrificing or self-aggrandizing heroics. It is more than likely that each of these alternatives to a primarily interpretive approach manifests countertransference.

Well-prepared analysts expect analysands to respond ambivalently and resistantly to analytic help because, as I shall continue to emphasize, unconsciously analysands can only view understanding and changing as dangerous. Analysts know that their analysands will live up to their agreement to abide by the fundamental rule and other practical arrangements of analysis only in the compromised ways by which they characteristically live up to all their other significant agreements. They know that they will have to direct many of their interpretations at these compromised, conflictual, resistant ways of collaborating.[1] Consequently, analysts expect their work to be demanding, and they anticipate that it will require full use of their intelligence, tact, empathy, vigilance, interpretive ingenuity, and patience.

Because the analytic attitude, therefore, has no place in it for undue therapeutic or didactic zeal, it provides no *work-appropriate* opportunity for the analyst to feel frustrated, disappointed, or impatient. This is so with respect to the consequences of a single intervention, a single session, or the entire course of the analysis. The analyst expects to find out only as the work proceeds what can be accomplished analytically. It is therefore puzzling, to say the least, when one hears an analyst complain about an analysand while conveying no recognition of the fact that he or she is ventilating a countertransference reaction. In such an instance, the complaining analyst does not see that therapeutic or didactic zeal has replaced the analytic attitude. In the cases in question, the analytic questions always remain (1) what can be learned from the unyieldingness of certain characteristics which have already been subjected to considerable analysis, and (2) what can be learned from the analyst's having begun inappropriately to feel frustrated, disappointed, angry, or impatient. Sometimes the lesson to be learned is that the analysis has gone as far as it can go (for the time being, anyway). In extreme cases, the lesson may be that analysis is not the method of choice. But very often, assuming that the analysand has been selected with some care and that the analyst is adequately equipped, the lesson is just that some negative countertransference has developed which calls for self-analysis or supervisory consultation.

A major feature of the analyst's helpfulness is the maintenance of a respectful affirmative attitude. Although this constituent of the analytic attitude will be described and illustrated in some detail in later chapters, a few words about it are in place here. Recognizing, as Freud did, that the analysand fears insight and change, the analyst is always

1. William I. Grossman, personal communication.

12

ready to view the difficulties presented by the analysand not in a negative light but rather as meaningful, even if still obscure, expressions
of the very problems that call for analysis. These difficulties are compromises. That is to say, they are ways in which, unconsciously, the
analysand simultaneously obtains gratification, maintains a sense of
security and integration, and satisfies needs to be punished. Because
the analysand has a large stake in maintaining the status quo, the analyst must approach the attendant difficulties respectfully. When, for
example, an analysand says, "Suspicion is the only way of looking at
the world in which I have confidence," the affirmative analytic attitude will be expressed not in trying to induce the analysand to give
up that conviction as soon as possible, but rather in trying patiently to
understand and interpret all the emotionally contradictory uses of that
conviction in the analysand's psychical reality. For the analyst, analyzing is not an alternative to being helpful, it is the analytic way of
being helpful. It is just that the manifest gains produced by this effort
to be helpful may not be immediate, unambiguous, of an expected or
easily recognizable sort, or instantly responded to by the analysand
with unbounded joy.

I lay no claim that this introductory outline of the analytic attitude
is particularly original, that it is adequately comprehensive and detailed, or that it is entirely incontestable. As I indicated earlier, it is
intended to convey as briefly as possible the ideal I have come to as-
pire to in my work as an analyst. This ideal selectively condenses the
best of what I have learned from my teachers, my reading, my clinical
work, and my previous efforts to teach or to write on topics that bear
on the analytic attitude. The extent to which I have approached my
ideal may be judged not so much from this introduction as from the
following chapters on theory, empathy, interpretation, and technique.

2

The Atmosphere of Safety: Freud's "Papers on Technique" (1911-1915)

Introduction

Today's psychoanalysts must deal with an ever-increasing number of challenges to the traditional or classical analytic method. On the one flank are the actively confrontational therapists and the sex therapists who, at least implicitly, claim to bring about structural changes (such as radical modification of defenses) that have been held to be the special achievement of the psychoanalytic method. On the other flank are those working within psychoanalysis who, while denying any revisionist orientation, are developing new approaches to technique with special classes of analysands. In the latter case, with which I am here concerned, reference is made to an increase in the number of severely narcissistic and borderline patients and phenomena, their refractoriness to the classical method, and the special requirements of doing analytic work with them. Inevitably, questions arise for analysts as to whether these challenges call for fundamental modifications of analytic attitude and technique or merely describe advances based on more sophisticated thinking through of the theoretical and technical implications of Freud's papers, perhaps especially his paper, "On Narcissism" (1914b).

In the face of such challenges, it is always useful to go back to Freud and review or reconsider the recommendations he made in his "Papers on Technique" (1911–1915; all page references below are to these papers in the *Standard Edition*, 12). Not that Freud insisted on absolute uniformity of approach—far from it. He presented his recommendations as being appropriate "on the average," and he warned against

14

"mechanization" of his method (p. 123). Although he said very little about specific variations on his ideal approach, he did refer in a general way to educative and also need-gratifying moves on the analyst's part. He also stated explicitly, even then, that one may expect to encounter comparatively few analysands who will prove to be suitable for the consistent carrying through of his recommendations (p. 131). It is, I think, warranted to assume that already at that early time he did not expect very many analyses to be carried through to some ideal completion. Much later, in "Analysis Terminable and Interminable" (1937a), he was explicit on this point.

Consequently, my review of Freud's recommendations is not presented as a reading which will definitely establish a prescription for a single, invariant, correct, and infallible technique. In undertaking this assessment, I hope only to define a number of reference points with respect to which those who are assessing these variations may differentiate them as to type and also estimate their extent. But however modest my undertaking, it must be an interpretation of Freud. This is so for three reasons at least. First, Freud made a number of dogmatic statements the appropriate qualification of which can only be achieved by interpreting the total context of his discussions. Secondly, he made a number of ambiguous statements which also call for interpretation in context. An important aspect of the total context is the manner in which Freud set forth his recommendations, that is, his consistently neutral tone and his dispassionate curiosity concerning the variety, complexity, and subtlety of the problems with which one must come to grips. Thirdly, even if Freud had recommended strict uniformity, the fact is that we have had a number of different readings of his text on technique, and it could not have been otherwise, for texts exist only in relation to the orientation and values brought to them by each reader. No text can anticipate and control advances in knowledge and skill and changing times and values.

It is my contention that throughout Freud's discussions there runs a concern with progressively establishing an atmosphere of safety in the analysis. I make this claim even though I found only the following single explicit reference to safety in these papers. In taking up the analyst's response to the erotic or romantic demands that the female analysand will make at the height of her positive transference to the male analyst, Freud pointed out that it is only by being proof against every such temptation that the analyst will make it possible for her to "feel safe enough to allow all her preconditions for loving, all the phantasies springing from her sexual desires, all the detailed charac-

15

teristics of her state of being in love, to come to light; and from these she will herself open the way to the infantile roots of her love" (p. 166). One does, of course, want to help open up this way to the infantile, for it is a fundamental aspect of carrying out an analysis. However, the project of progressively making the analysis safe is obviously far more complex than showing that one is proof against libidinal temptation.

Far more than frankly heterosexual demands are in question when one speaks of the temptations besetting the analyst. The analyst must be proof against temptations of every sort in every aspect of carrying out an effective analysis. To mention only a few other temptations: there is the masochistic analysand's "seduction of the aggressor" (Loewenstein, 1957); there is the temptation to enter into a bitter power struggle when the analysand shows the full force of his or her negative transference; there are seductions away from an empathic stance; and there are seductions into panic as when regressive self-experience is dramatically displayed.

In developing a reading of Freud's technical papers around the theme of safety, one runs a considerable but, I think, unavoidable risk of tediously reviewing what is already well known and has already been adequately reviewed and discussed in the literature. One hesitates to attempt to go beyond Leo Stone's excellent monograph, *The Psychoanalytic Situation* (1961), or Greenson's text (1967). Nor can one avoid the risk of reading more into Freud's words than he could have intended at that stage of his development. One also runs the risk of seeming to recommend an indiscriminately adulatory attitude toward Freud—the Freud who "knew it all," as is sometimes said. Well, I do believe that Freud already knew much that we now pride ourselves on having only just come to know, even though he did not know it, and could not have known it, in quite the way that we do today. And finally there is the risk of giving the impression that the atmosphere of safety was Freud's sole or major concern. It was not so. My claim is only that it was a steady concern that may be recognized, often between the lines.

Unless one reviews Freud's writings continuously, and from one or another point of view, one finds it difficult to maintain some organized and comprehensive conception of the fundamentals of the very technique by way of which he gathered the data that support or justify his theory of psychoanalysis. And there is always room in these reviews for some further penetration and amplification as well as critical discussion of Freud. In the final section of this chapter I shall take up briefly a few of the major points that today seem to be problematic.

I have organized my review of Freud's technical papers under five headings: the difficulties in the way of change; the complexity and the ambiguity of change and the attitude of finding out; the importance of a disciplined approach; the importance of an empathic approach; and the importance of the analyst's confidence in the analysand and in himself or herself. I shall not review systematically or exhaustively the many points Freud made about the handling of specific arrangements and problems which must be part of any attempt at analysis and which, each in its own way, may be shown to add to the atmosphere of safety.

In view of the general familiarity with Freud's papers that can be safely assumed, I shall use direct quotations sparingly, and then mainly to highlight some of Freud's less frequently cited, though extremely significant, observations and arguments. Page references to specific points will be appropriate only in certain instances.

The Papers on Technique

THE DIFFICULTIES IN THE WAY OF CHANGE

The adult analysand comes to analysis with a troubled life story, the beginning of which is gradually seen to extend back to earliest childhood. The formative influences of that early period play a part in virtually every important aspect of his or her life. The process of change during analysis must contend with a vast network of disguised expressions, derivatives, and reactions against them; of assets and achievements which have been developed out of these and subsequently have come to be valued in their own right; and of adjustments to personal limitations which go hand in hand with the strengths of the analysand and which he or she will not confront gladly. At the core of this formidable problematic life is extreme infantile anxiety or a sense of danger that serves unconsciously as a major rationale for the analysand's ever-present and ever-problematic resistance. Consequently, fundamental personality change can take place only slowly and in a manner that cannot be predetermined (p. 130), and an atmosphere of safety can only be developed slowly and uncertainly.

No single variable emerges with more force in these papers on technique than resistance. Resistance figures as the chief variable in the discussion of the handling of dreams, the dynamics of transference, and the approach to remembering, repeating, and working through. Resistance, Freud said, accompanies the analysis step by step (p. 103). This is to say that every advance enters into a new domain of opposition to the work of analysis. It is resistance that makes change slow and difficult. It is resistance that makes it possible for the analysand to know something consciously and yet not know if effectively (p. 142), and certainly the analyst's knowing something has little or no bearing on the question of whether the analysand knows it at all (p. 96).

Further, it is resistance that subverts the attachment to the analyst, making it into a source of opposition to the analysis itself by provoking irrational demands and hostility, as well as gross violations of the fundamental rule. It is resistance that has far greater power than the analysand's consciously cooperative attitudes, keen interest in intellectual understanding and collaboration, and even considerable subjective suffering. On this view, Freud maintained a benign scepticism toward the analysand's early improvement, friendly and helpful attitudes, rapid acceptance of interpretations and constructions, and ready production of apparently corroborative material (see, for example, p. 96).

One of Freud's most telling arguments in this connection was his pointing out how this same pervasive and oppressive resistance is encountered in the analyses of analysts. He said: "No one who is familiar with the nature of neurosis will be astonished to hear that even a man who is very able to carry out an analysis on other people can behave like any other mortal and be capable of producing the most intense resistances as soon as he himself becomes the object of analytic investigation. When this happens we are once again reminded of the dimension of depth in the mind, and it does not surprise us to find that neurosis has its roots in psychical strata to which an intellectual knowledge of analysis has not penetrated" (p. 126). In making this observation, Freud was talking about us and to us. He was urging us not to forget how resistant we ourselves were (or are) as analysands, and he was cautioning us not to place naive trust in the power of intellectual preparation and professional motivation.

It might, therefore, be interjected here that, in addition to the role played by the analyst's fantasized omnipotence in his or her intolerance of the analysand's resistances, there is also to be considered the role played by inadequate resolution of the analyst's own resistances. It is an expectable consequence of these inadequately resolved and continuing resistances that, inappropriately and defensively, the analyst will keep trying to prove something about the completeness of his or her own personal analysis. This may be attempted, for example, by developing an attacking, exhorting, or at least impatient attitude toward the analysand's resistances—none of which can contribute to the necessary atmosphere of safety. If, by definition, the still resistant analyst does not feel adequately safe, how can the analysand? Beyond the implication that one should not persecute the resisting analysand, there is the further implication that one should be satisfied with the limits of analytic achievement in each case. Admittedly, it is no easy matter to arrive analytically at a determination of these limits.

Freud recognized that the study of the resistance must itself play a central part in the analysis. That is to say, he recognized that there is something fundamentally antithetical to the analytic attitude in viewing the resistance as anything other than additional analytic material to be interpreted. It is material from which a great deal can be extracted concerning the history and current status of the analysand's problems. Freud went so far as to say that the greatest analytic gains will be made through the analysis of the resistance (p. 155). This emphasis only gained in force with the advent of the structural point of view and its technical implication of the need for thorough analysis of the ego, especially of preferred defensive strategies and their history. This productive, affirmative orientation toward resistance is essential in establishing an atmosphere of safety. Initially taken as a danger, the consistent, patient, and neutral analysis of resistance gets to be one of the analysand's criteria of the analyst's empathy and understanding, and thus a basis for consciously tolerating progressively less distorted derivatives of infantile conflict.

Anxiety as a motive for resistance came into its own in "Inhibitions, Symptoms and Anxiety" (Freud, 1926), ten to fifteen years after Freud wrote his papers on technique. At the time he wrote these technical papers, he was dealing with the role of anxiety in resistance mostly by implication, for he was then more concerned to emphasize the resistance to giving up the unconscious infantile gratifications obtained through symptoms, character traits, and other forms of repetition or acting out. There, he attributed this resistance to the unconscious infantile wishes (p. 103). He estimated that the strength of these infantile wishes and the depth of their unconscious gratification exert far more influence over the analysis than the conscious suffering that brings one to analysis (p. 143). It is in connection with this source of resistance that the promotion of the positive transference assumed such importance in Freud's discussion of technique. He even said that one must "compel" the development of the transference (p. 108).

Freud's principal points in this regard were these. During analysis, the analysand's continuing search for infantile wishful gratification has to be directed more and more toward the analyst. Ideally it culminates in a transference neurosis, that is, a centering of neurotic concerns or symptoms on the relationship to the analyst. This redirection will be accomplished chiefly through systematic interpretation of manifestations of resistance and transference. Only on this basis might one hope that the analysand will continue the often arduous work of analysis, for now he or she will tolerate the anxiety, frustration, and other painful affects entailed by analysis, and will do so on the strength of the hope that finally the analyst's transference-love will be obtained (p. 169). Many years later, in "Analysis Terminable and Interminable" (1937a), Freud emphasized the analysand's hope of finally obtaining the paternal penis or some symbolic equivalent of it, such as a baby. Only wishes with a force of such magnitude can be counted on to overcome the resistance. Hence the importance of proper and timely handling of the transference, particularly with respect to its subversion by the resistance (see, for example, pp. 162–163 and 167–168). The transference neurosis must be at one and the same time heightened *and rendered safe* by the interpretations and constructions developed from within the neutral analytic attitude. Only thus are the very great obstacles to change converted into agents of change.

THE COMPLEXITY AND AMBIGUITY OF CHANGE AND THE ATTITUDE OF FINDING OUT

Freud cautioned against taking anything for granted about the possibility of change, the direction in which change will take place, and the extent to which change will be effected. He spoke of analysis as a process which, once it is started with the help of the initial positive transference and the clearing away of preliminary resistances, will go its own way (p. 130).

It is, I think, appropriate to interpolate here a few remarks on analysis as a process that "goes its own way." According to my impression, too often analysts have used this notion to legitimize far-reaching inactivity on their part. One must remember that Freud did also refer to the "middle game" of analysis when he drew his famous analogy with the game of chess (p. 123). Although he said he could provide no guidelines for this middle game, he was obviously not envisioning inactivity as a regular and rigid practice. Rather, in speaking of a process that goes its own way, he was warning the analyst not to be too directive on the basis of preconceived ideas about technique, psychopathology, and desirable outcomes.

Freud intended to emphasize the complexity and novelty of the explanations that will have to be worked out during the analysis. He recognized that there is no simple truth about symptoms or developmental factors (p. 99). He discouraged the analyst from either defining particular sectors to work in or presenting specific goals to the patient. It is "evenly suspended attention" that is called for (p. 113), inasmuch as it is usually only after the initial communication of analytic material that its significance may be defined and estimated. And this significance may well be surprising. Clearly, any other approach forecloses the issues, which is to say that it fosters new compromise formations or intensifies old defenses. Freud also stressed the danger of the analyst's projecting his or her peculiarities into the analysand and then overgeneralizing to all analysands or all people from this already biased view of the analytic data (p. 117). His warning against one's getting too excited by apparently corroborative material dished up by the analysand may be recalled in this connection.

What these recommendations add up to is this. The appropriate analytic attitude is one of *finding out:* finding out what the analysis itself will be or be concerned with; where the principal work will be done, which, as he said, need not be in the same locale as where the principal conflicts are (p. 104); how this work will best be done; and, by implication, finding out when, why, and how to establish a termination of the analysis.

According to Freud, there are guidelines or constraints that must ordinarily be observed, such as the introduction of the fundamental rule, the recumbent position of the analysand, and the frequency and regularity of analytic sessions. But Freud was also indicating that these factors must be understood as helping to establish a framework within which the analysis will be jointly created by analyst and analysand. The analysis is created by a continuing examination and interpretation of its progress and the obstacles to its further progress. It begins to become evident how much in each case the psychoanalytic process is a study of itself as it is created in and through the analytic dialogue (see chapter 14). What else can it be if it is always a matter of finding out where one is going, how, why, and with which consequences?

Freud did not take for granted the usefulness of the initial anamnestic data or the correctness of one's initial diagnostic impression. Instead, he recommended a trial analysis of one or two weeks during which time the analyst could hope to identify what we might now call pseudoneurotic schizophrenics or borderline personalities, those patients who, in his view, are not adequately analyzable owing to their essential unrelatedness to other people.

Freud recognized that just as it is difficult to maintain an interpretive analytic attitude toward resistance, it is difficult to maintain the nondirective constituent of the analytic attitude. A part of the problem is this, that in a general way the analyst can often recognize a good deal of the primitive, conflictual significance of material being presented by the analysand and can anticipate its further elaboration. However, Freud saw that there was a long way between the analyst's knowing something and the analysand's knowing it. At the same time he saw that the analysand might know something consciously and yet at the same time not know it in the sense of having insightfully established meaningful connections with hitherto unconscious significant conflicts and their infantile origins. He was aware that the analysand could be frightened by too knowing a stance on the analyst's part or by too hasty, deep, or insistent an interpretation. Although Freud did not go into detail, he was making room for the unpredictable specifics of the analytic process, that is, for those turns in the work by way of which certain types of conflict in certain realms of life, certain dreams and symptomatic variations, and the like, prove to be the best routes to insight and working through.

Before finding and traversing these routes, the analyst can only have an intellectualized, incomplete, and relatively nonspecific or nonindividualized kind of insight. Although useful to the analyst while listening, it is not usable insight—or not yet that—and for the analysand its being verbalized can be frightening. Bringing it up explicitly may intensify resistances. The directive question, "How do you get from here to there?" is, therefore, usually less appropriate as a guide for implementing the analytic attitude than the questions, "Just where are we anyway and where will we get to from here?" It is the *finding out* questions that define the freest type of adherence by both analyst and analysand to the fundamental rule. What I am stressing is not so much a matter of technique as it is a guiding attitude toward the complexity and the ambiguity of psychoanalytic change. Arriving at the most individualized version of insightful change is, in the end, the only really safe and therefore effective analytic objective.

To refer again to the time when we ourselves were analysands, we need only think of just how great and unanticipated were the varieties

of content and the types of change that had to be dealt with before it
was possible to know at first hand our defenses, our Oedipus com-
plexes, our anality, orality, and narcissism. Only when the approach is
thus individualized can one arrive at the belief, and feel secure in the
belief, that one's own analyst is indeed an analyst and that the analysis
is indeed an analysis of oneself. The analyst's offering generalized
wisdom or universal insight can establish only the self-limiting, unstable, and resistance-intensifying security of submission to omniscience.

[handwritten margin note: it can also represent therapist's attempt to establish authority where his own is lacking, or to bolster interventions which aren't quite to the mark.]

THE IMPORTANCE OF A DISCIPLINED APPROACH

The topic of discipline as a constituent of the analytic attitude pro-
voked some of Freud's most dogmatic and ambiguous statements. He
urged, for example, that the analyst adopt the attitude of a surgeon
(p. 115); that he be only a mirror to the analysand (pp. 117–118); and
that he enforce abstinence (p. 165). Leo Stone (1961) did a good deal to
clear up the confusion engendered by these problematic statements.
More recently, in an analysis of Freud's analytic attitude, Samuel Lipton (1977) has clarified matters further, though perhaps not uncontro-
versially. In general, it can be said that the contexts and tones of
Freud's remarks made it clear enough that he was urging a *disciplined*
approach in which considerations of what will be most helpful to the
analysis, and therefore to the analysand, will always be foremost in
the analyst's mind. Thus, when recommending that the analyst remain
cold, he was thinking of the surgeon's skill and decisiveness. One
might say that he was distinguishing between sentimental or maudlin
analysis and analysis ruled by disciplined compassion.

Freud did not want the analyst to inject his own personality forcibly
into the analytic process, neither deliberately nor through blatant
countertransferences. He did not want the analyst to take the idealizing and erotic transference as a personal tribute. He did not want the
analyst to be guided rigidly by ordinary considerations of delicacy and
restraint in taking up what needs to be taken up and doing so in an
effective way. Freud stressed truthfulness as fundamental to the analytic attitude (p. 164), and he emphasized "honorable" procedure
when he spoke of preparing the analysand early for the rigors of analytic work (p. 129). One might add to this that it is only on the basis of
progress within an analysis that the analysand dares to believe deeply,
even if only intermittently, in this truthfulness, when it is there, and
to comprehend fully, even if unstably, the inescapability of the rigors
of the work. In the case of the analytic process, truly informed consent

23

can be established only step by step and on the basis of an increasing sense of safety.

Additionally, Freud did not want the analyst to yield thoughtlessly or too readily to the not infrequent demands for gratifications in the analytic relationship, for he understood that the analyst's doing so can only obscure resistances, make the analysis of transference all the more difficult, and diminish the motivation for further work. He did not want the analyst to give the analysand permission to suspend observance of the fundamental rule, that one report all of one's thoughts without regard to conventional standards of coherence, importance, or decorum; instead, the analyst should attempt to analyze the departures from frankness that invariably occur. He did not want the analyst to count on the usefulness of sharing confidences with the analysand as a way of promoting the analysis. Nor did he want the analyst to confuse personal and professional relationship on the one hand and analytic relationship on the other, for the distinction to be made is necessary to protect the analyst's own emotional life and the neutrality and objectivity of the work of analysis. Admittedly, the distinction between the two types of relationship is sometimes difficult to draw, but it is fully warranted at least to be concerned to draw it. Freud's consistent objective was to do as little as possible to further complicate the inevitably complex analysis of resistance and transference.

A word is in order here concerning the analyst's being a "mirror" and remaining "opaque" to the analysand. Freud's recommendation does not legitimize stiff formality, impassivity, and remoteness. The "mirror" refers to the analyst's reflecting back to the analysand, now in neutral analytic form, what the analysand has been showing unconsciously in his or her associations and behavior. It is an active, transformational mirror and so is not a mirror at all. The metaphor is not well chosen. It is better to call this mirroring a psychoanalytic reading of the analysand's text (see especially chapters 11, 12, and 16). In the same vein, "opaque" refers to the analyst's not using personal disclosure as a major tool of analysis. "Opaque" would be better called the subordination of the analyst's biography and personality to the task at hand. The term "subordination" is superior to "opaqueness" in two respects. First, it implies the recognition that total personal opaqueness is impossible to achieve and, owing to its artificiality, technically undesirable as a goal. Second, it indicates the continuing need for flexibility and imagination on the analyst's part in achieving, with suitable variation from one analysand to the next, an analytic version of himself or herself, a second self that integrates the analyst's own biog-

24

raphy and personality with the constraints of the analytic method and the needs of each analysand (see chapter 3).

There must be many reasons for the absoluteness with which Freud stated some of his recommendations on discipline. The dissensions in the analytic movement during the early teens of this century must be mentioned here. I would suggest that in part this absoluteness also be taken as a sign that Freud recognized how powerful are the analyst's defensive and transference needs as well as his or her narcissistic needs. The young analyst, he observed, is particularly vulnerable to heterosexual erotic transference. This point must be extended to include vulnerability to homosexual erotic transference, though in this respect the vulnerability is more likely to be shown by blind spots and defensive displacement of analytic interest than by manifest sexual arousal. One way or another, the analyst's temptation is to use the analytic work to get otherwise unavailable gratifications, support faltering defenses, enhance grandiose fantasies, and, in the end, to *use* the analysand rather than to *work for* him or her. How much the analysand's sense of danger within the analysis depends on the frequency and extent of the analyst's nonneutral violations of trust in this respect!

One need not be an apologist for Freud to read his strictures on discipline as statements of his recognition of, and respect for, the frailties of the analyst at work and the ambiguity of the work itself. It is even possible to infer that Freud had learned a great deal from errors of his own in these respects.

THE IMPORTANCE OF AN EMPATHIC APPROACH

In connection with empathy, though not expressly under that heading, Freud made a number of important recommendations. One should not rush to interpret everything one sees at any moment. One should avoid humiliating the analysand through responding nonanalytically to manifestations of transference, that is, by preaching, acquiescing, rejecting, etc. One should make interpretations that are but a step ahead of where the analysand is and, ideally, should make them in such a way as to let him or her get the solution (p. 140). The associative response to one's intervention should always be scrutinized in order to test out the intervention's correctness and to decide whether further interpretation is required. It is important not to overestimate the analysand's capacity for sublimation. Nor should one expect an unrestricted capacity for object relations on the part of analysands with significant narcissistic problems. One should demonstrate an attitude of sympathetic understanding and concern from early on in the relationship (pp. 139–140). It is essential to maintain an attitude of flexibility with regard to the analytic route that will be taken by the analysand and the level on which he or she will be functioning from moment to moment (pp. 123–124). One must always take into account the inevitability of ambivalence in human relationships. And one ought to be satisfied with whatever the fruits of the day's work may be.

In contrast to Freud's strict statements in connection with the disciplined approach, this set of statements suggests that the analytic attitude must include gentleness, undemandingness, open-mindedness, flexibility, patience, tentativeness, spontaneity and individuality (p. 111), and willingness to go along. What matters is not so much bountiful expressions of empathy as such, for these can be condescending, gratuitous, maudlin, overstimulating, or seductive. Rather, as in the case of resistance, what matters is an unflagging recognition that one must function essentially as an empathic, facilitating supervisor of the analysand's further development through analysis (see, for example, p. 130). I would not say the analysand's "guide," as that term implies both detailed knowledge of the terrain and preestablished goals. A better metaphor is the analyst as a seasoned and hardy coexplorer. In any case, a facilitating supervisor is neither a tyrant nor a martinet, neither a mindreader nor a controlling architect of the personality. Freud's steady preoccupation with resistance may be viewed in the light of the analyst's playing this helpful role. Elsewhere, as I mentioned, he emphasized the dread of change that underlies the resistance, indicating that the analyst's awareness of this dread can only add to empathic facilitation. As a facilitating supervisor, the analyst is safe; as an enforcer or mastermind, however manifestly benevolent in intent, he or she can only be experienced as dangerous by the analysand (for example, as a castrating, abandoning, or engulfing figure, one who is the external embodiment of fantasized persecutors or omnipotent infantile imagos).

THE IMPORTANCE OF THE ANALYST'S CONFIDENCE

Freud emphasized that everything that comes up in the analysis has an actual or potential analytic yield. The analysand must learn that this is so (p. 93), and the analyst must keep on relearning it. Everything can be put to use, including the resistance.

26

The Atmosphere of Safety

Freud took an impressively affirmative view of the trends which are being expressed in the neurotic symptoms. In connection with the importance of directing the analysand's attention to the phenomena of his illness, such as the precise wording of obsessional ideas, Freud said this: "His illness itself must no longer seem to him contemptible, but must become an enemy worthy of his mettle, a piece of his personality, which has solid ground for its existence and out of which things of value for his future life have to be derived" (p. 152).

Further, Freud encouraged the recognition of the continuity between the old and the new in transference, both within the analysis and within relationships in everyday life. He saw the necessity of tolerating the apparent aimlessness of the analytic work (p. 94). He appreciated how many, varied, and subtle are the forms of remembering through dreams, screen memories, repetitive acting out, character attitudes, and the like, which is to say that he was confident that the important life-historical material which is consciously unavailable permeates what often appear to be irrelevant or inadequate data. He urged confidence in the mutual understanding between analyst and analysand of unconscious mental processes (p. 115). He trusted in the persistence of dynamic contexts beyond the immediate time when they first come up, expecting that material of importance not arrived at during one day's session may very well be arrived at subsequently (p. 94).

Freud's brave view of the effects of constructions or reconstructions of the infantile past is striking (pp. 148–150; see also his later paper, "Constructions in Analysis" [1937b]). He asserted that it makes no difference whether the analysand ever gets to remember the early events or experiences that are constructed by the analyst. Here Freud showed remarkable confidence in determining the correctness and value of constructions. It is not conscious testimony that counts in what is recalled or reorganized and what is changed in feeling and behavior; it is *consequences*, that is, the consequences of constructions. Once a construction has been worked through adequately, the analysand knows and uses unconsciously something that, consciously, he or she can only assent to intellectually. Here is a significant reversal of Freud's usual emphasis on how much depends on making the unconscious conscious!

I want particularly to mention Freud's boldly saying that real life provides no model for the analyst's mode of response (p. 166). Here he seemed to mean more than the analyst's not responding in kind to the analysand, that is, not meeting hate with hate or hate with love and

this is very interesting in light of Watzlawick's constructionism. Why is a psychoanalytic construction not to be taken as on a par with a Watzlawickian construction, epistemologically speaking?! fascinating. epistemic issue. cf. hermeneutic elaboration

27

not entering into lengthy discussions of analysis with the analysand. He also meant a way of listening and understanding, and an appreciation of analytic meaning and value in everything that comes up, however negative its superficial appearance. One may say that Freud took an affirmative view of every phenomenon in the analysis. To say this is not equivalent to saying that he was blind to the potential for destroying the analysis contained in the various forms of resistance, including transference and acting out. With regard to these destructive potentials, he did not assume a pollyana role or a position of omnipotence. But unwaveringly he expressed his affirmative attitude through his confidence in the ultimate intelligibility of human activity. One may hope to develop a sense, or more likely a complex network of meanings, for everything in the analysis, even that which is most disruptive and apparently nonanalytic or antianalytic in appearance. This affirmative constituent of the analytic attitude must play a great part in building the analysand's sense of safety, for it establishes that he or she is totally welcome in the analytic relationship and that the analyst not only sits but stands behind the analysand.

Some Comments on Freud's Discussion of Technique

DISCLAIMED ACTION IN THE DISCUSSION OF RESISTANCE

In contrast to the way Freud described the relatives of analysands as people who may be expected to do a great deal to undermine the analysand's relation to the analyst (p. 120), Freud consistently described the analysand's own opposition to the work of analysis as work done not by a person but by "the resistance." For example, he referred frequently to how the resistance uses the transference for its own purposes. Similarly, he said the resistance follows the analysis step by step. In this respect he presented resistance in the same way that analysands often do, that is, as a species of disclaimed action—as a happening or as an alien force to be conquered at best or submitted to at worst, rather than as a personally intended activity. Elsewhere, in an earlier discussion of resistance (1973), I have discussed it as unconscious personal action rather than as force or mechanism operating impersonally and autonomously (see also chapters 6–10).

It is, however, suggested by a few of Freud's remarks that in the

28

clinical crunch he would have been inclined to deal with the resistance by interpreting it as unconsciously performed action. For instance, in his interpretations of resistance, he tended to link it with defiance of the father. Also, he took it as an expression of the analysand's dread of the unconscious material against which it is directed. In these respects he was viewing the analysand as a person who resists rather than as a locale of the operation of an impersonal process called "the resistance." Why, then, this discrepancy? Perhaps it was necessary for Freud, at least in his formal exposition of technique, to present resistance as an impersonal and autonomous force or mechanism with which the analysand, along with the analyst, must reckon. Whether knowingly or not, he may have had to do so during the time of his pioneering work in order to reinforce his empathy and extend his tolerance, for at that time his confidence in his own analytic attitude and method could not have been altogether secure. Both his own emotional safety and the protection of his new method and his analysands were at stake.

Be this as it may, Freud continued his implicit disclaiming of personal action when he attributed much of the resistance to the tenacious claims of infantile unconscious wishes. These wishes will not give up the gratifications they obtain through symptoms and character traits and blind repetition (see, for example, pp. 103 and 108). Yet, even though this theoretical lodging of power in the independently demanding wish rather than the wishful person further encourages a view of the analysand as an apparatus which is beset by resistance rather than as a person who is resisting, there is again reason to think that in practice Freud was inclined to refer to what the analysand wished rather than to the wish as autonomous agent in its own right. It was just that this way of thinking did not qualify as scientific in Freud's estimation, and perhaps additionally it supported his accepting attitude toward the difficulties presented by the analysand.

One can appreciate how, for a time, this disclaiming orientation does help analysands follow the fundamental rule with some sense of safety, thinking that they are studying how their minds work rather than how they live their lives, albeit largely unconsciously. They are in this respect consciously relieved of a frightening sense of responsibility, a responsibility they slowly and erratically assume with the progress of their analyses. But it must also be remembered that not every analysand progresses this way, and it may well be that one of the hindrances to working through to an appropriate sense of responsibility may be the reinforcement of disclaimers by the mechanistic terminology of metapsychology and its penetration into the analytic dialogue.

EDUCATIVE ASPECTS OF ANALYTIC TECHNIQUE

As I mentioned in the second section of my review of the technical papers, Freud presented analysis mostly as a matter of *finding out* the exact nature of the analysand's problems, the forms in which these will be accessible to interpretation and modification, and the individualized goals of the analytic process itself. True, he did make occasional unelaborated references to educating the analysand—for example, as to the fact of resistance—and he did speak of compelling the development of the transference neurosis by consistent transference interpretation. It is true, therefore, that in these respects he presented analysis as a process that cannot be pure exploration. Still, the view was encouraged that analysis is a naively empirical method. His metaphor of the analyst as mirror reflecting back only what is shown, neglecting as it does the transformational nature of analytic interventions, epitomizes this positivist stance, as does his recommendation that one should work without presuppositions (pp. 113–114).

It must, however, be recognized that Freud was always following certain lines of interpretation and construction in his establishing of "the facts" of the case. These were the lines that led to the full definition of the Oedipus complex, ambivalence, psychosexual stages of development, unconsciously guilty and anxious activity, and the intricacies of the entire family drama of early childhood, including birth of siblings and primal scene. Even the fostering of the development of the transference neurosis implies a shaping of the phenomena to be interpreted. This approach provides the analyst with a useful set of selective and organizing principles. These principles define the best form of material to deal with as well as a special slant on the implications of whatever the analysand does bring up under these conditions.

Consequently, the frequently observed neglect by analysts of adequate interpretation of transference need not be a matter of their missing the point altogether or ineptly finding nothing to interpret. The analyst can always attend exclusively to other aspects of the complex material in question, such as its developmental aspects, and can, in principle, always claim validity for these interventions. But what these alternative interventions so often lack is the immediate or long-range transformational efficacy of transference interpretation. For example, genetic or developmental material, however illuminating it may be, is often presented by the analysand as an escape from exploring transference (for example, displacement from the analyst to the parents), and the analyst who takes up such "past" material on its own terms, while not factually wrong, may be technically quite wrong and may further complicate the analysis of resistance and transference. But the main point I am making is not so much technical as epistemological. Analytic material always lends itself to multiple interpretation and is progressively shaped by the analyst's interventions.

Consequently, it seems appropriate to modify the conception of analysis as a purely exploratory or naively empirical procedure. It now seems more exact to say that, as Freud presented it, analysis is a matter of finding out how certain expectable and therapeutically crucial variables have figured in the development of a neurosis or character problem and its extension into resisting and transference. These expectable variables include the psychosexual phases of development in which current problems are anchored, the events to which they are tied, the unconscious fantasizing through which they remain continuing influences, the importance of all these variables relative to one another, and the accidental influences of life which, after the distinctive evolution of these psychosexual variables, have been used to give them their final form.

On this view, psychoanalysis emerges as an educative investigation, and one can accept that it is not paradoxical to call it that. Variations of analytic method and attitude represent different forms of educative investigation. Because it is educative or supervised in this respect, it shapes the phenomena to be analyzed, and it selectively accentuates and organizes them. So long as it remains within the bounds of reason, each analytic approach tends to be self-confirming, and its results cannot be easily compared to those obtained differently. This epistemological issue will be taken up in various places in the remainder of this book.

SAFETY

Let us return more directly to the theme of safety. There is no need to detail the many ways in which analysands will press for simple, magically effective interpretations or other interventions during the course of analysis; nor need it be emphasized how much they suffer consciously in response to the analyst's not yielding to this pressure—though often they are relieved, too. At the same time, analytic experience makes it plain that, with the progress of an analysis, and particularly as analysis moves toward termination, the analysand gets to appreciate how vital it always was that the analyst maintain the *neutral* analytic attitude, particularly in view of the atmosphere of safety that has been progressively, even if unstably, engendered thereby. If, as Freud described and I have emphasized, the analyst has been consistently, even if only implicitly, indicating his or her recognition of the difficulty of changing, the complexity and ambiguity connected with changing, the importance of a disciplined approach as well as an empathic one, and an abiding confidence in the analytic method and in both parties to the analytic relationship, then he or she has done all it is possible to do to establish and foster the atmosphere of safety in the analysis and to lay the groundwork for reestablishing it every time it is lost.

In turn, this proposition implies that analysands do recognize, at least in a rudimentary preconscious way, that this analytic attitude is a prerequisite of their taking the many chances that have to be taken in the course of adhering to the requirements of the analytic method. In this sense it emerges that these requirements are jointly defined, even though it requires the effectiveness of the analysis itself to make it plain that, all along, the analysand has had a vital stake in requiring the work to be done in this way. Were this not so, the analysand could not take on what he or she ventures to confront during the analysis, and instead would continue simply to feel injured, betrayed, threatened, seduced, or otherwise interfered with or traumatized. In other words, every significant lapse from the analytic attitude supports the analysand's expectation that it is dangerous to go any further with the work.

It is widely recognized that such lapses on the analyst's part cannot be altogether avoided. It is also widely recognized that the disruptive effects of these lapses can often be counteracted and even on occasion put to good analytic use, through self-analysis of countertransference by the analyst and through analysis of the analysand's responses to the lapses once they have been identified and perhaps confirmed by the analyst. For the moment, however, what matters is our recognizing the impact of these lapses on the atmosphere of safety that is fostered by the well-maintained analytic attitude.

Finally, there is this to be added to this discussion of safety. When Freud wrote his papers on technique, he had not yet systematically named, described, and arranged in developmental sequence the prototypical danger situations: loss of the object, loss of the object's love, castration, and superego condemnation (Freud, 1926; see also chapter 7 herein). Today, we would want to extend and better integrate this list to include, from the side of ego development, the dangers of loss of self-cohesion and loss of differentiation of the self from the object. These dangers are somehow implied not only by those that Freud described, but also by the primal traumatic state which, for Freud, was the ultimate referent of all danger situations. All of these dangers may be experienced in the analytic situation, and it is an essential part of analysis to analyze the infantile psychical reality they imply and the way they appear in the analysand's dread of the analyst and resistance against developing and exploring the relationship to him or her. Ultimately, the analysis of infantile danger situations is the most potent factor in establishing an atmosphere of safety. Nevertheless, the carrying through of this analysis of danger situations depends greatly on the analyst's readiness to conduct the analysis in such a way as to foster and sustain the atmosphere of safety against which the infantile fantasies may be crystallized, expressed, and tested. I am suggesting that we deal with a benign circle in this respect.

It is this step-by-step construction of a safe analysis, as described above, that establishes what has come to be called the therapeutic alliance. I have not mentioned the therapeutic alliance before this because it is my impression that in too many clinical discussions that concept is used in a nonanalytic way. That is to say, it is used in a way that denies the transferential elements of this alliance, or, if not that, then it is used in a way that tends to minimize the *interpretive* work required to establish and maintain the type of alliance without which an adequate analysis is impossible. But having said so, I will add in conclusion my recognition that, in one respect, this chapter may be read correctly as a contribution to the theory of the therapeutic alliance (Zetzel, 1965).

3

The Psychoanalyst's Empathic Activity

Introduction

Do psychoanalysts empathize with their analysands in a more sensitive, complex, sustained manner than they do with others in their nonanalytic personal relationships? In "The Metapsychology of the Analyst" (1942), Robert Fliess assumed that they do. In that paper he characterized the analyst's "work ego" as capable of special feats of empathizing. This capability is based on a permissive, work-justified, adaptive realignment of the analyst's superego relations with his or her ego. And this realignment allows the "work ego" to experience a great array of feelings and fantasies in relation to the analysand which might otherwise be experienced as inappropriate and reprehensible and therefore effectively blocked by the ego's usual defensive measures.

With Fliess, I believe that often, even if not always, analysts do empathize more freely and reliably in the analytic situation than they do in nonanalytic situations. But I also believe that the explanation of this discrepancy is more complex than the one proposed by Fliess and that it is amenable to profitable discussion in nonmetapsychological terms. Consequently, with the help of action language, I shall attempt in this chapter to develop further the psychology of the analyst's empathic activity, from here on to be designated *empathizing*. Although empathizing will remain the focus throughout, the following discussion should, owing to its wide range, also develop further the idea of the analytic attitude. No effort will be made to maintain a sharp line between empathizing and the analytic attitude as a whole, of which empathizing is a constituent. The cost in precision will be offset, I believe, by the gain in evocativeness and significance.

There exists now an extensive literature on the analyst's empathizing, and it is not part of my purpose to review this literature in detail or even to touch on every significant contribution to this important topic. Nor is it part of my purpose to suggest that the analyst's empathizing alone can cure or change people significantly, though I do believe that appropriate empathizing helps clear the way for, and also enhances, the mutative effect of interpretation. I shall be concentrating on four features of the analyst's empathizing. In my view, these features deserve more attention or amplification than they have received up to now. These features are, first, the analyst's construction of a mental model of the analysand; second, the modification of the analyst's activity that eventuates in what Fliess referred to as the "work ego" and what I shall call, provisionally, a second self; third, the fictive aspect of the analytic relationship; and fourth, the transformational as against the merely imitative or identificatory aspect of empathizing. In preparation for a discussion of these features, I will first review briefly three other topics: (1) some major problems which beset the discussion of analytic empathizing, (2) some of the ideas about the analyst's empathizing which deservedly have gained wide currency and which form the background of the present essay, and (3) those factors in the emotional position of the analyst relative to the analysand that seem to facilitate his or her empathizing.

PROBLEMATIC ASPECTS OF DISCUSSING THE ANALYST'S EMPATHIZING

To write on the nature of the analyst's empathizing is, for a number of reasons, a risky business. For one thing, no matter how carefully written they may be, essays on empathizing tend to be, or to seem to be, surrounded by a self-aggrandizing or exhibitionistic atmosphere. It is as though the author were proclaiming, "I got rhythm! Who could ask for anything more?," or, if not that, then it is as though one were applying to oneself the ancient saying, "Nothing human is alien to me"—quite a large claim to make, although, as I shall try to show later on, there *is* something to be said for it. The effect of this real or imagined atmosphere is threefold: the reader's attention gets fixed on the presenting analyst rather than on the topic being presented, the line between personal performance and the clarification of technical-conceptual issues gets blurred, and the theses being advanced may come across as stronger or weaker than they should.

For another thing, any review of the psychoanalytic literature on empathizing will show that one risks succumbing to and perpetuating various confusions. For example, confusions between empathizing and sympathizing or pitying, between the analyst's empathizing and empathizing in the great variety of ordinary human relationships, between empathizing implicitly and explicitly, between one's own empathizing as an analyst and that of other analysts, and between the origins or infantile prototypes of empathizing and its technical forms in analytic work. Additional risks include dwelling on disruptive influences on empathizing instead of on empathizing proper; and they include as well sentimentally limiting the contents of empathizing only to those emotional experiences that are, in one or another sense, usually considered "good" things to undergo in analysis, such as hopelessness and hope, conflict and mastery, and shame and joy, while forgetting about empathizing with avariciousness, overweaning pride, sociopathy, sadism, and the like. Empathizing with the struggles against these tendencies, yes; with the tendencies themselves, no. Can it be correct to think that the latter instances of empathizing are always and only based on countertransferences or pathological identifications with the analysand? I think not. I once discussed a similar issue and came to a similar conclusion in the case of the analytic psychology of ideals, ideal self, or the ego ideal. Psychoanalytic writers on this topic have tended to focus on lofty ideals and to neglect ideals, such as toughness, of a more earthy or even antisocial nature (Schafer, 1967).

BACKGROUND CONSIDERATIONS

There is a general consensus among psychoanalytic contributors to our topic that empathizing must be understood as an activity with complex cognitive aspects. (That empathizing has an emotional side is true by definition and so is taken as self-evident when the cognitive aspects are being articulated.) These cognitive aspects include the analyst's (1) constructing a mental model of the analysand, (2) being alert to his or her own "signal affects" and shared fantasies in response to the analysand's associations, and (3) being prepared to use these responses reflectively as cues to the emotional aspects and the significance of the analysand's activity in the analysis.

These cognitive elements, which include response to nonverbal as well as verbal cues or messages, have been considered to arise out of trial, segregated, partial, and transient identifications with the analysand. On their part, these identifications come about through projective and introjective processes or imagined merging of self and object.

The Psychoanalyst's Empathic Activity

In this, the analyst utilizes memories of personal experiences of a sort similar to the analysand's. The entire process may be described as one variant of regression in the service of the ego (Kris, 1952). And for the regression to take place smoothly and productively, it would seem to require, as Fliess pointed out, a relaxation of the analyst's superego standards. Superego relaxation may be needed not just for the content but for the meaning in psychic reality of the very act of empathizing. For, unconsciously, the process of empathizing may be invested by analysand and analyst alike with the meaning of nursing, seducing and penetrating, invading the object's body and robbing it of its contents, and other such archaisms. However, acute superego conflict will not arise for the analyst to the extent that these meanings are subordinated to others of a more neutral sort, such as their being means to the ends of understanding and therapeutic and generative benefit rather than their remaining primarily and crudely libidinal and aggressive. Among the previous contributors whose work I have been briefly summarizing, in addition to Fleiss (1942) and myself (1959, 1964), are Knight (1940), Kris (1952), Greenson (1960), Kohut (1971, 1977), and Arlow and Beres (1974).

FACTORS IN THE ANALYST'S EMOTIONAL POSITION WHICH WILL FACILITATE EMPATHIZING

What is it that facilitates the analyst's special feats of empathizing? Why is the analyst in his or her work, as compared to many non-analytic relationships, relatively more relaxed, poised, and patient; less easily gulled, bewildered, or stimulated to be mistrustful, irritable, judgmental, or helpless; more curious, tolerant of ambiguity and lack of closure, and working with a keener sense of the relevance of what is said from one moment to the next or one day, week, or month to the next; less inclined to form transferences and mount resistances readily, intensely, enduringly, and unreflectively; and readier to enter with no great trepidation into moments of extraordinary *analytic* intimacy of feeling, imagining, remembering, and anticipating?

I am sure many examples will "come to your mind" of analysts whose usual analytic competence and effectiveness you would not seriously doubt and yet who, in their nonanalytic relationships, including those with colleagues, seem to be one or more of the following: rigid, aloof, irritable, ruthlessly controlling, egoistic, flamboyant, shut in, timid, obsessional, paranoid, depressive, or hypomanic. Some would say that these analysts might be able to work well up to a point but be unable to carry their analyses through to optimal terminations. But to be realistic about it and also for heuristic purposes, I think it best to suspend judgment on this matter; for how many competent analysts come across as paragons of normality to those who know them best in their private lives?

Among the factors that have been said to facilitate the analyst's relatively secure and complex empathizing at work, the following seem to stand out. For the analyst, less is at stake personally in that the analytic relationship is not the repository of his or her major personal needs other than those directly involved in the subjective importance of working well as an analyst. Also, the analyst gets to know so much about certain intimate and crucial details of the analysand's life (for example, masturbatory practices and fantasies, transgressions and abuses of various kinds, long-smoldering resentments, etc.—and the conflictedness of it all!). Additionally, the analyst is not constrained to respond overtly in the ordinary social way and so may, and usually will, defer response while sorting out what is essential, timely, basic, or authentic, and is able on this basis to remain narcissistically and defensively secure and emotionally finely tuned. The analyst's primary responsibility is to formulate interpretations at appropriate times and not to respond in kind to what the analysand is bringing up. Further, as well as benefiting from a superego-sanctioned "work ego," the analyst can rely on what may be called a "work superego," one which, through training and identification with teachers, prohibits nontechnical erotic and hostile intimacies and thereby eases the strain on, and expands the limits of, ego functioning. Additionally, the analyst, through personal analysis and supervision, has weathered confrontations with regressive shifts of functioning and the primitive erotic and hostile pressures that will be experienced in regressive contexts. And finally, the analyst is protected by the knowledge that the specialized form of closeness that intensifies during an analysis will abate with its termination.

Owing to factors of these various sorts, the analyst in relation to the analysand will be less disposed than he or she would be otherwise to act ambivalently and anxiously and to introduce distortions. The analyst will need much less to be loved and cared for, less to be empathized with and appreciated, vicariously fulfilled or victimized, and so on. Occupying this relatively informed and disinterested position, the analyst is better prepared to work sensitively, generously, and reliably.

It has also been suggested that one must like someone in order to empathize with him or her. But as there are many kinds of liking, "liking" is too complex a topic to be taken for granted. Furthermore, I would suggest that a strong case can be made for the view that liking of any sort is based on empathizing rather than being its product. And perhaps an even stronger case can be made that liking and empathizing ordinarily contribute to one another in a benign circle.

The portrait I have sketched of the informed, disinterested, and empathic analyst is not an idealization. It has been presented here only to serve as an ideal form with reference to which one may hope to explain the often observed discrepancy I mentioned between the competent analyst's analytic and nonanalytic relationships. (As Cooper [1982] has pointed out with respect to what is ordinarily called "good character," many analysts show more of it in their work than otherwise—a discrepancy of the same sort which concerns us here.) Sketching this portrait is also the last part of my introduction to the points which I particularly want to consider at length: mental models, analytic modifications of modes of action, fictive aspects of the analytic relationship, and transformational against imitative aspects of the analyst's empathizing. It is in these four respects that I shall be attempting to add something to the already rich and clinically useful literature on our topic.

Constructing Models of the Analysand

To begin to consider the analyst's construction of mental models, one must first of all disregard certain positivistic assumptions, namely that subject and object are distinct entities; that there is a single, unambiguously knowable emotional reality with which to empathize; and that empathizing may therefore be judged simply right or wrong on the basis of objective criteria that exist free of theoretical presuppositions and interpretive grasp of context. If empathizing requires the analyst to construct a mental model or idea of the analysand to use as a framework or guide for responding empathically, then the analyst can only be empathizing with the analysand as he or she exists in this constructed model. That is to say, for the analyst the analysand is not someone who is somehow objectively knowable outside this model, whatever its nature. As an analyst, one empathizes with one's idea of the analysand. Certainly, over the course of an analysis, the analyst's

39

idea of the analysand may be revised extensively in the light of special developments and difficulties. But in principle some model, however incoherent, is always implied.

Consider, further, that not only is there considerable variation in the types of models that tend to be constructed by members of different schools of analysis, there is as well great variation in the models constructed by members of one school. Variation *among* schools reflects in large part different theoretical presuppositions concerning what is to be regarded as basic in child development and psychopathology and therefore in transference and resistance (or vice versa). This variation among systems also includes different ways of naming things and resulting different connotations and narrative consequences of the language used to establish the phenomena in question. Variation *within* a school reflects in large part differences in personality type and working style of analyst and analysand considered as a pair; it also reflects differences among analysts in intelligence, wit, training, professional identifications, and clinical as well as other life experience. Additionally, this variation reflects what is usually officially discounted, if not denied, that is, interpretive heterogeneity within each school. There is heterogeneity both in the hierarchical arrangement of explanatory variables such as hostility, sexuality, and narcissistic concerns, and in the descriptive terms considered most suitable for the phenomena under consideration.

The consequence of all of this variability is that there are numerous, perhaps countless, mental models of any one analysand that may be constructed, *all* more or less justified by "data" and by reports of beneficial effects on empathizing and the analytic process. Thus it is that, on the one hand, many analysts of different sorts and persuasions may empathize well and beneficially with a similar group of analysands, and, on the other hand, a second analyst may empathize with an analysand better than a first even though both analysts belong to the same school of analytic thought.

In connection with analysts' models of specific analysands, two sets of factors must be discussed here. One of these sets comprises, as I mentioned, the influences exerted by the analyst's theoretical orientation. For example, a Freudian analyst does and should construct Freudian models. With the help of these models, Freudian analysts do more than establish and order phenomena into some kind of coherent and intelligible account of the analysand. They also help create further analytic phenomena in the contexts of associating, dreaming, remembering, fantasizing, etc. These phenomena necessarily reflect the impact

The Psychoanalyst's Empathic Activity

of the analyst's Freudian way of making sense in the terms of infantile psychosexuality and other familiar variables. It is no joke—it is, in fact, an epistemological necessity—that Freudian analysts get Freudian material from their analysands while Jungians and others get other material, material not altogether different, to be sure, but different enough to require much careful reflection before one attempts to pass judgment on the superiority of one school over another simply on the basis of what the "facts" are.

Heinz Kohut, for example, essentially and necessarily tends to put in parentheses detailed exploration of the origins of various kinds of polymorphously perverse phenomena. He does so by regarding these phenomena as "disintegration products" (1977). In his writings, he is more interested in the factors that precipitate the disturbances of the cohesive self, which then produce these disintegration products, than he is in these products themselves. And one precipitating factor that he emphasizes again and again is empathic failure on the analyst's part that repeats similar, real or imagined failures on the part of the analysand's parents during early childhood. On this basis, Kohut not only organizes a model of the analysand to be empathized with, he also helps bring into being within the analytic situation a rich array of further phenomena. These phenomena then seem quite naturally to fill in critical aspects of the narcissistic or self-representational and self-experiential aspects of the analysand's development and disturbance. The vicissitudes of "selfobject" transferences reign supreme.

With Kohut, I believe that mainstream Freudians usually do not and cannot develop material of this kind in as great variety and in similar detail as he does. Consequently, for these Freudians the explanatory value of empathic interaction as a developmental and technical necessity, though it has always been affirmed and emphasized in one fashion or another, has never been the same or as prominent as it is in Kohut's scheme of things. On the other hand, Freudians have much more to say than Kohutians about such variables as, for example, formative bodily experiences and object love, variables that are themselves constituents of models which mediate differently focused acts of empathizing. This more traditional universe of analytic phenomena is just not the same as Kohut's. And so, in the end, it cannot be a question of one set of claims being simply right and the other simply wrong; nor can it be a matter of the phenomena being natural or analytic in the one case and artificial or nonanalytic in the other. Comparative assessments of the two approaches can only be carried out in terms of more or less integrated systems of assumptions, concepts, methods, and the phenomena defined in and generated by each type of analysis. Kohut's attempt at comparative analysis of this sort—his report of the two analyses of Mr. Z (1979)—is unsatisfactory in this respect. Among other problems, there seems to be, in the first "Freudian" analysis, little of the empathizing with which I am familiar in traditional analyses, including those that I have carried out myself. Additionally, Kohut presents his argument in purely empirical terms rather than in more appropriate systematic-methodological terms, a failing that I have discussed elsewhere (1980a).

A second set of factors involved in the analyst's construction of the analytic model of the analysand may now be taken up. In the analytic situation, the analyst never does see the analysand in his or her entirety. This is so because analysands, in fashioning their self-presentations, are always responding to the current structure of their analytic situations, to their own shifting aims, and to their analysts' modes of thinking and responding. Analysts do not, for example, always see the full range of the analysands' charm, wit, verbal facility, or their capacity to bear responsibility, assume leadership, or win love. In some cases they see very little of any of this, at least for a long time. Indeed, when the analysand's mode of resisting is of a certain kind, the analyst may be the last to see characteristics of this sort. In other cases the analyst can extrapolate with some confidence from whatever it is that is allowed to show in the analytic situation. Still, it *is* extrapolation in these cases. Many psychological studies have shown that, to a variable extent, behavior *is* a function of situations and relationships. In terms of their mode of understanding, analysts may include under "behavior" all that analysands unconsciously and repetitively enact in forming and revising transferences and in resisting over the course of the analytic work.

Analysts deal therefore with what may be called the analysand's organization and presentation of a second self. Of course, this second self necessarily amounts to a version of what the analysand presents in nonclinical relationships. It cannot be viewed otherwise. Psychoanalytic work presupposes this continuity. But the guiding principle that these selves must be continuous with one another does not show that they are identical, that they are equally accessible, or that it is only their sameness that counts. Freud came at this problem from the opposite direction when he noted that analysts see aspects of analysands that others never see.

If all this is so, if follows that the model of the analysand that is constructed is essentially a model of this second self, that is to say, the self in analysis with a particular analyst. And the changes that are observed and facilitated take place in the realm embraced by the model being used. All the analyst can ever know for sure is the analysand as his or her own analysand, and that is a lot to know and of no small beneficial consequence. My emphasis here is on what may be called the *fictive* aspect of the analytic relationship, an aspect to which I shall return in several places. (It is, I believe, an emphasis that is consistent with Freud's on the artificial aspect of the transference neurosis [Freud, 1914a], though it is not on that account consistent with Freud's usual positivist stance toward his "data.")

It is important to add that what is known, that is, the models that are developed, are evident primarily in what analysts *do* as analysts and not in what they *say* they do or *say* they believe. The analyst's consciously rendered accounts of his or her analytic beliefs and performances may involve self-misunderstanding. Thus, it is a generally accepted principle that analytic supervisors must be alert to such self-misunderstanding on the part of supervisees. But any account of what the analyst does do as analyst can only be developed coherently and instructively in the terms of a system of psychoanalytic thought and practice. Psychoanalytic narratives are system-bound.

To sum up this lengthy set of considerations: depending on many factors, including but not limited to interrelated theoretical and technical preferences, the cognitive models of analysands will vary and, varying with them, the occasions, forms, uses, and analyzable meanings of the analyst's empathizing. In the analytic situation, empathizing is *not* a cognitively innocent or naive activity, nor is it altogether comprehensive. Consequently, one cannot elucidate this activity well if, positivistically, one insists on a sharp distinction between subject and object and, with that, on the existence of facts or phenomena that are theory-free, method-free, and narratively complete.

The Analyst's Second Self

Turning now to the analyst, I propose that he or she, too, operates through what may be called the organization and presentation of a *second self*. Here, I return to my opening observations of the qualitative and quantitative differences between personal nonanalytic empathizing and analytic empathizing. Briefly, many analysts seem to be people who are not as much at ease and open to give-and-take in ordinary life situations as they are in the analytic situation.

I wish to emphasize next that this second self presented by the analyst is analogous to the second self (or "implied author") presented by creative writers. There are many writers, whether poets or novelists, who, from what is known about them, seem to be above average in their everyday misery, cruelty, greed, egocentricity, snobbery, self-destructiveness, and sociopathy. Nevertheless, these men and women may achieve in their writings the most sublime versions of emotional experience of every kind. Though they are not angels, they write like angels. At their best they make us wish we were like them—or that we had them for friends, parents, or lovers. But in responding so appreciatively, we are thinking in fact of authorial second selves, and we are recklessly creating an illusion (an arbitrary mental model) of what these writers are as social beings—tender, witty, compassionate, brave, heart-rendingly empathic.

It is possible to conceptualize these observations concerning analysts and authors in the metapsychological terms of psychic structure. One would have to say that there is a second psychic structure available to the analyst and creative writer alike. This second structure would be similar to what Robert Fliess (1942) called the analyst's work ego. And one would have to think that analyst and writer can shift from one structure to another, as required. But if psychic structure is so much a function of situation and task orientation, such as writing a love poem or conducting an analysis, then its generalized fixity—its very structuredness!—is thrown into question. Here, ego psychologists encounter a serious difficulty.

A partial explanation of the phenomena with which we are now concerned was proposed by Kris (1952) under the heading of "regression in the service of the ego." This regression makes possible the inspirational phases of work (relaxation of defense, openness to archaic experience, etc.). In the end, according to Kris, these phases must be succeeded and modified by elaborational phases (critical scrutiny, reworking, selection, synthesis, etc.). But Kris's discussion does not authorize one to view these regressively "inspired" phases romantically as wildly creative chaos. Writers consistently work within traditions. They are working in terms of traditions even when they are revolutionizing them. To the extent that they are working, their regressive phases are best understood as those of writers, not as those of analysands or dreamers. Like empathizing, creative writing is in this respect no innocent activity; it is thoroughly informed by existing systems of thought as these have been embodied in literary and other writings, past and present, including the author's own previous work. As an art historian of some merit, Kris knew all this; however, he was writing primarily for analysts, and so he devoted most of his discussion of inspiration to primary process modes of function and to infantile fantasy and wish fulfillment, such as oral and respiratory incorporation. On this account he sometimes seemed implicitly to be endorsing a naively romantic view of the matter—the very opposite of what he was depicting—equating inspiration with simple primitivization. In the same way, empathizing, like any *analytic* regression that is truly in the service of the ego, is informed in large part by the tradition of doing analysis.

Because I have for some time been exploring alternatives to the metapsychological mode of discourse, I would not now conceptualize these activities in the terms of multiple or self-modifying psychic structures. I now prefer the terms of action and stable patterning of action. I have explored the usefulness of this metatheoretical option in a number of previous discussions (1976, 1978; see also below, chapters 6–10). And on this account I have been using "empathizing" in preference to "empathy." I use the term "action" in a broad sense that includes more than motor activity; it takes in any goal-directed performance such as thinking in all its forms and the cognitive aspects of behaving emotionally. It covers whatever in ordinary language we could say someone *does* (for example, walk, talk, remember, repress). As yet, however, we understand imperfectly the mediating actions by which analysts and writers organize and present these second selves that can be so different from, even if not thoroughly discontinuous with, their everyday selves. I shall now go on to offer some reflections on these mediating actions.

Perhaps the most important feature of the analyst's second self is the analyst's affirmative orientation. This feature is highlighted particularly by Kohut whose psychology of the self is consistently growth oriented. Highlighting, however, is not the same as discovering. Freud (1923) had already pointed in this direction in his accounts of the embattled ego's striving for mastery, Hartmann (1939, 1950, 1951) had advanced in this direction in his discussions of adaptation, I (1959) had stressed the generative aspects of the analyst's empathy; and others had made similar contributions.

What is this affirmative orientation? One way of describing it is to say that in empathizing, the analyst assumes, at least implicitly, that whatever the analysand is doing or experiencing, it is what it is essential that he or she do under the extremely adverse circumstances that prevail unconsciously or in "psychical reality." These adverse circumstances center on the terrifying infantile danger situations that Freud described broadly in "Inhibitions, Symptoms and Anxiety" (1926), namely, total loss of the love object, total loss of love, castration, and archaic and crushing superego punishment. Behind these dangers, Freud claimed, lies the primal or traumatic anxiety state of infantile helplessness. We might now want to add the following dangers to this list, perhaps as components of primal anxiety or of total loss of the object: paranoid terror, depressive helplessness, fragmentation of the self, and loss of self in a dedifferentiation of self and object, all of which would to some extent be understood unconsciously in terms of devouring and self-annihilation, and all of which could certainly be counted as ultimate narcissistic shocks.

In creating analytic experience affirmatively, the analyst steadily recognizes that the analysand has unconsciously carried these dangers into the present and continues to impose them arbitrarily on the present or at least to exaggerate present dangers in terms of infantile dangers. Consequently, the analysand is viewed as living in dread, continuously anticipating or experiencing actual or potential agonizing conflict and loss. And in seeing the analysand as doing what it seems essential to do under these psychically real conditions, the analyst does not turn pollyanna and see the analysand as just wanting to love and be loved in the ordinary sense; rather, the analyst works with a tragic vision of human development and existence (Schafer, 1970). (This is not Kohut's idea of "tragic man" as a victim of lack of empathy, an idea that violates the entire critical tradition of the sense of the tragic as *conflictual*.) With this tragic vision, the Freudian analyst understands that intransigent mistrust and negativism, discouraging rigidity and inertia, relentless triviality and grandiosity, or apparently unmodifiable resisting of some other sort, are costly means of coping with the infantile dangers which we have all experienced and which we continue to recreate in our present lives. Unconsciously, we repeatedly enact infantile dangers and security measures.

Let me here return to the claim that "nothing human is alien to me." This claim may be made legitimately by any analyst who is not altogether unprepared for the psychoanalytic encounter, provided at least that this encounter is understood in terms of danger situations and traumatic anxiety, and the repetitive and formidable forms of resisting (and transference) to which they give rise. The claim requires only a shift to a higher level of abstraction than that occupied by the analysand's concrete accounts. Specific dangers and responses to them do, of course, vary from person to person, but typical dangers (for example, object loss) and responses have been delineated in fine detail. Unconsciously we are all members of an endangered community. Here is a basis for the analyst's appropriately identifying with the analysand in the partial, circumspect, empathic way that sustains and enhances good will toward the analysand and good work with him or her.

Notwithstanding this community of experience, the concrete definitions of danger and the disturbed modes of coping with it are not to be ignored. Even though these, too, may be shared to some degree by all analysts, they are not shared equally, and they are not utilized in the same way by all analysts. Here is where analysts differ from one another in empathic range and tolerance. Some can empathize with sociopathy better than others who, in turn, may empathize more fully with depression, while yet others know anxiety inside out. But in general, although each analyst may be prepared to view some things more affirmatively than others, all analysts, to the extent that they remain more or less consistently affirmative in their orientation, actualize the empathic second self.

Another aspect of the affirmative self is the analyst's following Freud in assuming coherence and potential intelligibility in everything the analysand brings up or refrains from bringing up. The analyst is prepared to see the analysand as a meaningful totality, that is, as someone whose actions require constant life-historical and contemporaneous cross-referencing in order to be defined most exactly through their mutual implications. Unlike analysands, analysts do not believe in randomness, nor do they believe in major or total personal incoherence and discontinuity. In the analysand's beliefs there is much magic, fragmentation, denial, timelessness, and negativity. In the analyst's beliefs, to the contrary, there is much affirmation.

To the extent that analysts approach the ideal implied in "nothing human is alien to me," that is, to the extent that they unflinchingly recognize and accept that unconsciously carried forward infantile danger and coping are part of the human condition, they remain, relatively speaking, narcissistically secure. This is to say that they will not be likely to wish desperately to establish omnipotent control, nor will they resort readily to mutually destructive strategies of helplessness and discontinuity. Remaining within the fairly strict limits required by neutrality, they will tend to work honestly, bravely, patiently, and nonjudgmentally. To use the terms tragic and ironic in the sense I have presented elsewhere (1970), I would say that the analyst will envision reality tragically, tempering this vision with the ironic realization that the danger situations, being conceived in infantile terms, are both fantastic and potentially modifiable. And as a further manifestation of these cohesive and affirmative and ultimately neutral modes of action, the analyst will manifest stamina.

It is worth spending some time on the concept of stamina. (In action terms, one might speak of empathizing sturdily, steadfastly, and patiently.) Like affirmativeness, stamina is a central feature of the analyst's second self. Analysts need stamina like they need oxygen. This is not only because they may be putting in long days or seeing very disturbed analysands. These facts of an analyst's life are, of course, important, but there is more. It is hard work to move empathically with analysands through their ranges of affective experience—or in some cases to live with their paucity of affective experience over long stretches of time. Human beings are not built to do so much improvising of the analytic second selves appropriate to different analysands. Empathically improvising different modes of organizing experience always makes for some identity diffusion. And although some of us analysts seem to forget that we, too, are human beings and not gods or machines, we all do need constantly to recreate the experience of self-cohesiveness and self-consistency. The analyst must therefore monitor his or her sense of being integrated or "together" while at work and must be prepared to carry out whatever self-analysis is indicated, not only to stay in good repair but to modify analytic activity appropriately (for example, by slowing down the pace or taking greater distance from the clinical interaction). Those analysts who maintain cohesiveness securely are not so endangered or confused by empathic excursions. Those analysts have stamina.

A second major factor making for the second self's stamina is anticipation. No matter what the analysand might confront the analyst with, it will have less shock value if the analyst works with a frame of reference that helps him or her anticipate, from the cues provided by the analysand and by self-understanding, the sorts of things that might happen next. The analyst's own personal analysis is essential in this respect. Other help derives from clinical supervision and experience, moderated therapeutic zeal, and a reasonably integrated, clinically rooted theory or system of concepts. Intelligence also helps, for one

48

of the signs of intelligence is the capacity to anticipate, which is to say, the capacity to establish and apply on appropriate occasions patternings of expectation. These patternings are essential aspects of what is meant when it is said that, in empathizing, the analyst forms a mental model of the analysand. In one fundamental sense, the model is a patterning of expectations. With it, the analyst is like a good tennis player who always seems to be waiting for the ball rather than scrambling after it and getting worn down.

But it is literature rather than tennis that should concern us here. I would say that in this regard the analyst is in a position analogous to that of an informed reader of literature, one with what has been called interpretive competence (Culler, 1975). Competent readers recognize the genre, the historical period, the formal constraints and opportunities of one or another type of literature. They do not approach a Cavalier poet, a Romantic poet, and a Symbolist poet with the same expectations, nor do they read in the same way a lyric, an epic, and an occasional piece, when all three have been written within the same tradition. In clinical analyses, too, the patternings of expectation vary from analysand to analysand and from context to context, and varying with them are the forms and degrees of analytic activity. Interpretive competence reduces the likelihood that, repeatedly, the analyst will be emotionally shocked or overextended and so suffer a loss of stamina.

One of the most important and frequent shocks the analyst must anticipate is the analysand's *attacks* on empathizing. In part, sometimes in large part, analysands fear being empathized with and so they attack the very thing they long for! (Kohut puts his own sort of special emphasis on this point.) Empathizing that is recognized as such stirs up conscious hope when, defensively, none is wanted. Being the object of empathizing can be disturbingly overstimulating especially when, consciously or unconsciously, the analysand invests it with erotic significance, perhaps homosexual or castrating significance. Being empathized with can intensify feelings of worthlessness or overwhelming indebtedness. And it can be deadening when the antagonistic analysand feels disarmed by it. I am not now speaking of conspicuous or heavy-handed shows of empathic power, many of which are, by common agreement, altogether misguided. The attacks in question are on the very possibility of being empathized with and on the empathizing that is an implicit component of any sensitive intervention—or nonintervention. Coolness can be as empathically appropriate in some clinical contexts as compassion is in others. For the

49

most part, however, I shall be referring in what follows to empathizing of the more compassionate sort.

Technically, the analyst cannot always anticipate—and will not insist on always being able to anticipate!—just how any explicit act of empathizing will be taken. It is, however, usually possible to analyze such disturbing reactions to analytic empathizing as feeling misunderstood, smothered, seduced, pressured to repress rage or anxiety, or invaded. It is perhaps best to think of these disturbing interventions as instances of incomplete empathizing, provided that they are not evidently inappropriate in context or countertransferential. Being prepared in the individual case to learn about empathizing while engaging in it, the analyst does not put the second self under the strain of being a know-it-all. Instead, the analyst maintains the proper focus on the vicissitudes of the analytic relationship.

Looking at attacks on empathizing from another angle, one sees that analysands often are unprepared to empathize with themselves. This unpreparedness may be based on a disposition to react guiltily or ashamedly and a correlated reactive policy of asceticism (Schafer, 1964). Being thus unprepared, these analysands may take the analyst's empathizing as an unwelcome stimulus to go easy on themselves, become self-pitying, or even become grandiose. Or else they may be afraid they will cry out their strangulated grief forever or become incontinent or do something equally disastrous. That analysands fear such developments is well known to psychoanalytic clinicians, though its relevance to self-empathizing may not be widely appreciated. As an aspect of his or her second self, the analyst is prepared to empathize with these dilemmas, too.

In yet another respect, analysands often fear empathizing with the analyst. They may prefer the posture of nonsentimentality, detachment, aloofness, or being the efficient, self-sufficient, properly self-absorbed patient. What they then dread is this, that from their end rather than the analyst's all the difficult issues of otherness, closeness, guilt, reparation, voyeurism, and envy and gratitude might be introduced into the analytic setting by their responding empathically to the analyst who, on occasion, will seem to them, and perhaps be, confused, troubled, ill, elated, or depressed. Good reality testing is often implicit in the analysand's way of perceiving the analyst, and the analyst's readiness to self-empathize is needed to make it clear that for the analysand conflicted reality testing is a live issue.

Fearing any or all of these three kinds of empathic interaction, the analysand will mount a sustained assault on any empathizing or even the prospect of it. The analyst will be worked on to become as moralistic, impatient, fragmented, fatigued, secretive, bored, discouraged, hostile, or sexually aroused as the analysands are or fear they might become. And owing to the analysands' having remained unconsciously desperate throughout their lives, and owing to the cunning strategies that, unconsciously, have been born of this continuing dread—strategies whose cunning it is impossible to overestimate—they skillfully sabotage the analyst's empathizing. Indeed, it is essential that the analyst empathize with the desperation implied by these very assaults. Otherwise, the most dreadful kinds of negative countertransference may ensue. Against these assaults, along with the other attributes of his or her empathic second self, the analyst requires stamina, staying power.

So far we have considered the following factors: maintaining a sense of self-cohesiveness, anticipating events with the help of an integrated frame of reference, learning while doing, and being alert to attacks on empathizing and being empathized with. There is one more important factor to consider, and that is the analyst's ability to maintain a long-range view of the analysis as a whole. At every stage of the analysis, the analyst must be ready to look ahead, from the beginning of the analysis to the present moment and beyond it, in order to locate the analysand in a context of dangerous change. Knowing the starting point and the route thus far helps maintain perspective on present and anticipated difficulty. This long-range aspect of empathizing, which makes analytic restraint more useful and less wearing than it would be otherwise, has been generally overlooked; in the main, analysts have focused on empathy of the moment, perhaps because of their conception of empathic response as imitative. I shall return to the question of imitation later in this chapter.

By emphasizing stamina as a feature of the analyst's second self that safeguards empathizing, I may seem to have shifted from the mediation of empathizing to its facilitation. But I would argue that the shift is more apparent than real in that, often, it is sustained empathizing in extended contexts that is in question, and sustaining an empathic orientation is a manifestation of stamina. Pressured, hasty, fragmentary attempts at empathizing frighten and wound analysands, as they do children, and they lead to renewed attacks on empathizing itself. Seen in this light, stamina and its constituents are essential features of the analyst's empathic second self.

THE ANALYTIC ATTITUDE

The Fictive Aspect of the Analytic Relationship

If, as I have proposed, the analytic relationship amounts to a meeting and a development of two second selves, defined to a large extent by the nature of the analytic project, then it follows that this relationship may be called *fictive*. Fictive, not in the sense of artificial, inauthentic, or illusory, but in the sense of a relationship constructed by two people under highly specialized dialogic circumstances. It is not, however, its approximation to uniqueness that makes it fictive. All relationships have a fictive aspect in that they are constructed by both parties involved; they are constructed out of what is conventionally realistic and expectable and what is fantasized unconsciously . Among other things, the word *fictive* means fashioned or invented by imagination, and within the psychoanalytic perspective, all relationships are necessarily approached as fictive.

I centered first on the analysand's second self and then on the analyst's. By calling them "second," I have not intended to distinguish them from some kind of real, uninvented, or unfashioned self. I have intended only to indicate their specialized nature. Nor did I mean by "second" that there is a single "first" self, monolithic and constant in all other relationships. It is just that the analytic second self is not identical with those constructed or narrated in nonanalytic relationships.

In order to clarify my point about the fictive analytic selves-in-relation I shall next discuss the second self in relation to action language and also in relation to values.

How does the second self stand in relation to action language? Let me remind you that, to begin with, I spoke of *organizing* and *presenting* a second self; also, that I emphasized that it is the analyst's performance rather than his or her consciously given testimony which counts in this regard. I made these points in order to indicate how the entire matter might be couched in the terms of action. In keeping with my recent theoretical work on the reconceptualization of psychoanalysis, I do believe that the second self—and the first self too, for that matter—are for systematic purposes better conceptualized as actions and modes of action. The analytic second self is a way of conducting an analysis. It does not refer to an essence that lies behind the actions and expresses itself through them. And it does not refer exclusively or without amendment to the analyst's self-descriptions. Indeed, the designation *second self* is best thought of as a narrative device, a form of description or interpretation of the analyst insofar as he or she is working effectively as an analyst, that is, in the fictive mode of working analytically. One could therefore dispense with the concept of self and speak only of the analyst who empathizes sensitively and in a sustained, informed, and coherent manner and who often performs better in the work context than in his or her purely personal situations.

Why, then, have I stayed with the idea of the second self? There are two reasons, the first being that from the standpoint of action language, the second self is preferable to the "work ego." It is preferable in that "work ego" stems from the mechanistic and anthropomorphic mode of conceptualization that characterizes traditional metapsychological language and which action language is intended to replace. The second reason is that, for the time being, I find much inspiration in the concept as it has been used in literary discussion of the second or implied selves of authors and readers (see especially Booth, 1961). There is much to be gained by establishing bridges between the two interpretive disciplines of psychoanalysis and literary studies. In many respects, literary critics are far ahead of psychoanalysts in their examination of the principles and problems of analyzing discourse and dialogue in terms of their transformational aspects. As a rule, psychoanalysts have been more concerned with the content of psychoanalytic dialogue and the long-range personal changes effected by this dialogue than they have been with the personal changes that *mediate* or *enable* effective discourse and dialogue of one kind or another.

With regard to values: I have been emphasizing that the empathizing analyst often performs better in work than in nonanalytic personal relationships. It does not follow from this proposition that the analytic second self is in some absolute sense a better self. It is better *for analytic purposes.* To claim for it any more than this would be to impose on the analyst a set of values or an ideology that favors something like saintliness or being a savior as a way of life. It would be to disregard the fact that it is precisely because the analyst is conducting an analysis that he or she must put in parentheses many aspects of the first self, that is, the self of his or her nonanalytic relationships. If they are not put in parentheses, then they must be consistently noted and reflected upon, often arduously, in order to sort out countertransference from appropriate analytic activity.

Idealizing the analyst's second self as a proper model for all human interaction can only have unfortunate consequences. Instead of all relationships becoming that much more exaltedly human, they become pseudo-clinical or pseudo-analytic relationships, and as such they are disruptive and often destructive. Family relationships, work relationships, the routine business relationships of everyday life, each calls for a type of dialogue in which the development and interpretation of unconscious resisting and transference are beside the point and most likely will be disturbing. The fictive elements and the aims of these relationships are not the same as those of the analytic relationship. On the other hand, I do not imply that the analyst ought never use his or her analytic understanding in everyday life. That restrictive policy would be self-crippling as well as inauthentic, and, in any event, impossible. In this respect, questions of balance and flexibility will always have to be dealt with, and they are not easy to answer.

Empathizing and Imitating

The best empathizing is not that which is undertaken in a deliberate way. In this respect, one may liken empathizing to flashes of wit. As Freud (1905b) pointed out and Kris (1952) elaborated, the work of wit is best performed preconsciously and unconsciously. We know empathic response not so much by the analyst's intent, or by its outward form, as by the developments to which it gives rise. As I mentioned, explicit and insistent empathizing might, among other things, mortify the analysand, in which case the model of the analysand at that moment may be considered flawed and the analyst's conduct not truly empathic. Often, in the course of analytic sessions, there is not even enough time for the analyst to cogitate briefly before responding, or not responding, to the analysand's self-presentations. Analysts feel their way, and often they learn after the fact, if they learn at all, when and how they have acted empathically. Sometimes analysands tell them only long after the event how important a response, a significant silence, or the maintenance of respectful distance was to their sense of being understood, appreciated, empathized with. It is easier to identify what is emotionally out of tune than what is exquisitely in tune. Consequently, there is a major retrospective aspect to the identification of empathizing.

Upon reflection, one may define here a major ambiguity of analytic work. The ambiguity attaches to the place of imitation in empathizing.

The Psychoanalyst's Empathic Activity

This ambiguity arises because the empathic value of an intervention or nonintervention may be appreciated only after the analysand has changed in some significant way. Having changed, the analysand will be using a new perspective on the history of the analytic relationship to date, and the original empathizing may have helped make that change of perspective possible, though it cannot be regarded as having been effective apart from the interpretation with which it was correlated.

Again, we may draw an analogy to art, more specifically to aesthetics. The analogy involves the much debated question of imitation. Does art imitate life, or is it the case, as Oscar Wilde (1889) suggested in earnest, that to a great extent life imitates art? In the latter case, art is viewed as the creation of new ways of constructing experience and thus as the maker of new modes of living generally and new retrospective considerations specifically. It should not be necessary to make the case for the proposition that we live in ways that to a noteworthy extent have been shaped, directly and indirectly, by the constructions of artists and other creative people. In this connection we must acknowledge the shaping and reshaping of our ideas of what love is or Nature, a self, a noble person, a beautiful woman, or a Jewish identity in America.

Returning now to the ambiguity I mentioned, one must ask to what extent empathizing is imitative and to what extent it is constitutive of new experience. To what extent does the fictive meeting of the two second selves in the analytic situation give rise to empathizing of a very special sort? This is empathizing that creates in the person of the analysand someone who has never quite existed before *for anyone* in that articulated form or with that intensity. To what extent does this encounter give rise to new modes of conceiving of self and others and thereby to a new possibility on the analysand's part of recognizing, appreciating, and performing specific acts of empathizing?

I think that the most conservative yet still adequate answer to these questions is that analytic empathizing cannot be, as Freud (1921) and Fenichel (1945) seemed to think, largely imitative. Among its other features, the imitative conception is restricted to only a few elements of what earlier I called empathy of the moment as against empathizing in extended contexts. Less conservatively, I would join with Oscar Wilde to the extent of emphasizing the creative cognitive aspects over the imitative while still acknowledging that, often, the imitative aspects remain important constituents of complex empathic actions. I would add to this that, whatever we do regard as new in the empathic construction, we should not view it as discontinuous with all that has come before it, that is to say, as understandable without reference to the past.

Presumably, the imitative aspects take in one person's immediate response, through an act of identification, to another persons's emotionally expressive physical changes, such as smiles, tears, tone of voice, and clenched fists, when these are part of the scene. Yet even here one does not respond altogether innocently. Each of us establishes and employs models not only of the particular expressive person and context but of expressiveness itself. We rely on these models to help us sort out the essential from the inessential, the intense from the mild, the straightforward from the ironic, and the authentic from the inauthentic. Some tears are crocodile tears, some laughter is derisive, some scoldings are affectionate, some affection is ingratiation. We have to be able to tell the difference.

In a transference-countertransference impasse, the analyst fails to see the difference. What is involved here is a faulty model constructed by the analyst. It may be a model that is out-of-date, that is, one that disregards important changes in the analysand, or it may be a model distorted by any number of other factors. It may take a crisis in the analytic relationship to make this discrepancy or lag clear and to open up the model for revision or correction (Schafer, 1959).

In any case, the purely imitative-identificatory view depends too much on the split between subject and object. The transformational view I am advocating emphasizes how, in empathizing, we reflect or imitate something we have already shaped, and in so doing shape it further.

I want now to relate a very short story told about Picasso. The story makes my point about the transformational and fictive aspects of empathizing far more succinctly than I have. When told at first that his now celebrated portrait of Gertrude Stein did not resemble her at all, Picasso replied simply and with enviable confidence, "It will."

The Analysand's Response to the Analyst's Second Self

In conclusion, I want to amend Freud's proposition that analysts should not be misled by their analysands' enthusiasm and desire for them. He argued that this love and this idealization are essentially transference phenomena; and he held to this view even though he recognized that the difference between "real" love and transference love is not nearly so great as it might appear. My amendment is this: a significant part of what analysands are responding to is the presentation of the analytic second self, through which analysts can sometimes empathize in so extraordinary and intense a fashion. Loewald's (1960) concept of the analyst as a new object, and my proposal (in chapter 8) that transference within psychoanalysis is a new form of experience for the analysand, however much it is unconsciously repetitive—these and other such ideas form the background of what I am saying now about empathizing through an analytic second self. In my view, my amendment enriches rather than diminishes our understanding not only of what goes into analytic collaboration or "alliance" but of the concept of transference itself. It is enriching in that it articulates the idea of the object of transference and thereby facilitates the essential analysis of transference's unconsciously repetitive aspects.

Looking at it from this point of view, one may say that there are three mistakes that we analysts are liable to make. The first is when we think we are necessarily as finely tuned empathically in our ordinary lives as we can be in our work; the second mistake, emphasized by Freud, is when we think that we are as special, even in our analytic selves, as our analysands sometimes say we are; the third is when we think that the analysand's love, respect, and gratitude are simply and only blind repetitions and therefore entirely unearned.

4

Appreciation in the Analytic Attitude

From the time of Freud's "Papers on Technique," analysts have been attempting to delineate the constituents of the analytic relationship. These constituents include the noncountertransferential and potentially beneficial ways in which analysts view analysands and engage in clinical relations with them—the so-called analytic attitude. A variety of terms have been proposed: respect, liking, and empathy (widely accepted and now elaborated in a special way by Kohut), benevolent neutrality (Jones), tact (Loewenstein), the diatrophic attitude (Gitelson), the work ego (Fliess), the therapeutic alliance (Zetzel) or working relationship (Greenson), the holding relationship (Winnicott), and the growth-fostering relationship that includes an analytic type of love (Loewald). From this list of overlapping terms I abstract the constituent element of appreciation in order to give it special consideration here.

By appreciation I refer to a family or spectrum of terms that range from the analyst's being mildly admiring to experiencing wonder that may border on awe. No doubt, appreciation may be a manifestation of, a screen for, or simply colored by disruptive value-laden identification in the countertransference. Being appreciative of the analysand may also amount to the analyst's adopting a defensive stance against consciously envying and derogating the analysand. But then any of the other constituents listed above (respect, empathy, etc.) may also involve transferential and resistant actions on the analyst's part, and it is generally accepted that the mere possibility of such involvement is no argument against the analytic usefulness of one or another constituent. Appreciation, a mode of engagement frequently expressed or implied in informal clinical discussion as well as published case reports,

58

is not usually taken necessarily to imply any lapse from the analytic attitude.

The guiding questions in the discussion that follows are these. What is it specifically that is being appreciated when the analyst appreciates the analysand? Is it that the analysand has successfully, even if in a costly and compromised way, struggled against adversity and suffering during his or her actual, public, behavioral life history? Or is it rather the analysand's struggling painfully but productively within psychical reality, an endeavor which does not always correlate closely with the public or so-called objective life-historical facts? Or is it perhaps a mixture of both of these that is appreciated? And if it is this mixture, do both kinds of appreciation belong, or belong equally, within the analytic attitude? Also, are there other factors that are being appreciated?

As to what it is that the analyst appreciates, one ready answer is this. Through recall, insight, and empathy, the analyst gets to understand the extent to which the analysand has managed to continue living hopefully, lovingly, and honestly, and also in a way that is dignified, proud, talented, and constructive when, considering all the relevant adverse life circumstances, the odds against this achievement have been very great if not overwhelming. The analyst will, of course, remain well aware of activities of the analysand that tend in the destructive direction. These destructive trends include living despairingly, hatefully, corruptly, self-abasingly, enviously, and wastefully with respect to personal potential and opportunity. Without this two-sided view and the empathic tension it implies, the analyst would, in a self-aggrandizing manner, be either idealizing or derogating the analysand.

The achievement of this analytic two-sidedness or many-sidedness is a function of the analyst's maintaining a vision of reality characterized especially by its tragic and ironic modes (Schafer, 1970). In different ways, these two modes simultaneously embrace the terror and wonder of being human. Analysands grow only slowly into being prepared to view themselves and present themselves in this balanced light. To begin with and for a long time, they simplify themselves, presenting now one side, now another, as they bring up the "good" and "bad" fragments of self and others in their reminiscences and current experiences. In their forming transferences and their resisting, they attempt to seduce the analyst into believing in these self-simplifications. Loewenstein took up one of these seductions—seduction of the ag-

59

gressor—in his notable discussion of masochism (1957). Analysts are familiar with many other types of seductive action, all of them equally simplifying and thus potentially unbalancing so far as the analyst's responding empathically is concerned.

In maintaining the analytic attitude, the analyst confronts, clarifies, and interprets these seductive strategies in a fundamentally neutral manner, thereby paving the way toward the analysand's believing that it may be safe to become a whole person engaged with whole others. In other words, the analysand becomes readier to experience and contain the tension of opposites within a unified self-presentation, however painfully this may be done. In time, if things go well, it is done much less painfully and much more stably.

The problem of the analyst's maintaining a balanced analytic attitude is, however, greater than that just described. One of the great tests faced by the analyst is to continue to respond empathically to the sick, miserable, helpless, and frightened aspects, and also to the rebellious, destructive, grandiose, and erotically seductive aspects of the analysand's self-presentations. Yet another great test is to begin responding empathically to the affirmative aspects of just these disturbed self-presentations. By affirmative aspects I am referring to the ways in which these negative-seeming self-presentations are, unconsciously, elements of a grand strategy both for protecting oneself in the infantile danger situations that, unconsciously, have remained as real as ever and for making the most of oneself in one's relations with others. For example, in the case of an analysand's adopting a rigidly defensive and oppositional course of action in the analysis, it often emerges that, unconsciously, he or she believes this course to be the only safe way to protect the beloved analyst or to forestall devastating personal regression.

The analyst cannot clarify and experience these affirmations empathically all at once. Understandably, it takes considerable analytic work, which means considerable development and interpretation of the forming of transferences and resistant strategies, before this work can be done genuinely and in a manner that is specific to each analysand. Before then, the analyst's affirmative appreciation must be mainly theoretical and anticipatory; however, even in that limited form, it will still be important and useful. In order to maintain this affirmative appraisal of the analysand's productions, both verbal and behavioral (as in acting out), the analyst must also view these productions from the vantage point of personal action or goal-directed activity. Otherwise, in viewing them too simply as afflictions, automatically operat-

60

ing mechanisms, and unfortunate accidents of development, the analyst only sets limits on their analyzability.

There is a third form of appreciation that enters into analytic work, in addition to the life-historical appreciation and the affirmative appreciation already mentioned. Analysts often express wonder and awe at the incredibly complex and ingenious workings of "the Unconscious," as it continues to be called. What is important in this respect is that this appreciation not be defensively intellectualized and displaced from the analysand to a topographic system. To claim simply to experience appreciation of the workings of a theoretical assumption is surely to reify that assumption. Nor is it any one of the metapsychological structures—id, ego, and superego—that one may legitimately claim to appreciate empathically, for the same problems of intellectualizing, displacing, and reifying would persist in this instance, too. Additionally, it is entirely inappropriate to speak of empathizing with entities and processes that have meaning only within an impersonalized natural-science model of mind. The object of appreciation to which reference is actually being made is not a mental apparatus but a distinct human individual. It is the analysand as person who is incredibly complex and ingenious in his or her mental or social activity. Moreover, in clinical work, it can only be a person who is the object of empathizing. Empathizing with the impersonal ego or mental apparatus would be like empathizing with a chemical undergoing transformation in a test tube.

Consider, for example, a not unusual response to dreams. Once one understands a dream analytically, one may well admire it as a creation. Alternatively, one may, as Freud (1900) did, admire the dream work as the creative process that fashioned it. How skillfully and imaginatively it has condensed, displaced, and symbolized conflictual issues; how versatile its use of dramatic and graphic representation; how much it "says" in disguise! At this moment of interpretive achievement, no longer fearing that one will not understand, one is, of course, pleased with oneself, even impressed by one's acumen; but it would be wrong to ignore on this account one's response to the thing itself, that is, to the dream or the dream work.

Within the framework of action language, which deals with persons rather than mechanisms, it is necessary to ask, Who does the dream work? The dream work doesn't just happen. It makes little sense to state or imply, as Freud did, that it just does itself. Saying that the primary process does the dream work is unacceptable. This is so not only because one would thereby remain in the realm of mechanistic discourse, but also because saying so would be inconsistent with one's being as impressed with dreams as one often is, in that the prevailing conceptualization of primary process emphasizes energic mobility and not creative synthesis. And in modern psychoanalytic theory there is, following Freud, no longer a hypothetical system *Ucs.* to do this work; metapsychologically, the matter must now be conceptualized structurally.

From the structural standpoint, then, one would have to invoke the principle of multiple function. One would say that all the constituent structures of the mind participate in the amazing end-result that one appreciates as a dream. The same might be said for a symptom, a good joke, a parapraxis, any important character trait, and the subtle manifestations of powerful transferences and resisting. Brenner (1976), for example, emphasizes the central role in analytic work of investigating neurotic compromises, but he does not say who effects these compromises. The ego does, he might say, but what then of the unconscious defenses? Although these defenses are constituents of the ego, they resist compromise. Perhaps it is certain superordinate organizing functions of the ego, as Hartmann (1939) suggested, that effect compromises, but then so much scope and authority would have to be ascribed to these functions that in the end they would come to stand for the person as agent. And the constituents of compromise are, after all, the various conflicting actions that the one person wishes to perform (see chapter 6). So at least one would speak if one were to be using action language consistently. It is, therefore, the analysand who compromises, to be sure mostly unconsciously in the case of both neurotic symptoms and dreams.

In his discussion of responsibility for dreams, Freud (1925a) had to say that the dreamer was responsible for the dream. Who else, he asked, dreamed the dream? Just as soon as notions of responsibility enter the discussion, one must depart from metapsychological impersonality and begin to speak of persons—the dreamer, the neurotic, the analysand, etc.—performing actions in characteristic ways.

Thus, if the analyst is to avoid mechanizing, anthropomorphizing, or intellectualizing the "parts" of the mind, especially the ego, and if the analyst is also to avoid taking too much distance as well as the wrong kind of distance from the analytic engagement by marveling at "functions" of the mental apparatus, he or she would do better to say that it is the analysand who is being regarded with wonder or awe for having effected this intricate achievement of dreaming. The analyst would still be accepting and using the proposition that much of this impressive work has been accomplished by the analysand unconsciously and preconsciously. It is not primarily a question of one's appreciating mental performances that have been carried out consciously and deliberately; as a rule these performances do not elicit the kind of appreciation being discussed here. The acid test of the analyst's believing in "the Unconscious" is his or her readiness to appreciate or otherwise empathize with those conflictual activities engaged in by the analysand of which the latter dares not be aware. It is, therefore, most important that the analyst appreciate what the analysand has done, mostly unconsciously and preconsciously, and how he or she has done it.

In the case of dreaming, the object being appreciated is no longer primarily either explicitly narrated conflictual life-historical achievement or the unconsciously affirmative aspects of negative self-representations.

Certainly, in one form or another, the general features of dream activity are universally encountered so that their significance extends beyond the immediate analysand to all people. Nevertheless, it is also true that the analyst is always dealing with particularized manifestations of these features and that these manifestations emerge only in the two-person context of analyzing, in which there is an immediate object of appreciation.

It is necessary to pause briefly in order to discuss the conception being invoked here of the person as unitary agent. To say "the person" or "the analysand" seems to suggest a denial of the subject's being unconsciously conflicted and thus a denial of the central subject matter of psychoanalytic work. But this inference is unwarranted. What is in question rather is the best way to reconceptualize what traditionally has been called unconscious conflict. In the mechanistic universe of metapsychology, unconscious conflict is a matter of clashing forces or of opposing, energized structures. In effect, each of these parties to conflict is conceived as an agent in its own right, and accordingly the mental apparatus is conceived of as an aggregate of such agencies. In the alternative action conceptualization being used here, one is always dealing with a single agent, the person, and one recognizes that this person simultaneously pursues incompatible and even contradictory goals. Additionally, one recognizes that the person defines and pursues many of the most important goals *unconsciously* and avoids and resists recognizing that this is the case. In other words, *the person acts conflictedly and unconsciously* rather than being the repository of conflicting and unconsciously operating forces or structures. Unitary does not mean conscious and perfectly integrated. In the instances that call for interpretation, the action ("ego function") of synthesizing is inadequately carried out, consciously, preconsciously, and unconsciously. Unitary, therefore, means only that it is *one* person doing lots of things at once, that is, performing very complex actions while defensively and in self-contradiction restricting his or her being consciously aware of what is being done and why. This is the analysand with whom one is emotionally engaged and to whom one speaks when intervening analytically, and this is the analysand who is appreciated.

It should be obvious that thinking of this third kind of appreciation in terms of personal actions within the analysis would tend to support and enhance empathic engagement with the analysand. In contrast, thinking of complex mental productions strictly in traditional metapsychological terms would tend to limit this beneficial engagement; it would do so by interposing a hypothetical mental apparatus between the analyst and analysand. It would be an instance of what might be called narcissism of theory as well as a conceptually incoherent attempt to humanize a natural-science model of the mind. Narcissistic-identificatory elements do, of course, always play a part in empathizing—one appreciates what one wishes one could do or what one prides oneself on having done—but object-related elements need not be excluded or minimized on that account.

More than imposing limitation on the analyst's empathizing with and engaging the analysand, the analyst bound to the metapsychological way of thinking will convey to the analysand a conception of both of them as passive witnesses of astonishing and impersonal mental events. This conception will be conveyed between the lines, as it were, through fluctuations and distributions of the analyst's interest, activity, excitement, and forms of expression such as "the analysis," "the process," "the mind," "the inner world," or "the Unconscious." And thus will resistant activity be reinforced, even confirmed, by the analyst's basic point of view on mental functioning, for the analysand will be encouraged to participate in dissociated, intellectualized, and passive experience of the analytic work. The problem may become critical during the termination of analysis, for then, more than ever before, the analysand will be speaking as a unitary person, however dramatic the temporary lapses into disclaimed action, conflictedness, and fragmentation may be. Especially at that time one can see that theory is indeed a technical issue. The day of reckoning has come.

I have already expressed the view that it is the analysand who is appreciated. In the context of action language it is more exact to say that what is appreciated is the repertoire of actions and modes of action of the analysand viewed always as a whole active person even when engaged in giving the most fragmented and contradictory accounts of experience. I have also referred to three different sets of factors that enter into appreciation, namely, the analysand's life history of achievement under adversity, the analyst's affirmative interpretation of the manifestly negative, and the marvelous intricacy of actions performed mostly unconsciously and preconsciously.

It is, however, not the appreciation of the analytically revised, coordinated, and filled-in biographies that is most consistent with the analytic attitude. This is so no matter what may be the share of adversity, suffering, handicap, and surmounted obstacle in each analytic biography. Although this life-historical appreciation is often felt by the analyst and no doubt plays some sustaining role in the analytic work, it falls at the periphery of the analytic attitude proper. What is most consistent with the analytic attitude is the appreciation of the analysand as analysand, that is, of the unitary, though conflicted, person living out all of this adversity and achievement during the analytic process itself and reflecting on it with benefit.

5
Resisting
and Empathizing

I shall be dealing here less with empathizing as such and more with resisting and its impact on empathic interactions. I have linked the two terms in my title because over many years of supervising analysis and teaching analytic technique and process in seminars, it has always seemed to me that certain things about resisting which ought to be well known, and are said to be well known and sufficiently appreciated and applied, are in fact not known well enough and not consistently attended to in practice. And it has seemed to me that this neglect of resisting has invariably functioned as one of the most powerful disturbers of the analyst's readiness to empathize.

The emphasis in clinical psychoanalysis falls, of course, on understanding and explaining the analysand's difficulties. And the goal of the analytic method is structural change. Structural change is shown not just by the analyst's getting back from the analysand insightful formulations. And certainly it is not shown by getting easy assent to the analyst's formulations, for if it were easy to develop mutative insight, if, that is, there were no resisting that achievement, there could be no analysand who needed expert analysis.

Structural change is shown by obvious differences in the way analysands conduct themselves in the analytic relationship as well as in other relationships. In particular, it is shown by the way they generate *independently* new kinds of life situations and new ways of understanding these situations, and their doing so in ways that are better for them (in whatever adaptive sense the word "better" may be applied in each instance). This change is possible only if there has occurred a significant reduction in resistant activity, for then the self-imposed and self-maintained limitations on how a life is to be lived will have been fundamentally altered. However desirable symptomatic improvement may be, it alone is not an index of structural change. Indeed, the disappearance of symptoms from interpretive scrutiny may be a form of resisting—sometimes called a flight into health.

Resisting is an extremely complicated concept, as I shall develop more fully in subsequent chapters. Usually (and not incorrectly), it is understood as a form of opposition to the analyst's exploratory or interpretive aims. But there are other ways to understand it, and some of these ways are so different from the oppositional way that one might not even want to go on speaking of resisting at all. I shall come back to this point later. For the present I want to emphasize that it remains technically and heuristically useful to retain the oppositional sense of resisting. Much of what I shall be saying next will refer to this sense of it.

In chapter 2, I emphasized that Freud, in his discussion of technique, insisted that the analysis of resisting is the most important part of the work. I know that he also made a similar point about the handling of transference, and it is this point, rather than the one about resisting, that seems to have had the greater influence on the way many analysts, both young and old, conduct their work with analysands. But to a large extent Freud was trying to get *at* transference *through* the analysis of resisting. He realized that in order to develop an effective analytic process—one in which the transference develops and emerges in forms that are transparent enough to be interpreted—the analyst must pay consistent attention to resistant activity. This is so, according to Freud, because resisting accompanies the analysis every step of the way—and he meant even into the final session of a beneficial course of analysis.

Freud insisted further that transference should itself be regarded as a form of resisting. It is resisting remembering, in that it takes the form of the analysand's insisting that all feelings toward the analyst, positive and negative, are fully justified or explained by the conventionally viewed here and now of the analytic situation and relationship. The conclusion that the analysand is driving toward is that there simply is no blind repeating of past patterns of relationship to be analyzed. Thus there is resisting the development and expression of transference, and there is resisting the analysis of transference. And, even further, as I shall explain later, there is what Freud called resisting the uncovering of resisting, some examples of which are facile acceptance of, or compliance with, the analyst's interventions.

Discussion of resisting necessarily overlaps discussion of what has traditionally been called analysis of the ego, of the ego's defenses, and of character. I shall not now try to stake out the boundaries of each of these concepts. There is quite enough to discuss in the extensive area of their overlap, and it can be covered this way without becoming technically confusing. I shall concentrate on one conception of resisting, which I shall designate as the analysand's difficulty in being and remaining an analysand. Once one pays attention to this difficulty, one sees that it permeates every aspect of the analysis.

Being and remaining an analysand in an analysis has a general form even though this form varies from analysand to analysand depending on what he or she is like as a person and the nature of the presenting problems. This form may, however, be obscured by the analyst's wanting the analysand to be an analysand of a particular sort, such as exciting or highly verbal, when it is not appropriate to expect anything of that sort in that case. Then the analysand may fight the analyst in all kinds of ways that seem to be simply expressions of resisting. In fact, however, much of this opposition will be an artifact of an inappropriate technical approach. Heinz Kohut (1971, 1977) has presented some valuable discussions of how this difficulty may arise in work with severely narcissistic analysands when they are approached technically as though they are ordinary neurotics. I shall not review his helpful remarks on this problem, for I want to focus on those appropriate approaches to analysands that do not seem to create iatrogenic difficulties.

What does one observe? Although analysands come asking for help, they repeatedly have problems in being or remaining analysands. They do not freely, consistently, or genuinely enter into what has been called a therapeutic alliance or working relationship. Blatantly or subtly, they obstruct any kind of open, direct, frank, feelingful, spontaneous interchange between them and their analysts. They rationalize and intellectualize, they act seductively, and they provoke fights. Some resist by trying very hard to be "good patients." Thus, they prepare an agenda of important or serious matters to discuss. Overconscientiously, they make a point of remembering and telling dreams. They labor to produce memories that corroborate the analyst's interventions. The alert analyst is bound to feel that something is wrong here, for on the face of it the analysis is proceeding too smoothly to make analytic sense, and the apparent change is occurring too easily to be convincing. Some of these analysands are unconsciously avoiding the erotically and/or sadistically exciting aspects of a free give-and-take. Others are being good clean anal children, the kind who never make a mess. Still others, both male and female, are unconsciously acting castrated in order to avoid loss of a real or fantasized penis. This type of resistant activity may carry other meanings as well.

There are many other forms of resisting to being or remaining an analysand, for example by maintaining attitudes of mistrust or overdependency, seeking to suffer the analysis in a masochistic way, or barraging the analyst with unconnected information. Then there is idealization of the analyst. In its resistant aspect, idealization puts the analyst out of reach of any kind of open human interchange. Both erotic and hostile expressions are excluded. Or if the analysand does not idealize the analyst, then he or she utterly impersonalizes him or her and so makes a machine or a textbook out of the human being occupying the analyst's chair.

I have not presented a complete list of resistant strategies as that would be impossible. When it comes to resisting, the ingenuity and the tenacity of analysands cannot be overestimated. But I do want to go on now to describe some versions of a particular, and sometimes particularly devastating, form of resisting. This form is the undermining of the analyst's readiness to empathize. (I have already discussed in chapter 3 some reasons for, and some manifestations of, this attack on empathizing, and here I develop that discussion further.) The attack is an attempt to stifle the analyst's hopefulness, enthusiasm, spirit of collaboration, and objectivity in estimating the extent to which the analysis is in fact going forward. The analysand does this by remaining superficially suspicious, derogatory, rigidly unemotional or saccharine or histrionic, tediously circumstantial, and so on and so forth. I make this point about underestimations of progress because, as a teacher and supervisor, I have often been told in advance by a student that a particular analysis is stalled, boring, confusing, or otherwise unsatisfactory. The student is listless or ashamed of the work, or does not think it is a "good case" to discuss. And yet, on my part, once I hear about the analysis in detail, I may well be impressed by it, despite its difficulties. Sometimes this more positive estimate reaches the point where I seem (wrongly) to be a pollyanna to the student. In any event, the student's empathically recognizing and appreciating the existence of an active analytic process may well have been undermined by the analysand.

To understand this undermining, it will be helpful to return once again to Freud, this time to his discussion of unconsciously maintained infantile danger situations in his 1926 monograph, "Inhibitions, Symptoms and Anxiety." These danger situations are fear of total loss of the love object or the love object's love, castration, and crushing superego condemnation. Freud saw fear of death or fate as reducible to one or more of these dangers. Today we might want to expand Freud's list to include additional dangers that are receiving much clinical and theoretical attention. These dangers include loss or fragmentation of the self and conscious exposure to one's own infantile grandiose and persecutory fantasies. It may, however, be argued that these additional dangers are reducible to Freud's four danger situations or, if not reducible to them, then better seen as cutting across them. The ultimate peril, according to Freud, is utter helplessness and catastrophic anxiety.

In developing his theory of danger situations, Freud was, among other things, aiming to improve the theory that defines and guides his principles of technique. This improvement affects especially those principles concerned with the analysis of resisting or, as Freud might have preferred to say in that 1926 monograph, the analysis of the defenses that make up much of what is called "the resistance." The specific point to be appreciated is that when one is dealing with analysands, one must never forget that, unconsciously if not consciously, they are living in terror. They dread every kind of fantasized calamity, each of which is, in their psychical reality, as real as any objective danger and, owing to its infantile nature, far more terrifying.

As Freud pointed out, it is largely on the basis of these unconsciously perpetuated infantile and fantastic dangers that analysands fear the prospect of changing and "getting well." For when they first become analysands, and for a very long time afterwards, they envision "getting well" only as a full actualization of these infantile danger situations. If, as we believe, they have developed their disturbing modes of functioning as static accommodations to such dangers, why should they risk changing and "getting well"? The analyst cannot empathize too strongly with this desperate, locked-in position.

Analysands indicate in all kinds of ways that they insist on inhabiting these closed, static, conflictual, and infantile worlds in order to remain "safe." For example, they convey that if they change for the better nobody will like them, everyone will turn against them, they or their parents will go crazy, someone will die, etc. However severe the suffering they consciously experience, the analyst must assume that it is less than what they unconsciously anticipate they would feel were they to "get well." So there they lie, on the one hand asking for help in changing and wishing consciously to be cured, and on the other hand protecting their closed worlds and undermining their analyst's empathic orientation.

Many of these closed worlds have been described. One of the very familiar and powerfully confining worlds is that based on the conviction that the self is unworthy: one is unlovable, undeserving, fraudulent; one has no right to love as well as no capacity to love; one may not make claims on anyone else, for one is of no account whatsoever, etc. Consequently, if someone likes an analysand of this sort, that only goes to show that that person is a fool or a dupe or is just pretending. This is how this type of analysand feels about the analyst's showing patience, interest, concern, and acceptance. The analysand will think or say, "It's your job to be that way, otherwise you would hate and loathe me and have nothing to do with me" or something equally discrediting.

It is, however, usually wrong to assume that these worlds are absolutely static and closed, or that the analysand is absolutely certain that the convictions on which they are based are incontrovertible. For if that were so, the analysand would not be coming for analysis or coming to sessions regularly. It is best for the analyst to assume incomplete closure even when all available signs point to the interpretation that the analysand is lingering on in the analysis just to prove how hopeless and worthless a case he or she is. The analysand's use of that self-presentation must be worked into the analysis; it is something to analyze, if possible. Before an analytic relationship can come into being and endure, there must be a sense on the analysand's part that there is another way to be, another way to construe things, another kind of emotional experience that may be hoped for, another self that, however rudimentary it may be, might be freed to develop in safety. Still, this sense may be almost entirely obscured by resisting and by the undermining of the analyst's readiness to empathize.

Another common type of relatively closed world often accompanies the "worthless" one. In this world, the analysand holds the conviction that he or she is a menace to others—ruthless, devouring, poisonously envious, immorally seductive, or volcanically enraged. Many resistant strategies of the schizoid, depressive, masochistic, or obsessional sort imply these convictions about the self.

But now it must be added that more than danger is involved in resisting. Analysands also prove to be attached to the very things that otherwise seem so terrible to them in their psychical reality. Freud was alert to this factor of gratification in what analysands present simply as suffering or dread. There is a kind of clinging to, even a love of, the suffering they complain of and the hazards they face. They are reluctant to give them up. As one analysand said (only half facetiously), "I have enough misery to keep me happy."

What sense can one make of this paradoxical behavior? Sometimes in the course of exploring this attachment to suffering and danger, the analyst may find that unconsciously it is the analysand's preferred way to continue an early emotional tie to his or her mother of infancy. Sometimes it is a way to be identified with her as a sick, suffering, castrated creature in her relationship with the powerful phallic father. It may be that the analysand does not want to give up this tie or this identification because, however consciously painful it is, it once was the whole world and the matrix of a developing sense of self. Thus it served as a guarantee of survival, continuity, or pleasure. Frequently there is also the factor of relief from unconsciously feeling guilty or of gratification of the analysand's wishing to be punished (Freud, 1923). And not infrequently one comes upon the aggressive gratification of defeating the analyst, perhaps castrating him or her as a representative of the phallic father or mother. Thus, the analysand is found to have a considerable stake in remaining "sick." It is safe, it is self-integrative, and it is erotically and aggressively gratifying. At one time or another, the analyst must empathize with each of these facets of resistant activity and must not rush the analysand into confronting any of them consciously, not to say giving them up prematurely.

From these general remarks it follows that the resisting implies or enacts every basic issue that, ideally, will be taken up in the analysis. Analysis of resisting now seems coterminous with the analysis as a whole. Wilhelm Reich's (1933–34) brilliant dynamic and genetic analyses of character resistances illustrate this point. For by the time Reich gets through explaining the dynamics and genesis of different types of resisting, he leaves little over that calls for further analysis. There are hardly any significant aspects of life history or unconscious fantasy systems which have not come up in his explanations of the analysand's difficulty in being an analysand, of his or her often silent and secret refusal to be or remain a true and faithful collaborator in the analysis. Even the transference will have been dealt with extensively. It is important to realize that by now one is no longer viewing "the resistance" simply as oppositional activity. Now one sees it as taking in virtually all of the analysand's psychical reality. The analyst's understanding that, as a focus for analysis, resisting transcends mere opposition makes much clear that otherwise would remain baffling.

It is all too easy for the analyst to lose sight of this broad and no longer purely oppositional conception of resisting and the importance of resisting to the analysand. The analyst's narcissistically needing to get "results" plays a big part in developing this blind spot. As the analyst loses sight of this broad conception, he or she begins to feel impatient with analysands who, despite analysis, further analysis, further clarification of origins, and obvious disadvantages and benefits of character traits, nevertheless continue to maintain certain forms of mistrust, affectlessness, intellectualizing, fear of rejection, scatteredness, or whatever other forms of resisting they insistently enact. Then the analyst's attitude tends to shift toward "attacking the resistance," and thus toward proceeding in a way that, at least implicitly, is alienated, irritable, and hopeless, and in any case unempathic. Reich himself shows in his militaristic metaphors of armor and attack how much one may fall into an adversarial view of the analytic relationship. Despite his rich understanding of the analysand's needing to resist and the complex meaning or function of this policy, he, like so many others, lapses into speaking of it as though it were a motiveless form of stubbornness or belligerence. What is forgotten is what is being unconsciously dreaded, loved, hated, and affirmed about the self. The analyst may end up insisting narcissistically that the analysand be another kind of analysand. The analyst then will have begun acting manipulatively rather than in an exploratory and empathic fashion. The analytic attitude will have been abandoned.

The so-called acting out analysand is a good case in point. As alienated analyst, one may forget not only that acting out is a form of resisting that calls for interpretation. One may also forget that, strictly speaking, the concept of acting out should refer to an analysand's enacting something in the world rather than remembering it in the analysis, and so is a concept that may be used to designate acts of kindness, pseudostupidity, and conscientiousness as well as acts that are directly provocative and disruptive. When empathizing fails, the analyst may begin to use acting out as a term of disparagement and disapproval. The analysand must be made to stop it. Interpretations become poorly veiled demands and criticism. The analysand may be incorrectly called passive-aggressive, sociopathic, or "borderline" simply because he or she is not being the kind of analysand the analyst wants. In part, the analyst will then be colluding in setting up a vicious circle, and much of the technical problem will reside in a narcissistic countertransference.

Another case in point is the so-called insatiable analysand. No amount or kind of attention, concern, or support seems to be "enough" for this type of analysand. But considered from the standpoint of psychical reality, rather than its being insatiability with which one is dealing, it is a form of resisting. This is so because anyone who is as conflicted as this sort of analysand is likely to be could not possibly tolerate enjoying gratification. In oral terms, that person is manifesting blocked incorporation (not ingesting), or else the turning of what is ingested into indigestible or poisonous matter and then symbolically expelling it as vomit or feces in order to get rid of it. A gourmet meal is a gourmet meal only if one is prepared to enjoy it in a relatively conflictless manner, which means that one is not maintaining the conviction that one does not deserve it, is too greedy, is spending too much, is being exploited by the restaurant, etc. One may eat many such meals and still end up unfed. Or, in the case of hypersexuality, end up sexually unsatisfied. As Abraham (1924) showed, analysands with depressive or manic features show that this is so repeatedly. And so it is in analysis, the analysand always feeling deprived, empty, and needful. But, unempathically, the analyst may miss the analysand's conflictual position and the resisting to which it gives rise, and in an alienated way may then dub the analysand "insatiable." It may, of course, be that the analysand is not analyzable, in this respect at least, but that is another matter and it is not an easy determination to make.

The analyst's own experience as analysand, while no absolute guarantee of anything, is likely to be a great help in dealing with these difficulties effectively. Freud said of those who are able to treat other people successfully, that when they become analysands themselves they show the same resistances as everybody else, and he cited this as evidence for the power of the infantile unconscious. Freud was indicating that it is only through personal analysis that the analyst will have come to moderate his or her own resisting through understanding its origins, its urgency, its pervasiveness, its complexity, and the personal benefit that may be extracted from its continued analysis. As a result, the analyzed analyst's empathizing should be less easily undermined by the resistant strategies followed by his or her analysands.

One of the rules of analyzing is that one should not take sides in the analysand's conflicts. As Anna Freud (1936) put it, one should take up a position equidistant from the id, ego, and superego. This means, among other things, that rather than setting oneself to "break through resistances," one should try to elucidate their role in the life that is being studied, and, one hopes, beneficially modified in the analysis.

Here I want to mention that one of the most common technical errors I have observed flouts this rule of equidistance. Often the error is committed without the analyst's becoming aware of it. The error is to try to elicit directly some kind of ideational or affective content that one senses is pretty close to being expressed but is being "warded off" by the analysand. It may be tears, anger, love, or gratitude; it may be a masturbation fantasy or a thought about the analyst; etc. The content seems to be there, waiting to be plucked off the branch, and impulsively the analyst reaches after it with a question or comment, not stopping to ask why it is that the content is still being warded off, why it is not being volunteered or displayed. Suppose the analysand is evidently struggling not to cry: Why the struggle? The analyst interested in resistant strategies will first want to know the answer to this question, for that answer will do more for the analysis than the crying itself. As Paul Gray (1973) put it in an excellent paper on this topic, analysis is primarily a study of conflict or of the working of the psyche; it is not primarily a cathartic method, or a study of the analysand's mental content, or of his or her life outside the analysis considered in and of itself. The crying, if it is genuine, will take place in good time, that is, in a context that will make it fruitful for the analysis.

There are many moments in the course of an analysis when analysands seem to dangle unexpressed content before the analyst. These are moments when the analyst is tempted to say, for example, "You are angry," "You are excited," or "You are ashamed." But if it is so obvious, why isn't the analysand simply saying so or showing unmistakably that it is so? To begin with, it is the hesitating, the obstructing, the resisting that counts. If the analyst bypasses this difficulty with a direct question or confrontation, the analysand is too likely to feel seduced, violated, or otherwise coerced by the analyst who has in fact, even if unwittingly, taken sides unempathically.

These remarks bring us to the precept of technique that stipulates that one should always take up the defense before taking up that which is being defended against. It is often possible to note defensiveness and to raise useful questions about it, so that there is much that can be said in support of this precept. Still, if this precept is followed rigidly, it can lead to awkward, artificial, offensive, and even meaningless distinctions and practices. In the case of the stifled crying, it is as a rule more effective to note that the analysand is *stifling crying*, and *to begin with* to center attention neutrally on the reason for the stifling. One is not then taking sides in the conflictual situation as one would be doing were one to encourage the analysand to cry, to "get it out," to "go on," or whatever. The analysand is left free to continue stifling the crying, but is encouraged to think and talk about why this is the necessary course of action. The approach is patient and respectful, and is empathic in the best analytic sense in its stressing above all the understanding of conflictual experience in the analytic session. It is therefore more consistent with the analytic attitude to say, for instance, "You seem to want to cry and yet you are stopping yourself," and perhaps to go on to wonder why this might be so. Or if the life-historical information is already available, to begin to explain why this is so.

Or take the case of irritation. For instance, the analyst has been very late for the appointment, and the analysand seems to be in a depressed mood and to be trying to suppress signs of this mood and to go on with "business as usual." In this instance the analyst has grounds for surmising that the analysand has adopted two resistant strategies, one being a depressive mood as a way of warding off complaining angrily and the other being "business as usual" as a way of eliminating any trace of reacting emotionally to the lateness. Optimally, the analyst would begin by taking up the analysand's resisting any affective display, then, perhaps, his or her resisting depressive display specifically; next, the use of depressed mood as a way of defending against recognizing and expressing that one is reacting irritably. And only then might the analyst take up the anger-provoking meaning the analysand has attached to the lateness, such as that the analyst is sexually interested in someone else. This series of steps and transformations cannot be gone through quickly, nor can it always follow a precise sequence, except perhaps toward the end of a very effective analysis; and it certainly cannot be gone through once and for all. Working through is important, and that means retraversing these steps again and again, patiently, through a seemingly endless series of repetitions, permutations, combinations, and variations. The effort is well worth it, but it can be sustained only if the analyst truly and empathically believes in the enormous importance of resisting and the desperation from which it derives, and if he or she has withstood the analysand's attacks on empathizing.

Let me now take up the point I only mentioned earlier, that, as Freud said, there is resistance to the uncovering of resistance. This point has an important bearing on technique. It should be evident from what I have already said why this second-order resisting is necessary. Briefly, it protects both the analysand's essential security and integrative measures, and it ensures achieving certain infantile gratifications on which the analysand depends. It follows from this that the analysand will not welcome and will attempt to defeat the analyst's interest in defining his or her resistant strategies, not to speak of analyzing them. The analysand looks for a way out. For example, and this is common, the analyst identifies signs of a conflictual position and raises questions first about the defensive or resistant side of that position, whereupon the analysand, in a countermove, proceeds to "spill the beans." If it is crying that is in question, the self-stifling analysand will often cry rather than discuss why it seemed necessary not to cry. If it is a masturbatory practice that is in question, the reluctant analysand will disclose that practice rather than discuss why he or she was backing away from disclosing it. One may think of these countermoves as *seductions by disclosure.* They are aimed at getting the analyst interested in "choice" content; they distract the analyst from the analysis of resisting.

Often the analysand construes the analyst's noting of resistant moves as a demand to cut it out, to come clean, to be good, or whatever, and there may well be much to discuss and interpret in this connection. It may, for example, turn out that the analyst's intervention has unconsciously been construed as a rape or an enema and so as a simultaneous genital or anal violation and gratification. Nevertheless, the premature disclosure of content must also be viewed as an instance of resisting the analysis of resisting. The analyst should not yield to this seduction by disclosure; rather, in a tactful but steadfast manner, he or she should return to the attempted warding off and should now, in addition, try to understand what it meant to the analysand to disclose the disagreeable content. The flow of tears or the revealed masturbatory practice will have its turn in the analysis, but not right away. Indeed, it is often the case that the analysis of specific instances of resisting and seductive disclosure shows them to have the same conflictual significance as the very content that was at first being "warded off." Thus, the masturbatory practice that is disclosed may involve rape fantasies. In first resisting and then disclosing the practice "under pressure," the analysand may be unconsciously enacting a rape in the transference. The interpretation of this repetition within the transference has the greatest chance of promoting genuine insight and structural change.

Analysts-in-training are likely to be particularly easy to seduce in this connection. They have not yet achieved adequately sustained mastery, sublimation, or neutralization of the voyeuristic aspects of analytic work. Often, they are uncomfortable when the analysand acts in an explicitly antagonistic way. They are impatient to get to the "hot" content, and they are eager for the analysand's good will and compliance. The really "hot" content, however, is not so much erotically or aggressively hot as it is technically urgent, and that content concerns how the analysand is setting limits on what can happen in the analytic relationship, and how the analysand is thereby setting limits on what can be accomplished independently in self-understanding. And that urgent material amounts not only to resisting itself but to resisting the analysis of resisting as well.

I want next to take up a couple of objections to the concepts and techniques I have been presenting. First, there is Heinz Kohut's (1977) objection. According to Kohut, the analysand is often justifiably angry when his or her acting resistantly is pointed out or interpreted, for in each such instance the analysand may in fact be a victim of a failure of empathizing on the analyst's part. Kohut was referring specifically to analysands with severe narcissistic problems, those who readily take these interventions as criticisms, but in his view most analysands have those problems, so that he was, it seems, really referring to most analysands.

Leaving aside insensitive or brutal approaches to the analysis of resisting, what is wrong with Kohut's objection? A full answer to this question would require extensive discussion of the interrelationship of theory, method, and phenomena in any clinical approach, and I cannot develop that discussion here. (See chapters 11 and 12; see also Schafer, 1980a.) But a partial answer is in order. If one recognizes that an analysand is unconsciously conflicted, then one must expect the analysand to respond angrily to any intervention that highlights one or another unrecognized constituent of conflictedness. For the analysand, it is as if the analyst *is* taking sides in the conflict by pointing out one of its denied elements. And for reasons that I have already explained, the analyst's highlighting resistant strategies will be particularly threatening and therefore angering. There is no way around hostile activity on the analysand's part. There is only seduction away from this activity, as when the analyst treats the analysand as a fundamentally *pre*conflictual being. This is the approach that Kohut recommended. That is, in effect he urged one to see the analysand as wanting only or fundamentally to complete the early narcissistic phase of development in a healthy way, and not to be retraumatized in the process by the analyst's failures of empathy. Kohut recognized narcissistic rage—his is not, as is sometimes asserted by critics, a theory or therapy that ignores aggressive activity—but he tends to explain this rage by labeling it a product of disintegration of the self and so not to be taken as a major component of a conflictual life. We have then what is at best a technique of limited interpretation and at worst outright denial of conflictedness, justification of ragefulness, and fostering of a persecutory orientation. In this way Kohut did seem to increase the chances of seducing the analysand into repressing or rerepressing some of the origins and meanings of the hostile actions and reactions that require extensive analysis. To some extent, Kohut seemed to be taking sides—specifically, the side of the analysand's narcissistic sensitivity. To be fair to Kohut, however, I want to add that he *did* call attention to the needless narcissistically traumatizing aspects of ill-advised analytic interventions, and, if studied in the right way, he had much to teach in this respect.

A second objection that has been raised against the trend of my discussion is this. Some analysts say that the analyst's paying close and sustained attention to resisting tends to reduce the whole world to what happens in the analytic relationship. They raise the same objection to a consistent emphasis on transference. And here I might point out, if it is not already clear, that consistently paying attention to resisting inevitably involves consistently analyzing transference, for the two are at bottom different facets of the same analytic relationship. As I said earlier, this was already apparent in Reich's discussions in 1933.

This objection to a strict focus on resisting (and transference) is not founded on direct observation. Observation shows that whenever analysands are confronting their resistant strategies, they will, as a rule, bring up analogous problems and impasses in their past and present extra-analytic relationships. Their difficulties in being and remaining analysands are at bottom no different from their difficulties in all their relationships, including their relationship with, or attitudes toward, themselves. These problems and impasses may center on their fearing intimacy, grief and loss, the conscious experience of ambivalence or self-satisfaction, or whatever. As for those analysands who do speak of nothing but the analytic relationship, they may be viewed as engaging in a special form of resisting, one by which they isolate the analysis from the rest of life, and it is usually possible for the alert analyst to help them work through this resistant strategy to some significant extent.

As a matter of fact, however, it is the opposite impasse that is encountered far more frequently. The analyst hears endless detail about the analysand's extra-analytic life, often detail of a terribly painful or threatening nature and sometimes detail of a thrilling and fulfilling nature, but all with little organization or drift to it and with no reference or even allusion to the analytic relationship. Inexperienced analysts often are seduced into running after all this exciting content, making interpretations whenever they have what seems like a good idea, and so being led by the analysand away from the analytic interaction and a sense of the analysis as a conflictual process or a series of conflictual contexts that are of pivotal importance. Consequently, a static analytic situation may persist for years. The analysand's presentation of a plentitude of past and present dramatic or chaotic life incidents is not recognized as a form of resisting and so is not taken up as such. Even scrupulous observance of the fundamental rule of free association may be used by the analysand in order to resist in just this way. It is made to seem that there are just too many events to report, too little time to do it, rationalization of inadequate receptivity to interpretation, too few signs of difficulty in being and remaining an analysand, and in a way too much confining of the analyst to the role of just being an idealized or inert empathic listener.

In order to concretize the complex considerations I have been presenting, I should like to conclude with a brief clinical sketch of some aspects of the resisting encountered in the analysis of a severely narcissistic professional man in his late thirties. Upon his very first entrance into the analyst's office, he was sure he could tell he was not welcome. For a long time afterward, he maintained this belief, and so he behaved as though he were on probation and might be "kicked out" at any time. This was a resistant stance in that it maintained enormous distance between him and the analyst. Among other things, it proved to be based on his conviction, for which it seemed he had some good evidence, that he had been an unplanned and unwanted child, though his parents had attempted to conceal their negative feelings (as he assumed the analyst was doing). His childhood solution was to live as if he were on probation in his own family. Additionally, in the analysis he was for a long time a nonstop talker who took any intervention by the analyst as a disruptive interruption, and he did so despite his assertions that he regarded the analyst as unusually empathic. Among other things, this resistant conduct was a form of showing that he needed nothing from the analyst. That he should need nothing from anybody was one of the terms of probation he had defined in his family setting—that is to say, he should believe that he was sensitively loved but should make no demands on his busy and unwelcoming parents.

At one point in the analysis, he recalled a time when as a child he had barricaded himself in his room out of fear of being punished for naughtiness. He described this move as "power in position," and he recognized that much of his walled-off behavior as an analysand, as in other areas of his life, was a replaying of this "power in position." Although he kept insisting that the analyst was not active enough, he dreaded the analyst's being forcefully and empathically active—breaking down the door, so to say (which he also experienced consciously and disturbingly as homosexual seduction). Also, he insisted that the analyst bring about quick elimination of some of his symptoms, specifically those which interfered with his work, rather than develop a wide-ranging exploration of his conflicts and their histories. And in thus trying to exclude from the analysis his general disturbance of self and object relations, he was, as it turned out later, in one respect wanting to be cured of a long-unmentioned minor birth defect which, he felt, had impaired the development of his masculinity. For him, the analysis of his resisting as part of his character was in this respect yet another castration, and so he fought it fiercely.

Material of this sort can certainly be discussed as characterological repetition and transference, but in this analysis it appeared most obviously as his resisting the development and interpretation of a relationship in which he was an acknowledged analysand working with a committed analyst. Many of his life-long conflictual actions could be taken up under the heading of his resistant strategies. But the strain on the analyst's empathic resources was, as might be easily imagined, considerable, and it was not always possible for the analyst to avoid feeling overtaxed and acting inconsistently, though it was often possible subsequently to include in the analysis in a useful way discussion of the analyst's technical or empathic lapses.

My summary of observations and principles of the technique of analyzing resisting is not part of a counsel of perfection. Analytic perfectionism has no legitimate place in the analytic attitude, for it is a form of narcissistic counterresistance, and as such it must lead to failures in empathizing and understanding. If taken in the right spirit, my summary ought to help identify, analyze, and put to some good use the mutually developed complications that inevitably arise in analytic work and that fall under the heading of resisting and its effects on empathizing.

6

Conflict as Paradoxical Actions

Introduction

The concept of conflict, especially *unconscious* conflict, is, of course, central to psychoanalysis. Conflict in the psychoanalytic situation is the source of psychoanalytic psychopathology, the psychoanalytic theory of the therapeutic process, and the psychoanalytic theory of individual development in the family and society. The analyst's attending carefully and impartially to signs of conflict is an essential feature of the analytic attitude. Psychoanalysis could not exist as a theory or a clinical method without constant reference to conflict.

Psychoanalytic theorizing about conflict has always adhered basically to Freud's metapsychological model and the language rules it dictates. We speak, for example, of dynamic conflict between drives and defenses, thereby agreeing to use a language organized around such terms as energy, force, and mechanism. We speak, too, of structural conflict between the ego and the id and between the ego and the superego, thereby agreeing to use a certain kind of structural language as well. The proposition will be developed here that it is both possible and desirable to develop a nonmetapsychological conceptualization of conflict that is still psychoanalytic and systematic. Conflict will be defined as a person's engaging in paradoxical actions. As will be explained later, action is to be understood in a broader sense than the usual one.

A need does exist to develop alternative conceptualizations of the central terms of psychoanalysis. This is so because in recent years metapsychology has been the object of a number of strong and effective fundamental criticisms (see, for example, Grossman and Simon, 1969; Klein, 1975; Gill, 1976; Holt, 1976), and in some cases suggestions for alternative approaches have been put forward. Especially under attack have been metapsychology's embodiment of a natural-science model that is obsolescent and inappropriate to the psychoanalytic method and the data it generates; also its producing hypotheses that are either untestable or contrary to fact and its reliance on ambiguous, even if appealing, anthropomorphic or otherwise blatantly metaphoric explanations.

I have presented my critique and proposal for an alternative in *A New Language for Psychoanalysis* (1976), and in *Language and Insight* (1978). I call this systematic alternative to metapsychological language *action language*. In this chapter I shall develop further some remarks in those books which point to the action-language conceptualization of conflict as paradoxical actions. But in order to do this job, I must first spend some time synopsizing some of the main features and rules of action language. The synopsis will prepare those readers not well acquainted with those books' extended argument to grasp the new approach to conflict that follows. That more of this chapter is devoted to the preparation than to conflict itself should not be taken as a structural imbalance in the presentation, for most of the necessary conceptual work is preparatory. The discussion of conflict proper will follow readily from the exposition of the basic assumptions, concepts, and requirements of action language. In conclusion, I shall apply the proposed reconceptualization of conflict to a summary of some major conflicts of one analysand.

Action and Its Modes

ACTION

By action I refer to human activity of every sort. Far more than motoric action in and on the environment, action takes in thinking, wishing, and every kind of emotional activity. Defense is action in this sense. It is an unconsciously performed action (a defensive measure) that ensures that one refrains from engaging in other actions that one views as dangerous in some way. Even though defense is identified and interpreted through its overt features, it is not a construct, for sooner or later, if all goes well, the analysand will consciously affirm it as his or her mode of operation with respect to certain problems or all problems. Fantasizing, too, is an action. Rather than its being a substitute for action, it is action of a certain sort; it is an action that initially the person may perform unconsciously and may not acknowledge consciously until and unless interpretation makes that possible.

BODILY HAPPENING

In contrast, the class of nonactions includes reflex movements, normal maturational change, bodily secretions and stimuli, and other such anatomical, motoric, and physiological processes. These are to be conceptualized as bodily happenings. Although they often provide the occasion of significant actions (for instance, during puberty) and although, in turn, they may be influenced by actions (for instance, in psychosomatic conditions), they are biological, nonsymbolic events, definitely not to be classed with the intrinsically meaningful or goal-directed performances that characterize specifically human activity. In giving meaning to a bodily happening, however, the person *is* performing an action. For purposes of interpretation, the analyst will be especially interested in the action aspect of this event. When, however, the bodily happening is itself extraordinary (for example, severe brain damage), the situation is radically compromised in that the analysand's entire mode of functioning may be drastically limited and distorted. Consequently, the ordinary criteria of action no longer apply. Discussion of action presupposes a relatively well-developed and unimpaired neurological substrate of behavior.

ENVIRONMENTAL HAPPENING

Independently occurring events in the environment are also to be conceptualized as happenings. It is the subject's specific action of giving meaning to these environmental happenings that is of particular psychoanalytic interest. Birth of siblings, deaths, poverty or plenty, these are happenings that the child transforms into actions or consequences of action, viewing them, for instance, as the results of having been good or bad. As development continues, the person has more opportunity to act so as to influence the occurrence of many environmental events, in which respect it is often hard to make and to sustain the distinction between action and happening. Analysts struggle with this distinction all the time. Nevertheless, the broad concept of action does not exclude the idea of necessity.

Conflict as Paradoxical Actions

VERBS, ADVERBS, AND PERSONS

In systematic propositions, *though not necessarily or even usually in clinical interventions,* actions are to be stated exclusively through the use of verbs and, when modes of action are in question, adverbs as well. The performer of actions is to be designated the person or agent, or in our particular context, the analysand. Thus, the prototypical action statement is that a person performs an action in a certain mode. For example, one may say that a person accepts an invitation happily, remembers a missed opportunity ruefully, wishes unconsciously for oedipally gratifying transactions in the transference relationship, or rejects an interpretation anxiously.

MULTIPLE DESIGNATION OF ACTIONS

Each action may be stated in an indefinitely large number of ways. It may be stated variously on the same level of abstractness, and it may be stated variously on different levels of abstractness. For instance, to act affectionately, to act tenderly, and to act compassionately: each may describe the same action from different points of view that are, roughly speaking, on the same level of abstractness. Moving to a lower level, one may say that acting affectionately is constituted by a family of actions that includes kissing, embracing, saying what one admires and desires, etc., though not every one of these actions need be performed before it will be appropriate to use the designation *affectionately.* Moving to a higher level, one may say that acting affectionately is one of a family of actions that constitutes object love, so-called, or seduction.

One corollary of multiple designation is that, without contradiction, one may speak of an action in three ways: as such, as a constitutive action, or as an action with its own constituents. In ordinary language and in psychoanalytic interpretation, one uses these three ways all the time, though perhaps often without recognizing that one is doing so.

A second corollary of multiple designation is that ultimately there is no one specific action to identify correctly, for the idea of the action will change with each change of context and of the locutions appropriate to that context. Within any one context, there may be right and wrong or better or poorer descriptions of an action; but this cannot be the case invariably and often it is not very surely the case even within given contexts. For example, when analysts disagree on the interpretation of some analytic material, they may disagree because they are working within different contexts of meaning or because, even within one context, they are always dealing with enough ambiguity and complexity to allow them to arrive at more than one statement of what the analysand means or what he or she is doing. Thus, we may not speak of a single ultimate action, that is, of *the* action simply. Nevertheless, we may say *an* action or *the* action, provided it is understood that we are speaking of a set of possibilities of description or, in other words, provided it is understood that we are speaking of something whose real existence we are asserting but of which, necessarily, we can only have versions. If I ask, "What is a knife?" and answer that it is a weapon, an eating utensil, a household possession, and a phallic symbol, I am giving a specific instance of what I refer to as sets of possibilities and versions of reality. The question of some one and only final truth does not arise.

A third corollary of multiple designation is this. One may simultaneously describe or name an action in divergent or contradictory ways. Thus, one may say of an action that it is simultaneously wish fulfilling, defensive, and self-punitive; and further, with respect to any one of these designations, one may correctly state the action in more than one way—for example, as wish fulfilling both erotically and aggressively. A seduction with oedipal significance is one of the many actions studied in analysis that are wish fulfilling in both of these ways. Obviously, this corollary deals with what, metapsychologically, analysts are used to calling multiple function and overdetermination. To speak of a person's complex multifaceted action is to refer in the terms of action language to the metapsychological "resultant" of forces. In action language, the person (or agent) performs actions, the meanings or goals of which are several or many and possibly unintegrated or paradoxical. Further, only some of these features may be realized consciously or preconsciously by the person, the remainder being enacted unconsciously.

NEW ACTIONS

This matter of multiplicity and contradiction may be put in another way. What we would call one action, according to common sense or convention, might be better designated as several actions. Just as many actions may prove ultimately to be most usefully described as versions of one action, one action may be analyzed into several or even many as we return to it again and again in many different contexts. One advantage we gain by viewing it as a set of actions is that we allow for an action's becoming a new action once it is seen in a new light.[1] This is so because it is often appropriate and useful to begin viewing a known action as a new action during clinical analysis. It is mistaken to assert that everything the analyst interprets refers to an already established but somehow hidden meaning; often the analyst's interpretations provide new connections, new perspectives, new ways of appraising consequences, and so new actions. What we call the Unconscious is not omniscient, and is certainly not an analyst under wraps, even though, upon analysis, people may be said to know a lot more about the infantile erotic and aggressive significance of their actions than they dare to realize consciously. Consider the case of an adolescent girl talking back to a parent: were she (or her parent) to realize that her talking back was defensive with respect to mourning the passing of her old relationships, hostile with respect to her oedipal rivalry, justified with respect to her developmentally necessary reactions against parental infantilizing, and affirmative of her new or revised ideals, she (or her parent) would no longer view it as "just" talking back or even as primarily talking back, even though it would remain useful to retain the initial designation of the action as "talking back."

Interpretation is more than uncovering; it is discovering, transforming, or creating meaning, too. What it refers to may not have been "all there but hidden" prior to its utterance. This means that analysands learn as well as admit, discover as well as recover. And, as is regularly the case when significant new learning or interpretation is in question, by introducing the new, one may throw much previous knowledge and understanding into a new light. Large segments of the analysand's life history may be changed in this way, and changes of this sort may be effected a number of times during an analysis. The life history keeps being rewritten, not just because there are fewer gaps, disguises, misunderstandings, and limitations, but also because there are more perspectives or strategies of definition and organization. In this way, new actions constantly come into being.

NONSPATIAL DESCRIPTION

Action language represents, among other things, an attempt to describe analytic data with as little use as possible of blatant unsystematized metaphors, especially those metaphors derived from, and con-

1. Robert Michels, personal communication.

ducive to, a model of a mind-machine or of a brute organism with a tamed mind. One of the blatantly metaphoric aspects of metapsychology is its use of spatial terms to describe mental activity. Mental activity does, of course, presuppose a human organism with a more or less adequately functioning and developed brain. But to say this is not to say that thinking and reacting emotionally exist in any kind of space. One need not say that they exist on levels or at distances from one another, and that they move from one level or place to another. Especially important is the consideration that actions are neither inner nor outer; they may, however be private rather than public. To say that they are private is not to say that others may not infer them correctly in one version or another. Psychoanalytic interpretation has always depended on the analyst's making such inferences, just as understanding of others in everyday life depends on it. But whether the actions are private and more or less inferable or actions that have been public from the first, they will not be public in the same way or to the same extent for every ordinary observer or, for that matter, for every psychoanalytic observer. The agent, in turn, may be oblivious of the fact that he or she is performing some action or performing an action that may be understood in more than one simple, commonsensical fashion. As we know so well from our analytic work, people are far from being expert witnesses of many of their most significant actions or modes of action. For example, projecting is an action one performs unbeknown to oneself; acting out and rationalizing are actions that the subject will view in some way that misses the point so far as psychoanalytic interpretation is concerned.

Consequently, if one accepts the proposition that it is better *for systematic purposes* not to refer to mental places, the term intrapsychic becomes problematic. Intrapsychic must now be understood to mean private, perhaps unconsciously private. Intrapsychic conflict is private conflict in this sense. Far from denying the phenomenon of conflict or minimizing its significance, one recognizes it under another aspect and in a more systematic fashion. Nor is one denying the importance in people's lives of physiological happenings. When a person recognizes these happenings, however, and gives them meaning (for instance, metaphorically, as driving forces), that person is to be seen rather as performing a descriptive action than discovering independently existing forces.

Conflict as Paradoxical Actions

AFFECTS AS ACTIONS AND MODES OF ACTION

I have been using adverbs to refer to affects. My doing so follows from the sections on verbs, adverbs, and persons, and on nonspatial description, above, which dictate the use of verbs and adverbs and require nonspatial designation of personal actions. The term *affects* refers to certain actions and modes of action—for example, loving, hating, and grieving, and acting lovingly, angrily, and mournfully.

TOPOGRAPHY

The topographic qualities, as we are used to calling them, are to be viewed as modes of acting and are to be differentiated with respect to consciousness as a reference point. For example, a person may strive to fail unconsciously or preconsciously or consciously. When Freud (1940, pp. 157–164) designated the topographical distinctions as *qualities*, he was in effect arguing both that they should not be treated spatially and that they should be treated adjectivally, that is, as properties of nonspatial events that occur in the spatially conceived psychic apparatus; whereas in my designating them nonspatial *modes of action*, I am arguing that they be treated adverbially. From a systematic point of view, no big change in formulation is entailed by this grammatical switch. The big change is metatheoretical; what is entailed is giving up substantive designations of mental activity. Revised accounts of the dynamic unconscious are therefore required and are possible, but will not be undertaken here (see Schafer, 1976).

SUBJECTIVE EXPERIENCE

Subjective experience is to be viewed as a construction. Experience is not given or primary; it is not unmediated information or static information that is accessible through introspection and that serves as a court of last resort in settling questions of fact or truth. One is required now to speak of experience as the person's action of reviewing other actions he or she has performed in various modes; among these reviewed actions will be the accounts one has already developed of what one has been doing and of the happenings one has been dealing with. Experience is always mediated by personal interpretation. Psychoanalytic interpretation has always depended on this recognition, though its metapsychological restatement has obscured the fact. Implicit in analytic interpretation are the following questions. What are the analysand's reasons for construing certain events in a certain way, for responding to them in certain emotional modes, and for bringing up this subject matter under the present analytic circumstances and doing so in a certain way? For example, the overly optimistic experience of one's situation that characterizes manic denial is something an analyst will interpret as being, among other things, the imagining of nondestructive oral abundance in order to reduce the possibility of responding depressively to a situation that otherwise would be viewed as ruined and barren. In this fashion, the analyst interprets the manic denial as an action taken by the analysand to accomplish something, that is, as a constructed experience rather than experience passively encountered and observed, which is to say as a happening.

INTERPRETATION IS REDESCRIPTION

Interpretation is designation of actions in other terms; it is a restatement of the meaning or goal that defines these actions. Interpretation is not causal. It is true that an interpretation may include or imply causal propositions. A case in point is the proposition that trauma causes, among other reactions, anger. But even in this instance, which seems pretty self-evident, the fully developed interpretation will refer to the personal, unconsciously elaborated meaning of both the trauma and the analysand's having responded angrily. We know that however extreme the physical or social trauma, one will view it in one's own way, depending on one's life history up to that point and on the context of action that one has defined and in which one has been operating. In many instances, not everyone will be traumatized by the same events, nor will those who are traumatized be equally traumatized, nor will everyone react angrily to trauma in the same way and with the same significance. Even when the traumatic circumstances and the reactions are apparently uniform, the analyst will still want answers to questions concerning their meanings to the "victim," for they may vary from one instance to the next.

To say that interpretation is statement of actions in other terms is to refer to the nature of psychoanalytic explanation, which is the nature of psychoanalytic answers to the question, Why? Whether they do so knowingly or not, when analysts answer "why" questions, they do so in terms of reasons, on the understanding that reasons are ways of stating actions in terms of their meaning or directedness. Take, for example, wishing or desiring: rather than saying that *a* wish or *a* desire *caused* anything, in using action language one would say that the analysand wished or desired to bring about a certain state of affairs. Thus, when one interprets an insulting remark as a castrating action, one is giving its reason, which is to say that one is stating in other terms its meaning or its directedness. Here, systematic formulation coincides with clinical practice, but it need not always do so, for there are many effective ways to make a clinical interpretation and only some of these will reflect clearly the rules one follows in making systematic theoretical statements about clinical phenomena.

SPECIFICALLY PSYCHOANALYTIC INTERPRETATION

It is of the utmost importance to realize that, ultimately, psychoanalytic interpretations are concerned with only certain kinds of reasons or certain views of actions. As was mentioned, any action may be viewed in an indefinitely large number of ways (see section on multiple designation of actions, above). As analysts we are always concerned to view actions in terms of infantile psychosexual and aggressive conflicts and the variations of these that the analysand has continued to fashion along with a suitable environment in which to enact them. Above all, the analyst is concerned with the versions of these conflicts that are presented in transference actions and resistant actions—the feeding, seduction, peeking, exposing, destroying, protecting, dirtying, withholding, impregnating, castrating, and so on and so forth that analysands enact, usually unconsciously, in the analytic relationship.

Conflict

With this preparatory synopsis of action language behind us, we may now turn to the discussion of conflict. The question to consider is this. How shall we speak of conflict in line with the rules of action language, which is to say in terms of actions and their modes?

First, a series of exclusions based on all the points made above. As we are not to regard conflict as an entity, we may not say that it is something one *has* or *deals with* in and of itself. Conflict now is neither internal nor intrapsychic. It causes nothing and has no independent life history of its own. It is neither a happening nor a raw experience to be consulted introspectively. There is no one formulation of conflict that is adequate to all occasions or correct in all contexts. There is no one all-purpose level of abstraction on which it is to be stated. The factors that constitute conflict are themselves not necessarily unidirectional; nor has every one of these factors necessarily existed unambiguously before being stated in an interpretation, at least not in the form defined by the interpretation. It is not ideas, affects, or drives that conflict with each other; nor is it mental structures, functions, mechanisms, and forces.

Turning now to the inclusions that follow from the twelve previous subsections: in the terms of action language, *conflict refers to a person's being engaged in a complex action the constituents of which the person views as standing in contradictory or paradoxical relations with one another.* The person may be performing some of the constituent actions in question unconsciously; others, preconsciously or consciously. A person may wish unconsciously to make a sexual advance while wishing consciously and anxiously to remain aloof; and in the action of wishing to do both simultaneously, that person is acting conflictedly. And the recognition of the paradox itself may be maintained unconsciously, preconsciously, or consciously, or in more than one of these modes simultaneously, in which case simultaneously the recognition will be made in different terms (for example, consciously as self-contradictory and unconsciously as destruction of a loved and needed person).

There are many actions one would perform under other conditions than those obtaining at the moment or enduringly. These other conditions may, of course, never be realized (for example, conditions under which one would literally consummate incest). In this respect, one is acting conflictedly, that is to say, simultaneously wishing, anticipating, fearing, and refraining. Metapsychologically, we are used to calling those actions we refrain from taking *impulses,* and we tend to portray them as propulsive entities with minds of their own (for example, the impulse to kiss or to kill). But the idea of impulse as autonomous propulsive entity is a commonplace not only in metapsychology; it pervades our civilization. Consequently, our analysands speak repeatedly of the experience of struggling with their impulses. Nevertheless, we are under no necessity to base our systematic propositions on these reports from the couch or, indeed, on our own accounts of *our* subjective experiences. In fact, it is hardly a theory of subjective experience to use unsystematically the terms of experience to explain experience itself. In action language, the impulse is the action one refrains apprehensively from taking while yet wishing to take it.

We are used to calling the action of refraining from other action something else. We call it delay, control, inhibition or, if it is performed unconsciously, defense. On this basis we are used to speaking of many conflicts as taking place between impulses (what is refrained from) and unconscious defenses (the refraining itself). In spite of this terminology, when we make optimal interpretations, we avoid any suggestion that we are speaking of happenings in the mind involving relentless impulses and unyielding automatic mechanisms. We do not want to refer to happenings with respect to which the analysand is merely the vehicle or observer, because to do so would probably reinforce certain resistant strategies. Rather, as an expression of our analytic attitude, we want to refer in one way or another and sooner or later to the analysand's being engaged in paradoxical or contradictory actions.

A word about anxiety is in place here. Anxiety (I would say acting anxiously) is not now to be viewed as being caused by a conflict, nor is it to be viewed as causing conflict; rather, acting anxiously is an essential aspect of what we mean by conflict both when we interpret it clinically and when we speak of it theoretically. Consequently, it is tautological to bring in notions of causality in this connection. The cause and that which it is supposed to explain are not logically independent and often they are identical—hence the tautology. Reports of anxiety indicate occasions when conflictual actions are being taken and viewed as dangerous. To remain logically coherent, one need only bring to bear the psychoanalytic categories of understanding and interpretation, that is, those that refer directly or indirectly to the two great classes of infantile, problematic sexual and aggressive actions and modes of action; these are the actions and modes that the analysand is continuing to perform more or less unconsciously and anxiously. Using these specifically psychoanalytic categories, we establish psychoanalytic contexts with their distinctive criteria of relevance and importance. What has just been said about acting anxiously applies as well to acting guiltily, ashamedly, or otherwise uncomfortably and erratically.

A Clinical Example and Its Implications for Theory

As an illustration of my theoretical position on conflict, I shall present a clinical case summary in the terms of action language. A young woman in analysis dreads taking examinations. In disregard of her own record of achievement and ordinary social standards, she thinks of herself as being inferior both intellectually and as a woman, that is, as being stupid and undesirable. According to the interpretations being developed during the analysis, exposing her stupidity means to her, unconsciously, also exposing her lack of a penis, in which connection, and again unconsciously, she has always viewed her brother enviously. As the test-taking situation may expose her imagined cognitive-phallic defect, she regards it as dangerous, resents it, and wishes to flee from it. She also expects her male professors to devalue her work, as she does herself. In this regard, she is viewing the academic situation projectively, although also with some accuracy (male professors so often acting as they do in relation to female students). In this instance it is, therefore, both correct and useful to say that she is using a partial truth in order to think projectively.

As to her judging herself inferior as a woman, it is, among other things, her way of leaving the oedipal field in favor of her mother; it is an act of renunciation and refraining from competition. However, her unconsciously viewing test-taking as exposing herself genitally does not tell the whole story, for, again unconsciously, she also views test-taking as acting seductively toward her father, represented (by way of transference) by her male professors. And so, again, though in a paradoxical sense, she enters a danger situation whenever she takes a test, and would be doing so all the more were she to take the test eagerly, excitedly, competently—winningly, one might say. Among other things, the victory would be a positive oedipal victory. Here is one more reason for her consciously resenting the test and wishing to flee from it.

Yet, at the same time, doing well on the test would also be finally to restore and show off her phallic intactness in the form of intellectual potency. By doing well, she would at last defeat her brother, surpass her mother, and even win her father's homosexual love, owing to his high estimation of "masculine" intellectual achievement; whereas by doing poorly on the test, she would damage herself instead of damaging her rival mother and brother, and she would lose her father's favor in the bargain. Consequently, she prepares for her tests conflictedly and takes them and assesses her performance on them conflictedly—all at once hopefully, excitedly, resentfully, anxiously, guiltily, and self-abasingly. But she does not do so consciously in every respect.

For her, being in analysis is such a test situation and danger situation. For her, free associating amounts to exposing simultaneously her defect, her desire, her phallic status, and her various rivalries and sexual goals. Is she doing analysis well or correctly? Am I (the analyst) approving, loving, disappointed, disparaging, taking too much interest, taking too little interest, favoring her achievement and attractiveness or deploring, fearing, and envying them? In the analysis, this paradoxical outlook is her way of resisting, often quite projectively, as well as enacting her paternal, maternal, and sibling transferences. Consequently, she thinks desperately about both remaining in her present undesirable position and getting cured. Her negative therapeutic reaction to interpretations is pronounced.

This analysand's problems are in fact more complex than just this much about her would suggest (for example, preoedipal issues are involved); however, my summary should suffice for present purposes.

What have I done in formulating this analysand's "conflicts" in the way that I have? In showing how taking tests and being in analysis are, *for her*, paradoxical actions in a number of ways at once, I have made use of certain categories of interpretation that are specifically psychoanalytic. These categories serve as selective and organizing principles for dealing with the wide variety of actions and modes of action in which this analysand characteristically engages. She performs all these actions and modes of action in her roles as daughter, sister, student, and analysand. Unconsciously, she views the four roles just mentioned as one complex and paradoxical role, and she plays this one role repetitively. Her apparent compulsion to repeat in this respect is her action. It is what she does unconsciously, not what she is driven to do; that is to say, it is her repeatedly defining the same paradoxical and dangerous situations, and, correlatively, doing only what is appropriate to those situations, that is, acting conflictedly.

Metapsychologically, the preceding account would be considered primarily a *dynamic* formulation of the case, that is, an account of forces in conflict. My claim, however, is that I have provided an example of psychoanalytic theorizing plain and simple. From the standpoint of action language, the *meta*theoretical language of metapsychology is superfluous and distracting as well as inconsistent with the analytic attitude. Psychoanalytic theory is to be seen as setting the rules for interpreting those events (actions, happenings) of a human life that are of special psychoanalytic interest and that are defined and organized through the psychoanalytic method. Nothing more is needed in the way of *meta*theory; what is needed is further reconceptualization of the basic events of the psychoanalytic situation and their implications for psychopathology, analytic process, and individual development.

7
Danger Situations

Introduction

"Inhibitions, Symptoms and Anxiety" (1926) is the most modern of Freud's theoretical treatises. In this work, Freud systematically introduced a new way of looking at the neuroses and their clinical analysis—a way so true, so useful, and by now so familiar that one all too easily underestimates its achievement. By formally defining danger situations, arranging these situations chronologically, and aligning them with the various neuroses, he developed a new perspective on the analysis of the neuroses. In that perspective, the analyst's goal is to help the analysand consciously recognize danger situations and to understand how in his or her life history these situations evolved and persisted and the means that were adopted to cope with them. In this last respect, the analysand's characteristic unconscious defensive activities are of particular significance. The entire treatise amounts to a major advance in the analytic attitude.

In what follows I shall justify this appraisal of "Inhibitions, Symptoms and Anxiety" while sorting out some of the weaker parts of Freud's argument. In executing this project, I shall make extensive use of action language. I shall develop further the concept of anxiety (and of all affects) as an action or mode of action best rendered through the use of a family of verbs and adverbs. In light of this conception, I shall review the key terms of Freud's treatise and discuss other key terms such as *character traits, defenses, diagnosis,* and *therapy.*

Danger Situations

Anxiety and Its Situations

Freud succinctly summarized the conclusion of his discussion of anxiety in the following words: "A danger situation is a recognized, remembered, expected situation of helplessness" (1926, p. 166). The sequence of danger situations, following the traumatic situations of helplessness at birth and during early infantile periods of intense bodily need, are loss of object, loss of the object's love, castration, and superego condemnation. Anxiety is the appropriate response to danger situations as it is to the initial traumatic situations. In danger situations, however, the ego attempts to restrict the anxiety response and to use it as a signal for instigating its own defensive measures. Anxiety functions, then, as the motive for defense; more exactly, it is the ego's anticipation of a traumatic situation of which the preliminary anxiety reaction is a portent, together with the ego's function of avoiding unpleasure, that establishes the occasion of defense.

First of all it is important to decide just what kind of theory this is. One must say that it is a cognitive and experiential theory of anxiety; certainly it is no longer purely or primarily an energic theory like Freud's earlier theory according to which anxiety is transformed libido that has accumulated in excessive quantity. Helplessness is experience, a view of one's position in the world. The new theory forces the economic-quantitative approach very much into the background. Even though Freud continued to mention that anxiety is a biological discharge phenomenon, he also argued against this idea when in the same work he refuted Rank's theory of abreaction of the birth trauma through anxiety. He was similarly uncertain or ambivalent with respect to his earlier idea that it is countercathectic energy that is discharged in anxiety. He seemed no longer sure that this energic bookkeeping mattered. Of course Freud was not then, nor was he ever, prepared to give up his postulate of psychic energy and his metapsychological vantage point of psychoeconomics (witness his final addendum to "Inhibitions, Symptoms and Anxiety" on the subject of pain and the pain of mourning [pp. 169–172]). Still, what was new and central in this anxiety theory was basically its cognitive and experiential slant, its consistency with the analytic attitude. The danger situation, which is the occasion of anxiety, is what is recognized, remembered, and expected. It is defined by ego functions or, as I prefer to say, by the actions of recognizing, remembering, and anticipating.

At this point I should like to introduce a superordinate conception of danger situations, one that encompasses this cognitive, experiential, ego-functional account. According to this conception, a danger situation corresponds to an action taken by a person to define situations from a certain standpoint. This action is constituted by particular actions, such as recognizing, remembering, and anticipating. To call it an action may be troubling, for it is customary to think of action as overt motor behavior in or on the environment. One thinks of it this way both in ordinary language and within the psychoanalytic tradition of distinguishing thought and experience from action. Yet it is legitimate to subsume the varieties of thinking and experience under action in that it is consistent with certain modern philosophical discussions of action. It is also consistent with some ideas that have always been implicit in the psychoanalytic theory of consciousness and ego functions. I am thinking, for instance, of the implicit idea that what Freud (1940, pp. 157–164) finally called the mental qualities— conscious, preconscious, and unconscious—are to be viewed as explainable activities in that they are features of the ego's shifting about of cathexes in keeping with its own interests. Thus, thinking in one or another mode of consciousness is something a person ("the ego") does or refrains from doing.

Another such instance is the idea we hold of ego functions as being activated or suspended by the superordinate organizing function of the ego. Implied in this idea is the notion that an ego function, too, is something one does or refrains from doing. As psychoanalysts we faithfully adhere to these ideas in our clinical work: we interpret why the analysand has or has not seen, recalled, or anticipated something, and why the analysand has or has not experienced it in a certain way.

Although an appreciation of Freud's forward leap does not depend on one's viewing it in terms of action language, I want to explain how the notion of situations, when carefully elucidated, is especially compatible with action language and even requires the development and adoption of some such language.

In Freud's new theory, everything turns on the concept of situation. As presented by Freud, the notion of situation implies several fundamental propositions that must be spelled out. On the most general level, the natural-science language of forces, energies, mechanisms, and the like, is now to be set aside in favor of a language devoted to meanings, for a situation is not an object or an environment or an ego function, but necessarily the individual version of reality that is currently understood and experienced by a person, especially unconsciously. Up to this point in the history of his theory-making, Freud had consistently treated meaning as phenomenon in a naive empiricist fashion; that is to say, although Freud was always concerned with the further definition of meanings and the specification of the life histories of meanings, he consistently viewed the job of scientific psychoanalytic explanation as requiring one to take a further step of translating phenomena into the mechanistic and organismic terms of metapsychology. In his revised theory of anxiety, however, he was unself-consciously reversing the explanatory priorities by placing meaning at the center of his theory. Even his continuing energic account of anxiety and its regulation depended on first defining the meaningful situation, while his purely instinctual account of the origin of danger situations could no longer be decisive. As he now pointed out, instincts are not dangerous in and of themselves; they become the occasions of danger when they are defined as such by the child or adult.

Once we develop our explanations in a universe of meanings rather than forces, we cannot avoid viewing the person as the interpreter of circumstances and needs, that is, as the definer and assigner of meanings. Danger situations are thus personal constructions, and whether or not a person constructs a danger situation will depend on his or her conceptions and estimates of self relative to circumstance. It also follows that, strictly speaking, the earliest traumatic situations, starting with birth, are not situations at all in that they refer to noncognitive events. A newborn cannot conceive situations, and physiological stress or disequilibrium is not yet a situation. With respect to that early point in development one can speak of helplessness only from the standpoint of an objective, independent observer, and that was not at all what Freud was referring to.

One might wonder if I am denying the place of the body and its maturation in psychoanalytic explanation. With reference to this conception of situation, I shall try now to show that no such denial is being fostered. As psychoanalytically oriented thinkers we are quite at home with the idea that people construct their own situations, but we consider it under other names: phase-specificity, and transference and resistance. Phase-specificity refers of course to the fact that, at each stage of bodily and cognitive maturation and development, the child will attribute meanings to self and circumstance appropriate to that stage. This observation puts us in the familiar clinical realm of oral meanings, anal meanings, phallic meanings, and genital meanings, and of the particular erotic and aggressive aims the person sets in terms of these psychosexual reference points. Today, we might add to this list separation-individuation conceived in bodily terms. But, historically, we can trace the idea of phase-specificity back to Freud's early emphasis on the delayed impacts of seduction during early childhood and the discovery of the anatomical difference between the sexes, and also on the dominance during childhood of early infantile sexual theories over enlightened sex education. A cardinal feature of the genetic approach of psychoanalysis is its recognition that bodily categorizations play a great part in the child's construction of reality. These categorizations are unconsciously carried forward into adult life. Psychosexual zones and modes continue to be used to construct situations. The point of phase-specificity, then, is that situations are never given. The child and later the adult fashion and perpetuate situations and do so unconsciously as well as preconsciously and consciously, and always in terms of the bodily and developmental issues and the level of cognitive maturity that predominate at the time.

A situation corresponds to an action. To say that the situation is defined, created, or constructed is to say that someone is doing something, that is, engaging in action. A situation, of course, is not created out of whole cloth. From the dawn of mental activity, each person takes into account necessity and accident, but he or she can only do so in phase-specific and individually characteristic ways. However much one agrees with others in certain "objective" respects, and however limited and directed one may be by bodily makeup, maturation, and the conditions and language of one's upbringing, one may still be viewed as authoring one's own life. Thus, transference and resistance are ways in which the analysand takes into account the necessities and accidents of the analytic relationship. As one analysand said, "Any question you ask me makes me anxious: I take it as a criticism." Transference and resisting are concepts that refer to the construction of situations.

I do not need to elaborate the point that our interpretations of transference and resisting consistently demonstrate that the analysand is repetitively constructing his or her archaic versions of the analytic relationship. But my thesis applies to more than the construction of a situation. It applies as well to the actions of the person in the situation thus defined. For an essential aspect of maintaining the nonbehavioristic orientation of psychoanalysis, of its concern with psychical reality or unconscious fantasizing, is to remember always that what to an outside observer might look like identical items of behavior may mean different things to different agents or to one agent at different times. Here we come directly to the way in which the concept of action is integrally related to the concept of situation.

100

Danger Situations

As I mentioned earlier, action refers to all behavior performed in a personally meaningful, purposive, or goal-directed fashion and includes all the forms of thinking and feeling as well. Action does not imply conscious awareness. It cannot be fully described by an independent observer acting alone, for it is not exclusively or mainly a social psychological concept. For instance, unconsciously the same insult may be an excremental action for one person, a castrating action for another, and perhaps both for a third. Similarly, solving a puzzle may be an action by which one unconsciously seeks to answer the question of where babies come from or how it is that women do not have penises. Or solving a puzzle may be mental masturbation, or an action that helps master one's wishing to be fed, or a step in the passing of an examination, or several or all of these actions at once. We refer to this recognition of the variable and multiple meanings of specific actions as their overdetermination or their multiple function, such terms representing the metapsychological way of talking. In effect, however, in elucidating these meanings or these multiple actions implied by one action, we are giving psychoanalytic answers to the questions, "What is this person doing?" and "Why is he or she doing it and doing it just that way?" Psychoanalysts are especially interested in certain definitions of actions, namely those that convey the infantile erotic and aggressive sense in what the analysand is doing and the infantile hazards and protective measures connected with this sense.

With this much understood about the technical notion of situations, we may return to the danger situation specifically. I want to point out that the idea of a danger situation and the idea of what one is doing in it or would like to do about it are correlative. Each implies the other. To say something about one is necessarily to say something about the other. For example, the danger situation of castration exists when one views one's actual or potential actions as the kind that will create that danger; for example, actions of oedipal seduction and attacking the paternal phallus are both danger-creating actions. Therefore, if one is in a situation that clearly seems to threaten retaliatory mutilation or impairment of prowess, one will define one's actions accordingly: one's conception of them will be situation-bound; they will be intelligible only in terms of that situation. The castration anxiety of Little Hans (Freud, 1909a), is a case in point. We are used to dealing with stimulus-response relations in this way, that is, to see in each case that the stimulus has already been defined in ways which imply the response to be made to it.

Another important correlative of action and situation is affect. Affect enters into the experiential conception of danger situations. Throughout the ages and throughout the history of psychoanalytic theory, affects have been treated nominatively, that is, as independent entities with which the person, ego, or self must cope. Our ordinary language is rich in words, phrases, and figures of speech that teach us to think this way about affects and steadily reinforce our doing so. We think of affects as coming and going; we think they overwhelm us or support us or enrich us; we believe that we hold them in, that we get rid of them in catharsis, that they get under our skin, and so on. Even when they are viewed metapsychologically, as the quantitative aspect of instinctual drives whereby they seem to be established as aspects of our selves, these aspects are still often said to impinge on the ego and thus to be encountered as something other than our selves. They remain entities we must contend with or independent processes we must suffer or enjoy as the case may be. Especially in the case of moods and pathological emotional states, such as depression, we, equally as lay people and analytic observers, ordinarily view affects in this anthropomorphic and disclaimed way. It is, I should emphasize, a way that sets up the person as inherently passive and reactive in relation to affects.

But I think it is not necessary and no longer helpful to think this way, for this view of the matter does not conform closely to essential aspects of psychoanalytic interpretation. Analysts do not hesitate to raise questions as to why someone feels a certain way and why he or she even makes sure to feel that way or not feel that way. By doing so, analysts reject the conventional disclaiming separation of the person from his or her affects.

For example, analysts view neurotic depression as an aspect of the person's actions, and thus they follow the clinical explanation Freud (1917) advanced concerning mourning and melancholia. Quite apart from Freud's extensive and unproductive psychoeconomic speculation about the painfulness of the depressive affects, speculations he then regarded as his scientific metapsychological account of these matters, he was developing an account of mourning and melancholia that tells what people are doing when they mourn or are depressed. They introject and punish other persons whom they regard ambivalently, meanwhile sparing them from direct attacks, or they slowly face up to the reality of an actual loss and do so by reviewing and reliving the multitude of memories of the relationship that has, in the commonsense view, ended. In these activities, they regard themselves reproachfully or hatefully, or they remember sadly in order to face facts and go on living. For better or worse, they conduct their lives painfully. According to this clinical explanation, depression, far from being an entity to be encountered, is war conducted by other means while mourning is reality testing conducted reluctantly and miserably, but usefully as well.

I have just used a number of adverbs to characterize the affective states of the mourning and melancholic person—reproachfully, hatefully, sadly, painfully, etc. To return again to the danger situations outlined in "Inhibitions, Symptoms and Anxiety," which is to return to the neuroses and specifically to anxiety, I would say that Freud was necessarily talking about the person considering certain situations anxiously; he could not be referring to the entity, *anxiety*, passively encountered by a person or ego. I say this for several reasons. My first reason is to modify my previous description of ordinary and psychoanalytic language, for it is not the case that we invariably designate affects as entities not of the self. The fact is that we also have a large and well-used stock of verbs and adverbs by which to designate affects. We say "to love," and "lovingly," "to hate" and "hatefully," "to fear" and "fearfully," or that one climbs "anxiously," reminisces "nostalgically," loves "passionately," etc. In these locutions we specify affects not as disclaimed entities but as personal actions or modes of action. It is this aspect of our thinking about affects that has been directly incorporated into action language. In action language there are no personified and autonomous mental entities, emotional or otherwise. Nouns and adjectives give way to verbs and adverbs. Far from being merely a stylistic change, action language establishes an entirely different view of existence or of what it is to be a person. Persons are no longer regarded as the arenas and resultants of mental forces; they are their own actions and the modes in which they perform these actions. Their identities reside in what can be said in a general way about their actions. Action, it must be remembered, is not restricted to overt behavior or conscious thinking.

My stressing this conception of situations and actions constructed anxiously, and thus the verbal and adverbial version of affects, is not so far as it might seem from Freud's theory of psychic structure. Freud's new anxiety theory presents the ego as the seat of anxiety. Not only does he argue that the ego perceives the anxiety and uses it as a signal, he also argues that the ego defines the danger situation to begin with. In the structural theory, what else but the ego would and could recognize, remember, and expect situations of any kind? It is the ego, that coherent group of functions, that does so. Anxiety is thus an activity of the ego or, in other words, acting anxiously is a defining feature of what we call the ego (the id and superego do not, by definition, act anxiously).

My stressing the verbal and adverbial conception of danger situations ties in with my assertion that affect is a correlative of action and situation. For if affect or emotion may be stated as action, and if action and situation are correlatives, then affect is a correlative of both. The meaning of this statement is quite in line with the usual clinical way of understanding affects.

How do we know that someone is in a danger situation? Of course people may tell us that they feel unaccountably frightened or apprehensive, but we do not have to depend on their report, and anyway they may be pretending or trying to mislead us. Also, people are often unaware of anxiety signals. When, according to usual criteria, a person is fleeing or getting ready to flee from a scene, or reports such action in a convincingly agitated fashion, or acts in ways that imply fleeing, or perhaps shows some of the familiar physiological signs that accompany flight reactions, it is safe to infer that the person is in a danger situation. And when, objectively, there seems to be no danger to flee from, we assume we are dealing with an unconsciously defined danger situation and with "neurotic anxiety." For example, the person dreads a friendly embrace or an open street or an ordinary horse; the action and mode of action implies the danger situation. The action may be an emotion-action ("to fear"), or the mode might be an emotion-mode ("to run fearfully").

Danger situations can be identified in other ways. When we observe a person rigidly avoiding certain objectively innocuous situations, we infer that the person unconsciously views them as danger situations; emotion-actions and emotion-modes need not be evident. If our inference is correct, these "anxious" actions and modes will be evident whenever that person is compelled to enter or stay in that situation— for instance, forced to go out in the street, or to part from mother in the nursery school, or to talk about a certain topic. Thus, how a person acts or what a person now does overtly that before he has done only privately, can be used to establish the existence of a danger situation. On this basis the analyst can say to an analysand: "You are afraid even though you deny it. You wouldn't be acting defensively if you weren't afraid." Or the analyst can say, "You would be frightened to think so and even more frightened to do so."

If anxiety, danger situation, and action are correlative, the idea that the ego perceives a danger situation and then gives itself a signal of anxiety is tautological. We are dealing here not with causes but with codefining features of a psychological event. To say that the ego perceives anxiety would be to make a category mistake, for defining situations anxiously in one of the things we refer to by the abstract term *ego*. It is true that people often consciously deny being in danger situations and only admit it to themselves after they notice signs of agitation; but rather than establish a case for the anxiety signal, these observations show that people sometimes revise their defensive orientations in the light of new, even if unwelcome, evidence, that is, new developments in their construction of danger situations.

We use action language in commonsense fashion in our clinical interpretations, though perhaps we do not realize we are doing so because our metapsychology stands in the way. I for one feel better using action language because I no longer have to try and make sense of the proposition that the ego signals itself. I cannot picture it except as the ego rushing from one end of a telephone line to the other in time to catch its own message.

Inhibition

Inhibition must be approached as we now approach anxiety, that is, it must be rendered as a verb, "to inhibit," or an adverb, "inhibitedly." According to Freud, the reason for inhibiting or acting inhibitedly is to prevent the stimulation and experience of anxiety by avoiding a danger situation. What is to be inhibited or done in an inhibited fashion may be a specific action, such as showing sexual interest in another person, or a whole class of actions and modes of action that, metapsychologically, might be subsumed under one or more of the ego functions involved in performing certain tasks skillfully or at all. Further, one's neurotically inhibiting specific actions or classes of action in order to avoid a danger situation is to be explained, according to Freud, in the following manner: unconsciously, the actions and modes in question gratify impulses the expression or conscious experience of which it is anticipated would establish a danger situation; thus, only manifestly is it ever an action or class of actions that one inhibits; ultimately, one aims to inhibit a latent impulse or group of impulses. We should, therefore, pause at this point to examine once more, the fundamental psychoanalytic concept of impulse from the vantage point of the rules of action language. Much of the new anxiety theory turns on this concept.

A cornerstone of the structural and dynamic theory of psychoanalysis is the proposition that conflict exists primarily between the ego and the impulses of the id. To make this statement is not to deny the great importance of the ego's internal conflicts and its conflicts with the superego; nor is it to deny that these conflicts must be clarified in their own terms. It is to recognize that (1) id-ego conflicts are almost always implied in these other conflicts, and (2) the conceptualization of these other conflicts follows the lines laid down for speaking of the antagonistic relations of id and ego.

What, then, is an impulse in the terms of action language? More exactly, how shall we speak of an impulse verbally and adverbially? As I pointed out in the preceding chapter, an impulse is an action one wishes to perform but refrains from performing. It is an action or course of action one would perform in a certain mode (for example, cruelly, seductively) if it seemed safe enough to do so. We know, for instance, that almost all people regard certain actions as never safe enough to perform, whether overtly or in a fantasy; among these are incestuous, parricidal, and cannibalistic actions. These actions remain unthinkable, where "unthinkable" can only mean consciously unthinkable, for we know that, unconsciously, people must wish to perform the actions on which they impose taboos. One refrains forever from taking these actions.

If an impulse is viewed as an action one wishes to take but refrains from taking, then the experience of impulse can only be a manifestation of already existing "conflict"; it is the "conflict" between doing and refraining. Otherwise the person would simply perform the action in question. This conclusion, although I have not stated it metapsychologically, is in line with what Freud called functioning according to the primary process that characterizes the id, that is, imposing no delay on discharge and executing no experimental action in thought prior to discharge or, as I would say, prior to immediate action. Thus, what we or our analysands call inhibiting impulses amount to *further* inhibiting of actions or further refraining from performing them, however much one continues to wish to perform them. In this light, when we consider a manifest instance of inhibiting, we are dealing with someone's refraining from actions that he or she merely designates as impulse expressions. Metapsychologically, we would say that the inhibited ego function has been libidinized or aggressivized, whereas in action language we would say that, unconsciously, what one inhibits amounts to some sort of aggressive or erotic action or mode of action.

Although at this point we are far from the metapsychological way of conceptualizing id, instinctual drives, and psychic energies, we are, I submit, at the very center of clinical interpretation. For explicitly or implicitly we center our interpretations on actions and repudiated actions and their modes, and especially on their unconsciously implied meanings. Clinically, we also center interpretations on the defensive disclaimings analysands engage in when they speak of struggling with their impulses, for we understand that by putting it that way they are excluding these impulses from their own ideas of themselves and are disavowing having any responsible part in them. In this respect the analyst tries to show the analysand that he or she would like to perform the actions in question but does not dare do so and refrains from doing so. The analyst also tries to establish why the "impulse" is present and how the "inhibition" is accomplished. Thereby it is brought home to the analysand that he or she is as implicated in the "impulse" as in the effort to control or repudiate it.

In action language, one does not struggle with one's id or one's unconscious as autonomous entities; one struggles to choose between paradoxical actions or somehow to combine them or go on doing both in self-contradiction.

If the words I have just used are not the very words of clinical interpretation, they convey their sense. During the progress of an analysis what is to be noted is the ever-increasing presentation of oneself as the agent of one's current life. Less and less do analysands present themselves as lived by impulses, emotions, defenses, or conflicts; more and more do they present themselves as the authors of their existence. For even when all the necessities or terrible happenings of their past and present existences have been taken into account, analysands come to realize how much has always depended on what they have made of these factors, whether they be family constellations, traumas, infirmities, losses, or sexual anatomy. In fact, it is only on the basis of this arduously achieved realization that analysands can sort out their personal irrational constructions from rationally appraised necessity or accident—sorting out, for example, unwarranted ideas of unworthiness from more objectively considered parental neglect that occasioned them. To go further into the theoretical fates of drives, energies, motives, external reality, and determinism in the scheme of action language would require a discussion too lengthy for this chapter. I have attempted to deal with these crucial issues in a number of other discussions (1976, 1978).

One final consideration about inhibition. I prefer to say *refraining* from taking certain actions rather than *inhibiting* them because refraining is more consistent with action language. To say inhibiting is to imply the existence of both agentless independent forces and some concept of "inside" in which these forces can be located or contained. Both of these implications can be shown to be logically problematic even within the traditional metapsychological framework. That they are inconsistent with the requirements of a systematic action language should by now be evident.

Symptoms

In reconceptualizing symptoms as actions, the first job is to realize that what we are used to calling overdetermination or multiple determination and multiple function of symptoms may now be designated as complex actions. In clinical interpretation we attempt to make symptoms intelligible; we do so by progressively bringing them into the realm of claimed or acknowledged actions that the analysand is performing. Specifically, we try to ascertain in what ways symptoms are wishful activities such as enactments of primal scenes, in what ways they are self-punitive activities such as enactments of castration, and in what ways they are defensive, organizing, and adaptive activities. Thereby we take into account their so-called multiple function with respect to id, superego, and ego, respectively. Also in each of these structural respects we attempt to identify the many different wishful, self-punitive, and other meanings they carry; thereby we take into account their so-called overdetermination.

In working out these interpretations we progressively establish the following point: far from being afflictions visited on the hapless "patient" which must be "cured," neurotic symptoms are actions in which, unconsciously, the analysand has a definite stake and is most reluctant to give up. The stake and the reluctance are intimately related to his or her unconsciously expecting to be left exposed to those danger situations which the symptom was designed to forestall in the first place.

108

Danger Situations

It is important to recall in this connection that much of the analysis of symptoms is not conducted explicitly in relation to them; rather, it is conducted in terms of content far afield from them, perhaps in relation to certain neurotic character traits or certain features of transference and resisting. It is also important to recall that it is not unusual for analysands to mention, late in the treatment, the alleviation or disappearance of certain symptoms that have not figured prominently in the work and may never have been mentioned at all. These symptoms include headaches, constipation, dysmenorrhea, gastric distress, and minor phobias and compulsions. The significance of these clinical observations lies in their close connection with the analysis of danger situations, for wherever and however the analysis of chronic, characteristic danger situations has been successful, the analysand's stake in maintaining symptoms will have been diminished or eliminated. He or she will no longer have good and sufficient reason to act symptomatically or to act in ways that provoke or aggravate the physical aspects of his or her disturbances. Moreover, even when we take up symptoms directly, we find it especially useful in working out our interpretations of them to follow their exacerbations and alleviations; we do so on the assumption that these changes correspond to the waxing and waning of the danger situations for which they have been designed and so point to the constituents of danger. The case is the same when we analyze defenses: we depend on their diminution and intensification, their flux; for when they remain static, we are left in a poor position to discover their specific point and are in no position at all to make clear that they are actions, that they have reasons, and so are intelligible and modifiable after all.

Character Traits

In action terms one would speak of neurotic character traits as one would speak of inhibitions and symptoms, that is, as complex actions (see chapter 9). They can be analyzed insofar as they show the flux I referred to in discussing symptoms. They are chronic features of the analysand's existence. Typically they extend back to early childhood, even though their manifest form may not have been consolidated until adolescence. They imply chronic danger situations. The more disabling or disruptive they are, the more drastic or imminent the dan-

109

gers they imply. What I chiefly want to emphasize here is that, in thinking of them as traits, we commit ourselves to viewing them as properties one possesses, like facial features, whereas in thinking of them as actions and modes of action, we more usefully regard them as things one does consistently with reference to unconsciously defined and continuously maintained danger situations.

Defenses

The great advance Freud made in "Inhibitions, Symptoms and Anxiety" with respect to defenses was not his definitively sorting out repression as merely one mechanism of defense among others, although to be sure this contribution was an advance. More important, he leaped far ahead of himself in his mode of conceptualizing by interpreting mechanisms as expressions of unconscious fantasizing, that is, as meaningful or personal actions. He did this in his discussion of the relation in the obsessional disorders between isolation and touching and between undoing and anal blowing away. By analyzing the unconscious fantasizing or the psychical reality of the defensive activity, Freud was able to say more fully and with more analytic effect what the obsessional patient does when engaging in isolating or undoing. In this respect the notion of a mechanism of the ego gave way implicitly to the notion of the person as agent—the right step for Freud to take in a treatise devoted to danger situations. If touching becomes dangerous because of its anal-masturbatory significance, and if, unconsciously, thoughts and affects have come to be regarded concretely as anal-masturbatory substances or objects that are dangerously assaultive and seductive in themselves or that may be used in one of those manners, then the thing for one to do is to refrain from touching—at least one should refrain from touching in those areas of one's life where it would be most dangerous to touch at all. As we know, even thoughts, words, or letters might have to be kept from touching.

The regression that brings about this anal-masturbatory concern with touching is a regression from the oedipal danger situation to an earlier anal danger situation. In this connection Freud referred to the regressively debased Oedipus complex of the obsessional neurotic. And if the regression moves, as he said, to a point of fixation, then it is implied that certain anal-masturbatory danger situations have always figured significantly in the obsessional patient's actions even though less so before the neurotic regression. But here Freud referred mechanistically (hydraulically) to a regression to old channels of discharge.

It seems that Freud was not ready to recognize the nature and the extent of the forward leap I have been describing and so did not draw its implications. In his treatise, he neither analyzed the unconscious fantasizing involved in each of the defenses nor appreciated that he had embarked on an inherently nonmechanistic and nonorganismic course of conceptualization. Otto Fenichel (1941), while shrewdly emphasizing defense as personal activity, also did not make the most of this advance. It remained for Melanie Klein and others working with her to capitalize on Freud's great advance. They have done so by insisting that all mechanisms be analyzed in terms of unconscious fantasy. However, they have interwoven this illuminating development with elaborations of metapsychology that are even more problematic than Freud's. Thus, in my view, they have taken the wrong turn and missed the opportunity to develop a unitary theory in terms of unconscious fantasizing (Schafer, 1968b).

Diagnosis and Therapy

The implications of the preceding discussion for the idea we hold of diagnosis should be apparent by now. The word *diagnosis* is not problematic for action language as it means "to distinguish," and we make such distinctions. It is the usual contexts of this word that are problematic.

We say we diagnose psychopathology; however, by the word *pathology* we refer to that which one suffers, thereby implying passivity and affliction. The word *patient* makes the same reference and has the same implications, and the word *symptom* means anything that has befallen one—again, the same view of things. But what Freud began to establish clearly in "Inhibitions, Symptoms and Anxiety," even though he did not systematically develop it, is the proposition that it is wrong to think that a neurosis befalls one. A neurosis is created and arranged and protected. It is, correlatively, the construction of danger situations and the construction of emotional actions to take in these situations.

Consequently, the diagnosis of neurosis is the diagnosis of the actions we are used to calling symptoms, neurotic character traits, impulses, defenses, affects, and functions.

If by a diagnosis we refer to what someone is doing, then we may designate a psychoanalytic therapy in comparable action terms. In the case of neurosis, the service we render is inappropriately called the cure of pathology. Rather, we should say it consists of clarifying what the "patient" is doing, and to make sense of it in terms of unconsciously defined danger situations. Then, by sorting out the past from the present and the imagined from the actual, the "patient's" sense of danger is diminished and he or she can open as well as reopen the possibilities of action. Increasingly during this process, the "patient" will present apparent demonic forces and unyielding structures as personal actions and begin to live his or her life less painfully, apprehensively, self-deceptively, and unintelligibly. The "patient" will construct other and better situations to live in and will do so with an enhanced and more rational sense of personal responsibility. The "cure" will be this personal transformation from "patient" to conflicted agent engaged in a personal analysis.

I do, however, believe that the etymological implications of *pathology*, *patient*, and *symptom* do apply to certain aspects of constitutional problems and hardships suffered by infants and young children—the factors that independently predispose them toward constructing certain worlds as against others. But one must question whether we could ever "cure" these predispositions and whether it even makes sense to think of them as something to which the word *cure* could rightly be applied—as though it would make sense to speak of curing history.

8

The Interpretation of Transference and the Conditions for Loving

Introduction

The progress of the discipline of psychoanalysis is expressed perhaps most obviously in its theory of transference and the therapeutic effects of the interpretation of transference. The theory of transference rests on assumptions concerning repetition and regression or the influence of the past on the present; the roles of activity, passivity, and defensive measures; and the content of unconscious fantasy and conflict. The theory of the therapeutic effects of interpretation rests on these same assumptions and on others concerning the nature of insight, the role of the therapeutic relationship, the accessibility of unconscious fantasy and conflict to conscious influence, and the balance in the psychoanalytic process between, on the one hand, reliving and reexperiencing of the past and, on the other, new experience.

Clearly, the topic is vast, and one cannot hope to do justice in any single discussion to all the valuable contributions to the extensive literature on it; nor can one cover all that is widely understood and accepted in ordinary good practice. In this chapter I shall limit myself to reexamining some of the assumptions I just mentioned, doing so from the standpoint of action language.

In particular, I shall attempt to clarify the relationship between relived experience and new experience within the interpreted transferences, for the question of what it is in these transferences that is real, artificial, or mere stereotyped repetition has not yet been satisfactorily settled. I shall point out how Freud was indecisive in this respect. In order to trace Freud's thinking on this topic, and also to anchor the discussion in the psychoanalytic situation, I shall take up what Freud called the conditions for loving as well as his direct remarks on transference; I shall also introduce a clinical example as a concrete reference point for some of the theoretical considerations to follow. For present purposes, I consider it unnecessary to take up the problematic distinction between transference and transference neurosis; I shall simply refer to those major transference phenomena that call for interpretation.

On the assumption that it is arbitrary to separate consideration of transference from consideration of its interpretation, much of the following exposition will deal with certain aspects of the logic of interpretation and the question of how it is possible for the act of interpretation to break into the closed circle of unconsciously fantasized situations and make possible significant new experience. To this end it will be useful to discuss briefly fresh metaphor as a step toward new experience, unconscious "certainty," and the contribution made to insight through the coordination of the terms in which the past and present are to be understood. Despite their brevity, these discussions should enhance our understanding of the interpretation of transference and the conditions for loving.

Freud on the Conditions for Loving and Transference

Freud's views on the matters under discussion may be best approached through his introduction of the idea of conditions for loving in the course of his discussing the analysis of tranferences. For example, Freud says in this context that "each individual . . . has acquired a specific method of his own in his conduct of his erotic life—that is, in the preconditions to falling in love which he lays down, in the instincts he satisfies and the aims he sets himself in the course of it" (1912b, p. 99). In another place, Freud is advising the analyst to adopt a special attitude toward erotic transferences. This is the attitude that combines attentiveness, neutrality, nongratification, and insistence on analyzing the erotic feelings as "unreal" but necessary features of the treatment. He goes on to describe the consequence of maintaining this attitude in the following words: "The patient, whose sexual repression is of course not yet removed but merely pushed into the background, will then feel safe enough to allow all her preconditions for loving, all the

Transference and the Conditions for Loving

phantasies springing from her sexual desires, all the detailed characteristics of her state of being in love, to come to light; and from these she will herself open up the way to the infantile roots of her love" (1915a, p. 166). And in a number of papers dating from about the same time, that is between 1910 and 1922, he describes particular conditions for loving. Among these are the man's condition that the woman he loves sexually must somehow be degraded or in need of rescue or that there be an injured third party in the interpersonal configuration (1910b, 1912a). Also, in the instance of male homosexuality, in addition to the partner's possessing a penis, there is the condition that the young man who is loved be the same age that the lover was when he developed his now dominant identification with his mother (1922).

Freud described many such conditions throughout his writings. Although he was obviously intent on particularizing the conditions for loving, nothing stands in the way of our including under that designation the general or universal conditions for loving on which we now put so much emphasis, especially in our analysis of the preoedipal phases of development and their sequelae. Freud set forth a general outline of development (for example, in the "Three Essays on the Theory of Sexuality" [1905a]) that easily accommodates this general extension of the idea of conditions for loving.

I have been using Riviere's translation "conditions for loving" in preference to Strachey's "preconditions for loving" for two reasons. The first is that Freud's word for it was *Liebesbedingungen*, not *Liebesvorbedingungen*. My second and more important reason is to minimize the suggestion that Freud was here referring to causes of loving. The word *conditions* does have a causal ring. Nevertheless, although Freud was somewhat ambiguous in this respect—he did distinguish these "conditions" from "behavior in love"—one may assert that, logically, the points he made are descriptive in character rather than causal. That is to say, far from being about the causal conditions of loving, they describe actions, what one does in loving or how one does it, and these, in turn, include the people one chooses to love and the conduct one exhibits in loving them. Viewed in context, to "lay down" a condition, as Freud put it, can only mean to love in one way rather than another or to choose in accordance with certain rules rather than others. It is the clarification of these rules and choices, or the analytic translation of these regulated and consistent actions, that establishes the infantile prototypes or "roots" of loving.

It should go without saying that one must always take into account the darker side of loving—its fearful, mistrustful, hateful features; for my purposes, however, I shall speak mainly of the positive side of transference love.

But now, in order to understand Freud's account of loving, one must move on to his views on transference repetitions. When Freud discussed the transference love that brings to light these conditions for loving he seemed to be groping his way toward an adequately complex conception of it. Sometimes he says it is mere repetition. For example, "the transference itself is only a piece of repetition" (1914a, p. 151). And he says this of transference: "While the patient experiences it as something real and contemporary, we have to do our therapeutic work on it, which consists in a large measure in tracing it back to the past" (1914a, p. 152). But then, in the same paper of 1914, when speaking of the transference neurosis specifically, he modifies his account: "The transference thus creates an intermediate region between illness and real life, through which the transition from the one to the other is made. The new condition has taken over all the features of the illness; but it represents an artificial illness which is at every point accessible to our intervention. It is a piece of real experience, but one which has been made possible by especially favourable conditions, and it is of a provisional nature" (p. 154).

Another of Freud's suggestions that transference refers to more than repetition of the past is this description of the analysand: "He repeats everything that has already made its way from the sources of the repressed into his manifest personality—his inhibitions and unserviceable attitudes and his pathological character-traits" (1914a, p. 151). A year later, Freud adds this important point: "It is true that the [transference-] love consists of new editions of old traits and that it repeats infantile reactions. But this is the essential character of every state of being in love. There is no such state which does not reproduce infantile prototypes" (1915a, p. 168). And he emphasizes that this transference love is genuine even though it is greatly intensified by resistance, more unrealistic than normal love in its disregard for consequences and its idealizing features, more clearly dependent on its infantile prototypes, and so the less free, adaptable, or modifiable of the two.

Thus, in Freud's view, the differences between transference love and normal loving are quantitative rather than "essential," and the repetitiveness of transference love pertains to features of current life as well as to the repressed past. And yet, only a few years later, Freud shifts the emphasis back to the earlier type of formulation when he says this of the analysand: "He is obliged to *repeat* the repressed material as a contemporary experience instead of, as the physician would prefer to see, *remembering* it as something belonging to the past. These reproductions, which emerge with such unwished-for exactitude, always have as their subject some portion of infantile sexual life. . . . what appears to be reality is in fact only a reflection of a forgotten past" (1920, pp. 18–19).

These shifts of emphasis indicate that Freud had not thought through something essential. He was in effect juxtaposing and accepting two views of the matter without integrating them. On the one hand, transference love is sheerly repetitive, merely a new edition of the old, artificial and regressive (in its ego aspects particularly), and to be dealt with chiefly by translating it back into its infantile terms. (From this side flows the continuing emphasis in the psychoanalytic literature on reliving, reexperiencing, and recreating the past.) On the other hand, transference is a piece of real life that is adapted to the analytic purpose, a transitional state of a provisional character that is a means to a rational end, and as genuine as normal love. (From this side flows the emphasis in our literature on the healing powers inherent in the analytic relationship itself, especially with respect to early privations and deprivations.) We are not in a position to disagree entirely with either conception of transference, transference neurosis, and transference-laden therapeutic effects. The problem is, how to integrate the two.[1] In tackling this problem, I shall be drawing especially on the classical discussions of transference and interpretation presented by Strachey (1934), Kris (1956a), Rycroft (1958), Loewald (1960, 1971), and Stone (1961, 1967). More recently published papers by Blum (1971), Gray (1973), Leavy (1973), and Schimek (1975) present orientations that are relevant or similar to the one that follows here. But first a clinical example to serve as a point of clinical reference for the theoretical analysis to be undertaken.

A Clinical Example

A young man in analysis had been realizing in an ever more agitated fashion how disturbed and confined he had always felt in connection with certain characteristic features of his father's conduct. His father

1. It has been suggested, correctly, I think, that Freud's stress on repetition was in part a response to real and threatened public disapproval of the erotic transferences that female analysands developed in relation to their male analysts (Charles Rycroft, personal communication).

followed the strict policy of always behaving sensibly, responsibly, gently, and kindly; the man thus fit the familiar pattern of reaction formation against anal-sadistic and phallic-sadistic modes of action. As is usually the case with marked reactive practices of this sort, these modes of action were cruel in their effects, for they stimulated the son to think himself especially unworthy and unable to love, and so, in keeping with Freud's generalization, "to doubt every lesser thing as well." But, as is also usually the case in such family contexts, the boy himself became more and more disposed to act sadistically, especially in the wishful fantasies he unconsciously elaborated.

One main reason for this development was, of course, that he identified himself unconsciously with his father as a sadistic figure. Another reason was that he angrily regarded his father as castrating in several ways: for one thing, he saw his "blameless" father as setting a standard of controlled manhood he could never hope to meet; for another, he experienced a seduction into loving this paragon in what was for him a passive-feminine manner. Additionally, he came to view the masculine sexual role as one that was intolerably dirty, exhibitionistic, selfish, and rapacious, and so felt cut off from ordinary sexual activity. And to top it off, in a reaction against his painfully guilty, doubt-ridden daily activities, he virtually ceased working and was forfeiting his young manhood in this respect, too. Understandably, he had presented himself for analysis as a dispirited, cynical, indecisive, apathetic, melancholy person. Consciously, he professed only love and esteem for his father, while attacking unmercifully the rigid postures of tolerance and forbearance adopted by his humanistically oriented friends.

Before going any further, I should clarify a number of features of my exposition of this bit of analysis. First, when I say "his father," I am referring to the father imago, which I take to have been only partly faithful to the father more objectively considered. It was an imago maintained mostly unconsciously and built up during different phases of psychosexual development. Second, this imago had been defined principally through close inspection of his various father-transferences and my countertransference reactions to them. Third, it had been possible to define these transferences at all clearly only by sorting them out from an array of mother-transferences, each with its own developmental and attitudinal complexity. Fourth, the relevant analytic data included the usual wide range of phenomena: they extended from bodily fantasies and enactments, such as constipation, masturbation, and archaic ideas of retribution and damage, to sober attempts to remember, reconstruct, and organize just how events, long remembered in a neurotic way, had actually transpired. Finally, my explanatory account, since it is not a complete synopsis and analysis of the analysis itself, can give only a limited picture of the multiple meanings of those details I do mention.

Returning now to the young man: one day when he was well into the analysis, he experienced one of his most anguished yet liberated and liberating moments during the analysis. He was recounting once again, but more insightfully than ever before, a scene that had been serving as a prototype of his childhood relation with his father. In this scene, his father had forbidden him to do something because it would have upset his mother. Thereupon the boy had stormed off to his room. His father had followed him and taken a long time, patiently and calmly, to explain and to justify his having issued the prohibition. It seemed that this father had determined, for his own neurotic reasons, to get his young son to agree that issuing the prohibition had been the right, kind, rational thing for him to have done. But the son, already going round in a vicious circle, had reacted to these acts of coercion and seduction ever more angrily, erotically, and guiltily. It had been, as he now portrayed it in some detail, slow torture under paralyzing conditions. At this point, the analysand half sat forward on the couch, clutched the empty air in front of him, wept miserably, and pleaded—to himself, his father, me, the gods above—"What could I tell him? What could I say to him?" *Then,* as a boy, he had been inarticulate. *Now,* as an advanced analysand, he had answers to these questions and could see how impossible it would have been to think them or utter them in that situation.

As he now viewed the matter, he had found his father wanting in the capacity to tolerate or contain his enraged mode of reacting. In Winnicott's terms (1971), this father had not provided him with the safety of a holding relationship in which he could remain, as long as need be, the frustrated, angry child and not lose his father in the process. His father had characteristically abandoned him at those moments of experienced need for a father that are so important in a child's development.

The son had experienced these abandonments all the more painfully in the context of his mother's failings as a mother. In his presentation of her, she was a pleasant but ineffectual woman who required constant support and protection from her husband and children; left to her own resources she would soon react anxiously and depressively herself. It seemed that reacting that way had been, among other things, her way of controlling the family. Thus the mother imago was

119

that of the inadequate holding mother of infancy and childhood. Not only had this figure deprived her son of his developmentally necessary early experiences of distress-in-safety; additionally, she had enforced, unconsciously, that terrible reversal of generations in which the child must hold the mother. It was this reconstructed relationship that had been established as the original context of his reacting depressively and his turning desperately to his apparently motherly father to get the parental holding he urgently wished for. But, in our reconstruction, his father, too, had failed him in this respect. In relation to these parental imagos the son had established a mistrustful, despairing, and hateful outlook on himself and others.

This analytically established picture of a boyhood illustrates how a familiar condition for loving was not met: the condition of the convincing, sustained readiness of those who are loved to contain one's more or less projective assaults on them, to tolerate the role of bad breast or phallus, arbitrary authority, or villain of some other kind, and to endure being abandoned.

Ideally, the analyst provides this containing, tolerating, and enduring within the transference relation. The analyst even fosters these crises through interpretation of the defensive measures by which the analysand forestalls making this crucial test of the relationship. And the analyst passes this test, not through ordinary loving-kindness, but by standing fast as the interpreting analyst, recognizing the assault frankly, allowing it to be developed and sustained in the light of its developmental importance, and helping the analysand to endure it through understanding it more fully in all its crucial contemporary as well as infantile significance. Having met this condition for loving, the analyst is loved gratefully as a good mother, father, breast, womb, phallus, friend, and analyst. Not all at once, of course, not once and for all, and not altogether, for this is only part of the work.

To mention one additional and essential factor, in achieving this experience within the transference relationship, the analysand engages in less "splitting of ambivalence" and idealizing, and so begins to view the analyst, and each parent, more objectively, openly, and sturdily as a whole figure. A whole figure is one that is "good but also bad," to use Jacobson's (1964) phrase for it, which is to say a stable one that can be loved and hated. Being better loved than before, the analyst is more freely attacked. The analysand now tolerates his or her experiencing of relationships ambivalently, thereby demonstrating that new and more inclusive conditions for loving have been developed. This development bears as much on loving oneself as on loving others. That is to say, tolerating the ambivalent mode is, correlatively, a condition of healthy "narcissism" and "object love." (The one implies the other rather than being at its expense, as Freud assumed, or rather than, as Kohut [1971] assumes, an independent line of development.)

In his analysis, the young man of my example had reached his climactic questions and this turning point, that had a tragic quality in its being simultaneously terrible, wonderful, and irreversible, through the sustained analysis of his transferences. As one might expect, he had, among other things, been construing my consistently trying to understand him neutrally and impartially as a replication of his father's guilt-inducing and castrating actions, and he had been dealing with my interventions accordingly. That is to say, either he had been attacking me scornfully and vituperatively, as he had been doing to his tolerant friends, or he had been acting despondently, ruminatively, and inertly, sometimes concealing the latter by forcing himself to act jovially and zestfully, as he had been doing for his father. All of which I had been pointing out on numerous occasions and in various ways. It should be added that in part he was still enacting his father-transference when he clutched the air in his agitated way, for by that gesture at that moment he was shaking, perhaps choking and silencing, me as well as his father, and he was reaching out to both of us to be held in the right way at last. But consciously and genuinely, the accent had by now shifted to his hitherto idealized father, and he was on new ground, for he had slowly seen the point of these transference interpretations as his various ways of resisting had been taken up. Now, at last, he had integrated hitherto unintegrated bodily, emotional, and verbal constituents of experience. His conditions for loving had been significantly modified.

The Interpretation of Transference Repetitions

That the transference repetitions are unvarying cannot, of course, be true in any ordinary descriptive sense. *They appear as unvarying only upon interpretation.* It is interpretation that redescribes actions in the terms of one or another transference theme. For example, the dominant transference theme during one phase of the analysis of the young man of my clinical example was unacknowledged rebellion against his father's coercion. In this connection, the analysand's acting raucously, impulsively, negligently, selfishly, unproductively, and hurtfully to women all counted as repetitive instances of rebelliousness against the father—*but only through redescription.* And that line of interpretation was only one of the strategies of redescription I followed during the analysis as I tried to work out the multiple meanings and life-historical background of the analysand's transferences. Freud's designation of transferences as "new editions" does, after all, contain the word *new,* thereby recognizing that there are other, commonsense descriptions of the transference actions in question.

This redescription according to transference themes must be characterized as a simplification of what is said to be going on. It is an act of subtraction, abstraction, or analysis of form, depending on how one wants to view it. It simplifies the variously presented dramas of life—the individuating baby with its bodily modes of comprehension and experience, and the changing, conflictual, irrational relations of family members during one's psychosexual development. Interpretive simplification in terms of these dramas makes for that one kind of intelligibility so distinctively psychoanalytic and unquestionably essential to the analytic work. Far from being simple minded, it is, when rightly applied, a sophisticated and imaginative model of understanding. Simplifying in this way does not destroy some absolute truth; rather, it develops the psychoanalytically necessary version of the truth. Although it is reductive, it is not crude or unthinking reductionism. In fact, sooner or later, in and out of the transferences, it is the source of new complexities.

As the analysand manifests transferences and finds them redescribed as such by the analyst's interpretations, he or she goes on to enact them in ways that are progressively more concentrated and transparent within this interpretive context. The reasons for this change are many. They range from the analysand's identifying with the analyst to the implicit and effective reassurance provided by the analyst's conduct that it is safe, even if painful, to change in this way. It is a change that brings one subjectively closer to the fantasized paternal phallus and maternal breast, face, womb and "wound." In this connection, the analyst must, of course, sort out genuine change from the analysand's perseveratively resisting through compliantly delivering what seems to be expected. While this sorting out is no easy task, it can usually be performed well enough to allow the analysis to be developed further. The analyst performs this task through transference interpretations of the resisting itself. For example, he or she may interpret the overly compliant analysand's resisting as a matter of taking the part of a good, castrated boy-girl or latency child acting now on behalf of the father-analyst by dwelling on the theme of transference.

Increasingly, the analytic relationship is installed as the framework and the reference point for everything of which special note is taken. For example, it is the reference point for the topics introduced and avoided, together with their timing and their emotional qualities, and for overt behavior in and out of the sessions. The analysis of transferences promotes two developments: first, especially during the sessions themselves, the world most real and of most concern is the analytic relation itself, and second, that world is of most interest and value when it can be interpreted as the analysand's own construction. That is to say, the analysis becomes primarily the contemplation of the fantasized or invented aspects of the analysand's relationship to the analyst. This is so even when the analysand has temporarily succeeded in forcing or seducing the analyst into actualizing some assigned countertransference role in the relationship.

The analysand invents many versions of the analytic relationship in the transference fantasies. Sooner or later, however, all these versions are redescribed through interpretation as sheerly repetitive. It is this way of analyzing transferences that seems to warrant calling them "artificial" and "new editions." But these designations are tied to the interpretive method being used, and one would be wrong to attribute an "as if" character to the development of the transference neurosis. Nor would one be correct in saying that the relaxation of defense against the transference involvement brings the analysis closer to the truth, for the defensive features are themselves parts of the truth or part of the transferences, too. Rather, the change that takes place is an altered version of reality based on another way of apprehending self and others in relationship. There are only *ways* of apprehending reality, there being no single, authoritative, context-free reality to use as a criterion or to be held fast no matter what one is aiming to understand. As Grossman (1967) pointed out, the introspectible world reflects the purposes for which one is introspecting. Although the version enacted in the transference neurosis includes many infantile, irrational features, it is as real as any other version.

To return now to the analysand's getting to be increasingly preoccu-

123

pied with the fantasized transference relationship: this preoccupation establishes a special atmosphere of solitude in the analytic setting. Paradoxically, this solitude plays an essential role in the fullest possible expansion of the analysand's conditions for loving. The paradox is perhaps best described in Winnicott's phrase, "being alone together" (1958; see also Green's recent development of the idea of "absence" in the analytic relationship, 1975, esp. p. 12). The solitude captures that essential tension generated in the psychoanalytic situation which Freud devised. It is both the foundation and the summit of the analytic relationship, for if two people can be alone together, they are in the best position to develop freely the emotional and cognitive possibilities of the relationship. The idea of solitude takes in the deprivation in the two-person relationship described so well by Stone (1961, 1967). And it includes the solitariness so vividly presented by Thomas Mann in "Death in Venice." Speaking of the solitary person, Mann writes:

A solitary, unused to speaking of what he sees and feels, has mental experiences which are at once more intense and less articulate than those of a gregarious man. They are sluggish, yet more wayward, and never without a melancholy tinge. Sights and impressions which others brush aside with a glance, a light comment, a smile, occupy him more than their due; they sink silently in, they take on meaning, they become experience, emotion, adventure. Solitude gives birth to the original in us, to beauty unfamiliar and perilous—to poetry. But also, it gives birth to the opposite: to the perverse, the illicit, the absurd (1913, p. 26).

"Being alone together" adds this to the accounts of Stone and Mann, that a shared reality is developed in which new transference interpretations, jointly developed, stated by the analyst and uniquely modified by the analysand, become the basis of enriched, intensified modes of constituting experience in the life of the analysand. These constitutive modes, too, will be redescribed as repetition so far as that seems possible and useful.

The major transference phenomena represent the achievement of such simplified, focused ways of defining and acting within the analytic relationship that there can be no mistaking their meanings or avoiding their emotional manifestations or implications. The mode of experiencing is clear, compact, intensified. Here, as Freud emphasized, is the ground for conviction: nothing important is being dealt with *"in absentia* or *in effigie"* (1912b, p. 108).

Transference and the Conditions for Loving

Unconscious Certainty

The idea of ground for conviction implies not doubt but convictions or certainties unconsciously maintained by the analysand. These are the convictions—for example, that the analyst is indeed persecutory—that stand in the way of the analysand's taking the transference interpretations for what they are rather than as further evidence in support of the convictions themselves. It is essential to hold a correct view of the status unconsciously accorded these convictions by the analysand. They are far from being merely anxiously and rigidly held positions, though they are these, too.

In this regard, one may bring into consideration an adaptation of Wittgenstein's discussions in "On Certainty" (1969; see also Morawetz, 1978). The transference interpretation is an attempt to correct certain beliefs about self and others to which the analysand has been holding fast against all evidence. The analysand has been holding these beliefs so fast that he or she gives every appearance of using them as methodological principles or principles of knowing. This is to say that, for the analysand, these beliefs must be taken as true if he or she is to be able to make judgments or claims about anything else, for nothing else is more certain than they are. They serve as tests of what is true. One such belief might be, "I am worthless." That it is held fast is made evident by how the believer will judge anyone who thinks otherwise to be a fool, a dupe, a manipulator, or another worthless person who cannot know any better.

Thus the person in question will reinterpret all contrary evidence in the light of this belief rather than begin to question the belief itself. One's entire idea of reality and of one's relation to it is at stake. In this context, for the analyst to respond in kind by agreeing or disagreeing with the belief would be to discredit himself or herself as a person and analyst. Further, as Strachey (1934) has pointed out, the analyst would be providing a good magical introject to counter a bad one, and in doing so would be making a poor move in the game of analysis. The transference interpretation is a good move in a game different from the analysand's. This is a game or a set of practices into which the analysand must be initiated and ultimately become an expert. But it is, in Wittgenstein's sense, only a game, that is to say, an approach to reality that consistently uses one language or one set of rules or practices, thereby making a more adaptive reality in which a certain mode of experiencing is extended in scope, intensified, and made amenable to further transformation. To call it a game is, of course, not to say that it is frivolous, merely pretense, or a nonanalytic social psychological interaction.

In making transference interpretations, the analyst attempts to throw into question these certainties or beliefs unconsciously held fast. The analyst as analyst takes nothing presented by the analysand for granted. It is inherent in the analytic attitude that it is only by finding other ways to understand what the analysand holds to be both unquestionably true and damaging that it will ever be possible to develop and carry through an analysis. In saying why they are treated as certainties and how that came to be so, in pointing out the analysand's uses of these convictions and their consequences, and, above all, in showing how they shape what is painful, pleasurable, and limiting in the analytic relationship, the analyst tries to help the analysand become more genuinely a co-worker in the analysis.

But for the analysand, this attempt on the analyst's part represents for a long time an assault on his or her idea of reality. As such, it is to be resisted strenuously, even if subtly. It is not only the specific sense of the interpretation that is threatening; it is also the interpretation's throwing into question the analysand's entire mode of making sense. Here the analyst counts on the analysand's having been making more than one kind of sense of the events of his or her life, that is, of having multiple, *conflicting* conceptions of what is real or true, based on other infantile psychosexual convictions as well as more or less rational, communally shared conceptions of the real and the true. Were the analysand to be maintaining only one self-enclosed set of convictions, he or she could never consider the interpretation as such. If, for example, persecution were the issue, then every interpretation of persecutory fantasizing would be experienced merely as further persecution. And we do know that every analytic process goes through phases during which each intervention is regarded as a seduction, a castration, etc., according to the unconsciously maintained certainty that is dominant at the time. At least for the time being, though perhaps forever, the analysand's interpretive circle is closed—or appears to be.

Yet, given a reasonably well-chosen analysand, the reductive transference interpretations do seem to make a difference, and so we must pursue the question of how the ground for conviction referred to by Freud does develop during the analysis. Perhaps the old relationships that serve as prototypes in the transference interpretations were not identical with all that is now being lived, interpreted, and believed in the transference. Perhaps *in principle* they could not be identical. If this were so, to formulate manifest transference interpretation simply in reductive terms would be to obscure the many other factors that play an important part in the changes that are observed. In this regard it is worth considering whether new experience, far from being only a consequence of transference interpretation, is somehow inherent in the developing repetitive transferences themselves.

Metaphor and New Experience

In taking up these questions, we are entering an area of life in which things are also other than themselves, where meaning is multifaceted, and where the line between the old and the new is blurred. It should, I think, help develop answers to these questions to consider briefly some interrelated aspects of the psychology of metaphor. In the psychology of metaphor we shall find a useful analogy to the psychology of transference interpretations. My focus will be on newly encountered good metaphors, those in response to which we say "That's it exactly!" or "That really captures it!" or "That says it all!"

Some literary and linguistic analysts (see, for example, Lewis, 1946; Snell, 1953), and also people in everyday life, believe that there are experiences that can only be expressed metaphorically. And it is for this achievement that these metaphors, which may be entire poems as well as lines or even words, are so highly valued. But how can this be so? Just what is the "it" that the metaphor "is" or "captures" or "says"? If this "it" or this "experience" can only be rendered metaphorically, then we can know it only as such, that is, as the metaphor itself. In this I agree with the position put forward by T. S. Eliot (1933) and D. W. Harding (1963) in their discussions of poetry. For in these instances we are granting that there is no known and logically independent version of the experience that can serve to validate the metaphor. Whatever the metaphor makes available to us depends on it and so cannot be used to prove its correctness.

It seems justified to conclude that the metaphor is a new experience rather than a mere paraphrase of an already fully constituted experience. The metaphor creates an experience that one has never had before. It is an experience one has not realized by oneself. The metaphor does, of course, suggest certain constituent experiences of which one

127

may have been more or less dimly aware. And as Ella Freeman Sharpe (1940), among others, has argued, metaphor is derived from and touches on certain unconsciously elaborated, wishful psychosexual events and fantasies. One may say, therefore, that the metaphor *speaks for* these constituents, on the existence of which much of its appeal depends. But in its organizing and implicitly rendering these constituents in its new way, it is a creation rather than a mere paraphrase or new edition. Paraphrases and new editions never speak as forcefully as good new metaphors, nor could they facilitate further new experience. One analytically familiar feature of these creations is that they make it safe and pleasing to experience something that otherwise would be considered too threatening and so would be kept in fragmented obscurity through defensive measures.[2]

Thus, when one says, "That's it exactly!" one is implicitly recognizing and announcing that one has found and accepted a new mode of experiencing one's self and one's world, which its to say, asserting a transformation of one's own subjectivity. Something is now said to be true, and in a sense it is true, but it is true for the first time. Nothing just like it has ever happened before. And nothing just like it can ever happen again, for the second time cannot be the same as the first. One can't step into the same river twice. A revelatory metaphor reencountered or repeated later may lose some of its force. Alternatively, it may gain in significance, but it cannot serve to mobilize an experience identical with the first. The point applies as well to new metaphors that are similar to familiar ones; they have to be judged or experienced through their conventionalized predecessors, as through methods of knowing or already proved instruments of perceiving. The audience and the performer, who may be one person, have not stood still.

Interpretation and New Experience

What I have said about the psychology of metaphor is analogous to the transformational aspects of developed transferences and the steadfast interpretations that both facilitate and organize them as transferences.

2. My formulation of this point does not fundamentally clash with the established psychoanalytic proposition that art is a means of mastering emotions through some relaxation and realignment of defense that permits expression and gratification of instinctual drives in relative safety. It is just that I am no longer viewing emotion as an inher-

Transference and the Conditions for Loving

Allowing that these transferences and "remembered" experiences come into existence over a period of time, nothing that is identical with them has ever before been enacted, and nothing identical with them will ever be enacted again. They are creations that may be fully achieved only under specific analytic conditions. For example, at the time of his childhood scene with his father, the young man of my clinical example could not have had the specific experience I recounted. Strictly speaking, he was not reliving that moment. As a boy, he must have experienced some of the main precursors and constituents of his present mode of experience, but he could not have done so in the present articulated and integrated manner. That present manner was the basis of his anguished outcry. Words such as recreating, reexperiencing, and reliving simply do not do justice to the phenomena. It is not paradoxical to say that, in the way he was doing it, *he was living that past moment for the first time.*

In making this claim, I am not contradicting some of our well-established ideas about interpretation and insight. I am not, for example, disputing the point that insight refers to more than the recovery of lost memories, and takes in as well a new grasp of the significance and interrelations of events one has always remembered. It is in the latter connection that the analysand will say, as Freud pointed out, "As a matter of fact I've always known it; only I've never thought of it" (1914a, p. 148). But the young child simply does not have the means of fully defining what we later regard as its own life experiences. It takes an adult to do that, especially with the help of an analyst. It was, after all, Freud's analysis of adults that made it possible to define infantile psychosexuality. In this respect, but without disrespect, child analysis always retains a quality of applied psychoanalysis. The adult definition of infantile psychosexuality is "artificial" in the same way that the interpreted transference neurosis is. Both are ways of describing as true something that was not true in quite that way at the time of its greatest developmental significance. This apparent paradox about "remembering" as a form of creating goes a long way, I think, toward saying what it is that is distinctive about psychoanalytic

---

ently autonomous and quantitative entity or process of discharge that must be mastered by the psychical functions we ascribe to the ego structure. In the alternative terms of action language, it would be preferable to say, with regard to mastery, that it is the person enacting emotional experience in a manner that he or she now views as less threatening because it implies less in the way of drastic action, both in what is privately or unconsciously imagined and in what is publicly performed. In this view, far from being encountered passively and only then dealt with as happenings, affects are features of actions or aspects of personal agency.

interpretation. Freud's (1899) discussion of screen memories laid the foundation for this proposition.

In steadfastly and perspicaciously making transference interpretations, the analyst helps constitute new modes of experience and new experiences. This newness characterizes the experience of analytic transferences themselves. Unlike extraanalytic transferences, they can no longer be or remain sheerly repetitive or merely new editions. Instead, they become repetitive new editions understood as such because defined as such by the simplifying and steadfast transference interpretations. Instead of responding to the analysand in kind, which would actualize the repetition, the analyst makes an interpretation. This interpretation does not necessarily or regularly match something the analysand already knows or has experienced unconsciously. Although the analysand does often seem to have already represented some things unconsciously in the very terms of the interpretation, equally often he or she does not seem to have done so at all. To think otherwise about this would be, in effect, to claim that, unconsciously, every analysand is Freud or a fully insightful Freudian analyst. And that claim is absurd.

It would be closer to the truth to say that, unconsciously, the analysand already knows or has experienced fragmentary, amorphous, uncoordinated constituents of many of the transference interpretations. Alternatively, one may say that, implicitly, the analysand has been insisting on some as yet unspecified certainties and, in keeping with this, following some set of as yet unspecified rules in his or her actions. These the transference interpretations now organize explicitly. Each transference interpretation thus refers to many things that have already been defined by the analysand, and it does so in a way that transforms them. That's why one may call it interpretation; otherwise it would be mere repeating or sterile paraphrasing. *Interpretation is a creative redescription.* Each interpretation does, therefore, add new actions to the life the analysand has already lived.

Technically, redescription in the terms of transference-repetition is necessary. This is so because, up to the time of interpretation and working through, the analysand has been, in one sense, unable and, in another sense, unconsciously and desperately unwilling, to conduct his or her life differently. In and of themselves, the repetitions cannot alter the symptoms, the subjective distress, the wasting of one's possibilities; rather, they can only perpetuate a static situation by repeatedly confirming its necessity. They reinforce once again the unconsciously maintained, damaging certainties. But once they get to be viewed as historically grounded actions and subjectively defined situations, as they do upon being interpreted and worked through, they appear as having always been, in crucial respects, inventions of the analysand's making and, so, as his or her responsibility. In being seen as *versions* of one's past life, they may be changed in significant and beneficial ways. Less and less are they presented as purely inevitable happenings, as a fixed fate, or as the well-established way of the world.

Coordinating Past and Present Experience

One major point remains to be made about the logic of viewing transference interpretations as simplifying yet innovative redescriptions. This point is that the interpretations bring about a coordination of the terms in which to state both the analysand's current problems and their life-historical background. As far as possible, the analysand's symptoms and distress are described as actions and modes of action, with due regard for the principle of multiple function or multiple meaning. In coordination with that description, the decisive developmental situations and conflicts are stated as actions and modes of action. Continuity is established between the childhood constructions of relationships and self and the present constructions of these. Interpretation of transferences shows how both are part of the same set of practices, that is, how they follow the same sets of rules. Past and present are coordinated to show continuity rather than arranged in a definite causal sequence.

In the same way, the *form* of analytic behavior and the *content* of associations are given coordinated descriptions, say, as being defiant, devouring, or reparative. Or, in the case of depression, the depressive symptoms, the depressive analytic transference, the themes of present and past loss, destructiveness and helplessness, all will be redescribed under the aspect of one continuously developing self-presentation. And this coordination will be worked out in that hermeneutically circular fashion in which the analyst defines both the facts to be explained and the explanations to be applied to these facts. In the end, as is well known, both the paramount issues of the analysis and the lead-

131

ing explanatory account of them are likely to be significantly different from the provisional versions of them used at the beginning of the analysis.

This is the sophisticated cognitive simplification that promotes the convincing development and recognition of transference and the emotional experiencing of the past *as it is now remembered*. The coordination of terms is the only way to break into the vicious circle of the neurotic disturbance and reduce its unconsciously self-confirming character. New meaning is established by steadfast interpretation of transferences and the conditions for loving of which they are enactments.

That this kind of analytic work is not simply intellectual is shown by the analytic example presented above. My analysand was now operating according to rules which, through previous transference interpreatations and coordination of terms, had changed. The changed rules were implicit in this hitherto avoided experiencing of the past. It was not reexperiencing, or not mainly that. In its special way, it was experiencing that past in an articulated emotional fashion for the first time.

Conclusion

I should like to mention two implications of the foregoing remarks.

1. The transference phenomena that finally constitute the transference neurosis are to be taken as regressive in only some of their aspects. This is so because, viewed as achievements of the analysis, they have never existed before as such. Rather, they constitute a creation achieved through a novel relationship into which one has entered by conscious and rational design (in part). The analytic definition of the conditions for loving has never been arrived at before; they have never been so simplified, organized, intensified, and transparent as they get to be in the analytically circumscribed and identified transference neurosis. It seems a more adequate or balanced view of transference phenomena to regard them as multidirectional in meaning rather than as simply regressive or repetitive. This would be to look at them in a way that is analogous to the way we look at creative works of art. We would see the transferences as creating the past in the present, in a

special analytic way and under favorable conditions. Essentially, they would then represent movement forward, not backward.

2. It is wrong to think that interpretation deals only in what is concealed or disguised or, what is its correlate, that "the Unconscious" is omniscient. In particular, it cannot be the case the "the Unconscious" knows all about transference and repetition. By establishing new connections, comprehensive contexts, and coordinated perspectives on familiar actions, interpretation creates new meanings or new actions. Not everything that is adequately organized has been actively kept apart by defensive measures; not everything that has failed to be recognized has been denied. This point is obvious, really, but it is often obscured by formulations, some of Freud's among them, which suggest that interpretation is just uncovering (see in this connection Fingarette, 1963).

I mentioned earlier that Freud was groping in these connections. I would now suggest that he had to grope owing to his having drawn a sizable number of distinctions too sharply: past and present, old and new, genuine and artificial, repetition and creation, the subjective world and the objective world, dream and reality, solitude and intimacy, and union and separation. He also distinguished too sharply between the psychoanalytic method and its results, and between psychoanalytic description and explanation. Each of these pairs we may now view differently on the strength of Freud's discoveries taken together with advances made by others in psychoanalytic theory and the general theory of knowledge. We may view them, that is to say, as *features* of action or experience rather than as mutually exclusive types of action or experience. And we may realize that they are such features only as described or redescribed and organized by an observer following a plan. For us today, these distinctions are simultaneously more uncertain and less conducive to needless uncertainty than they were for Freud in his day.

9

The Analysis of Character

Introduction

Perhaps the first question to raise in a theoretical and clinical discussion of character is whether it is worth bothering with the concept at all. Unlike the ego, which, as a systematic concept, came after it, character has never been provided with either a satisfactory conceptualization or a definite place in psychoanalytic theory. Moreover, in an amorphous way character overlaps the concept *ego*. In other respects, character overlaps both the concept *self*, which is now very much in theoretical vogue, and the free-floating concept *style* or "neurotic style" as elaborated by Shapiro (1965). But conceptualizations of *self* and *style*, in turn, usually overlap those of the *ego*. For these reasons alone, one remains uncertain of one's theoretical ground when referring to character.

One feels better positioned with respect to character when the discussion turns to clinical or technical matters and centers on such issues as resistance, defense analysis, conflict resolution, ego-syntonicity, and subtle expressions of maladaptiveness. It is, however, questionable whether this security is any more warranted than theoretical security in regard to the concept of character. This is so because for some time there have been at hand the theoretical and technical concepts of ego analysis, defense, intersystemic and intrasystemic conflict, acting out, multiple function, the synthetic function of the ego, secondary autonomy, and others of that order, and these, far more than character, have an established place in systematic psychoanalytic discussion of clinical phenomena and methods.

It would seem, then, that one might do better to forget about a systematic approach to character and do what is so often done, discuss other matters, such as the development and analysis of the total personality, under the title *character*. As a rule, in fact, analytic writing on character has tended to deal with the development and analysis of the total personality. But one need not follow this evasive precedent, nor should one, for the concept of character seems to have so strong a hold on the psychoanalytic imagination that one is obliged to try to determine the source of its power or the good uses that have been found for it. One might even hope to discover additional work that can be done in the name of character.

There seem to be a number of important and more or less interrelated reasons why character has been such a viable concept. They include, first of all, the opportunity it affords to discuss the development and analysis of the total personality; second, the contribution it makes toward satisfying the ever present urge toward nosology, especially in relation to the problem of asymptomatic neuroses; third, the way in which it takes into account the inevitably fluid but seemingly important boundary between form and content in the understanding of human action, as in the understanding of art; and finally, the freer access to experiential aspects of human contact generally, and the clinical encounter specifically, that is provided by characterological terms as compared to the more austere and confining terms of metapsychology. Some of these reasons will be touched on in the course of the following discussion. Reference will also be made to some important theoretical problems—specifically, to the tension within psychoanalytic theory between, on the one hand, persistent and unquestioned naive empiricist or positivist attitudes and, on the other, the more sophisticated epistemological conceptions that are available today; also, to the questionable status of certain theoretical assumptions which dictate that a mechanistic theory of energy and structure is required to explain both the occurrence of human activity and the continuity, consistency, and coherence of this activity.

For the general organization of my discussion I have used the following five headings: The Metapsychological View of Character, Character as Action, Ego-Syntonicity, Technical Considerations, and Character Change. In the first section I shall state and criticize the metapsychological conceptualization of character and shall try to show how it refers to actions. In the second section, I shall restate the concept of character in action language. In the third, I shall take up the concept of ego-syntonicity as the pivotal concept in clinical and theoretical discussions of character; in the fourth, some major features of the method and content of the clinical analysis of character; and finally, I shall formulate in action terms the reasonable claims that can be made about character change through psychoanalytic treatment, and in this connection I shall discuss briefly both the usefulness and the ambiguity of the distinction between content and form or structure.

The Metapsychological View of Character

One may take as a representative instance of the metapsychological view of character the careful and extensive definition offered by Moore and Fine in *A Glossary of Psychoanalytic Terms and Concepts* (1968). It is a definition that incorporates the earlier contributions of Freud, Reich (1933–34), and Fenichel (1945), among others, and it is altogether compatible with later discussions, such as that by Blos (1968). To quote from Moore and Fine (p. 25) incompletely, though not, I think, unfairly:

CHARACTER: That aspect of personality . . . which reflects the individual's habitual modes of bringing into harmony his own inner needs and the demands of the external world. It is a constellation of relatively stable and constant ways of reconciling conflicts between the various parts of the psychic apparatus to achieve adjustment in relation to the environment. Character therefore has a permanent quality that affects the degree and manner of drive discharge, defenses, affects, specific object relationships, and adaptive functioning in general. . . . The integrating, synthesizing, and organizing functions of the ego are significantly involved in determining character. Through these functions stimuli and impulses are sifted and organized. Some are permitted to find expression directly while others are tolerated only in altered form. Permanent character traits are either perpetuations of original impulses in modified form, sublimations of them, or reaction formations against them. Thus, some character attitudes or traits are defenses, others not, but none are completely independent of instinctual conflicts. (Various forms of glossary-style emphasis deleted.)

This definition includes at least several category mistakes which seem to be consequences of the pressure toward deterministic formulation that inheres in metapsychological discussion. A category mistake confuses an abstract term and its referents. For instance, logically the concept of character must *include* "the degree and manner of drive discharge, defenses, affects, object relationships, and adaptive functioning in general"; yet, in the definition offered by Moore and Fine, character is said to *affect* these very features of the personality. Similarly, in logical terms the concept of character must *include* the type and degree of "integrating, synthesizing, and organizing" that distinguish the individual; yet, they say that character is *determined* by the ego functions of integration, etc. These objections are not mere quibbles; they point to confusions encountered commonly and perhaps inevitably even in the most serious attempts at metapsychological precision. But let us leave these objections aside and consider the definition from the standpoint of action.

"Modes of bringing into harmony" and "ways of reconciling conflicts": these are modes of action, that is to say, these phrases refer to the ways in which people get problematic things done, whether in thought or overt deed.

"The various parts of the mental apparatus": this is a mechanistic theoretical (metapsychological) way of sorting out constituent aspects of the complex actions that people perform or would perform under safe enough circumstances. These aspects include, among others, infantile wishful actions and archaic moral actions.

"The integrating, synthesizing, and organizing functions of the ego.": this is a set of biological-adaptational terms. It refers to the observation that people do attempt, with varying degrees of success, to integrate, synthesize, and organize what they do.

But these metapsychological terms no longer indicate that they pertain to symbol-using people who are engaged in human action. Instead, they convey that organismic functions play their role in the mental apparatus and that they do so under the guidance and control of higher-order functions which set priorities and rule the mind. I shall return to this point. Here I am just trying to bring out the human referents of the metapsychological terms, or, in other words, to emphasize what one sees when one observes people psychoanalytically. One does not see metapsychological entities; one sees actions being performed in various modes, some in the form of thinking, some in emotional form, some in motor performances, and most of them in complex forms.

It is neither *a*theoretical nor *anti*theoretical to insist on remaining close to the observational base of psychoanalysis, for there are many ways of designating what one observes, and one of the systematic and therefore theoretical ways of doing so is to formulate psychoanalytic data as actions. One may go further and group these actions through the introduction of higher-order concepts, such as infantile sensual and hostile actions (id impulses, so-called); defensive actions (ego mechanisms, so-called); or synthesizing actions (ego functions, so-called). Returning to one's observational base does not mean limiting oneself to atomistic descriptions. Action language can be used as abstractly as the language of psychic structure.

This systematizing project entails dropping the usual stock of nominatives and their associated adjectives from the descriptive-explanatory language of psychoanalysis and relying instead on verbs and their adverbial modifiers. That is to say, it entails giving up the idea that one understands more or explains more by saying that mental entities and functions, working autonomously and in some hierarchic arrangement, somehow produce a more or less continuous, consistent, and coherent psychological existence. It is eminently theoretical to proceed on the basis of an alternative assumption, namely, that it is sufficient to state, from the specifically psychoanalytic point of view and on an appropriate level of abstraction, what people do, how they do it, and their reasons for doing so. And at the same time it is eminently clinical to proceed in this manner; it is in fact the way that analysts do proceed in practice, however figurative the manifest language they use in making their interpretations.

It is essential at this stage of the argument to emphasize several more points. First of all, if one notices in Moore and Fine's description how broad a scope and how determining an influence is being attributed to the "integrating, synthesizing, and organizing functions of the ego," one must realize that these are functions of so high an order that they amount to a central agency in the personality; that is, they amount to a person regulating his or her existence in some kind of continuous, consistent, and coherent fashion. This central agency is the reified and anthropomorphized ego acting as a whole person, even if a conflicted one, or else it is a functional nucleus of that ego acting as a whole person. Here, in headquarters, is what I have called "the mover of the mental apparatus" (1976, chapter 5). This problem of reification and anthropomorphism was not adequately resolved in Hartmann's great monograph on adaptation (1939), and it has never been adequately dealt with by the best of metapsychologists. (See, in this regard, Grossman and Simon, 1969, and Schafer, 1976, chapter 4.) Additionally, this "mover" must be viewed as acting freely or autonomously, whatever its history. A central and superordinate regulatory agency does not fit into the deterministic scheme of metapsychology, for if it, too, were determined in the usual way, it would amount to no more than another one of the constituents of the psychic apparatus that required regulation by yet other higher order "integrating functions" of the free or autonomous kind. These functions would dictate when synthesizing functions, for example, would be activated. The chain of determinism snaps at this point.

It is worth mentioning that Heinz Kohut began to address these problems in his 1977 book. Coming at them from a different but related direction—that of the introspective-empathic method and the unique reality it establishes—he too found it necessary to reject a totally and strictly deterministic, mechanistic-functional approach. Kohut spoke of the coherent self as *being*, as well as *being experienced as*, a center of free initiative. This self is similar to what I have been referring to for some time as the person as agent.

The second point to be considered before returning to the concept of character is this: metapsychology rests on what may be termed a quasi-physical principle of inertia. It holds that no one would ever do anything unless made to do so by some underlying force; even psychological development depends on the force of frustrated drives. It only seems that something is being explained by the idea of necessary propulsive force, when actually one is witnessing an after-the-fact introduction of an assumption masquerading as a finding. It is, moreover, an assumption whose necessity has not been demonstrated. In the alternative terms of action language, it is sufficient to state that people perform actions for reasons, the reasons being immanent in the actions and definers of them. I am referring here to the *interpretive* principle of intelligibility of actions that is the cornerstone of Freud's method. This principle is indispensable in clinical work and daily life. It is presented here as a theoretical *alternative* to the mechanistic principle of inertia rather than, as Freud saw it, a prelude to formal theorizing.

The third theoretical point to consider is that metapsychology rests on what may be termed a quasi-physical principle of structure. It holds that some entity must exist in the mind that guarantees the continuity, coherence, and consistency of action. It leads one to take it for granted that in order to act rationally and adaptively one must have an ego that makes possible and ensures just this kind of activity. In action terms, however, whatever a person does may, *when viewed in a certain way*, be said to show more or less continuity, coherence, and consistency. I am referring here to an equally indispensable principle of seeking, specifically for purposes of psychoanalytic interpretation, the best description of the way a person organizes or patterns his or her actions. Psychoanalytic redescription is distinguished by its focus on certain aspects and implications of present actions, such as the sexual, the

139

aggressive, the defensive, the infantile, and the unconscious; it is also distinguished by its encompassing the antecedents of these actions in the multiple and circular life-historical accounts which psychoanalysis makes possible (Schafer, 1978).

Reference was made earlier to the metapsychological notion of a structured hierarchy of functions. This notion depends entirely on the fact that people can be shown, through interpretation, to be following certain complex rules in their actions and adhering to certain priorities they have set. Nothing indispensable is added to the explanation of the actions by introducing metapsychology's quasi-physical principle of structure. It is a unitary person who acts, conflictedly or otherwise, and not a something else *within* him or her that impels action and guarantees its organization. Seen in this light, character cannot be an entity that determines behavior; it can only be a form of explanation through systematic redescription of action in the broad sense in which I am using the term.[1]

Character as Action

Character refers to the actions that people typically perform in the problematic situations that they typically define for themselves. It thus refers to what they regularly do when they experience danger or when they must choose between or accommodate courses of action that they view as desirable though incompatible. Character also refers to just what it is that these same people regularly define as dangerous, the conflictual courses of action they regularly envisage, and the reasons why they have established these regularities. Additionally, character refers to the typical ways in which people organize what they do, for they do not ordinarily act piecemeal. Rather, they act within complex, more or less stable and coherent contexts of meaning which they develop and maintain continuously. They strive to act as consistently and as unconflictedly as possible. Individual psychoanalytic investigation is necessary to show how this is so, for the larger and most important part of all these actions is performed unconsciously.

It is, of course, true that many situations are encountered rather

1. See also the illuminating comments on character in the critical dictionaries by Rycroft (1968) and by Laplanche and Pontalis (1973), and the promising approach to character as communication to self and others by Bollas (1974).

than contrived or arranged. Nevertheless, analysts are always concerned with individual subjective definitions of these "objective" circumstances. Analysis centers on psychical reality.

Character is a dispositional or predictive concept. It tells what someone may ordinarily be expected to do. The designation of this or that type of character is arrived at only through a process of selection and abstraction that is carried out by an observer who has adopted a certain point of view; for example, the Freudian psychoanalytic point of view and, within that and more narrowly, the instinctual point of view ("oral character") or the diagnostic ("obsessional character"). The point of view will reflect the theoretical, technical, and literary choices of the observer. (By "literary choices" I refer to such masterful designations as Freud's: "those wrecked by success" and "the exceptions" [1916].) Contrary to the assumption of the naive empiricist or positivist, there are no simple characterological facts waiting to be gleaned, for each observer, too, is constructing a reality. I shall develop this point more fully in later chapters.

As a dispositional concept, character is not the name of an entity that organizes or stabilizes. It is the name given to the particular way in which a person may be said to organize and stabilize his or her actions. Consequently, character *development* is not the development of an entity, but a progressive change in the way someone both defines and acts in his or her problematic situations. It is the sort of development which renders previously adequate descriptive terms—for instance, infantile or unstable—no longer applicable; at least they can no longer be applied to the same extent or with no significant qualification.

As a dispositional concept, character is closely related to the concept agent or person in action language. In action terms one would say that the observer focuses on the actions of a unitary person. A person is defined by the appropriate description of his or her actions. The idea of a person embraces someone's typical way of constructing realistic and unrealistic situations and viewing oneself and others in these situations (for example, as an innocent person dealing with anal-sadistic persecutors); it also includes typical ways of behaving emotionally (for example, savagely beating enemies to the punch); and typical perspectives that are developed on the past, the present, and the future (for example, a hell behind and a heaven ahead). As was mentioned, much action is performed unconsciously, and the many actions each person is always performing are imperfectly coordinated—if not incompatible with one another.

141

This relation between character and agency may account for much of the abiding popularity of the concept of character. That is to say, much of the appeal of character may stem from its closeness to clinical work, and particularly from its suggesting the chief business of clinical interpretation, which is to define how and why each person systematically makes the life that he or she does. This clinical emphasis is precisely what I have been attempting to capture theoretically by giving a central place in action language to the person as agent.

It is necessary to underscore the idea of the person as *unitary* agent and to repeat that "unitary" does not imply perfectly coordinated actions or the absence of contradictory actions—what we are used to calling conflict. One speaks of the unitary agent in order to avoid positing the existence of a mental apparatus and then attributing to it a multiplicity of more or less independent constituent agencies. As soon as the idea of multiple agencies is invoked, one is inevitably commited to a mechanistic view of human psychology, and it does not then matter much whether those constituents are called different mental structures, such as the id, ego, and superego, or different selves or fragments of self. In the mechanistic conception, people are lived by their parts acting more or less autonomously, each according to its nature (for example, the cruel superego or the grandiose self); here it is very much as if each of these parts is some kind of single-minded person who at best will accept some compromises. It is this conception that is epitomized in Freudian metapsychology.

Many analysts find it difficult to accept the idea of the unitary person as agent. This view of agency seems to deny conflict, that most central of all psychoanalytic concepts. But this is a mistaken understanding of action language. What is being urged is a different way of conceiving of conflict; it is being proposed that this way makes more theoretical and clinical sense. The proposed change requires one to give up thinking on the model of an energically closed physical system with parts (drives, structures, etc.) that conflict with one another more or less autonomously and produce resultants. Instead, one now must think of a person pursuing incompatible and contradictory courses of action or wishing to do so, experiencing distress in this regard, and attempting to carry out renunciations or develop compromises or highly synthesized solutions of the dilemmas being both created and confronted.

Among the many reasons why analysts find the unitary agent a difficult concept is their own responsiveness to what I have termed disclaimed action (Schafer, 1976, chapter 7; 1978). Disclaimed action takes many forms, but what runs through all these forms is the exclusion of certain actions from the concept of oneself and others as active and responsible beings. Typical disclaimers in the verbal realm include such statements as "The impulse overwhelmed me," "His feeling slipped away," and "My thoughts are running away with me." Each such statement is a condensed narrative. Each narrative is a construction of experience rather than a factual introspective report of events in an inner world. Disclaimers are deeply rooted in our metaphoric language, and they are highly useful for certain adaptive as well as defensive purposes. Analysts and analysands alike have learned to think in these terms from the time of their earliest acquisition of language, and, for analysts, this way of thinking has been reinforced by the terms of metapsychology.

But metapsychology repeats rather than explains these narratives of a self that, far from always being the agent of its own experience, is often merely a helpless, passive observer of mental activity. It is *always* the agent of its experience, for it always gives one or another set of meanings to those circumstances that are encountered rather than actively brought about (for example, economic depression and loss of job viewed alternatively as "hard times," "persecution," or "proof of unworthiness"). And yet, contrary to the language of metapsychology, good interpretations do not ever basically incorporate these disclaimers. Who would be proud of having said to an analysand *in an interpretation*, "Your impulses overwhelmed you"? Although one might say such a thing quite usefully during preliminary empathic exploration of reports of subjective experience, especially if these are the disclaiming terms in which the analysand begins to give access to painful matters, one would not say it in a good interpretation. One way or another, a good interpretation conveys the idea that the impulse and the person are one, that the analysand cannot accept the insight that he or she wished to do the very action that is being disclaimed or has constructed a certain version of a traumatic experience, and that there are intelligible reasons why this is so. Ultimately, psychoanalytic interpretation is not *analysis* in the sense of decomposing material into its elements. Although it is true that such teasing apart of themes or issues does take place along the way, fundamentally analytic interpretation is *synthesizing* in that it demonstrates the analysand's participation in every significant event, including the very action of disclaiming. In psychoanalytic work, synthesis does not follow analysis into parts; synthesis and resynthesis are inherent in interpretation.

On the basis of these considerations, it may be claimed that action

143

language elucidates the messages conveyed by traditional analytic interpretation; it does not amount to a new, strange language of clinical intervention and certainly not to a hectoring attitude toward the analysand. The present attempt to elucidate the concept of character, long familiar and useful in clinical work, is being made in the same spirit. Rado (1954), among others, approached the idea of the unitary person as agent, but his other theoretical commitments blocked his way to an adequate development of it.

Ego-Syntonicity

For purposes of clinical interpretation, the key constituent of the concept of character is ego-syntonicity. This is so because the psychoanalytic modification of character depends on transforming activity that is, or at least seems to be, nonconflictual into conflictual activity.

Ego-syntonicity must not be conceived either superficially or in a biased manner. It will be conceived *superficially* whenever it is simply equated with what is consciously self-syntonic. This equation cannot hold, first, because too many important aspects of self are maintained unconsciously (for example, the grandiose self of many narcissistic characters) and, second, because what is consciously self-syntonic may, unconsciously, be exceedingly dystonic. And ego-syntonicity will be conceived in a *biased* manner whenever it is simply equated with what is syntonic in relation to one aspect of the ego system, such as the defensive ego or the adaptive ego or the relatively autonomous ego functions. When Moore and Fine (1968), in their definition of "character disorder" (p. 26), explain ego-syntonicity on the basis of rationalization, idealization, and adaptive realistic gains, they manifest both of the problems I just mentioned, for even though they recognize that they are referring to conflictual matters with major unconscious elements, they overemphasize conscious experience and certain interests of the ego as against others. In this way they misrepresent a part as the whole, and they seem to say that there is unity when that is not what they mean.

It is indeed difficult to know just how to conceptualize this key constituent of the concept of character, ego-syntonicity. I want now to propose a way out of this difficulty. I suggest that the concept of ego-syntonicity has always referred to those principles of constructing experience which seem to be beyond effective question by the person who develops and applies them. There seems to be virtually no way in which these principles can come into question, and this for two reasons: first, they are applied mostly unconsciously and pervasively, and so require extensive interpretation and working through before they can even become a significant part of the analytic dialogue; and second, these principles are so fundamental that the mere raising of a question about them will itself be understood in their very terms. They are the person's fundamental grounds of understanding and certainty. Metaphorically, they are the eye that sees everything according to its structure and cannot see itself seeing.

A simple, common example of these characterological certainties is the basic, unconsciously pervasive conviction that one is unlovable and undeserving of love. The person who holds this conviction consistently constructs all possibly relevant experience in its terms and thus is always confirming its correctness and adequacy. That person not only assiduously collects obvious signs of dislike, but interprets actions of others that are indifferent in this regard, or even loving, as being other than they are, seeing them, for example, as exploitative seduction or as overestimation of his or her true self. Similarly, paranoid persons construct experience in terms that confirm grandiose and persecutory expectations, and they view anyone who dares raise a question in this regard mistrustfully as a deliberately or unwittingly dangerous enemy; in this context, an interpretation of a fear of being poisoned will be experienced unconsciously as a poisonous act or substance. One might say that these principles are beyond question in so far as the person treats the relevant questions about them *not as questions but as evidence.* In this way, questions are not allowed to exist outside the system of fundamental beliefs. The person's unquestioning and pervasive application of these principles thereby establishes a personal closed system.

On this view of ego-syntonicity it would seem a hopeless task to attempt modification of character. And there are, of course, those who maintain that fundamental character change is never achieved, not even by the best of analyses. An obsessive character once is an obsessive character forever: ambivalence, anal-sadism, passive homosexuality, isolation of affect, and reaction formation continue always to be hallmarks of the obsessive character's activity. Change can only be quantitative, never qualitative. One may therefore only become *less* extremely obsessive, *less* self-destructively and painfully obsessive, and the like. I shall return to the question of how best to conceive of

145

character change in the final section. For now, I want only to link this conservative view of the matter to the *apparent* implication of my preceding remarks that ego-syntonicity implies a closed, perpetually self-confirming system of basic principles for constructing experience.

I speak of the *apparent* implication of my remarks, for I believe that in practice we encounter many characterological actions whose organizing principles are not perfectly uniform or integrated and whose heterogeneous composition is interpretively accessible, the result being that during the course of analysis these analysands do get to be seen, and to see themselves, as constructing different types of experience simultaneously (for example, in oedipal *and* preoedipal terms). Further, we come to recognize that at least some of these types of experience are of a more neutral kind or developmentally more advanced; of these developments we say that they show good reality testing. It is this heterogeneous composition that provides the fulcrum with the help of which it is possible to move the subjective world. The system is not closed, except perhaps under conditions of great stress, which, when they abate, no longer preclude the development of more realistic perspectives. The analysands of whom this is true can hear an interpretation as such, at least some of the time, however else they hear it (for example, as criticism). Those who cannot are unanalyzable—at least during that attempt at analysis. Any theory of effective interpretation or transformational effect must allow for an interpretation's being heard in more than one way.

In undertaking the analysis of a character problem, one counts on there being some diversity of experiential principles, even if the nature of this diversity is not clear at the time and will not become clear until some point of access to them is discovered by the analyst. The point of access may be some well-guarded form of thinking hopefully, some shrugged-off way of esteeming oneself realistically, or some shyly hidden but stable kind of loving. Here, by the way, is where variations among analysts in skill, patience, compassion, sensitivity, and imagination make a difference, as do variations in the goodness of fit between particular analysands and analysts.

It is important to be clear on one point especially: not just any diversity of experiential principles will do. This is so because in analytic work one always encounters some diversity of primitive principles, such as archaic oral, anal, and phallic ways of constructing experience, and also archaic defensive and superego ways. And, if this were all that there was to encounter, as might be the case in certain borderline conditions, one would have an unanalyzable person shifting around among equally irrational constructions—for instance, between feedings and enemas or between gross indulgences and cruel punishments. What is required of the analysand, therefore—and analysts have always known this—is some degree of development of neutral, rational experiential principles. The analysand need not be acting manifestly and consciously according to these more realistic principles; some analysands desperately guard against this possibility owing to their fearing that terribly destructive consequences will ensue if they manifest accurate and neutral reality testing. It is especially the analysands with borderline features who are likely to repress, project, negate, or represent in dreams their truest perceptions of their analysts and their own families; in these cases it is correct to say that character analysis must be constantly focused on the way these analysands consistently and violently attack their own sense of reality and at the same time express it in obscure forms.

Another common type of diversity is encountered in analysands who seem so thoroughly narcissistic in their construction of experience that they never show concern for others except as the doings of these others bear directly on narcissistic issues. However, as Ruth Easser (1974) has already argued, this is not necessarily a true picture of the state of affairs. Rather, it is often the case that these analysands go to defensive extremes in order to obscure the extent to which they do or might concern themselves with others empathically. Much of their activity in analysis only becomes fully understandable when one takes into account that actual or prospective involvement with others is a danger situation in which they live constantly. Additionally, their blatantly unconcerned, egocentric activity must be viewed in part as a form of vigorous assault on the analyst's empathic participation in their subjective experience; this is an assault that is intended to forestall the dreaded recognition of mutual concern. Their relatedness to other people, far from being exclusively one of the fruits of the analysis, is a large part of the problem to be disclosed and analyzed.[2] The analysis of the narcissistic character disorder requires a slow, patient approach to this diversity within an apparently monolithic closed system.

My conclusion with respect to ego-syntonicity is that any effective character analysis depends on some unintegrated features of the pathological character-actions. These actions must be performed con-

2. Kernberg (1975) recognizes this, in a way, in his emphasis on defensive splitting, while Kohut (1971, 1977) seems either to bypass the issue or to deny it.

flictually. Metapsychologically, one would say that some rational ego or ego functions must be collaborating with the analyst if any analysis of character is to be effected and any character change accomplished. In action terms, however, one would say that the person must be applying incompatible principles simultaneously—using more than one eye, so to speak—and must be able, by way of some of these principles, to recognize an interpretation as just that.

Technical Considerations

I shall discuss interpretive and technical issues in character analysis from three points of view. First, I shall take up the role of identification in character, then the interpretive and empathic usefulness of an affirmative orientation to character; by emphasizing character's value to the analysand in his or her psychical reality, this orientation avoids the kind of adversarial orientation on the analyst's part which centers on the ways in which character functions as resistance. And additionally, intermingled with the first two points, I discuss the interpretive and technical importance of focusing on flux and contradiction in the analysand's mode of activity in the analytic situation. Although these three points of view do not encompass the entire subject of character analysis, they should serve to illustrate concretely the methods and the types of phenomena which are the principal features of character analysis.

IDENTIFICATION AND CHARACTER ANALYSIS

I shall speak nominatively here of "identifications" in preference to what would be more consistent with the rules of action language, namely, unconsciously maintained identificatory actions in the realms of overt behaving and private fantasizing. The exposition will proceed more smoothly this way, and anyway I have already emphasized sufficiently the description of character in terms of action language.

The analysis of identifications characteristically used by the analysand for coping with problems and in the solutions that he or she characteristically aims at do not for the most part appear to be created de novo. Rather, they have been prepared and presented by the analysand's parents during his or her early development; not in what the parents preached, of course, but in what they practiced; and not, of course, in what they practiced as seen through the eyes of mature and compassionate observers but in what they practiced as construed by the analysand when he or she was a sexually and aggressively ambitious, but frightened and confused young child. Thus, as Freud (1923, 1933) noted, the degree, type, and integration of superego activity, which play large parts in defining character, are modeled on the unconscious superego identifications of the parents as distorted by the child's projections and introjections.

Many of these distortions and identifications are predictable on the basis of the psychosexual stages of development, the sequence of infantile danger situations associated with these stages, and the typical conflictual and fantasy activities of childhood. But there is always room for novelty, for some aspects of identification do reflect features peculiar to the child's own parents, and in any case the child faces the problem of synthesis that arises out of his or her bisexual identifications. These childhood identifications affect alike id, ego, and superego activity, for basically all identifications must be understood in terms of the principle of multiple function (Waelder, 1930; see also my *Aspects of Internalization*, 1968a).

Thus, the child takes on the archaically construed characters of both parents and then is faced with the life-long problem of reconciling these components. Other figures may also be involved, of course, such as siblings or other relatives. This problem of reconciliation is all the more difficult when the parents are deeply at odds with one another or severely conflict-ridden in their own right, or, as is so often the case, both.

What this issue of reconciliation entails is that one of the central developmental problems is how to define one's own gender identity. As part of the attempted resolution of the Oedipus complex, this gender definition typically involves struggle *against* identification with the parent of the opposite sex. More exactly, the struggle is against consciously enacting or even recognizing the existence or extent of that cross-sex identification. The common result of this struggle is a pronounced rigidity in manifest character organization along the lines of the same-sex parent. But even then, analysts frequently observe struggles *against* that same-sex identification as well. In this case, the analysand will be attempting to escape his or her life history entirely or, in other words, to claim to have invented himself or herself entirely; this is an effort and a claim which require considerable self-deception and personal disharmony. By rigidly adhering to the acceptance

149

of some identifications and the repudiation of others, one hopes to avoid all of one's fears of castration or homosexuality, engulfment or triumph over one or another parent seen as a symbiotic or oedipally rivalrous figure. The extent to which fears of homosexuality enter into one's acting this rigidly will depend on the predominance of infantile, archaically sexualized imagos of the opposite-sex parent, and that predominance in turn will depend on such factors as early fixations, object loss, and other traumata.

Whatever the case or pattern may be in the individual instance, in times of stress or adversity, such as those brought on by being in analysis, the analysand will fall back all the more on these infantile identifications and cling to them tenaciously. The analysand will view them unconsciously as the only way to become or remain masculine or feminine or in some respects both or neither. It is not that masculinity and femininity are the only considerations to be kept in mind when considering the place of identification in character, but I follow Freud in thinking that gender identification is almost always essential and serves as the ground for other character traits such as moral masochism, exhibitionism, and chronically low self-esteem.

For the analyst, one great interpretive problem is to establish just which identifications have been made and how they have been patterned. Identifications do not always meet the eye. Especially the problematic identifications, such as those with the parent of the opposite sex, are often expressed in obscure, misleading, or reversed ways. For example, meekness may obscure a grandiose identification and modesty an exhibitionistic one, while masochistic submissiveness may obscure identification with a fiercely controlling parent. In one case, a quality of rough edges indicated a major father-identification on the part of a woman who, in effect, paraded an identification with a seductive mother and who did so in large part to obscure the father-identification. In this instance, it was to begin with useful to emphasize the awkward efforts to smooth over these rough edges and then to go on to raise a question as to the reason for the implied discomfort.

Another great interpretive problem will then be to recognize and interpret the real and imagined benefits the analysand believes are being derived, or can be derived, from the usually desperate and desperately hidden identifications. In the case of paternally based rough edges previously mentioned, activity of considerable strength was one such benefit, so that unconsciously this identification was greatly valued by the analysand as well as feared and abhorred. The analytic inquiry defined, first, her fearing to let this trait show, then its link to her image of her father, and later her priding herself on the strength she derived from it. Sometimes, however, the sequence may be different, as when the pride is plain and apparently unconflicted until its isolation from the father imago is reduced by interpretation. I shall return to the question of benefits later in this chapter.

A third interpretive problem is that of not being misled by the overemphasis analysands commonly put on *interpersonal* transactions within the family and on the continuation of these transactions in fantasy or in the so-called real world. It is important to emphasize this point today when there is such extraordinary enthusiasm for object-relations theories and emphasis on "real" preoedipal events. The analysand's emphasis on interpersonal transactions can only go so far as an explanation in that, as a rule, this emphasis is being used to obscure the extent to which the analysand is identified with the ostensible antagonist in the overt family drama. Being thus doubly identified (as sadist and masochist), the analysand is unconsciously conflicted as to the way to be and is not simply a reactive product of experience with one "external" person. This is well known from analysis of the projective aspects of the transferences, whereby the analyst is used by the analysand to embody one of his or her current conflictual courses of action (for example, being assigned the role of critic or devil's advocate).

In this connection the analyst's neutrality toward all the parties concerned in the family drama will serve the analysis very well. At least implicitly the analyst must convey an interest in understanding why the other figures are or were the way they are now being presented, because to some extent they have entered in that form into the character of the analysand through identification. The analyst's departures from neutrality inevitably are experienced as condemnation of some aspect of the analysand's "self."

But this concern with identification raises a fourth problem of interpretation, the last to be mentioned here. The problem is that of making sure of the validity of the picture of parental character on which one bases interpretation of identifications. It is well known that, as an analysis progresses, the pictures of parents tend to change radically, especially in the direction of complexity and conflictedness. Also, attributes that seem initially to have derived from one parent may prove to have had their solid foundation in identification with a long-denied characteristic of the other parent. For example, one man's disturbing feminine identification with a bisexual father proved to be secondary to an earlier identification with his constantly thwarting mother.

Interpretively, the analytic work benefits from the flux of identifications and the contradictions among them that become evident as the analysis progresses. So long as there is no flux and all appearance of contradiction is carefully avoided, there is no basis for interpretation. The characteristic modes of action that are in question are being presented by the analysand as fully syntonic with the ideal self or at least the self that one is ready to settle for. In this context, just about any comment on that trait by the analyst is likely to be felt as an assault, and to some extent rightly so. It is when the analysand erratically betrays the maintenance of other and unintegrated identifications by acting in self-contradiction, as she or he is likely to do as the transference develops, that the analyst will be in the position to formulate interpretations of characteristics which hitherto have seemed analytically untouchable. The flux and contradiction may be evident, for example, in sudden bursts of silliness on the part of a rigidly sober person or in a seductive posture adopted by a determinedly asexual person, either of which manifestation is likely to be quickly and anxiously repudiated by the analysand as incomprehensible, absurd, or the fault of the analyst's expectations or interventions.

To conclude this part of my discussion, the analyst may be able to get beyond the attitude commonly expressed by analysands, "That's the way I am and always have been or want to be," and open up such questions as, "That's the way who else was?" "What other ways are you, and why do you have to repudiate them and why do you have to repudiate them in the way that you do?" "What's in it for you to continue to be the way your model was?" When it comes to the analysis of the role of identification in character, flux and contradiction are signs of progress and levers for further progress. It should be added that each identification may be made with only certain aspects of one or the other parent and, in any case, will be further analyzable as a compromise formation as well as a party to compromise itself.

THE NONADVERSARIAL APPROACH TO CHARACTER ANALYSIS

I have already indicated the main features of this approach, and in chapter 10 I shall develop these features further in the context of discussing the analysis of resisting. These features are crucial aspects of the analytic attitude.

The affirmative approach focuses on the analysand's view in psychical reality of the uses and benefits of the traits in question. The analyst waits until flux and contradiction have become apparent; further, the analyst does not neglect to point out and interpret the defensive and hostile reactivity that are regular features of those occasions when the analyst emphasizes those inconsistencies which the analysand would prefer to ignore or rationalize. Nevertheless, for maximal analytic effectiveness the leading question the analyst should pose is what it does for the analysand to affirm or to deny the traits in question. What is their value in psychical reality? Leo Stone, in his paper on resistance (1973), has already commented on the integrative value of these characteristic means of coping and the sense it therefore makes to expect the analysand to be resistant to analytic attention to them. It is implied in this orientation that the analyst has no business deciding unilaterally that one or another character trait or larger-scale character organization is undesirable in and of itself and is therefore to be "attacked" (as some analysts put it). This is so even when it is apparent to the analyst that the characteristic in question is detrimental to some of the analysand's stated goals in life and also that it is serving a resistance function, that is, blocking certain otherwise expectable and presumably necessary developments in the analysis.

A common instance of what I am referring to is the analysand's resisting the emergence of transferential material. This resisting the analysand can carry out only in terms of his or her character. Character is being manifested in resisting. To the extent that the analyst is working neutrally and empathically, he or she will recognize that the resistant course of action must seem fully justified to the analysand, justified, as I mentioned earlier, in terms of the basic, unconsciously held convictions about self, others, and the world. The conviction may be, for example, the familiar one that all intimacy is ultimately dangerous, although the type of danger and its reasons and its origins will vary to some extent from one analysand to the next. On this basis, the analyst will be primarily interested, often for considerable periods of time, in the importance to the analysand of both that threatened construction of experience and of avoiding giving reports of transferential phenomena. Indeed, a great part of the analysis may consist of this phase of the investigation, as may be seen in some of the better examples in Wilhelm Reich's book *Character Analysis* (1933-34). And even in this respect it will be useful for the analyst not to become impatiently and relentlessly insistent on the matter of the analysand's resisting the transference.

The chief technical point I wanted to make in this connection is the undesirability of the analyst's forcing the issue of characterological change. Not really that the analyst can enforce such change; inevitably, misguided therapeutic zeal increases the extent of the analysand's fright, alienation, and characterological rigidity, whatever might otherwise be suggested by overt appearances. So far as possible, the analyst should remain a neutral and empathic participant and not (in the many subtle ways available in this kind of work) an enforcer or a bully.

It is not being implied that the analyst's posture should be one of passive and intellectualized acceptance of whatever is. If there are significant disadvantages to the characteristics in question, or if they are intimately linked to the severe problems already acknowledged by the analysand, they will be defined most clearly, considered most seriously, and analyzed most fully in the safe context of mutual understanding of why the analysand has also deemed these characteristics indispensable. And here the matters of flux, contradiction, and signs of unintegrated identifications take their most useful places in the analytic process. Typically, these instabilities and fragmentations increase as the affirmative understanding of character deepens. Identifications wax and wane, and with them the prominence of certain defensive, transferential, and sublimatory patterns of action. This one may count on in most cases.

And in time the instabilities will become distressing enough to the analysand to give rise to professions of shame, guilt, anxiety, and persecutory and depressive beliefs and experiences. In the most general way, they will give rise to professions of dissatisfaction with the life the analysand is leading in terms of his or her overt character. To recall the old analytic adage, the character trait will begin to feel like an ego-alien neurotic symptom, an affliction, and it is when this occurs that the analyst is technically correct to "treat" the character itself. It becomes the analyst's business to treat it, for it is now a mutually recognized part of the analysand's "patienthood." Treating it does not, of course, imply advice and exhortation. It implies working through, so far as possible, all the currently active and developmentally based conflictual solutions that militate against other, more adaptive solutions. Also, it means working through many of the thousand and one ways in which these hitherto characteristic solutions have been covertly embedded in all aspects of the analysand's life. For example, all the hiding places of continued seeking of masochistic gratification, all the conflictual enactments of symbolic parricide and incest that the analysand performs in work and in relations with peers, spouse, children, and parents. And it means working through the revision of so-called internal object relations so that the analysand may, for example, come to terms with feared, hated, and intensely sexualized parental imagos.

In this sense, it is never too late to revise a relationship: to begin or begin again to love and to mourn, to be grateful, to hate and to repudiate, or simply to accept that which in the so-called real world is no longer revisable. And no matter whether it is done purely subjectively or in overt, current interactions with others as well, it is always possible for the analysand to make a genuine effort to bring out the best in others or at least to stop bringing out the worst in them in order to confirm as necessary his or her type and rigidity of characteristic modes of actions (the "character").

The context of safety in which one may achieve these goals is based on the idea (to restate what I said before in other terms) that what initially seems to be character *disorder* is unconsciously and understandably an inescapable attempt as a certain sort of character *order*. I have tried to indicate that this order is not superficial but rather describable only in keeping with the principle of multiple function.

My remarks so far may seem to have been based on the hope of avoiding the hostile aspects of transference by coming across to the analysand as a good soul. This is far from my intention. In my experience, the emphasis I am advocating, if implemented neutrally and skillfully, facilitates the appearance of negative transference *in a form that is analyzable*. There is no way the analyst can avoid being hated, though there are many ways to provoke unanalyzable hostile reactions or else to duck the issue and instead help the analysand to continue to repress it. Even to begin with, the analyst will be hated for daring to try to understand and formulate anything at all about the analysand, for any such activity threatens the status quo and is experienced as an attack. This fantasized attack is usually analyzable in a way that begins to clarify conflictual issues involved in transference and in resisting. Among other things, conflicting patterns of identification may emerge. For example, being in analysis may be, for the analysand, too "feminine" or too "masculine" or too "passive"; and these ideas will prove to be linked on the one hand with infantile sexualized models of the parents and on the other hand with current attempted syntheses of identification fragments in which one fragment is being played off against the other (for example, when interpersonal passivity may be tolerated only under conditions of absolute control).

Another way to put this is to say that any neutral analytic activity, including appropriate listening, is bound to be represented in the

155

analysand's psychical reality as a confrontation and provocation. For it introduces a new way of seeing things and experiencing them emotionally which, try as the analysand might, does not adequately conform to his or her desperate attempts to repeat the past over and over again.

Direct confrontation of the analysand is often mentioned in connection with analyzing ego-syntonic character traits. There is always a place in analytic work for confrontation, but much depends on the spirit in which it is done. It is one thing to point out neutrally that a characteristic pattern of action seems to be blocking analytic progress or even seems designed to block that progress; it is quite another thing to become adversarially challenging. In the former instance, *analytic* questions will arise as to why progress is envisaged as a danger, and since when and why the analysand has used a particular strategy to block that progress. In the latter or adversarial instance, the analyst is *nonanalytically* expressing personal frustration and dissatisfaction. Then the analyst is taking a narcissistic stand and departing from neutrality, acting as though it is to be taken for granted that the analysand is obliged to change in a certain way even though, as I said, it is not the analyst's business to decide these matters unilaterally.

There is, of course, no approach that is guaranteed to work in all instances. Some problems remain beyond the reach of analysis, and a time may come when the analyst has to name and face these limits together with the analysand. This may require considerable tact and preparation. But working within the analytic attitude, the analyst is obliged to do his or her best to help create the most favorable conditions for change; the analyst is not obliged to succeed in bringing about change. Accepting the obligation to succeed in bringing about change is a sign of countertransference, a departure from the analytic attitude, and so will be a source of much difficulty in attempting to do analysis.

Character Change in Analysis

It is more a matter of definition than anything else whether or not one may speak of character *change* through analysis. A definition that stresses broad stylistic aspects makes it difficult, if not impossible, to speak of fundamental character change. In contrast, a definition that stresses the constituent actions that are subsumed by the term character gives one more latitude in this regard, for these constituents surely do often change to an appreciable degree. And an appreciable quantitative change may also be described as a qualitative change even when there is no precise or generally accepted convention specifying at what point quantity becomes quality.

Certain quantitative changes in action are seen commonly enough. For example, analysands no longer imagine their infantile danger situations as readily, for as long a time, and in such extreme terms as they did earlier; they show that this is so by their dream reports, the errors they commit, their speaking frankly about an ever greater range of troublesome issues in the transference relationship, their moderating their defensive measures, and their manifesting and reporting fewer actions performed in severely anxious, guilty, or ashamed modes. Nor are effective functioning, secure relationships, and pleasurable and joyful actions so consistently excluded from their activity and from their experience of their activity and the activity of others. On these grounds they may be said to become appreciably less hysterical, obsessive, masochistic, or narcissistic, enough so to warrant speaking of their having achieved change of character. What was regularly disturbed or pathological before is no longer so; the expectations of the analytic observer concerning action are now different, even if the analysand's initial style of action remains recognizable. That style will, of course, be particularly recognizable in stressful situations.

But there is a better way of addressing the question of character change. It depends on the earlier discussion of ego-syntonicity, and especially on the emphasis put there on the diversity of principles by which experience is organized. For it is possible on the basis of this diversity to modify the more archaic, less neutral principles in such a way that they no longer seem to lie beyond effective question. The analysand gets to experience them conflictedly after all. And the analysand no longer consciously fears and disclaims other well-defined ways of constructing experience to such an extent that he or she never undertakes such constructions long enough to make a real difference. It is this kind of change that is meant when one speaks of genuine insight and of the development through analysis of a continuing capacity for self-analysis. Thus, late in effective analyses and in postanalytic sessions, one sees analysands still beginning to create or accept crises of the old sort and then catching themselves in the act, questioning what they are up to—that is, asking themselves how they are threatened and why—and then going on to consider alternative views

157

of their situations and the courses of action open to them. All of this, taken together, would have been unthinkable during early stages of their analyses. What seemed then to be closed systems and were, in fact, pretty closed, are now evidently and often much more agreeably open systems.

Character change lies, then, in the analysands' now living in vastly more complex worlds with vastly more complex repertoires of action, including the actions of representation of self and others in relation. They give different accounts of their lives and prospects. They believe in nonincestuous sexuality, in vaginas that are either cloacal nor containers of teeth or hidden penises, in love that is not devouring, etc. And at the same time they know or, when necessary, they rediscover that they still employ the old contradictory principles and that they still refer to them, for example, when dreaming and when beginning to feel seriously endangered. Shouldn't these changes be granted the name of character change? To deny them this name would be to mistake a part (the remains of the past) for the whole (the new, enlarged context) and thus to commit a reductionistic error. It would also be to set up a simplistic and perfectionistic ideal, adherence to which can only becloud the most interesting and significant analytic issues.

This conception of character change in action terms might seem to be mistaking change of content for change of structure in that it puts so much emphasis on subjective experience. One cannot take up the topic of character change for long without introducing the long-familiar analytic distinction between change of content and change of structure. Change of content is exemplified by a swing from predominantly submissive modes of action to predominantly tyrannical modes of action; this is a change of content *only* in that the prevailing orientation of action and its representation remains authoritarian or sado-masochistic. Another frequently observed change of this sort is from manic to depressive or depressive to manic modes of action. Here, the prevailing orientation remains oral-devouring, reparative, and focused on guilt, whether by proclamation or vehement denial. Analysts have learned not to be impressed by such changes of content; for more convincing signs of enduring and adaptive change, they have looked to change of structure.

Change of structure may be defined in traditional metapsychological terms as change in the pattern of ego functions. This change includes lasting modification of preferred defensive measures, the direction being from more to less archaic and ego-limiting defense; more command on the ego's part over modes of activity previously dominated by id and superego trends; decreased inter- and intrasystemic conflict; improved efficiency of such ego functions as reality testing and synthesis; the attainment of stable and gratifying relations with others; also, increased reserves of neutralized energy and improved capacity for neutralizing the energies of the id and superego, as manifest in reduced regression-rate and decreased power of infantile instinctual and ascetic fixations. Reference might also be made now to maturer forms of narcissism and the completion of separation-individuation and the attainment of object constancy. If one recalls the typical traditional definitions of character, one readily recognizes that these features of *structural* change also imply *character* change in a progressive developmental direction.

I tried to show earlier that the metapsychological account of character is translatable into action terms, and I shall not extend that demonstration now in connection with the closely allied concept of structural change. But I do want to show that there are complexities concealed and ignored in the distinction between structure and content as it has usually been made. The complexities are these. Thematic analysis of content is a form of structural analysis, and the tripartite structural classifications have always depended on prior appraisal of content. One does not, after all, see the ego or superego, nor does one see systems in conflict or mechanisms of defense coping with impulses. Rather, the analyst defines different types of content in the ideational and emotional aspects of action, including action in fantasy. As analysands change, analysts find them developing certain themes less often, less extremely, and with less distress, and they are able to define new themes in their analysands' actions. These are themes that imply a more stable, differentiated, and unified sense of self and others, a more consistent and coherent defensive strategy, and so on. These themes are, of course, defined with respect to both verbal and nonverbal evidence. The metapsychological structures that have always been referred to in discussions of change of structure are formalized and abstract theoretical accounts of the changes of action and the experience of action, and these changes imply that different principles of constructing experience ("content") are being employed by the person under study.

Whether one calls it structure or content thus depends not on what one observes or can observe, but on the kinds of questions one is asking, the kinds of things one wants to say, and, ultimately, the kind of

159

psychological reality one wants to define and work in. All change of content is redescribable as change of structure and vice versa. On this account, it is closer to clinical interpretation and the clinical situation generally to attempt to describe or name those changes of content that may safely be taken to indicate change of a stable and beneficial sort. And for theoretical purposes, it is best to remain as close as possible to the clinical. For example, when a fantasy of exalted power replaces a fantasy of utter helplessness, one is observing a change of content with little gain in adaptiveness and long-range stability; so our analytically constructed experience tells us, and so any sophisticated way of making sense of human beings tells us. In contrast, when an analysand steadily maintains and implements ideals of realistic appraisal of what he or she can and will do reliably, when earlier that analysand communicated only fantasies of helplessness or of grandiose power or swings between the two, one is observing a change of content with considerable and observable adaptive consequences. In the same way one might observe a change in both the construction and content of the predominant danger situations and of preferred modes of gratification, and one may then justifiably speak of structural or character change.

The preceding account of change of content and structure is relevant to the broad principles of action language in the following way. Action language takes account of the fact that each action lends itself to multiple descriptions. It may be described on various levels of abstraction (for example, as a simple act or as an expression of a broad pattern), and it may be described from different points of view (for example, as transferential, resistant, adaptive). Although the formalistic description of actions in terms of id, ego, and superego has some uses for purposes of generalization, it is only one kind of account of actions, and it has some of the difficult consequences of being tied to a mechanistic view of people as mental apparatuses. Consequently, it is useful to develop other, more clinically anchored, accounts of people as agents.

The account I favor is that character change is change of action such that descriptions of the analysand which earlier were reliable, comprehensive, and analytically very much to the point, no longer apply or at least are no longer adequate. Thus, one must still describe a tyrant-analysand in very much the same authoritarian or sadomasochistic terms as one uses to describe the analysand in the role of slave or mouse; however, one cannot justifiably continue to describe that analysand in the same set of terms when he or she has begun reliably to include loving others relatively consciously, unanxiously, and pleasurably, in an overall scheme of living. Character change, then, is a required change in the psychoanalytic description of the analysand's typical, expectable ways of unconsciously constructing conflictual situations, of acting in these situations, and of developing experiential reports of these situations and their correlative actions.

10
The Analysis of Resisting

Introduction

There is a way to approach the analysis of resisting that is particularly valuable to the analysis as a whole. The analyst takes up the problematic actions in question simply as further analytic material of a conflictual nature. For even though it may be necessary to show that many of these actions have been unconsciously designed to be obscure, opaque, or stereotyped, and so to appear at first and second glance to be only limiting and disrupting the work of analysis, in time it will be possible and more useful to interpret them by applying the same principles used to deal with any other conflictual material. Indeed, it is often just this interpretive approach that is being used, knowingly or not, when resisting does get to be analyzed successfully. If this is so, then many of the textbook discussions of resisting are conceptually and technically incomplete, if not confusing, for they bog down in an approach to resisting simply as oppositional activity and thereby isolate that activity from other analytic material.

I have done some of the spadework for this thesis in two earlier papers. In "The Mechanisms of Defense" (1968b), I argued that the clinical analysis of defense mechanisms requires that they be approached from the standpoint of their fantasy content, as when projecting is interpreted as unconsciously expelling (usually) noxious figures and substances from the self. And in Part V of "The Idea of Resistance" (1973), I argued for an affirmative theoretical and clinical approach to resisting. This affirmative approach focuses largely on what resisting is *for* rather than simply what it is *against*. Although my characterizing it as affirmative grew out of my theoretical work on action language (1976, 1978), this was not really a new idea, and it entailed no departure from standard technique. Stone (1973), for example, emphasized at around the same time the role of resistance in the analysand's cohesive or self-integrative striving; he too spoke of an affirmative aspect of resistance. Nor is it a new idea to analyze defensive activity in terms of its fantasy content. In support of this point (1968b) I cited statements of principles and practices previously offered by Freud, Anna Freud, Wilhelm Reich, Fenichel, Melanie Klein, Waelder, and others.

I have already introduced the general thesis to be developed here in earlier chapters of this book. There I tried to show how empathizing, the understanding of defensive measures, and the technique of character analysis may benefit from the analyst's maintaining an affirmative attitude. And in chapter 14, below, I shall continue this discussion when I take up the narrative aspects of the analytic dialogue.

I should also mention at this early point that, at least since the appearance of Reich's *Character Analysis* (1933–34) and Fenichel's *Problems of Psychoanalytic Technique* (1941), it has been appropriate to regard resistance as personal activity. That is to say, resistance is to be seen as actions carried out by the analysand consciously, preconsciously, and unconsciously. "The resistance" refers to an analysand's resisting.

In this chapter I shall first briefly discuss how the concept of resisting is mostly inconsistent with the way in which the analytic process has been conceptualized. Next, I shall show how the concept of resisting tends to precommit the analyst to an undesirable combative or adversarial view of the analytic relationship. In this connection I shall return to the analytic attitude, especially to the neutrality it requires; additionally, I shall try to show that the affirmative approach does not, as it should not, require the analyst to deny the analysand's combative view of the relationship. Then I shall present a series of technical suggestions and clinical examples. Although suggestions and examples like these may be found in our textbooks of technique (see, for example, Reich [1933–34], Fenichel [1941], Glover [1955], and Greenson [1967]), and although material of this sort may already be quite familiar to readers with analytic training and experience, I shall include it here for a particular purpose: namely, to show how the analyst may not even mention resisting or any of its correlated terms while still carrying out effectively what is traditionally called the analysis of resistance. Finally, I shall take up some reasons for the relative neglect of the analysis of resisting that one often observes in case presentations of analytic work.

The Problematic Concept of Resisting

Resisting is conceptually problematic in that it is defined from the standpoint of consciously stated aims. It designates opposition to the plan, consciously agreed upon, to collaborate fully and freely with the analyst in order to get to the bottom of things and thereby effect substantial amelioration of suffering and functional impairment. Even though the analyst recognizes that the most important acts of resisting are carried out unconsciously, by resorting to the concept of resisting the analyst has limited the focus to manifest behavior. The analysand is to be regarded as not behaving in the way he or she has consciously agreed to behave.

In this important respect, resisting differs from other major analytic concepts, such as transference, repetition, acting out, and regression. These concepts are defined essentially from the standpoint of unconsciously maintained aims and objects and unconsciously significant consequences. If what we call resisting and view as oppositional activity were to be approached in the same way as the phenomena designated by these other concepts, it would be worked with as a matter of course in terms of ultimately infantile and conflictual "dynamics" or meanings or wish-fulfilling actions. The analyst would remember Freud's having pointed out that there is no No in the Unconscious (1915b), and he or she would then also interpret what the analysand *is* doing as well as what he or she is *not* doing. As I said, on my understanding this is how analysts do often develop interpretations of resisting even though they may do so without clearly conceptualizing for themselves the connection between what they do and the core of the theory of the analytic process.

On the face of it, the analysand is, of course, frequently behaving in ways that are readily describable as oppositional, recalcitrant, or obstructive. These actions include withholding associations, disrupting the continuity of the analysis, using free association evasively, or insisting against all evidence and common sense on the completely "realistic" justification of transferences. But the analyst cannot be satisfied with superficial appearances or manifest content and so cannot take violations of consciously stated aims and attitudes for granted. Here is where the affirmative approach becomes relevant.

As I have tried to make clear, the affirmative approach is not implemented by seeing everything through rose-colored glasses or regarding whatever happens as a good thing. The analytic attitude proscribes any such denials and value judgments. The affirmative approach refers to the analyst's taking manifestly oppositional forms of conduct as indications of unconsciously significant and conflictual projects that require interpretation. What appears as opposition is to be taken as an interpretable striving after something else. The behavior that gives the appearance of opposition is like manifest dream content: it is a starting point for analysis.

The Adversarial Conception of the Analysis of Resisting

Let us turn next to the combative or adversarial conception of the analysis of resisting. We find this conception of the analytic interaction in, to name only a few such places, Reich's (1933–34) numerous militaristic metaphors (armor, breakthrough); Menninger's (1958) use of such phrases as "never-ending duel," the analyst's "attacks on resistance," and the analysand's "intrinsic negativism"; and the simple definition of resistance offered by Moore and Fine in their *Glossary* (1968) as "opposition" to the analyst and the analysis. Glover (1955) was able to avoid this issue by correctly referring resisting partly to the negative transference and partly to intrapsychic defensive activity.

Greenson (1967), in his clinical examples, favored terms like "running away," "avoiding," and "hiding." Although these terms are ostensibly empathic in recognizing the analysand's flight from danger, often they are experienced by analysands as humiliating and coercive. They are experienced as demands or commands to stop acting in a cowardly, castrated, or infantile fashion. Their adversarial thrust is not eliminated, for, as we know, what the analyst intends and what the analysand experiences need not, and often do not, coincide. Of course, it goes against analytic understanding even to try to eliminate these discrepancies from analytic work; however, it is consistent with analytic understanding to avoid needlessly provocative interventions that can only validate the transferences and defensive strategies that are indicated by these discrepancies between the analyst's intent and the analysand's reaction.

Basically, Greenson was following Fenichel's commonsensical suggestion (which, incidentally, derives from Reich) that first of all the analysand must be made aware *that* he or she is resisting; or, in the

THE ANALYTIC ATTITUDE

case of ego-syntonic character resistances, the resisting must first be made ego-alien, that is, experienced by the analysand as something like undesirable symptomatic actions. On this basis Greenson repeatedly emphasized the intervention called confrontation, itself a term with some adversarial force. And Reich and Fenichel on their part were only following one of the lines laid down by Freud when he introduced the adversarial term *resistance*, and when he said such things as "whatever interrupts the progress of analytic work is a resistance" (1900, p. 517).

It must be remembered that Freud often used combative metaphors when discussing the work of analysis. For example, in his discussion of transference, he said that the enemy cannot be slain in effigy (1912b, p. 108), and he analogized the tactics of analyzing transference resistances to engaging in great battle over small ground (1912b, p. 104). It is true that Freud came to appreciate that resisting is to be expected and welcomed on the analytic scene; it was he who discovered that there is much to be learned from its analysis. Today, we might want to say that much of "the analysis of the ego" is accomplished around the study of resisting. Nevertheless, the work of analyzing resisting has continued to be viewed as the analysis of activity that is solely oppositional in nature: its wheres, whys, hows, and since whens. In this way, resisting has been isolated from the rest of the analytic material.

Let us consider next the recommendation that the first step in analyzing oppositional activity is to demonstrate to the analysand *that* he or she is resisting. Contrary to expectation, this move often fails to open up the topic, serving rather to drive that activity from view and, as a consequence, sometimes giving rise to the erroneous impression that resisting has abated or has been dispelled. When this vanishing act takes place, it may turn out later that the analysand has interpreted the analyst's intervention as a command to cut it out or has used it as a cue to wise up and become a subtler opponent. Often, the analyst's intervention is taken as criticism, whereupon the analysand, feeling hurt, misunderstood, unfairly treated, or confused, behaves in a submissive, enraged, defensive, or fragmented manner.[1]

Many of the responses I am citing are made by the analysand uncon-

1. Kohut (1977) has made much of these analytic events—too much, I think, owing to his having first placed the analyst's real and imagined empathic failures in the center of his principles of technique for selected cases, and then gone on to use this technical contribution to formulate a general, though narrow, theory of the analytic process and individual development.

sciously. The alert and skillful analyst may, of course, try to analyze these responses by means of versatile and sensitive follow-through or second effort. But even though this follow-through is sometimes productive, often it only compounds the immediate difficulties by threatening to turn the analysis into a noisy or silent contest of wills; that is, the second effort is experienced by the analysand as just another demand or criticism, just another twist of the arm or the knife. An impasse may result. Here, the analyst is up against one version of what Freud called "resistance against the uncovering of resistances" (1937a, p. 239); this second-order resisting is not adequately taken into account in the advice to begin the analysis of resisting by demonstrating to the analysand *that* he or she is resisting.

We are left then with some noteworthy questions of technique, some answers to which ought to be arrived at through reviewing our conception of the analytic attitude as it applies to the analysis of resisting.

THE ANALYTIC ATTITUDE

As was brought out in chapter 1, one of the key terms used to characterize the analytic attitude is neutrality. It may be defined in a number of complementary ways, of which I shall review and add only a few. In one way, the term neutrality specifies that the analyst should not take sides in the analysand's conflictual or paradoxical courses of action. Anna Freud (1936) put it in *inter*systemic terms when she said the analyst should occupy a position "equidistant" from the id, ego, and superego. Following Hartmann's (1950) discussion of ego psychology, we would want to add to this an *intra*systemic supplement and speak also of equidistance from conflictual activities "within the ego," such as struggles between ambition and altruism or between truthfulness and the need for security. Neither the view of resisting as opposition to the analysis and the analyst, nor the view of the analysis of resisting as an attack, can be easily accommodated within this conception of neutrality, for both amount to taking sides, that is, to preferring one kind of analytic material to another.

Another useful way to define neutrality comes closer to the analysis of resisting: the analyst does not unilaterally try to make anything happen. That is to say, the analyst does not decide to bring about certain personality changes just because as a matter of general principle he or she thinks it will be good for the analysand to change in those ways. In contrast, when the analysand is evidently and conflictedly

167

avoiding or deferring change which, on the basis of explicit discussion, already makes analytic sense, that *is* a matter for the analyst to try to understand and then, if the time is ripe, to convey that understanding in a tactful, even if somewhat confronting interpretation. On the whole, however, the analyst must always be careful not to impose his or her value judgments on the analysand by unilaterally prescribing change. Not only must the analyst appreciate the extraordinary difficulties that stand in the way of significant change, he or she must allow for the possibility that change in one or more major respects is not routinely to be expected in any single case. In those respects, it helps to recall Freud's emphasis on the analysand's dread of "getting well" and on the danger of the analyst's overestimating the analysand's capacity for sublimation; also, that he came to emphasize the unyielding influence of early deformations of the ego (1937a).

Moving next to a conception of neutrality that is even closer to the topic of resisting, one may say that the position of neutrality or equidistance implies total repudiation of any adversarial conception of the analytic relationship. This position is, however, easier prescribed than maintained, not only because inevitably the analysand will repetitively construe the relationship as a fight and ingeniously try to seduce the analyst into sharing this construction; the difficulty exists also because, as I indicated earlier, the analyst has been authorized to share this combative construction by the prevailing conceptualization of the actions in question as *resisting* or as *opposing* rather than as conflictual or paradoxical actions aimed toward other goals that remain to be interpreted.

At this point my major thesis becomes relevant. The most consistent way of maintaining the analytic attitude is to approach what traditionally has been called resisting in an affirmative manner, that is, to approach it not as resisting or opposing but as puzzling or unintelligible behavior that requires understanding. The analyst should not even think of this reorientation to resisting as a ploy or a means to the end of getting the resisting out of the way so that the analysis can proceed. Thinking of it in this way is incorrect, for not only does it rule out of court an important part of "the analysis of the ego," it also comes perilously close to the analyst's unilaterally trying to make something happen. And what right has the analyst to try to do that? In the absence of adequate understanding, it is inappropriate to do so. The means adopted may easily be poorly chosen, and the goal set for the analysand by the analyst may easily be biased, misguided, or beyond the analysand's reach at that time or ever. In this respect, adherence to the ideal of neutrality safeguards the analyst against making reckless, assaultive, and value-laden interventions. To make this point in a more general form: by what right does the analyst insist that the analysand do anything other than what he or she is doing? Not understanding the actions in question—what they are *for*—does not confer that right.

More usefully, the analyst might venture to point out and raise questions about apparent and ununderstandable contradictions, for example, between the analysand's frequent silences and his or her agreement to follow the fundamental rule, or between presenting oneself for analysis and then disputing or ignoring everything the analyst says. The analyst might proceed similarly with respect to gross omissions or gross discontinuities in mood or content. But even these very provisional moves only sometimes succeed in opening up an avenue toward understanding; just as often they are taken as criticism or impatient demand, with ensuing unproductive strain on the analytic relationship. As I pointed out earlier, interpretive follow-through at these points may intensify rather than reduce the strain. Often the analyst is better advised just to proceed patiently and unpresumptuously and not harass the analysand in his or her difficulties and inconsistencies. I touch here in passing on other attributes of the analytic attitude.

To carry this line of thought further, I would make two assertions about resisting that complement one another. The first is that one should avoid drawing hasty conclusions that the evidently resistant aspects of certain analytic behaviors, such as withholding associations or arriving late, render them useless for purposes of analytic understanding and necessarily and altogether undesirable. Instances of what appears to be blatant resisting of this sort might, for example, prove to be the first signs of hitherto rigidly repressed negative transference, which should be welcomed by the analyst; or they might prove to be a way of making visible a pattern of masochistic "seduction of the aggressor" (Loewenstein, 1957); or they might be a way of inaugurating a significant and, for the analysand, bold advance in self-authorization and self-definition. In one case, beginning to come late for appointments was, among other things, an early sign of having attained some confidence in the analyst and, along with that, an increasingly conscious sense of hitherto remarkably absent self-determination.

The second and complementary assertion about resisting is this: often it is not at all clear or even suggested by the analytic material that resisting is in question. Indications of resisting will be absent, not because something is being effectively concealed (as in the instance of the secret inner smile of scorn and disbelief that Reich described), but because what was collaborative activity at one time later proves also to have been serving a resistant function. This was the case, for example, when one analysand's faithful and useful attention to implied transferences proved later on also to have been a reactive form of anal cleanliness, a "coming clean" that helped the analysand repress anal-sadistic material. Generally speaking, *to each form of analytic collaboration there correspond significant possibilities of resisting.* This statement is only a variation on Freud's theoretical point that to every advance to a higher stage of psychical organization, there corresponds a new censorship (1915b, p. 192); it also restates Freud's emphatic point that resisting accompanies the analysis every step of the way (1912b, p. 103).

Other familiar examples of this dialectic include the analysand's unconsciously producing valid oedipal material in a way that plays down preoedipal issues and vice versa; or engaging in productive analytic explorations of heterosexual difficulties in a way that plays down homosexual issues and vice versa; or emphasizing significant narcissistic themes of a damaged self in a way that excludes the theme of a damaged penis and vice versa. I am quite serious about all these vice versas, for it is well known that, unconsciously, anything can serve to reduce or eliminate the analytic visibility of something else.

In all these respects the analytic attitude requires that the analyst not decide rapidly or one-sidedly what is resisting, what is analytic progress, and what is collaboration or working alliance. At least, one should not reductionistically mistake a resistant aspect or a collaborative aspect of the analysand's actions as representing the entire set of meanings, functions, potentials, or consequences that must be taken into account.

It is perhaps obvious by now that the adversarial view of resisting is not only too negative but too narrow. It is, I think, not too much to say that inevitably the concept of resisting is imbued with some countertransferential coloring, some element of overzealous psychotherapeutic attitude, some impatient and intolerant version of analytic omniscience and omnipotence. In this regard I am questioning the inadvertent authorization of this countertransferential coloring by the literature which has grown up around the concept of resisting. I shall have more to say about this problem at the end of this chapter.

At this point, however, the objection might be raised that I am encouraging or rationalizing countertransference of an opposite sort. This countertransference—perhaps one should say *counterresisting*—

170

would feature reaction formation against the analyst's sadistic aims and denial of the analysand's sadistic aims. It might even be objected that I am advocating the supportive psychotherapeutic attitude with which Heinz Kohut is frequently charged (unfairly, I think, though the case examples provided particularly by his followers [Goldberg, 1978] do leave one wondering). To these objections I would answer that, far from playing down the theme of sadism, which theme requires a prominent place in any well-conducted analysis, I am laying the groundwork for analyzing it in a clear and effective fashion. For the analytic questions now become these. What is this apparent opposition for? What is it in the service of? What new material is it introducing into the analysis? Which opportunities for further analysis does it open up? And sadism, along with masochism, is one of these opportunities.

To be more exact about the consequences of my discussion, it is not that this is what the questions now *become*, it is what they *remain*. I say so because close examination of detailed examples offered by major writers on resisting shows that either implicitly or explicitly these are the questions that guide the analytic work that is being reported. One common and simple example of what I mean is the interpretation of the withholding of associations as an unconscious form of anal retentiveness in the transference. And in Reich's examples, so many major psychodynamic variables get to be taken up in the course of analyzing resisting that resisting emerges in the end as no different in its "multiple function" or "overdetermination" from a dream, a symptom, or the whole of the transference. In effect, resisting is not taken as opposing the analysis or the analyst but rather as *the analysand's next significant step in the analytic process.*

Technical Suggestions and Clinical Examples

Next I want to advance some technical suggestions, similar to the suggestions I made in the preceding chapter on character, as to how the analyst might take an affirmative approach to the analysis of resisting. Let us begin with a few ways of starting to define the existence of a problem of intelligibility. The analyst might maintain a focus on its not being understandable why the analysand finds it necessary, say, to fall silent or to evidently suppress a show of feeling. Sometimes the

171

analyst might draw on his or her cognitive and emotional reactions in formulating comments that imply analytic questions; then, for example, the analyst might say that the analysand's affectless tone of voice leaves it unclear how important the matter at hand is to him or her or how seriously one should take it. Sometimes the analyst might just state an impression or hunch of implied shame, dread, avoidance, provocativeness, helplessness, or something of that sort.

These three types of intervention are similar in one important respect: careful not to address the analysand in a controlling and alienating way as an object being scrutinized from on high, the analyst is speaking provisionally and in the first person (for example, "I think," "It puzzles me," "I get the impression," "The way it seems to me," etc.). If for the moment we disregard those analysts who follow this course rigidly, in the manner of reaction formation, we could say that the analyst's speaking provisionally and in the first person does not corner, impale, or scoop out the analysand. More exactly, it does not lend itself so easily to the analysand's attributing that hostile significance to it. For this reason, speaking provisionally is less likely than other kinds of interventions to intensify or seem to "objectively justify" analytic combat. It makes the inevitable discrepancy between intent and reaction potentially more analyzable in terms of transference.

An oblique form of this relatively noncombative form of address is to ask the analysand from time to time what he or she makes of the current difficulty. Or the analyst might refer the analysand back to a point in time prior to the apparent attitudinal change and wonder aloud what stimulated the change at that time. In any single analysis it is, of course, unnecessary to be utterly aseptic in this connection, especially once the analyst has gained some familiarity with characteristic forms and occasions of resisting. But new or newly emphasized resistant actions do keep appearing, and, as Reich advised, it may be technically advisable to go back over old ground and, I would add, revert to provisional, first-person interventions. It is always risky to take the analysand's collaborative attitude for granted in any respect. Resisting *does* accompany the analysis every step of the way.

The analyst might carry this type of intervention further by adding some mention of signs of conflict, distress, danger, or dread that stand out in the manifestly disrupted analytic behavior. Here one calls attention to an unexplained stammer; some half-hidden embarrassment surrounding a slip; a euphemistic, apologetic, or defensive tone; a gross omission; an abrupt and blatant switch to a passive stance; or an implied or stated refusal to go further with a certain topic, as when the analysand says, "I don't know where I'm going with this," and then falls silent, or else says, "I don't want to think about that any more." Although the analyst might choose to say nothing at these moments, or to say only that something seems to be troubling the analysand, the guiding analytic question then becomes, "What can be the meaning or the source of this disruptedness and discomfort?" Being more explicitly empathic than the first type of provisional and relatively indefinite intervention in that it refers to distress or conflict in an open-ended and neutral manner, this type of intervention is less likely to be automatically, heatedly, and entirely opposed by the analysand; and it does often bring forth transference fantasies or clues that the analysand is distressed because in fact or fantasy the analyst has, in some other connection, missed an important point or has acted unempathically or because the analysand is approaching a difficult topic.

At just these moments, however, the so-called resistance against the uncovering of resistances may appear in one of its most beguiling forms. Once the analyst has called attention to some signs of conflict, distress, disruption, and avoidance, the analysand may rush into disclosing what was being withheld. It seems then that the analysand would rather ignore the anxiously resistant behavior and instead hurriedly disclose the troublesome content, say, a personal thought about the analyst or a detail of a sexual experience or a request for something. Thereby it becomes evident that it is less threatening to confess the troublesome content than it is to examine the initial distress and reserve. Here, second effort on the analyst's part is, as a result, analytically useful. Instead of succumbing to the analysand's seduction by disclosure, the analyst should bring the analysand back to the prior question about the difficult moment and underline the importance of understanding it fully. As usual, tact and timing are important in these interventions. If the second effort is not made, the confessing analysand is all too likely to feel "really" violated or self-sacrificing, or else to believe erroneously that a "real" breakthrough has been accomplished. The seduction by disclosure must also be made part of the analysis, for it may enact a fantasy of being raped or of being administered a gratifying enema or something of that sort. It is unlikely that the content that was too eagerly confessed will be lost to the analysis if this course is followed. It is more likely that it will reappear, perhaps very soon, in a coherent context that lends itself to confident interpretation. In contrast, the seductive disclosure can only be made under the constraints of unanalyzed resisting and so in a psychologically incoherent context.

Alternatively, the analysand might resist the analysis of resisting by denying the occurrence of any noteworthy or analysis-worthy disruption. In this instance the analyst might be well advised to wait for similar and perhaps clearer occasions and even then not intervene too soon, letting the analysand get to know the resistance better, as Freud advised (1914a, p. 155).

There is yet another response available to the analysand at these moments. The analysand might acknowledge that a difficulty does exist and then set about trying to analyze it, but, still being resistant in attitude, produce only unenlightening associations or say that nothing or nothing important comes to mind. Then the analyst might just point out that the difficulty seems to be continuing or that the analysand seems to feel threatened by what might come to mind next or what might be felt next; or, when it is appropriate, the analyst might take an interest in what *would* qualify as "important." In another type of follow-through the analyst might note that the analysand has suffered a change of feeling, a cramping of freedom, maybe even a loss of mental clarity at just that moment and then go on to express interest in that functional change. Still, the analyst may seem to be facing a stone wall and may have to curtail further inquiry at that point. If the analysand makes too much of the analyst's alleged coerciveness at these times, and especially if he or she does so emphatically and repetitively, the analyst might try to explore the possibility that the analysand is intent on feeling coerced, or intent on getting the analyst to feel guilty over the alleged coerciveness, or at least trying to stifle the analyst's participation in the analysis.

I turn next to some clinical illustrations, beginning with two instances of seduction by disclosure. One analysand could "work well" only "under the gun," that is, while believing that the analyst would throw her out if she didn't cooperate. Upon analysis, this "working well" involved a transference repetition. She was repeating a show of submission to a controlling and rejecting pseudophallic father. On this account the work was not adequately experienced by her as "really" analyzing anything at all; that is to say, her defiant pseudosexual and partially masochistic strategy prevented the content under discussion from reaching analytic significance. What was significant and usefully interpretable was the way she was unconsciously using the analytic sessions to engage in repetition.

In another case, the analysand could "work well" only if the analyst's interventions were brief, tentative, and few and far between;

otherwise the analysand functioned as though a message scrambler in his head prevented him from understanding even the simplest sentences or the most familiar words uttered by the analyst. Over considerable time it was possible to analyze this resisting as involving all of the following: a virtually lifelong need for omnipotent control; a defensive pseudostupidity that served to castrate him, enabled him to avoid emotional distress, and obscured his reliance on grandiose fantasies; a curb on what he experienced as his profound greediness; and an anal shut-down that prevented, though it also was meant to entice, homosexual rape by the analyst. It is important to add, however, that if left to himself this analysand would not only bring up significant analytic material but use it in his own way to understand and modify some of his severe neurotic difficulties. His apparent resisting was not simply opposing analytic progress; it was also establishing conditions under which he could work analytically, even though with significant built-in limits set on how far he could go.

In both of these cases, as in the cases to follow, the analyst placed little or no explicit emphasis on resisting or some equivalent term of opposition. The tone of the analytic work was simply that of trying to understand lifelong problems as they appeared in the analysand's functioning in the here and now of the analytic relationship.

The next case is that of a young woman being seen for less than full fee who takes six months before she reports a significant increase in income. She says that although she has had thoughts of bringing up the question of her fee, somehow she never has. She is ashamed of her lack of integrity. Taking into account work done in the earlier years of this analysis, the following set of interpretations and constructions is then organized and developed over a number of sessions.

1. She feared that the analyst would raise the fee to a level that would "devour" the entire increase in income; consequently, by not mentioning the increase, she was able to conceal from herself as well as the analyst her continuing mistrust of him throughout a period of ostensible positive transference and enthusiastic working alliance.

2. Her use of the word "devour" was based on her greedily wishing to keep all the money for herself and to avoid a situation in which she would openly protest having to pay anything at all. In this respect she was showing how, from early in life, she had painfully built her personal integration and family adjustment around the defensive identity of the undemanding, uncomplaining, self-sufficient, and faultless child. This orally depriving identity was tied in with an extreme ideal-

izing of her mother that had helped her survive her emotionally disappointing childhood. By all accounts, her mother was for the most part an emotionally shut-in, unhappy person. Making virtues out of necessities, the analysand had, as a very young girl, taken being shut-in, discontent, and ungiving as signs of strength—as constituents of an ideal self. Thus, for her, it would be not only weak and shameful to have a generous attitude toward paying for her analysis, it would also be disloyal to her idealized mother and undermine her own strengths and aspirations. And it would expose her to further oral deprivation.

3. Additionally, she feared that talking about money at all would intensify the analyst's hatred of her, for in her fantasy she was a burden to him. She was a major burden not just because of the reduced fee but more generally because she could not dare to imagine the analyst's deriving any satisfaction from working with her. She had, she felt, imposed herself on the analyst, and all she could now do was preserve the tenuous relationship by avoiding the subject of money. In this connection the analyst offered the construction that she was repeating the infantile experience of having to make reparation for ever having been born, while feeling that in fact there was no way to make adequate reparation for this depleting and damaging imposition. Unconsciously, she had made her choice: it was safer to think that the problem was a bad child and not a bad mother.[2]

Throughout this period of analysis it was not resisting that was the focus of the dialogue. It was desperation, idealization, need, greed, depletion, integration of self, protection of relationships, and repetition. Nevertheless, I present this analytic fragment as being in one of its most important aspects the implicit analysis of a complex pattern of resisting. That it takes in transference as well should be obvious.

The next example concerns a female college student. After the analyst inquired into some hesitant associating early in one session, she reported that earlier in the day she had decided not to tell the analyst about a pleasant time she'd had with her "boyfriend." Recently she had confined her remarks about the boyfriend to vehement and an-

2. As we see all too often, this is the conclusion typically arrived at by children who experience themselves as orally and emotionally deprived. When, later in life, these children are in analysis, they structure the transference around the conclusion that they are unworthy. Their holding resistantly to this conclusion is, unfortunately, self-validating inasmuch as deprivation and self-imposed deprivation combine to intensify normal need and greed and also promote compromises of personal integrity. At one and the same time these analysands emerge in the analysis as both victims and in the conventional sense "guilty as charged."

guished complaining. She says that she imagined that the analyst would merely grunt approval if she reported the pleasant time and that then she would get mad because the analyst would not be reacting jealously. And she dared not get openly mad at the analyst. She had, she adds, imagined another possibility. The analyst would "analyze the shit out of it" and thereby deprive her of her happy experience. Without mentioning her resisting as such, the analyst directs his comment at one of the resistant implications of this material. He says that secretly she would take his analytic interest in the pleasant time she'd had as an expression of jealousy, she would then get mad at him in order to disguise her gratification, and she would then suppress her anger in order to protect him and take the resulting misery on herself, as she characteristically did in other relationships.

In an earlier period of this young woman's analysis, following a stretch during which, in a relatively affectless way, she had been wandering unproductively in her associations, it became possible to develop the following set of interpretations (which here have been condensed for the sake of conciseness). She was anxiously avoiding what was for her "messy" and "unbecoming" anxiety; she was sadistically tormenting the analyst; she was engaging in a "tight-assed" holding onto whatever feeling she did possess; and she was maintaining a closed-mouth stance in relation to the possibility of her taking in anything good from the analyst. Some of these actions expressed her having identified with a sadistic, "tight-assed" father and some of them an early defensive resolve to need nothing from either of her parents. In part she implemented this resistant strategy by taking whatever the analyst said as a critical attack (she literally cringed whenever he began to speak); and at the same time she was concealing two attitudes, one being the anal-sadistic one according to which analysis was just so much "garbage" and the other being a narcissistic one according to which analysis was merely "trendy self-indulgence." Both attitudes manifested her having continued to identify with corresponding features of her parental figures. Often what seems to be only analysis of identifications is simultaneously, though implicitly, analysis of resisting. Hartmann's (1951) "principle of multiple appeal" of interpretations should be mentioned in this connection.

Another example concerns a young man of aristocratic American background who had been brought up to think of himself as princely. He was, in fact, handsome, intelligent, athletic, and brave—Prince Valiant himself. The trouble was that this upbringing was excessively in the service of what seemed to be his mother's coldly narcissistic character. She could not tolerate anything unruly, uncouth, or autonomous in his conduct; just his being a boy was bad. This at least was what he conveyed in his maternal transference. However much he consciously hated this princely role, he had also eagerly adopted it, among other reasons in order to promote the mutually narcissistic love affair with his mother. Accordingly, he felt obliged to repress rageful and depressive reactions to the extreme demands and deprivations that were entailed by this love affair. As might be expected, his athletic prowess and his courage proved to be both counterphobic and unconsciously suicidal. But princely he was, and on this account, though he consciously disavowed the attitude, he regarded the analysis as an affront and a degradation imposed by a vulgar commoner and an obscene and mercenary Jew.

In the course of analysis of some aspects of this attitude, he dreamed that he was in a stall in a public toilet and was disgusted by the stench coming from the next stall. His associations helped establish the following interpretation. He had to believe that his shit didn't stink. Here, shit served as a point of confluence for all his repressed activity of a loving, lustful, vengeful, rebellious, depressive, and self-destructive nature. The interpretation, however, was directed chiefly at his resistant posture. In this respect he unconsciously equated being expected to free associate with his being forced to shit in public and so he had to make sure that his associations didn't stink—as indeed they did not by ordinary social standards, for they were as dry and hard and controlled as could be. That he also wanted to "let go," come what may, was given split-off representation in the dream (the two stalls), as was an ambivalent attitude toward the analyst composed of contemptuous father-transference and homosexual love (disgust in a homosexual "scene"). The interpretation, however, said only that his shit mustn't stink, and it was soon extended to show that he equated shitting and associating. Following this interpretation, he brought up useful genetic material that included family records of very early and severe toilet training and recall of his having been "treated like shit" by his mother whenever he broke her rules; literally and figuratively she turned her back on him in the most contemptuous and expulsively abandoning way. Now, in identification with this figure, he was giving the analyst the same treatment—or the same shit.

In the case of another young man it developed that he always entered his analytic hours in a particularly downcast and listless way following his having scored some kind of victory in his work or his social relationships. And he would never spontaneously mention the victory. Unconsciously, this conduct amounted to more than defensive self-castration designed to forestall the analyst's "really"castrating him in response to his oedipal presumption in the transference. For this resistant self-presentation proved to have significant preoedipal as well as oedipal implications. One such implication was his anticipating that the analyst, acting as a depriving mother-figure, would pull the rug out from under his enthusiasm and pride if he dared to show them. It turned out that he had experienced his mother as always acting in this dampening and infuriating way. Another preoedipal implication, that of grandiosity, was tied in with his oedipal problems. In his triumphant fantasies he was a god, a king, a tyrant, and he feared the destructive effect of these fantasies not only on his liberal social values but on his relation to reality itself. Resisting was given the dispirited form in order to deny his feeling of sexual potency, his wishing to be crassly selfish, and his megalomanic imaginings. Insofar as he also intended to dampen the analyst's enthusiasm, he was reversing passivity to activity by acting in identification with his mother. It was clear that he was doing more than beating the oedipal father to the punch or anticipating an oedipal put-down by his mother. That is to say, from a technical standpoint it was clear that some further preoedipal explorations, experiences, and explanations would be necessary before he could feel it safe to begin to change his ways.

My final example concerns a young man with severe narcissistic, masochistic, and paranoid problems. For a long time he represented his best reality testing only in his dreaming. That is to say, only in his dreaming did he verbally and pictorially represent certain plain truths about himself, his parents, his friends, and his analyst. These were truths he did not dare consciously recognize and explicitly affirm while awake. We learned that by day he would often represent these truths by what were for him their opposites; he would, for example, emphasize only the kindness of others and his own selfishness. That it was a matter of resisting the daytime representation of reality testing became evident through careful analysis of his responding by reversal to instances of the analyst's countertransferential and counterresistant obtuseness, insensitivity, impatience, and ingratiation. This careful analysis of reversal required a good deal of honest, even if reluctant, self-observation on the part of the analyst. The interpretation that had to be developed was this: the analysand was dismissing his reality testing as only a dream and substituting waking dreams for reality testing. It developed subsequently that for him clear-sightedness and frankness amounted to loss of control over anal-sadistic and castrating attacks on others; also, a destructive differentiation of his self from a symbiotic and crippling mother; additionally, a sign of castratedness in its being based on "feminine" intuition; and finally, a sign of great superiority over others who, he felt, would not be able to stand up under his powerful "truth-telling."

In this case, as in all the others, it was technically essential that the analyst be ready to switch the focus from content to process in order to analyze the resisting. This switch amounts to noting and pointing out certain signs that inevitably appear during the exploration of any major form of resisting; these are signs that that very form of resisting is being repeated in the way the exploration is being carried out. Thus, this young man would suddenly begin functioning obtusely, slow-wittedly, and self-punitively when the disavowed reality testing was being taken up: for example, when the analyst would recognize in the analytic material and then acknowledge a countertransference lapse of his own. In the case of the young man mentioned earlier who had to disavow his enthusiastic and proud reactions to success, it became apparent that he was doing the very same thing in order not to respond enthusiastically to the liberating effects of the continuing analysis of this problem. And in the case of the message scrambler, he scrambled more than ever when his pseudostupidity was being interpreted. Fenichel (1941) long ago commented on how valuable it is for the analyst to make this switch from content to process in order to demonstrate the analysand's repetition of what is being analyzed in the very moment of analyzing it.

The Neglect of the Analysis of Resisting

Wilhelm Reich (1933–34) spoke of the neglect of the clinical analysis of resisting in his book, *Character Analysis,* and it is my impression that what he said then is still too often true: analysts often pay only lip service to the analysis of resisting (see also Gray, 1973).

Much of the resistance to the uncovering of resistances stems from the analyst. Why should this be so? According to my observations of my own work and the work of colleagues and candidates in supervision, the major reason is that the analyst fears that his or her inadequately neutralized erotic and hostile reactions to the analysand will get out of hand. With regard to hostile reactions, the analyst fears that he or she will bring up the topic of resisting tactlessly, irritably, or coercively; or the analyst fears that he or she will respond in a counteraggressive way to the fairly expectable combative reaction of the analysand. Thinking of resisting in adversarial terms and lacking confidence in his or her readiness to maintain a neutral, exploratory, affirmative analytic attitude, the analyst will not make the kind of second effort or follow-through I described earlier and will too quickly conclude that taking up resisting is "not getting anywhere"—as though "not getting anywhere" is itself not analytic material to begin to take up, or as though there is no readiness on his or her part to switch from content to process. And with regard to the erotic reactions, it often seems to be the case that the analyst secretly prefers an atmosphere of strained distance and veiled antagonism to the stimulating atmosphere of positive sexual transference, both heterosexual and homosexual.

I am referring to the analyst insofar as he or she too often and too insistently wants to come across as a reliably benevolent, "noninstinctual," and reparative figure; that is, I am speaking of the analyst engaged in reaction formation as a substitute for affirmative neutrality. The analyst's needing narcissistically to feel in good rapport is also related to factors that have frequently been emphasized in the literature on countertransference. These include experiences of loneliness and deprivation, and depressiveness and grandiosity, in the course of doing analytic work. For all these reasons and more, it may become too important to the analyst to keep the peace by resisting the analysis of resisting. Consequently, the analytic scene may be tranquil but very hazy. It is a case of collusion. It takes two to blur the view.

If one takes seriously Freud's summary statement that analysis should "secure the best psychological conditions for the functions of the ego" (1937a, p. 250), one is obliged to attend vigilantly to the analysis of resisting; otherwise, the unanalyzed and implicitly derogated resisting will remain unmodified and continue to limit and cancel out the most adroit analytic work on other aspects of transference and on genetic constructions. After the termination of analysis, analysands must be as free as possible to face and deal with the conflictual aspects of their actions, to develop and independently affirm important insights, and to make their important life choices. This outcome is what

181

the thorough analysis of resisting is aimed at ensuring. Yet in saying this I would not want to downplay my thesis that much of the most influential analysis of resisting is not, and should not be, carried out under that heading. It is often sufficient that the analyst think through the resistant aspects of whatever unconsciously conflictual material is being dealt with at the time and then frame his or her affirmative interventions in the light of this understanding.[3]

3. Obviously, I have not attempted to give a broad review of the analytic literature on resisting; nor have I presented a comprehensive survey of the principal forms of resisting or taken up in detail the relation of resisting to the infantile danger situations that Freud outlined in "Inhibitions, Symptoms and Anxiety" (1926; but see in this connection chapter 7 herein). There is much more I have not done. The existing texts on analytic technique provide excellent summaries and many helpful suggestions in all these respects. I also want to mention once more the articles by Paul Gray (1973) and Leo Stone (1973): not only do they deal in a particularly searching and helpful way with many of the issues taken up here, they also illustrate the analytic attitude at its best.

11
Psychoanalytic Interpretation

Introduction

I begin with two concretely oriented analytic questions concerning time and place, the answers to which also touch on substance, person, and activity as they appear in analytic interpretation. Following this relatively informal introduction, I shall move on to a systematic review of some of the main features of the construction of analytic interpretations.

The two questions are these: When is a phallus? And where is a phallus? These questions should not seem at all odd to anyone who is used to working within the second reality or so-called psychical reality that is constituted by and within the psychoanalytic dialogue. In the same vein, one could just as well ask when and where is a baby, a breast, a bowel movement, or a self. For expository purposes, however, phallus will do to make my point.

For the psychoanalyst, a phallus is *whenever* the analysand confronts, imagines, or construes a self, an activity, or a substance in what may credibly be taken as his or her phallic terms; and it is *wherever* he or she seems to locate that self, activity, or substance. For example, for one woman in analysis a phallus was whenever she thought intelligently; correlatively, its location was in her thoughts, her brain, or her impressive self-presentations through writing and speaking. On this understanding, which she had maintained unconsciously, she could enact irremediable castratedness or punitive self-castration by behaving stupidly, being surprisingly at a loss for words, damaged in syntax, unable to get the point of a simple idea, diffuse in her writing, or simply by beating her head in apparent frustration. Meanwhile, she concealed and protected her unconsciously fantasized intact phallic status. Unconsciously, she followed this strategy repetitively, for she found it intolerable to give the least appearance through functioning intelligently of being what was, for her, mannish or aspiring to be like a man, anatomically especially. In the account of her past and present life that was being developed during the analysis, there were many reasons why, for her, it was that kind of appearance, and why this appearance was so intolerable to her; but it is not to the point to go into them here. Before going any further, however, I do want to say that the kind of sexualization of intelligence I have just described is not gender-specific. Many men, as well as many women, undergoing a Freudian analysis prove to have been chronically and unconsciously confronting, imagining, and construing the use of their intelligence in very much the same frightened, guilty, secretly self-protective but nevertheless self-damaging phallic way. Work inhibition is thus presented as a genital affliction by members of both sexes, and often it can be explained *in part* on the basis I have just described.

In other aspects of this woman's life, a phallus was, as might now be expected, whenever she took initiative, established a commanding presence, or simply gave up her sometimes blatant and sometimes subtle role of being sick, suffering, and helpless. At these times, one could say that she was locating the phallus in directedness, in her body as a whole, or in her manifest well-being.

But just who is it that decides on the when and where of a phallus? Traditionally, analysts have maintained a simple positivist stance in claiming that they observe their analysands making these phallic reductions or being controlled by these unconscious phallic fantasies. In this view, the analyst's inferences are determined or compelled by the data; it is said that the conclusions are inescapable. The data emanate from the analysand's unconscious, and the analysand's unconscious is, of course, in the analysand. Today, however, this positivist stance in relation to data seems obsolete. I think it is now necessary to accept some form of the following interrelated propositions: one cannot distinguish sharply what the analyst finds and what the analyst introduces as a narrative organization; no absolute distinction between analytic subject and object is tenable; all perception is interpretation in context; and all proposed analytic interpretation is therefore reinterpretation that requires both recontextualization of what has been told and reduction of that telling to one or another psychoanalytic storyline. In my relatively more formal exposition of clinical interpretation, to which I now turn, I shall develop these last points further. And I shall return to them in the following chapter on reconstruction.

Interpretation

The way in which one defines clinical psychoanalytic interpretation depends on one's general conception of the events that take place in the psychoanalytic situation. Therefore, I shall introduce my understanding of interpretation by setting forth my conception of these events.

At the beginning of analysis, the analysand is introduced to the fundamental or free-association rule. No matter how this rule may be stated, and in some cases it may be only implied, its fundamental intent is subsequently made clear by the analyst's responsiveness. The analyst responds to the analysand as someone in a dilemma, as someone who, though encouraged to speak as frankly and unselectively as possible, is from the first giving many signs of finding it difficult to carry on in this manner consistently. As a rule, this difficulty seems to be all the greater when it comes to voicing thoughts, feelings, and bodily experiences that, in the analysand's consciously constructed experience, appear to intrude into his or her mind while talking. These intrusions violate the analysand's sense of what it is safe, appropriate, or coherent to say. The analyst takes these signs of difficulty as evidence that these "intrusions" violate some rules which the analysand is following in talking. To say that the analysand is following rules does not imply that he or she has consciously formulated these rules and is consciously resolved to abide by them; it is to say only that these rules may be formulated through analysis (Schafer 1978, lecture 2). In one of its major aspects, Freud's postulation of unconscious mental processes was his way of providing for these rules in his explanations.

Sooner or later, these "intrusions," the rules they violate, and the analysand's modes of coping with them must be formulated by the analyst, who will have been observing all of these mainly from one standpoint, namely that of their repetitive, unconsciously resistant, and transferential significance in the here and now context of the analytic relationship. They are resistant in that they limit what can come up and be considered in the analysis; they are transferential in that, unrealistically or inappropriately, they introduce into the analytic relationship passions and problems that repeat patterns of relationship established with significant figures in the analysand's past, especially his or her very early past.

In adopting this observational standpoint, the analyst is in effect regarding both the analysand's talking and his or her disruptions of talking as a species of narrative performance, that is, as a way of telling or giving an account of life events in the past and present. (It is in a closely allied sense that Freud [1914a] regarded repetitive action and acting out as forms of remembering. In this broad, interpretively useful conception, remembering need not be consciously identified as such by the subject.)

When the analysand is viewed as being engaged in narrative performance, he or she will be understood to be giving only one of a great number of possible accounts that could be given of these life events. Indeed, on this view, one can never have unmediated access to these events, for the events can exist only in narrative accounts that have been or may be developed by the analysand or analyst for different purposes and in different contexts. On my understanding, this pluralistic and relativistic conception of "events" is put forward in many modern theories of knowledge. In psychoanalysis, the versions of significant events change as the work progresses, and with these changes go changes in what is called the experience of these events, for the narrative accounts and the experiences are inseparable. Contrary to the plans and fears of analysands, the analyst never takes immediately available or emphasized subjective experience as the final or definitive version of anything, for the analyst views that experience as always being constructed or reconstructed; it can be encountered only in explicit or implicit narrative accounts. Once this is assumed to be the case, subjective experience is always (in principle, if not in practice) open to further interpretation. Clinical analysis is terminable; it is analytic interpretation that is interminable.

It is characteristic of analytic technique that the analyst scrutinizes the analysand's narrative performances for signs of unintelligibility or less than desirable intelligibility. The analyst pays close attention to contradictions, gaps, evasions, overreactions and underreactions, oversimplifications, non sequiturs, and bewilderment; also, to absent beginnings, transitions, and endings and to absent events, times, and characters, and so on. It may be recalled in this connection that Freud repeatedly formulated the rationale of the analytic method and of the necessity of postulating unconscious mental processes as doing what is required to make the unintelligible intelligible (for example, in analyzing dreams, symptoms, and parapraxes). The analyst also scrutinizes these narrative performances for cues as to the most timely, effective, and beneficial interventions to make. In this respect, the analyst attends not only to content but to nonverbal motoric and affective signs, selective use of figurative language, and many other features of the situation, including his or her own fantasizing and countertransferences. The analyst's fantasizing and countertransferences are useful, though not infallible or sufficient guides to effects on the analytic relationship that unconsciously are being achieved by the analysand; or at least they are guides to cues that are being responded to by the analyst before the corresponding narratives have been formulated.

If it is agreed that the analyst is working with narrative performances, then, in formulating interpretations and the confrontations and clarifications that lead up to interpretations, the analyst may be said to be engaging in acts of retelling or narrative revision. The concept of retelling subsumes four overlapping terms: redescribing, reinterpreting, recontextualizing, and reducing. These terms overlap because, according to modern theories of interpretation, every description is necessarily an interpretation, and from this it follows that every redescription is necessarily a reinterpretation. The four terms overlap also because a description or interpretation makes sense only in some context within which it attains distinctiveness, relevance, and significance, and from this it follows that reinterpretation necessarily recontextualizes that which it is designed to make more intelligible. And finally, they overlap because retelling requires reduction of meaning to the confining terms of another narrative. To give a schematic example of what I mean: in an analytic interpretation that deals with reaction formation against sadism, the analyst is *redescribing* ostensible kindness as a defensive move, or *reinterpreting* as defensiveness what the analysand has already interpreted and presented as evidence of sheer kindness, or *recontextualizing* ostensible kindness by placing it in a setting of infantile as well as current danger situations, or *reducing* the manifest forms and occasions of forced kindness to prototypic childhood situations of danger and defense (for example being good out of fear of abandonment).

In interpreting or retelling the analysand's narrative performances, the analyst follows certain storylines of personal development, conflictual situations, and subjective experience that are the distinguishing features of his or her analytic theory and approach. In the case of the mainstream Freudian, for example, these storylines are the familiar ones of the developmental vicissitudes and derivatives of conflictual infantile situations concerning sex and aggression. These storylines necessarily take into account the formative influence of early maturational and familial events, and they do so always in terms of more or less typical, phase-specific, and gender-specific ways in which the analysand-narrator may be said to have experienced these events, many of which have been simply imagined. The analyst's storylines also take into account the analysand's historical account of what analysts traditionally call the development of the ego's interests, defenses, and functions; the ego ideal or ideal self; and the superego or archaic moral principles. The role of identifications will be especially stressed in these connections (Schafer, 1968a). Whatever may be retold as having been unconsciously, conflictedly, and archaically carried forward into present activity will be given a prominent place in the analyst's redescriptions, reinterpretations, recontextualizations, and reductions. For example, the analytic situation may be interpreted in one of its aspects as a pregnancy, a feeding, a toilet, or a primal-scene chamber.

In developing interpretations, the analyst works in two directions: from the here and now of transference and resisting into the analysand's past, and from that past into the here and now (Schafer, 1978, lecture 1). The past is used to make the present more intelligible, and the present is used to make the past more intelligible, which is to say more coherent, continuous, and convincing. Thus, the analyst may use a history of past neglect to focus on the experience of being neglected in the analytic relationship, and this focus, in turn, may bring to the fore specific painful memories of actual or imagined past neglect, and so on, until past and present seem as one or "timeless." In this respect the interpretive process is circular, though it is not on that account a vicious circle. Rather, it is a process of filling in one repetitive narrative of being neglected.

Additionally, with respect to the analyst's having from the first accepted certain theory-dictated storylines as the ones to develop systematically, though always in a highly individualized and particularized manner, the process of interpretation does not conform to the official and traditional epistemological model of psychoanalysis, that is, the model of positivism. As I mentioned earlier, according to the positivist model, the investigator discovers, studies, and theorizes about facts that exist as such apart from the investigator's interrelated theoretical and methodological precommitments. What is being asserted or reasserted here, to the contrary, is that there can be no sharp split between observer and observed or between subject and object; for in psychoanalysis, as in all other fields of inquiry, there can be no theory-free and method-free facts. The purported life-historical facts that are initially presented by analysands become *psychoanalytic* facts only after they have been systematically retold by the analyst, who, it must be added, is more and more, even if erratically and only implicitly, joined in this project by the analysand as the analysis progresses. One might say that in the end the interpretations must be seen as coauthored.

In working out interpretations in this inevitably circular, nonpositivistic, and collaborative manner, the analyst coordinates the terms in which past and present are to be described. This coordination is inherent in the analyst's formulating the *repetitive* aspects of the analysand's present analytic behavior along with the reasons for this repetitiveness, that is, its "motivation" or "unconscious dynamics." I mentioned earlier that, in addition to its other features, interpretation is reductive. To a significant extent the coordination of terms of which I am now speaking is reductive. Reductiveness is not to be deplored, for it is inherent in any tracing of significant themes or developmental sequences in psychoanalysis as in all other interpretive disciplines. Thematic reduction should not be confused with the arbitrary reductionism or "nothing but" approach that instantiates the "genetic fallacy," that is to say, the claim that everything "really" is only what it once was; for in emphasizing sameness within apparent difference, the analyst need not forget that other narratives may have to be developed that give due weight to "changes of function" over the course of a life, as of an analysis. It is the analytic search for continuity and coherence that entails the strong emphasis on sameness over difference.

A fifth feature of interpretation may be singled out at this point: it is the adultomorphic aspect of the interpretation of experience in early childhood. It is not to be deplored that some adultomorphism is characteristic of analytic interpretation (Schafer, 1980a). Adultomorphism enters the interpretive process, at least in its final stages, through the indispensable use of the complex language and perspectives that are aimed to ensure maximal intelligibility of the evolving life history. Adultomorphism is involved, for example, when reference is made to infantile feelings and fantasies of "rejection," "abandonment," "starvation," or "loss of self (or self-boundaries)." These terms for infantile experience are not in accord with any developmental-psychological account of cognition in early childhood. But the analysand's infantile modes and contents of experience can only become analytic data in formulations that necessarily recognize and enhance the continuing activity of both the analyst's and the analysand's "observing ego" or "mature psyche." One may, therefore, say of analytic interpretation that, far from unearthing and resurrecting old and archaic experiences as such, it constitutes and develops new, vivid, verbalizable, and verbalized versions of those experiences. Only then can these new versions be given a secure place in a continuous, coherent, convincing, and up-to-date psychoanalytic life history. This is the history that facilitates personal change and further development.

Personal Agency

Interpretation refines and stablilizes the way in which the analysand experiences and expresses his or her personal agency, especially in relation to what have come to be defined, through interpretation, as critical life situations, such as the danger situations outlined by Freud (1926) of loss of love and love objects, castration, and superego condemnation. In the following remarks I shall try to clarify what I mean by personal agency. Refined and stabilized personal agency is one way—the action language way—of referring to what is more familiarly known as increased autonomy of adaptive, self-reflective, and synthesizing ego functions; as moderation of superego functions and defensive ego functions; as mature narcissism and increased cohesiveness of the nuclear self; as genitality or postambivalent object love; as the further development of separation-individuation and object constancy; or as development through and beyond the infantile depressive position. Personal agency is refined and stabilized by the analyst's insightful retelling of both disclaiming and excessive claiming of agency (Schafer, 1976). Instances of disclaiming include not only fate neuroses, as Freud (1920) asserted, or a passive attitude toward one's own defensive operations, as Fenichel (1941) showed; on Freud's own arguments, they also include, to name only a few of many factors, moral masochism, the ego-alien aspects of neurotic symptoms, and all those instances where the neurotic analysand defensively insists on the powerful influence of developmental deficits and goes on to attribute these deficits to constitutional factors and early, irremediable traumatization at the hands of the environment. Excessive claiming of agency is implied in neurotic guilt reactions and the construction of omnipotent fantasies, both of which are implicated in the analysand's irrationally assuming responsibility for family catastrophes, among other things.

In the reductive emphasis on repetition that characterizes analytic interpretation, the analyst steadily attributes agency to the analysand as against sheer victimization.

In developing action language, I have not been prescribing the language to be used by analyst or analysand in the clinical setting; rather, I have been developing a coherent, nonmechanistic account of the way in which analysts and analysands *do* traditionally interact and the way in which analysands *do* customarily change for the better as a result of being in analysis. So long as it does not insistently reinforce the analysand's disclaiming and excessive claiming of action, the everyday, more or less figurative, individualized language that analysts use in developing their interpretations does not seem to be decisive, for analysts who vary in their rhetorical preferences do seem to be able to get satisfactory analytic results in many cases. My point is this: however they may be worded, the interpretations will redescribe, reinterpret, recontextualize, and thematically reduce conflicts that the analysand has unconsciously defined, and compromises that the analysand has unconsciously arranged; and to say this is to say that, through interpretation, the great extent to which the analysand is unconsciously the agent or author of his or her life gets to be established beyond doubt. The analysand emerges as deeply implicated in his or her suffering even if not as the only agent or source of the pain. On this basis, though not in any strict sequence, the analysand is better able to envision and pursue desirable alternatives to those aspects of existence that heretofore and consciously were passively suffered or at least perpetuated in an unquestioning manner.

But the beneficial change brought about by analysis involves more than recognizing and accepting how much one has been implicated in developing the meanings, the forms, and the continuation of one's usually lifelong difficulties, and it involves more than recognizing the extent to which one has inappropriately assumed responsibility. For what has also changed is the analysand as life-historian, as maker of sense, as definer and designer of possible futures. I have described what amounts to a cognitive revolution on the part of the analysand. Although it is universally accepted by analysts that the analysand can accomplish this revolution only with considerable emotional travail (as well as relief), I have not dwelled here on these emotional aspects of the analytic process and its outcome as I have been aiming chiefly to clarify the *thinking* that goes into the making of analytic interpretations and to show that this entire project is hermeneutically conceived and executed.

Also, I have not dwelled on necessity, harsh fate, or traumatic events. In one respect, these features of a life over which one has not had control and for which one is not responsible get to be clarified through the analysis of excessive claiming of action (for example, fantasizing of omnipotence and guilt reactions), but in another respect the analysand has been helped to see how, unconsciously, he or she is implicated even in these events, for according to the psychoanalytic narrative, necessity and such are individually assimilated in the terms of predominantly unconscious fantasizing and its storylines (for example, in the terms of badness or helplessness). In the end, everything of significance will have been taken up, so far as possible, in terms of some aspect of the analysand as agent—even, as I illustrated in my opening example, the anatomical difference between the sexes.

I would mention in conclusion that a number of the major theories of the tragic in literature center on the many forms in which conflictual agency participates in the simultaneously terrible and wonderful aspects of life. In this respect, psychoanalysis has a tragic cast, though not on that account a gloomy one. One might say that analysis raises the melodramatic or pathetic to the level of the tragic and so changes the atmosphere or the quality or the dignity of an entire life (Schafer, 1970). Those who benefit from analysis gain an examined life which, whatever its continuing problems, is experienced not only as worth living but as worth improving.

12
Psychoanalytic Reconstruction

Introduction

There is no longer any need for an analyst to argue or to demonstrate that transference interpretations are relevant to the reconstruction of early development. The urgent question today is how the interpreting analyst establishes their relevance. And that question implies another. How does the analyst define *what* is to be related to something else or, in other words, how does the analyst establish contexts of significance? I am attempting here to set forth some partial answers to these complex questions. My approach makes use of ideas about the narrative aspects of psychoanalysis and the relativistic point of view on interpretation that I shall develop more fully in chapters 14–16. A clinical example will be included here.

Accounts of the Past

Each account of the past is a reconstruction that is controlled by a narrative strategy. The narrative strategy dictates how one is to select, from a plenitude of possible details, those that may be reorganized into another narrative which is both followable and expresses the desired point of view on the past. Accordingly, this reconstruction, like its narrative predecessor, is always subject to change. For whenever new explanatory aims are set and new questions raised, new slants on the past will be developed and new evidence concerning the events of the past will become available. Change of this sort typifies historical narratives of every kind.

193

In psychoanalysis, this new evidence becomes available primarily through remembering, or, in connection with strategically redistributed emphases and interpretively revised connections, through remembering *differently*. What the analysand remembers newly or differently is based on the utilization of new criteria of relevance (making analytic sense), personal benefit (gratification and synthesis), and safety (being less concerned with taking defensive measures against remembering whatever one anticipates will be remembered painfully).

When it is seen in this light, each analytically revised account of the past is necessarily a reconstruction of that which has already been constructed differently. The reconstruction is achieved by various interrelated interpretive means: thematic revision (for example, retelling inexplicable irritability as a means of warding off loving feelings), filling in (for example, acknowledging painful or apparently paradoxical details), recontextualization and reduction (for example, placing chronic problems of the recent past in the context of early family relations), and reassessment (for example, recognizing the adaptive significance of past actions which have seemed to be only bad choices).

By these means the psychoanalyst helps his or her analysands develop multiple life-historical narratives each of which is specifically psychoanalytic (see chapter 13). Analysts with different points of view on theory and technique employ different narrative strategies, and so they develop analytic histories of different types and with more or less different content. Members of other disciplines (sociology, biology) develop nonanalytic histories.

Some interpretive answers concerning the past will not be based on, or seemingly directly corroborated by, content that is consciously remembered by the analysand. These "constructions in analysis" (Freud, 1937b) are required for the coherence, followability, and further development of the analytic life histories, and ideally they will withstand the challenge posed by alternative interpretations.

Because the reconstruction of the psychoanalytic past necessarily takes place in the here and now clinical dialogue, it remains an interpretable and reinterpretable feature of that here and now. This means that the past is always taken as that which is currently being told in one or another conflictual analytic context. Ideally, in each analytic undertaking, one continues to interpret the biases and limits not only of histories initially presented but of those that have been developed previously in that very analysis and have now come into question. No analytic history can ever be completely taken for granted.

Psychoanalytic Reconstruction

Accounts of the Present

Accounts of the present (the here and now) are reconstructions in the same way as accounts of the past, as described above, except that they feature acts of perceiving rather than remembering. If it is accepted that every perception is itself a construction (an interpretive selection, organization, and formulation), the perceived present may not be regarded as a reality that is simply given, self-evident, or prenarrational. Like the facts of the past, the facts of the here and now exist only in narrated versions of them. They are organized selections from the plenitude of the present. Thus, formulating the here and now of each analysis is an interpretive or narrational project in the same way that reconstructively formulating the past is. For example, manifestations of transference in the here and now are reconstructions in this sense. Far from being narratively unmediated and unmodifiable facts, transference manifestations are psychoanalytic versions of facts that are told (by the analysand), retold (by the analyst), and always could be told (by anyone) in other ways.

Some interpretive answers concerning the transferential present will not be based on, or seemingly directly corroborated by, content consciously perceived by the analysand. These interpretations, like their past-historical counterparts, deserve to be called reconstructions in analysis in that they serve the same analytic functions and give rise to the same sorts of analytic developments as reconstructions of the infantile past. An instance of this kind of reconstruction is the interpretation of shame before any shame has been consciously experienced; the interpretation will be based on phenomena that, upon analytic retelling, foreshadow shame as a consciously experienced reaction.

From this point on, it will therefore be consistent to speak only of *reconstructions in analysis,* indicating, where appropriate, whether the reconstruction is the analysand's or the analyst's, or a joint product of both.

The Interrelationships of Accounts of the Past and the Present

Reconstructions of the infantile past and the transferential present are interdependent. This is so because, upon reviewing what is at any moment taken to be true of the past, one raises questions and suggests answers concerning features of the transferential present. Similarly, in reviewing what is at any moment taken to be true of the transferential present, one raises questions and suggests answers concerning the infantile past. For example, present feelings of inadequacy direct the inquiry toward life-historical prototypes, and accounts of a never-satisfied father direct the inquiry toward transference fantasies of a never-satisfied analyst; and the yield of both inquiries directs attention to new or unremarked features of past and present; and so on throughout the analysis.

In this way, analytic work is temporally circular rather than unidirectionally retrospective, and the so-called past and present may not be regarded as independent variables that are testable one against the other.

In addition to this circularity, interpretation is characterized by the analyst's utilization of specifically psychoanalytic abstracting and organizing concepts (for example, sadism, regression, orality, danger situations), and by the analyst's effort to identify sameness or repetition over the course of a life (for example, repeated provocation of rejection). Through this reductive categorization, concrete aspects of the analysand's past and present get to be defined in closely coordinated, if not identical, terms. *Thereby, the "timelessness of the Unconscious" is actualized in the analysis.* In the psychoanalytic life history, what was, is, and what is, was. The narratively reconstructed present originates in the narratively reconstructed past, and vice versa.

Consequently, for working purposes, that is, in order to develop the transference neurosis as fully as possible, it becomes less rather than more important to think in terms of conventional linear time, less rather than more important to distinguish between past and present. (I am stating in other terms what I take to be one of the main theses of Freud's [1914a] "Remembering, Repeating and Working-Through.") To Freud's unquestionable conclusion that the indispensable emotional aspects of insight and working through can be developed and interpreted only in the transferential here and now, one must add this: increasingly, as the transference neurosis develops, the here and now becomes a condensed, coordinated, and timeless version of past and present.

Rather than its being a product of regression, this timeless mode of experiencing and understanding is an achievement within a controlled analytic situation. Consequently it is to be regarded as a new mode of experiencing. Now, the past appears as never before experienced, and the present as it never could have been experienced were it not for analysis. On this account, what has hitherto been looked at as analytic regression is more correctly and usefully looked at as the kind of personal development that is peculiar to analytic work.

The analyst properly accords technical priority to the development, through interpretation, of this timeless account of the analysand's moment-by-moment transferential enactments. At the same time, in keeping with Kris's (1956a) discussion of the matter, the analyst continues to pay close attention to the analysand's shifting emphases on the content of the past and also to the shifting functions of the analysand's narrating the past at all (for example, defensive, seductive, or narcissistic functions of so doing). This close attention is required lest the analytic work itself be subverted unconsciously into a repetition of that which must be analyzed (for example, the analysand may be dwelling on the painful past *masochistically*). This is to say that to a significant though varying extent the analysand tends to engage in the analytic work in a manner that can be taken to express the same problems or characteristics that are under analytic scrutiny at that moment. Thus, if it is anxious seductiveness that is in question, it may be expected that the analysand will participate in its analysis in a more or less anxiously seductive manner. Analysis always bends back on itself in this way and so becomes in large part a reflexive study of itself.

None of the above has been presented as describing the entirety of analytic work, not even of its temporal dimension. The analyst also recognizes that, from the standpoint of what is called the secondary process and adaptation, there is a good deal of sorting out of the past and present that must be accomplished. But, in ways that I shall not detail here, as they have been amply described and illustrated throughout the psychoanalytic literature, the effectiveness of that conventional sorting out depends on the analysand's achieving the timeless mode of experiencing that characterizes the transference neurosis.

A Clinical Example

A clinical example will illustrate concretely some of these abstract, programmatic considerations. The analysand was a successful attorney who specialized as a consultant on bankruptcy problems. According to the line of interpretation that was developed in the analysis, he had unconsciously chosen this realm of work because, among other things, it represented dealing continuously and only half hopefully with death, the threat of death, and the making of reparative efforts. These were matters with which, unconsciously, he had been chronically concerned in an intensely anxious and guilty way. Analysis defined two leading reasons why he preferred the role of consultant. First, the restrictiveness of that role was one of its main advantages; for not only did it restrict the extent of his personal involvement with clients who, considering their extreme circumstances, could be expected to be highly emotional and demanding, it also restricted the extent to which he would have to be in on the often inevitable demise of their business ventures. The second leading reason was this: the role of the consultant allowed him much free time to pursue a wide range of legal interests and so to become very well versed in the law as a whole while at the same time concealing this interest and competence from his colleagues and, through denial and minimization, preserving his own view of himself as a mediocrity.

In the initial history-taking, he portrayed his parents as enemies to one another: his father, chronically angry and remote; his mother, chronically unhappy. He said that as a child he had always and only feared his father, and now he asserted he could dismiss him as irrelevant. His mother, in his account, had been a disturbing and growth-retarding influence. For some months during his preschool years and for undisclosed or unremembered reasons, he had been placed with distant relatives. His mother could not visit and his father visited seldom, which was, he said, a relief, for there was nothing to be gained from these visits. Although the analysand's developmental history included noteworthy disturbances in the oral and anal spheres, and although he reported some persisting difficulties in these spheres, he had gone on to establish some stable and self-enhancing, though not entirely conflict-free, sublimated oral and anal interests and achievements.

He had come for analysis complaining of depressive mood swings,

198

irritability, concern over his impact on his children, and doubts about his future. Early in the analysis he began to conceive of the analyst as depressed in carriage, manner, and outlook. In making this construction of the analyst, he used some gross misperceptions (for example "seeing" tears in the analyst's eyes) and also exaggerations. The question was posed why he would need to see the analyst in this way. His subsequent associations could be interpreted (retold) in the following way. He was presenting his depressiveness as a form of wooing the analyst and also as an implicit affirmation of a special bond, if not identity, with the "depressed" analyst. Meanwhile, he was making frequent slips of the tongue in which he referred to himself as his mother and vice versa. Using this and similar material, together with his history of pregenital disturbances and his consistent picture of his mother as unhappy, the analyst offered the following reconstruction. His mother had been depressed during his early years, and he had found that the best way to maintain contact with her was through cultivating a depressive identificatory rapport of the sort he was now imagining existed between him and the analyst. Subsequently, he brought into the analysis preschool memories of himself and his mother frequently and jointly bemoaning their fates. He also recalled his having vowed to himself during the preschool separation from his mother that he would never be a burden to her again, as though blaming himself for having damaged her and thereby having caused the separation or "rejection."

Gradually, what could be taken as signs of father-transference became discernible. These often took the form of his conceiving of the analyst in the same terms he had used initially to describe his father: angry, threatening, and unavailable. But at the same time he began to drop hints, inadvertently as it were, that there was more to his father than that, more than he could dare to recognize consciously or clearly. After exploring at length his being resistant in this respect (for example, his fearing to like or respect the analyst), it became possible to offer the following reconstruction. He had once felt love and admiration for his father but had dreaded his mother's hatred if she should see signs of these feelings It then became increasingly evident in his analytic sessions that he tended to panic and become uncomprehending, cold, and rejecting whenever he perceived the analyst as empathic or helpful, and that he intended thereby to rebuff the analyst and stave off positive feelings in the transference. The reconstruction of his early positive tie to his father was developed further. By the time of the preschool separation he had already begun to spurn his father's efforts to be close and helpful, and he had done so particularly—and with particular poignancy—when his father visited him in the home of the distant relatives. Subsequently, the analysand brought in memories of having looked forward, though only briefly and secretly, to his father's visits; and he related additional memories of various efforts, some of them obviously self-sacrificing, that his father had made over the years to help him develop intellectually, culturally, and professionally. It now seemed to be the case (that is, the "right" way to reconstruct this chapter of his history) that his father had been attempting to rescue him from the depressive entanglement with his mother and that, as a son, he could only respond ambivalently, that is, gratefully and fearfully. In response to these reconstructions, the analysand became better able to recognize and acknowledge his experiencing the analyst as concerned, responsive, and helpful.

Working directly within the transference, the analyst was able to go on to develop interpretations of passive homosexual love—of the analysand's wishing to be impregnated anally by the analyst but having to defend against showing that this was so by rebuffing the analyst's interventions and maintaining a detached manner. This theme, too, was then referred to the past (for example, rivalry with his mother for his father's love and babies). Yet another function of his detached position in the transference and his correlated dismissal of his father's importance to him was to disavow and continue to repress his having wished in his early years to be his mother's lover and his father's successful rival. In this connection he had begun to recall signs of sexual interest in his mother. It seemed then that, emotionally, there had been lots more to their relationship than their crying together. Additional pieces of evidence for these interrelated reconstructions of past and present included frequent slips in which he would call his mother his wife and vice versa and, similarly, in a reversal of generations, call his one daughter his wife and vice versa.

The last part of this schematic and incomplete clinical example concerns the place in the changing life-historical narrative that was given to death, dying, and reparation and to the hiding of his intellectual breadth and competence. As he recalled it, his mother had not only explicitly expressed death wishes against him when exasperated by his infantile excesses and fears, she had implicitly indicated these same wishes when, by inattention, she had exposed him to grave physical danger on several occasions. In the context of these experiences, he had imagined himself living under the constant threat of dying if he "grew up." To him, growing up meant breaking away from his mother's influence and revealing that he had a will, feelings, and paternally supported competence and interests of his own. If he exposed himself in this respect, rapprochement with her would be out of the question. But at the same time, he had had to go on making reparation for damaging his mother, for what he felt was his responsibility in driving her to distraction and her death wishes. This he did in the present by rescuing the bankrupt mother-surrogates he dealt with in his work. Additionally, he feared being killed or castrated by his forever angry oedipal father and killed in the extreme violence of a primal scene involving parents at war with one another in the bedroom, no matter whether he took in fantasy the masculine or feminine role. By keeping his thoughts and feelings apart and thereby remaining emotionless, he was unconsciously keeping his parents apart and saving himself. Unconsciously, he had continued to live in this complex danger situation from early childhood up to the present.

In the here and now of the transference these factors were expressed variously: for example, by the idea that the analyst wished to be rid of him as an exasperating patient; by the idea that the analyst was exposing him to deadly danger by not rushing to rescue him from his depressiveness; and by the idea that the analyst resented any show of intellectual independence or rivalry, as when the analysand used a psychological term or, worst of all, dared to arrive at an analytic interpretation on his own. Along the same line, it was unpardonable to be curious about the analyst's personal life, especially his sexual life but also his intellectual life as an analyst. He had to keep a low profile in analysis as in life, and for him a low profile signified both defensive and wish-fulfilling self-castration and nonindividuation. One might say it was a living death that guaranteed survival and gratification.

What I have wanted to show in reviewing this clinical material is that some reconstructions of current material followed from reconstructions of the past and some reconstructions of the past followed from reconstructed current material. Some reconstructions led from mother-transference on to father-transference and then back to mother. Much of the material was opened up by close attention to resistant activity in the realms of will, desire, ideas, feelings, competence, and their interrelations, and the connections of all of these to "growing up" and being condemned to death for that. This clinical material has its own individual slant; however, when it is considered in its broad outlines, it is not unique in that it includes themes often developed in analytic work. In the present context, its interest lies in its illustrating the complex circularity and narrativity of working simultaneously with the here and now reconstructions of transference and resisting and the then and there reconstructions of the vicissitudes of early development. Those then and there reconstructions remain, however, part of the here and now of the analytic narrative enterprise. How else could it be?

Theory and Reconstruction

Ordinarily it is difficult if not impossible for the analyst to distinguish purely imaginary infantile events from infantile perception of actual events (for example, early primal scenes). It is equally a problem to sort out and locate in linear time memories that probably date from different phases of early development but have been collapsed into one another. And in any case it is extremely difficult to verify or falsify analytic claims of correct or exact reconstruction of actual or imagined early infantile events.

As a rule, and as in my clinical illustration, the analyst reconstructs along lines laid down by preexisting theoretical commitments or life-historical strategies. These commitments or strategies control the analyst's general line of interpretation, which in turn influences the form and content of the analysand's associations. In their turn, the form and content of the analysand's associations provide the suggestive evidence for the concrete reconstruction of infantile psychical development. And yet the theoretical commitments have been worked out, mainly by Freud, so that they fit the material that analysands typically and *spontaneously* (to the extent that that is possible), present in analysis. More exactly, the theory fits what analysands typically select from the plenitude of possible versions of possible or probable events in their lives. As Freud noted, it is inherently unclear in psychoanalysis where observation and theory begin and end.

That the analysand reacts in illuminating ways to the analyst's reconstructions of both the here and now and the infantile past shows, not that those reconstructions are the only ones or the best ones possible, but merely that they are serving well as guides to the analysand. Consciously, preconsciously, and unconsciously, the analyst's reconstructions guide the analysand in reconstructing early significant memories, perceptions, and connections in the here and now of the analysis. Obviously, the beneficial developments to which this guidance by reconstruction gives rise are to be highly valued, but just as obviously analysts do vary among themselves in the amount and type of reconstructions of the infantile past they venture to make or expect to make with clinical confidence. In the realm of life-historical narration, there is always more than one way to tell what is the case now and so what the case must have been in the infantile past—and vice versa.

Thus, in considering analytic knowledge, we confront this triple circularity: conventional distinctions between subject and object, between observation and theory, and between past and present no longer hold. From this one may conclude that reconstruction of the infantile past is a temporally displaced and artificially linearized account of the analysis in the here and now. That this is so does not seem to point to any technical problem other than the familiar danger of dwelling on reconstruction of the infantile past in isolation from the current state of the transference. Within the analytic dialogue, it seems to be the case that the narrative reconstructions of the past may be spun out usefully in the form of evolving psychoanalytic life histories that are being repetitively and unconsciously enacted in the transferential here and now.

The usefulness of that narrational project is not being thrown into question by these remarks. But the preceding description of analytic work does have consequences for the epistemological aspects of analytic theory. It does not follow from these remarks that all strategies of interpretation, whether Freudian or non-Freudian, have an equal claim on our attention and respect, for I believe that it can be shown (though it would take extended discussion to make this demonstration), that some of these strategies are more penetrating, coherent, comprehensive, and mutative than others. What does follow from the foregoing discussion is this: for purposes of clinical consistency and assessment of competing points of view, we cannot do without a clearer understanding than we now have of the close and complex interrelationships between analytic theory, methods, and data.

13

The Construction of Multiple Histories

It will be argued in this chapter that there is no single, all-purpose psychoanalytic life history to be told, for the account of that life keeps changing during the course of analysis. This continuous change occurs not only because the history gets to be told more insightfully, that is, from the psychoanalytic point of view told more completely, more consistently, and with a greater sense of relevance regarding the variables that are crucial in analysis, such as the varieties of sexual, aggressive, and defensive activity during different phases of development. If it were just this kind of change, one could still end up with a single coherent history, as Michael Sherwood, for example, assumes to be the case in his important book *The Logic of Explanation in Psychoanalysis* (1969). But it is not just this kind of change. The historical account also changes whenever the major questions change; for in the context established by each such question, different aspects of events and people and conflictual compromised activity come to the fore in distinctive ways. One sees that this is so when new, surprising, and long repressed or neglected details of the life history are told with special significance as different analytic questions are pursued in depth. One also sees how remembering is so largely a function of the context established by one or another question.

More than being oversimplifying, it is often meaningless and confusing to discuss certain life-historical facts without referring to the analytic context within which they have been established, that is, without referring to the questions for which they are the answers. The intellectually unassimilable nature of so many synopsized case reports in the analytic literature is often due to neglect of contextual location, which is to say, neglect of the fact that analytic data are always functions of the method and of their place in the analytic process. Analytic case summaries purport to say what is true of the individual when they should say what is true according to the details of the different investigations that have been carried out within each analysis. More than being dreary and static catalogues of dynamic formulations, these summaries are wrongly construed and therefore misleading versions of psychoanalytic knowledge.

The proposition that there is a single life history may be questioned on another basis. The same stretch of life history reads one way when it is formulated looking backward from present adult activity, and it reads another way when couched in the forward-looking terms of an earlier phase of development. For example, the adult analysand may breathe a great sigh of relief upon understanding the good fortune of not having been the symbiotic favorite of a disturbed mother, while at the same time understanding how intense were the childhood feelings of deprivation at not having been the child who was "loved" the most or even "loved" equally or at all. The relief does not wipe out the sense of deprivation and its consequences, including the present yearnings, but it does signify their modification and reduced significance once they have been integrated into a better understood, more complex, psychoanalytic life history—one which, though open to continuous revision, is inherently a contemporary look at the past rather than a prospective view of future development.

One arrives then at various histories of the past just as one establishes different versions of the present. Each of these histories may be convincing. It is not that these different accounts are independent of one another, for certainly the questions being addressed are themselves interrelated. Rather, any question or any perspective implies a selective organization of the data specific to it; like an intellectual system, it enforces a figure-ground organization of the data. Thus it is that an individual analysis produces not one history but a set of more or less coordinated accounts of life history. And thus it is that different analytic approaches based on different assumptions produce different sets of life histories that support these assumptions.

Beyond this consideration, however, is the question of how justified analysts ever are to make fully confident historical judgments or reconstructions based primarily on an analysand's account of the remote past or on his or her apparent repetition of temporally remote events and then, going further, to claim to be responding directly to this view of things. It is not plausible that the analyst is directly experiencing the analysand as simply an infant or young child who is reliving ancient events and the reactions they evoked. The analyst gains whatever empathic confidence he or she does from what happens in the analytic session, most of all in connection with the analysand's resisting and forming transferences and getting to understand and modify them. Looking at these events from the unique analytic perspective, the analyst knows *first hand* just what the analysand endures and achieves in the course of working analytically. The analyst draws on the analysand's tellings of the past to elucidate these experiences and accomplishments in the here and now of the analytic sessions. The infant or young child of the remote and reconstructed past is rather more of a hypothetical being lacking in individual "feel" than a concrete presence, and this is so no matter how vividly and empathically the analyst may imagine this past. Consequently, the analysand imagined as infant or child plays a part only in the analyst's directing and focusing participation in the present analytic situation.

In this light, the history that the analyst comes to believe in with most justification is the history of the analysis itself. That history includes the varied tellings and contemporary reconstructions of the past. These tellings and reconstructions are both verbal and nonverbal, and both explicit and implicit, and they occur both within the bounds of the sessions and, through acting out, beyond these bounds. But to take account of the multiple nature of historical accounts, one should not speak of *the* history of the analysis; it should be said that it is the several or many histories of the analysis that must be told.

It must be asked next whether these histories comprise a set of new personal myths. To assert that they are myths is equivalent to saying that a history of any kind is a myth. This nihilistic (or pretentious?) conclusion does not follow from the preceding discussion; nor is it supported by the excellent essay on personal myths by Kris (1956b), which was written to develop another point altogether. What does follow is that it is in the nature of historical accounts to be subject to challenge, revision, and extension in the light of new questions and the new data that they establish or bring to the foreground. That no history is the single and final one does not mean that each history is a mythic creation which is exempt from the rules of verification, coherence, consistency, and (for the time being) completeness. In this sense, the psychoanalytic life histories are versions of the truth, and the analyst at any rate regards them as more efficacious in bringing about beneficial personal change than those established by other clinical methods. They are new, never before possible versions of the truth and therefore new truths; on this account, they may be said to enhance the life that is being examined.

It is only by extrapolation that one draws conclusions (constructions or reconstructions) about what is called the actual or biographical past, for the past could never be real to the analyst or analysand were it to be considered in isolation from the convincing histories of the analysis itself. These reconstructions do, of course, add to the ongoing analysis, enriching the understanding of what is being enacted in the present, but they always remain more provisional than the interpretation of the present.

During termination of a beneficial analysis, the analyst and analysand confidently believe that they have shared a profound experience. They have shared in the emotionally arduous and exhilarating construction of a more or less coordinated set of histories of their relationship; only secondarily have they shared in the relatively more cognitive task of constructing the analytically illuminated and reconstructed biographies.

Although it is true that much of the content of an analysis concerns events in the analysand's current life which are manifestly at some remove from the transference, and although it is also true that the analyst may and often does interpret this material without explicitly and immediately linking it to transference and resisting, it may still be asserted that ideally all such material should be at least implicitly interpreted with reference to its function in the analytic dialogue and thereby maximized in its significance and utility. There are no "other issues" pure and simple; there are only alternate, even if often tangential and delayed, approaches to the issues of the analysis itself. Thus it is that any analysis of a dream that is not located at least implicitly in the context of the current transference and resisting must be incomplete and potentially misleading or intellectualized.

There are two major implications of the foregoing discussion of the construction of psychoanalytic histories. First, by emphasizing the here and now actions that make up the analysis, the discussion reinforces the already generally accepted assertion, initially and frequently made by Freud, that the defining issues of the psychoanalytic process are transference and resisting and their interpretation and relative resolution. Second, it reveals the analyses of transference and resisting not merely as technical issues and contents of interpretation, nor as means to the end of "cure," but as issues of psychoanalytic epistemology. Primary psychoanalytic knowledge consists in the psychically real histories of individual psychoanalyses.

The second of these implications has important technical consequences of its own to which I shall devote the remainder of this chapter. My view of primary psychoanalytic knowledge implies a priority in interpretation that is not always fully appreciated or, if appreciated, not consistently observed in practice. The highest priority goes to arriving at the fullest possible understanding of the psychoanalytic encounter itself. Developing the psychoanalytic biography retains great importance, but what is more clearly recognized now is that the importance of this biography depends on the extent to which it enhances the understanding of the analysis itself.

If it is correct to define primary psychoanalytic knowledge in this way, then it would seem that all along analysts may have been taking a mistaken view of their interpretive work and its transformational consequences. The view customarily taken has been that one learns about the life history from the analysis of transference and resisting, that is, from the analysis of the analytic encounter itself; further, this knowledge of the life history is held to be in itself a final criterion of insight and an essential determinant of analytic results. On the present view, however, things are turned around. It seems now that the analyst goes on learning about the analytic encounter as he or she goes on developing the psychoanalytic life histories. The more freely and completely one knows relevant versions of the past, the richer one's empathic comprehension of what is taking place in the psychoanalytic sessions and the keener one's interpretations of transference and resisting. The convincing emotional experience of analysis, which is so essential to its results, lies in the present, as Freud emphasized long ago in his technical papers. In his role of investigator, however, Freud saw this experience as a means to the ultimate end of reconstructing a single past.

It might seem that the point of view being advocated here would establish a solipsistic conception of psychoanalysis. This is far from being the case in that, in any event, past and present life circumstances and events "outside" the analysis are continuously being taken into account along with estimates of change in these areas. But they are only taken *fully* and *effectively* into account when linked to the development of transferences and forms of resisting. It is, for example, implausible that an analysand can have entered into good, significant, and stable relationships with others while yet having desperately to omit reference to this change in the analytic sessions and to deny vehemently their continuity with previous work on his or her transferences and resisting.

One must allow for the fact that, over the course of an analysis, one both looks backward from the present and forward from the past, past and present shedding light on one another in what is a circular rather than linear development of interpretations (Schafer, 1978, lecture 1). The investigation of the past is conducted in the light of what is observed in the present, and at the same time what is known about the past leads to a specialized interest in the present. To give a crude example: present rebelliousness, in the transference raises questions about the history of personal rebelliousness, while existing or newly established knowledge of an earlier period of rebelliousness alerts the analyst to rebellious undercurrents, potentials, and meanings in the present.

I am, however, concerned here with something that goes beyond these considerations and bears on the transformational action of psychoanalysis. This issue may be put in the form of a question: what is it ultimately that one wants to arrive at? Is it full understanding of how the analysand got to be a "patient" or is it full understanding of what happens during the attempt at analysis? If it is the former, then one would be hoping to arrive ultimately at the interrelated life histories or biographies that were mentioned earlier. On balance, this emphasis on the yield of the analytic process characterizes Freud's writings. But if it is the latter, then one would be hoping to arrive ultimately at the interrelated psychoanalytic histories of the psychoanalytic process in each case. The current histories (one may call them by that name) would and do, of course, incorporate a great amount of biographical data, but they do so as part of the explanation of the analysis itself, and they amount to psychoanalytically formulated and arranged versions of these data.

Clearly, the preceding discussion favors the latter viewpoint. Psychoanalysis as a study of itself cannot be conducted and worked out without reference to changing and alternative versions of past events; more precisely, the analytic process depends both on repeated examination of how the telling of the past changes over the course of an analysis and on an attempt to explain how, when, and why the telling of the past changes in the process. Telling is a present action, and it is an action that cannot be divorced from the way the analysand subjectively experiences the telling; for the analyst understands this narrative action as much through its emotional mode, form, and sequelae as through its content. In psychoanalysis, it is the elucidation of the present that retains top priority. In the process of trying to explain how the analysand got to be "that way" in the present, one keeps on finding out what "that way" is, that is, how to characterize it or what it means. The analysis progressively defines the problems to be analyzed while analyzing them.

Consider, for example, the common complaint that one has always been an empty person. An analyst should regard this complaint as the analysand's way of telling about himself or herself. It is a telling that is, in the first place, self-contradictory, in that a truly empty person, if there could be such a person, could not pass that judgment and suffer accordingly. The question of emptiness would have no meaning to a truly empty person and so could not be raised and reacted to.

In the second place, the description "empty" is a spatial metaphor for the self as a quasi-concrete place that can be filled with substances such as ideas, feelings, interests, or relationships. But for theoretical purposes it would seem wiser to maintain that there is no such place and there are no such substances except in blatantly metaphoric, quasi-theoretical narrations of a mode of existence (Schafer, 1972).

"Emptiness" is established consciously, preconsciously, and unconsciously. Consciously and preconsciously, its referents ordinarily include a lack of enthusiasm, of commitment to goals and relationships, of ordinary reactivity to events, and the like. Unconsciously, the referents of "emptiness" include many factors: oral deprivation, castration, failure to be impregnated by father, excessive projection of feelings onto others, extensive or "depleting" repression, profound feelings of helplessness or hopelessness, fears of being invaded and robbed of one's contents, unattainable ideals, tremendous anxiety about loving others or oneself, etc. A special referent of emptiness is the (usually unconsciously made) demand that the analyst fill one up with whatever is thought to be lacking.

As a rule, the chronically "empty" person does manifest significant arrests in the development of agency and relationships. Nevertheless, the word "empty" is part of a narration that is simply unacceptable as a theoretical or clinical account of the actual state of affairs. Consequently, the autobiographical narration of emptiness calls for analysis and reconceptualization just as much as does the manic narration that one is filled to overflowing with good feelings, objects, etc. The analyst's knowledge of the development and past uses of the analysand's giving this account will help clarify the place of "emptiness" in his or her present life and most of all in the analytic relationship itself. In the course of analyzing the history of subjective emptiness, one gets to understand all that emptiness has meant in the life of the analysand, much as one may get to understand what a symptom or chronic daydream has meant.

As with every other problem presented in analysis, the analyst may be able to carry the analysis of the "emptiness" narration only so far.

210

The Construction of Multiple Histories

Developmental arrests may preclude adequate analysis of the narration. As a matter of procedure, however, the presentation of deficits is an action that is rather to be empathized with, understood, and interpreted than accepted at face value. This is so no matter how long and well documented the account of deficits may be. In some instances, the analyst may decide not to undertake an analysis at all, the prospective analysand's self-presentation being of a sort that indicates that other sorts of clinical measures are appropriate. Still, a history of emptiness is a present telling about oneself. As such, it is not independent biographical material. From the analytic point of view, there is, strictly speaking, no independent biographical material that counts.

14

Narration in the Psychoanalytic Dialogue

Psychoanalytic Theories as Narratives

Freud established a tradition within which psychoanalysis is understood as an essentialist and positivist natural science. One need not be bound by this scientific commitment, however; the individual and general accounts and interpretations Freud gave of his case material can be read in another way. In this reading, psychoanalysis is an interpretive discipline whose practitioners aim to develop a particular kind of systematic account of human action. We can say, then, either that Freud was developing a set of principles for participating in, understanding, and explaining the dialogue between psychoanalyst and analysand or that he was establishing a set of codes to generate psychoanalytic meaning, recognizing this meaning in each instance to be only one of a number of kinds of meaning that might be generated.

Psychoanalytic theorists of different persuasions have employed different interpretive principles or codes—one might say different narrative structures—to develop their ways of doing analysis and telling about it. These narrative structures present or imply two coordinated accounts: one, of the beginning, the course, and the ending of human development; the other, of the course of the psychoanalytic dialogue. Far from being secondary narratives about data, these structures provide primary narratives that establish what is to count as data. Once installed as leading narrative structures, they are taken as certain in order to develop coherent accounts of lives and technical practices.

It makes sense, and it may be a useful project, to present psychoanalysis in narrational terms. This I have already begun to do in the preceding chapters. In order to carry through this project, one must, first of all, accept the proposition that there are no objective, autonomous, or pure psychoanalytic data which, as Freud was fond of saying, compel one to draw certain conclusions. Specifically, there is no single, necessary, definitive account of a life history and psychopathology, of biological and social influences on personality, or of the psychoanalytic method and its results. What have been presented as the plain empirical data and techniques of psychoanalysis are inseparable from the investigator's precritical and interrelated assumptions concerning the origins, coherence, totality, and intelligibility of personal action. The data and techniques exist as such by virtue of two sets of practices that embody these assumptions; first, a set of *practices of naming and interrelating* that is systematic insofar as it conforms to the initial assumptions; and second, a set of *technical practices* that is systematic insofar as it elicits and shapes phenomena that can be ordered in terms of these assumptions. No version of psychoanalysis has ever come to close to being codified to this extent. The approach to such codification requires that the data of psychoanalysis be unfailingly regarded as constituted rather than simply encountered. The sharp split between subject and object must be systematically rejected.

In his formal theorizing, Freud used two primary narrative structures, and he often urged that they be taken as provisional rather than as final truths. But Freud was not always consistent in this regard, sometimes presenting dogmatically on one page what he had presented tentatively on another. One of his primary narrative structures begins with the infant and young child as a beast, otherwise known as the id, and ends with the beast domesticated, tamed by frustration in the course of development in a civilization hostile to its nature. Even though this taming leaves each person with two regulatory structures, the ego and the superego, the protagonist remains in part a beast, the carrier of the indestructible id. The filling in of this narrative structure tells of a lifelong transition. If the innate potential for symbolization is there, and if all goes well, one moves from a condition of frightened and irrational helplessness, lack of self-definition, and domination by fluid or mobile instinctual drives toward a condition of stability, mastery, adaptability, self-definition, rationality, and security. If all does not go well, the inadequately tamed beast must be accommodated by the formation of pathological structures, such as symptoms and perversions.

Freud did not invent this beast, and the admixture of Darwinism in his account only gave it the appearance of having been established in a positivist scientific manner. The basic story is ancient; it has been told in many ways over the centuries, and it pervades what we consider refined common sense.

Refined common sense structures the history of human thought about human action. It takes into account the emotional, wishful, fantasy-ridden features of action, its adaptive and utilitarian aspects, and the influence on it of the subject's early experiencing of intimate formative relationships and of the world at large. The repositories of common sense include mythology, folk wisdom, colloquial sayings, jokes, and literature, among other cultural products, and, as Freud showed repeatedly, there are relatively few significant psychoanalytic propositions that are not stated or implied by these products (Schafer, 1977). Refined common sense serves as the source of the precritical assumptions from which the psychoanalytic narrative structures are derived, and these structures dictate conceptual and technical practices.

But common sense is not fixed. The common sense presented in proverbs and maxims, for example, is replete with internal tension and ambiguity. Most generalizations have countergeneralizations (A penny saved is a penny earned, but one may be penny-wise and pound-foolish; one should look before one leaps, but he who hesitates is lost; and so on). And just as common sense may be used to reaffirm traditional orientations and conservative values (Rome wasn't built in a day), it may also be used to sanction a challenge to tradition (A new broom sweeps clean) or endorse an ironic stance (The more things change, the more they remain the same). Since generalizations of this sort allow much latitude in their application, recourse to the authority of common sense is an endless source of controversy over accounts of human action. Still, common sense is our storehouse of narrative structures, and it remains the source of intelligibility and certainty in human affairs. Controversy itself would make no sense unless the conventions of common sense were being observed by those engaged in controversy.

Psychoanalysis does not take common sense plain but rather transforms it into a comprehensive distillate, first, by selection and schematic reduction of its tensions and ambiguities and, second, by elevating only some of these factors (such as pleasure versus reality and id versus ego) to the status of overarching principles and structures. Traditionally, these elevations of common sense have been organized and presented as psychoanalytic metapsychology.

As more than one such distillation of common sense has been offered in the name of psychoanalysis, there have been phases in the development of psychoanalytic theory, and there are schools of psychoanalysis, each with a distinctive theory of its own. Each distillation (phase or school) has been elaborated and organized in terms of certain leading narrative structures that are to be taken as certain.

For Freud, the old story of the beast was indispensable, and he used it well. His tale of human development, suffering, defeat, and triumph was extraordinarily illuminating in its psychological content, scientifically respectable in its conceptualization and formalization, dramatically gripping in its metaphorical elaboration, and beneficial in his work with his analysands. Because this archetypal story has been mythologically enshrined in the metaphoric language that all of us have learned to think and live by, it is more than appealing to have it authorized and apparently confirmed by psychological science. At the same time, however, it is threatening to be told persuasively how much it is the beast that pervades, empowers, or at least necessitates our most civilized achievements. Except when moralizing about others, human beings do not wish to think consciously of having bestial origins, continuities, and destinies, and so they develop defenses and allow themselves to think only of certain aspects of their "natures." Through his uncompromising effort to establish a systematic psychoanalytic narrative in these terms, Freud exposed this paradoxical attitude toward his fateful story of human lives.

Freud's other primary narrative structure is based on Newtonian physics as transmitted through the physiological and neuroanatomical laboratories of the nineteenth century. This account presents psychoanalysis as the study of the mind viewed as a machine—in Freud's words, as a mental apparatus. This machine is characterized by inertia; it does not work unless it is moved by force. It works as a closed system; that is, its amount of energy is fixed, with the result that storing or expending energy in one respect decreases the energy available for other operations. Thus on purely quantitative grounds, love of others limits what is available for self-love, and love of the opposite sex limits what is available for love of the same sex. The machine has mechanisms, such as the automatically operating mechanisms of defense and various other checks and balances.

In the beginning, the forces that move the machine are primarily the brute organism's instinctual drives. Here the tale of the mental apparatus borrows from the tale of the brute organism and consequently becomes narratively incoherent: the mechanical mind is now said to behave like a creature with a soul—seeking, reacting, and developing. The tale continues with increasing incoherence.

To sketch this increasing incoherence: in the beginning, the mental apparatus is primitive owing to its lack of structure and differentiated function. Over the course of time, the apparatus develops itself in response to experience and along lines laid down by its inherent nature; it becomes complex, moving on toward an ending in which, through that part of it called the ego, it can set its own aims and take over and desexualize or neutralize energies from the id. At the same time, the ego takes account of the requirements of the id, the superego, external reality, and its own internal structural problems, and it works out compromises and syntheses of remarkable complexity. When nothing untoward happens during this development, the machine functions stably and efficiently; otherwise, it is a defective apparatus, most likely weak in its ego, superego, or both. A defective apparatus cannot perform some of the functions for which it is intended, and it performs some others unreliably, inefficiently, and maladaptively, using up or wastefully discharging precious psychic energy in the process. Its effective operation depends on its mechanisms' success in restricting the influence of the archaic heritage of infancy. This machine is dedicated to preserving its own structure; it guarantees its own continuity by serving as a bulwark against primal chaos, and changes itself only under dire necessity. This mechanistic account accords well with the ideology of the Industrial Revolution. We still tend to view the body in general and the nervous system in particular as marvelous machines, and traditional metapsychologists still ask us to view the mind in the same way.

Both of Freud's primary narrative structures assume the thoroughgoing determinism of evolutionary necessity and of Newtonian forces. No room is left for freedom and responsibility. Those actions that appear to be free and responsible must be worked into the deterministic narrative of the beast, the machine, or the incoherent mingling of the two. Freedom is a myth of conscious thought.

Freud insisted on these two narrative structures as the core of what he called his metapsychology, and he regarded them as indispensable. But, as I said at the outset, Freud can be read in other ways. One can construct a Freud who is a humanistic existentialist, a man of tragic and ironic vision (Schafer, 1970), and one can construct a Freud who is an investigator laying the foundation for a conception of psychoanalysis as an interpretive study of human action (Schafer, 1976, 1978). Although we can derive these alternative readings from statements made explicitly by Freud when, as a man and a clinician, he took distance from his official account, we do not require their authority to execute this project; and these alternative readings are not discredited by quotations from Freud to the opposite effect.

That Freud's beast and machine are indeed narrative structures and are not dictated by the data is shown by the fact that other psychoanalysts have developed their own accounts, each with a more or less different beginning, course, and ending. Melanie Klein, for example, gives an account of the child or adult as being in some stage of recovery from a rageful infantile psychosis at the breast (Klein, 1948; Segal, 1964). Her story starts with a universal yet pathological infantile condition that oscillates between paranoid and melancholic positions. For her, our lives begin in madness, which includes taking in the madness of others, and we continue to be more or less mad though we may be helped by fortuitous circumstances or by analysis. Certain segments of common speech, for example, the metaphors of the witch, the poisonous attitude, and the people who get under your skin or suck out your guts, or the common recognition that we can all be "crazy" under certain circumstances, all support this account that emphasizes unconscious infantile fantasies of persecution, possession, and devastation.

To bypass many other more or less useful narratives that over the years have been proposed in the name of psychoanalysis, we currently have one developed by Heinz Kohut (1971, 1977). Kohut tells of a child driven in almost instinctlike fashion to actualize a cohesive self. The child is more or less hampered or damaged in the process by the empathic failures of caretakers in its intimate environment. Its growth efforts are consequently impeded by reactive and consoling grandiose fantasies, defensive splitting and repression, and affective "disintegration products" that experientially seem to act like Freud's drives or else to take the form of depressive, hypochondriacal, perverse, or addictive symptoms. In truth, however, these pathological signs are, according to Kohut, bits and pieces of the shattered self striving to protect itself, heal itself, and continue its growth. The ending in Kohut's story is for each person a point on a continuum that ranges from a frail, rageful, and poverty-stricken self to one that is healthy, happy, and wise.

For the most part, Kohut remained aware that he was developing a narrative structure. He went so far as to invoke a principle of complementarity, arguing that psychoanalysis needs and can tolerate a second story, namely, Freud's traditional tripartite psychic structure (id, ego, superego). On Kohut's account, this narrative of psychic structure is needed in order to give an adequate account of phases of development subsequent to the achievement, in the early years of life, of a cohesive self or a healthy narcissism. This recourse to an analogy with the complementarity theory of physics fails to dispel the impression one may gain of narrative incoherence. The problem is, however, not fatal: I am inclined to think that complementarity will be dropped from Kohut's account once it becomes clear how to develop the tale of the embattled self into a comprehensive and continuous narrative—or once it becomes professionally acceptable to do so (see also Schafer, 1980a).

My schematization of Freudian narration and of Klein's and Kohut's alternatives can be useful. Schematization, when recognized as such, is not falsification. It can serve as a code for comparative reading in terms of beginnings, practices, and possible endings. It can clarify the sets of conventions that govern the constituting and selective organizing of psychoanalytic data. And in every interesting and useful case, it will help us remain attentive to certain commonsensically important events and experiences, such as the vicissitudes of the development, subjective experience, and estimation of the self or the vicissitudes of the child's struggles with a controlling, frightening, and misunderstood environment. Let us say, then, that some such code prepares us to engage in a systematic psychoanalytic dialogue.

I shall now attempt to portray this psychoanalytic dialogue in terms of two agents, each narrating or telling something to the other in a rule-governed manner. Psychoanalysis as telling and retelling along psychoanalytic lines: this is the theme and form of the present narration. It is, I think, a story worth telling. This introductory section has been my author's preface—if, that is, a preface can be clearly distinguished from the narration that it both foretells and retells.

Narration in the Psychoanalytic Dialogue

We are forever telling stories about ourselves. In telling these self-stories *to others* we may, for most purposes, be said to be performing straightforward narrative actions. In saying that we also tell them *to ourselves*, however, we are enclosing one story within another. This is the story that there is a self to tell something to, a someone else serving as audience who is oneself or one's self. When the stories we tell others about ourselves concern these other selves of ours, when we say, for example, "I am not master of myself," we are again enclosing one story within another. On this view, the self is a telling. From time to time and from person to person, this telling varies in the degree to which it is unified, stable, and acceptable to informed observers as reliable and valid.

Additionally, we are forever telling stories about others. These others, too, may be viewed as figures or other selves constituted by narrative actions. Other people are constructed in the telling about them; more exactly, we narrate others just as we narrate selves. The other person, like the self, is not something one has or encounters as such but an existence one tells. Consequently, telling "others" about "ourselves" is doubly narrative.

Often the stories we tell about ourselves are life historical or autobiographical; we locate them in the past. For example, one might say, "Until I was fifteen, I was proud of my father" or "I had a totally miserable childhood." These histories are present tellings. The same may be said of the histories we attribute to others. We change many aspects of these histories of self and others as we change, for better or worse, the implied or stated questions to which they are the answers. Personal development may be characterized as change in the questions it is urgent or essential to answer. As a project in personal development, personal analysis changes the leading questions that one addresses to the tale of one's life and the lives of important others.

People going through psychoanalysis—analysands—tell the analyst about themselves and others in the past and present. In making interpretations, the analyst retells these stories. In the retelling, certain features are accentuated while others are placed in parentheses; certain features are related to others in new ways or for the first time; some features are developed further, perhaps at great length. This retelling is done along psychoanalytic lines. What constitutes a specifically psychoanalytic retelling is a topic I shall take up later.

The analyst's retellings progressively influence the what and how of the stories told by analysands. The analyst establishes new, though often contested or resisted, questions that amount to regulated narrative possibilities. The end product of this interweaving of texts is a radically new, jointly authored work or way of working. One might say that in the course of analysis, there develops a cluster of more or less coordinated new narrations, each corresponding to periods of intensive analytic work on certain leading questions. Generally, these narrations focus neither on the past, plain and simple, nor on events currently taking place outside the psychoanalytic situation. They focus much more on the place and modification of these tales within the psychoanalytic dialogue. Specifically, the narrations are considered under the aspect of transference and resisting as these are identified and analyzed at different times in relation to different questions. The psychoanalytic dialogue is characterized most of all by its organization in terms of the here and now of the psychoanalytic relationship. It is fundamentally a dialogue concerning the present moment of transference and resisting.

But transference and resisting themselves may be viewed as narrative structures. Like all other narrative structures, they prescribe a point of view from which to tell about the events of analysis in a regulated and therefore coherent fashion. The events themselves are constituted only through one or another systematic account of them. Moreover, the analysis of resisting may be told in terms of transference and vice versa.

In the traditional transference narration, one tells how the analysand is repetitively reliving or reexperiencing the past in the present relationship with the analyst. It is said that there occurs a regression within the transference to the infantile neurosis or neurotic matrix, which then lies exposed to the analyst's view. This is, however, a poor account. It tells of life history as static, archival, linear, reversible, and literally retrievable. Epistemologically, this story is highly problematic. Another and, I suggest, better account tells of change of action along certain lines; it emphasizes new experiencing and new remembering of the past that unconsciously has never become the past. More and more, the alleged past must be experienced consciously as a mutual interpenetration of the past and present, both being viewed in psychoanalytically organized and coordinated terms. If analysis is a matter of moving in a direction, it is a moving forward into new modes of constructing experience. On this account, one must retell the story of regression to the infantile neurosis within the transference; for even though much of its matter may be defined in terms of the present version of the past, the so-called regression is necessarily a progression. Transference, far from being a time machine by which one may travel back to see what one has been made out of, is a clarification of certain constituents of one's present psychoanalytic actions. This clarification is achieved through the circular and coordinated study of past and present.

The technical and experiential construction of personal analyses in the terms of transference and resisting has been found to be therapeutically useful. But now it must be added that viewing psychoanalysis

Narration in the Psychoanalytic Dialogue

as a therapy itself manifests a narrative choice. This choice dictates that the story of the dialogue and the events to which it gives rise be told in terms of a doctor's curing a patient's disease. From the inception of psychoanalysis, professional and ideological factors have favored this kind of account, though there are some signs today that the sickness narrative is on its way to becoming obsolete. Here I want only to emphasize that there are a number of other ways to tell what the two people in the analytic situation are doing. Each of these ways either cultivates and accentuates or neglects and minimizes certain potential features of the analysis; none is exact and comprehensive in every way. For example, psychoanalysis as therapy tells the story from the standpoint of consciousness: consciously, but only consciously, the analysand presents his or her problems as alien interferences with the good life, that is, as symptoms in the making of which he or she has had no hand; or the analyst defines as symptomatic the problems the analyst consciously wishes to emphasize; or both. In many cases, this narrative facilitates undertaking the analysis; at the same time, a price is paid, at least for some time, by this initial and perhaps unavoidable collusion to justify analysis on these highly defensive and conscious grounds of patienthood.

My own attempt to remain noncommittal in this respect by speaking of analyst and analysand rather than therapist and patient is itself inexact in at least three ways. First, it does not take into account the analyst's also being subject to analysis through his or her necessarily continuous scrutiny of countertransferences. Second, during the analysis, the analysand's self is retold as constituted by a large, fragmented, and fluid cast of characters. Not only are aspects of the self seen to incorporate aspects of others, they are also unconsciously imagined as having retained some or all of the essence of these others; that is, the self-constituents are experienced as introjects or incomplete identifications, indeed sometimes as shadowy presences of indeterminate location and origin (Schafer, 1968, chapters 4 and 5). The problematic and incoherent self that is consciously told at the beginning of the analysis is sorted out, so far as possible, into that which has retained otherness to a high degree and that which has not. A similar sorting out of the constituents of others' selves is also accomplished; here the concept of projecting aspects of the self into others plays an important role. The upshot is that what the analysand initially tells as self and others undergoes considerable revision once the initial consciously constructed account has been worked over analytically. A third inexactness in my choice of terminology is that the division into analyst and analysand does not provide for the increasing extent to which the analysand becomes coanalyst of his or her own problems and, in certain respects, those of the analyst, too. The analysand, that is, becomes coauthor of the analysis as he or she becomes a more daring and reliable narrator. Here I touch on yet another topic to take up later, that of the unreliable narrator: this topic takes in analyst as well as analysand, for ideally both of them do change during analysis, if to different degrees, and it leads into questions of how, in the post-positivist scheme of things, we are to understand validity in analytic interpretation.

If we are forever telling stories about ourselves and others and to ourselves and others, it must be added that people do more than tell: like authors, they also show. As there is no hard-and-fast line between telling and showing, either in literary narrative or in psychoanalysis, the competent psychoanalyst deals with telling as a form of showing and with showing as a form of telling. Everything in analysis is both communication and demonstration (cf. Booth, 1961).

Perhaps the simplest instances of analytic showing are those nonverbal behaviors or expressive movements that include bodily rigidity, lateness to or absence from scheduled sessions, and mumbling. The analyst, using whatever he or she already knows or has prepared the way for, interprets these showings and weaves them into one of the narrations of the analysis: for example, "Your lying stiffly on the couch shows that you're identifying yourself with your dead father"; or, "Your mumbling shows how afraid you are to be heard as an independent voice on this subject." Beyond comments of this sort, however, the analyst takes these showings as communications and on this basis may say (and here I expand these improvised interpretations), "You are conveying that you feel like a corpse in relation to me, putting your life into me and playing your dead father in relation to me; you picture me now as yourself confronted by this corpse, impressing on me that I am to feel your grief for you." Or the analyst might say, "By your mumbling you are letting me know how frightened you are to assert your own views to me just in case I might feel as threatened by such presumption as your mother once felt and might retaliate as she did by being scornful and turning her back on you." In these interpretive retellings, the analyst is no longer controlled by the imaginary line between telling and showing.

Acting out as a form of remembering is a good case in point (Freud, 1914a). For example, by anxiously engaging in an affair with an older married man, a young woman in analysis is said to be remembering, through acting out, an infantile oedipal wish to seduce or be sexually loved and impregnated by her father, now represented by the analyst. In one way, this acting out is showing; in another way, it is telling by a displaced showing. Once it has been retold as remembering through acting out, it may serve as a narrative context that facilitates further direct remembering and further understanding of the analytic relationship.

The competent analyst is not lulled by the dramatic rendition of life historical content into hearing this content in a simple, contextless, time-bound manner. Situated in the present, the analyst takes the telling also as a showing, noting, for example, when that content is introduced, for it might be a way of forestalling the emotional experiencing of the immediate transference relationship; noting also how that content is being told, for it might be told flatly, histrionically, in a masochistically self-pitying or a grandiosely triumphant way; noting further the storyline that is being followed and many other narrative features as well. The analyst also attends to cues that the analysand, consciously or unconsciously, may be an unreliable narrator, highlighting the persecutory actions of others and minimizing the analysand's seduction of the persecutor to persecute; slanting the story in order to block out significant periods in his or her life history or to elicit pity or admiration; glossing over, by silence and euphemism, what the analysand fears will cast him or her in an unfavorable light or sometimes in too favorable a light, as when termination of analysis is in the air, and, out of a sense of danger, one feels compelled to tell and show that one is still "a sick patient." All of which is to say that the analyst takes the telling as performance as well as content. The analyst has only tellings and showings to interpret, that is, to retell along psychoanalytic lines.

What does it mean to say "along psychoanalytic lines"? Earlier I mentioned that more than one kind of psychoanalysis is practiced in this world, and so I will just summarize what conforms to my own practice, namely, the storylines that characterize Freudian retellings. The analyst slowly and patiently develops an emphasis on infantile or archaic modes of sexual and aggressive action (action being understood broadly to take in wishing, believing, perceiving, remembering, fantasizing, behaving emotionally, and other such activities that, in traditional theories of action, have been split off from motor action and discussed separately as thought, motivation, and feeling). The analyst wants to study and redescribe all of these activities from the standpoint of such questions as "What is the analysand doing?," "Why now?," "Why in this way?," and "What does this have to do with me and what the analysand fears might develop between us sexually and aggressively?"

Repeatedly the analysand's stories (experiences, memories, symptoms, selves) go through a series of transformations until finally they can be retold not only as sexual and aggressive modes of action but also as defensive measures adopted (within modes of response commonly called anxiety, guilt, shame, and depression) to disguise, displace, deemphasize, compromise, and otherwise refrain from boldly and openly taking the actions in question. The analyst uses multiple points of view (wishful, defensive, moral, ideal, and adaptive) and expects that significant features of the analysand's life can be understood only after employing all of these points of view in working out contextual redescriptions or interpretations of actions. Single constituents are likely to require a complex definition; for example, sexual and aggressive wishing are often simultaneously ascribable to one and the same personal problem or symptom along with moral condemnation of "self" on both grounds.

The Freudian analyst also progressively organizes this retelling around bodily zones, modes, and substances, particularly the mouth, anus, and genitalia; and in conjunction with these zones, the modes of swallowing and spitting out, retaining and expelling, intruding and enclosing, and the concrete conceptions of words, feelings, ideas, and events as food, feces, urine, semen, babies, and so on. All of these constituents are given roles in the infantile drama of family life, a drama that is organized around births, losses, illnesses, abuse and neglect, the parents' real and imagined conflicts and sexuality, gender differences, sibling relations, and so on. It is essential that the infantile drama, thus conceived, be shown to be repetitively introduced by the analysand into the analytic dialogue, however subtly this has been done, and this is what is accomplished in the interpretive retelling of transference and resisting.

Drives, Free Association, Resistance, and Reality Testing

To illustrate and further develop my thesis on narration in the psychoanalytic dialogue, I shall next take up four concepts that are used repeatedly in narrations concerning this dialogue: drives, free association, resistance, and reality testing.

Narration in the Psychoanalytic Dialogue

DRIVES

Drives appear to be incontrovertible facts of human nature. Even the most casual introspection delivers up a picture of the passive self being driven by internal forces. It might therefore seem perfectly justified to distinguish being driven from wishing, in that wishing seems clearly to be a case of personal action. The distinction is, however, untenable. It takes conscious and conventional testimony of drivenness as the last or natural word on the subject; but to take it that way is to ignore the proposition that introspection is itself a form of constructed experience based on a specific narration of mind.

The introspection narrative tells that each person is a container of experience fashioned by an independently operating mind, and that by the use of mental eyes located outside this container, the person may look in and see what is going on (cf. Ryle, 1943). The introspection narrative has been extensively elaborated through a spatial rendering of mental activity, perhaps most of all through the language of internalization and externalization. This spatial language includes: inner world, inwardly, internalize, projection, deep down, levels, layers, and the like (Schafer, 1972; see also chapter 15 herein). Thus the introspector stands outside his or her mind, thinking—with what? A second mind? We have no unassailable answer. The introspection narrative tells us that far from constructing or creating our lives, we witness them. It thereby sets drastic limits on discourse about human activity and responsibility. The uncritical and pervasive use of this narrative form in daily life and in psychological theories shows how appealing it is to disclaim responsibility in this way.

The drive narrative depends on this introspection narrative and so is appealing in the same way. It appeals in other ways as well. As I mentioned earlier, the drive narrative tells the partly moralistic and partly Darwinian-scientific tale that at heart we are all animals, and it sets definite guidelines for all the tales we tell about ourselves and others. By following these guidelines, we fulfill two very important functions, albeit often painfully and irrationally. We simultaneously derogate ourselves (which we do for all kinds of reasons), and we disclaim responsibility for our actions. Because these functions are being served, many people find it difficult to accept the proposition that drive is a narrative structure, that is, an optional way of telling the story of human lives.

Consider, for example, a man regarding a woman lustfully. One might say, "He wishes more than anything else to take her to bed"; or one might say, "His sexual drive is overwhelming and she is its object." The wishing narrative does not preclude the recognition that physiological processes may be correlated with such urgent wishing, though it also leaves room for the fact that this correlation does not always hold. In case the physiological correlates are present, the wishing narrative also provides for the man's noticing these stimuli in the first place, for his having to give meaning to them, for his selecting just that woman, and for his organizing the situation in terms of heterosexual intercourse specifically. From our present point of view, the chief point to emphasize is that the wishing narrative allows one to raise the question, in analytic work as in everyday life, why the subject tells himself that he is passive in relation to a drive rather than that he is a sexual agent, someone who lusts after a specific woman.

A similar case for wishful action may be made in the case of aggression. In one version or theory, aggression is a drive that requires discharge in rages, assaults, vituperation, or something of that sort. In another version, aggression is an activity or mode of action that is given many forms by agents who variously wish to attack, destroy, hurt, or assert and in each case to do so for reasons and in contexts that may be ascertained by an observer. The observer may, of course, be the agent himself or herself.

In the course of analysis, the analysand comes to construct narratives of personal agency ever more readily, independently, convincingly, and securely, particularly in those contexts that have to do with crucially maladaptive experiences of drivenness. The important questions to be answered in the analysis concern personal agency, and the important answers reallocate the attributions of activity and passivity. Passivity also comes into question because, as in the case of unconscious infantile guilt reactions (so-called superego guilt), agency may be ascribed to the self irrationally (for example, blame of the "self" for the accidental death of a parent).

FREE ASSOCIATION

The fundamental rule of psychoanalysis is conveyed through the instruction to associate freely and to hold back nothing that comes to mind. This conception is controlled by the previously mentioned narrative of the introspected mind. One is to tell about thinking and feeling in passive terms; it is to be a tale of the mind's running itself, of thoughts and feelings coming and going, of thoughts and feelings pushed forward by drives or by forces or structures opposing them. Again, the analysand is to be witness to his or her own mind. The psychoanalytic models for this narration are Freud's "mental apparatus" and "brute organism."

If, however, one chooses the narrative option of the analysand as agent, that is, as thinker and constructor of emotional action, the fundamental rule will be understood differently and in a way that accords much better with the analyst's subsequent interpretive activity. According to this second narrative structure, the instruction establishes the following guidelines: "Let's see what you will do if you just tell me everything you think and feel without my giving you any starting point, any direction or plan, any criteria of selection, coherence, or decorum. You are to continue in this way with no formal beginning, no formal middle or development, and no formal ending except as you introduce these narrative devices. And let's see what sense we can make of what you do under these conditions. That is to say, let's see how we can retell it in a way that allows you to understand the origins, meanings, and significance of your present difficulties and to do so in a way that makes change conceivable and attainable."

Once the analysand starts the telling, the analyst listens and interprets in two interrelated ways. First, the analyst retells what is told from the standpoint of its content, that is, its thematic coherence. For example, the analysand may be alluding repeatedly to envious attitudes while consciously portraying these attitudes as disinterested, objective criticism. By introducing the theme of envy, the analyst, from the special point of view on analytic narration, identifies the kind of narrative that is being developed. (Of course, one does not have to be an analyst to recognize envy in disguise; but this only illustrates my point that analytic narration is not sharply set off from refined common sense.) The specific content then becomes merely illustrative of an unrecognized and probably disavowed set of attitudes that are held by the analysand who is shown to be an unreliable narrator in respect to the consciously constructed account. Ultimately, the unreliability itself must be interpreted and woven into the dialogue as an aspect of resisting.

The analysand's narrative, then, is placed in a larger context, its coherence and significance are increased, and its utility for the analytic work is defined. The analyst has not listened in the ordinary way. Serving as an *analytic* reteller, he or she does not, indeed, cannot coherently, respond in the ordinary way. Listening in the ordinary way, as in countertransference, results in analytic incoherence; then the analyst's retellings themselves become unreliable and fashioned too much after the analyst's own "life story."

In the second mode of listening and interpreting, the analyst focuses on the action of telling itself. Telling is treated as an object of description rather than, as the analysand wishes, an indifferent or transparent medium for imparting information or thematic content. The analyst has something to say about the how, when, and why of the telling. For example, the analyst may tell that the analysand has been circling around a disturbing feeling of alienation from the analyst, the narration's circumstantial nature being intended to guarantee an interpersonally remote, emotionally arid session; and if it is envy that is in question, the analyst may tell that the analysand is trying to spoil the analyst's envied competence by presenting an opaque account of the matter at hand.

In this way, the analyst defines the complex rules that the analysand is following in seeming to "free associate" (Schafer, 1978, lecture 2). There are rules of various kinds for alienated discourse, for envious discourse, and so on, some very general and well known to common sense and some very specialized or individual and requiring careful definition in the individual case, but which must still, ultimately, be in accord with common sense. The analyst treats free association as neither free nor associative, for within the strategy of analyzing narrative actions, it is not an unregulated or passive performance.

The analysand consciously experiences many phenomena in the passive mode: unexpected intrusions or unexpected trains of thought, irrelevant or shameful feelings, incoherent changes of subject, blocking and helpless withholdings of thoughts, and imperative revisions of raw content. The analysand consciously regards all of these as unintentional violations of the rules he or she consciously professes to be following or wishes to believe are being followed. But what is to the analysand flawed or helpless performance is not that to the analyst. In analysis, free associating is a no-fault activity. What is consciously unexpected or incomprehensible is seen rather as the analysand's having unconsciously introduced more complex rules to govern the narrative being developed: the analysand may have become uneasy with what is portrayed as the drift of thought and sensed that he or she was heading into danger, or perhaps the tale now being insistently foregrounded is a useful diversion from another and more troubling tale. In the interest of being "a good patient," the analysand may even insist on developing narratives in primitive terms, for instance, in terms of ruthless revenge or infantile sexual practices, when at that moment a more subjectively distressing but analytically useful account of the actions in question would have to be given in terms of assertiveness, or fun-lovingness, or ordinary sentimentality. Whatever the case may be, a new account is called for, a more complex account, one in which the analysand is portrayed as more or less unconsciously taking several parts at once—hero, victim, dodger, and stranger. These parts are not best understood as autonomous subselves having their say ("multiple selves" is itself only a narrative structure that begs the question); rather, each of these parts is one of the regulative narrative structures that one person, the analysand, has adopted and used simultaneously with the others, whether in combination, opposition, or apparent incoherence. The analyst says, in effect, "What I hear you saying is . . ." or "In other words, it's a matter of . . . ," and this is to say that a narrative is now being retold along analytic lines as *the only narrative it makes good enough sense to construct at that time.*

RESISTANCE

Resistance can be retold so as to make it appear in an altogether different light; furthermore, it can be retold in more than one way. Before I show how this is so, I should synopsize Freud's account of resistance (see, for example, Freud, 1912b). For Freud, *"the* resistance," as he called it, is an autonomous force analogous to the censorship in the psychology of dreams. The term refers to the many forms taken by the analysand's opposition to the analyst. The resistance, Freud said, accompanies the analysis every step of the way, and technically nothing is more important than to ferret it out and analyze it. The resistance is often sly, hidden, secretive, obdurate, and so on. In the terms of Freud's theory of psychic structure, there is a split in the analysand's ego; the rational ego wants to go forward while the defensive ego wants to preserve the irrational status quo. The analysand's ego fears change toward health through self-understanding, viewing that course as too dangerous or too mortifying to bear. These accounts of resistance establish narrative structures of several pairs of antagonists in the analytic situation: one part of the ego against another, the ego against the id, the analysand against the analyst, and the analyst against the resistance. The conflict centers on noncompliance with the fundamental rule of free association, a rule that in every case can be observed by the analysand only in a highly irregular and incomplete fashion. Presenting the resistance as a force in the mind, much like a

229

drive, further defines the form of the analytic narration. Resistance is presented as animistic or anthropomorphic, a motivated natural force that the subject experiences passively.

How does the story of resistance get to be retold during an analysis? In one retelling, resistance transforms into an account of transference, both positive and negative. Positive transference is resistance attempting to transform the analysis into some repetitive version of a conflictual infantile love relationship on the basis of which one may legitimately abandon the procedures and goals of analysis itself. In the case of negative transference, the analyst is, for example, seen irrationally and often unconsciously as an authoritarian parent to be defied. Through a series of transformations, and with reference to various clues produced by the analysand, the opposition is retold by the analyst as an enactment of the oral, anal, and phallic struggles of infancy and childhood, that is, as a refusal to be fed or weaned or else as a biting; or as a refusal to defecate in the right place and at the right time, resorting instead to constipated withholding or diarrheic expelling of associations, feelings, and memories; or as furtive masturbation, primal scene voyeurism and exhibitionism, defensive or seductive changes of the self's gender, and so on. Thus the distinction between the analysis of resistance and the analysis of transference, far from being the empirical matter it is usually said to be, is a matter of narrative choice. Told in terms of transference, resistance becomes disclaimed repetitive activity rather than passive experience. And it is as activity that it takes its most intelligible, coherent, and modifiable place in the developing life-historical contexts. Resist*ance* becomes resist*ing*.

There is another, entirely affirmative way to retell the story of resistance. In this account, the analysand is portrayed as doing something on his or her behalf, something that makes sense unconsciously though it may not yet be understood empathically by the analyst. The analyst may then press confrontations and interpretations on the analysand at the wrong time, in the wrong way, and with the wrong content. Kohut's account of narcissistic rage in response to such interventions presents the analysand as protecting a fragile self against further disintegration in response to the analyst's empathically deficient interventions. Or the analysand may be protecting the analyst against his or her own anticipated ruthless, destructive, or at least permanently alienating form of love. Matters of personal pride and honor may be involved. In one instance, the analysand's resisting was understood as

230

Narration in the Psychoanalytic Dialogue

a form of self-abortion and in another instance as a refusal to be forced into what was taken to be a phallic role.

Whatever the case and whatever the manifestly oppositional attitude, the analysand is portrayed as engaged in a project of preservation, even enhancement, of self or analyst or both. The project is one that the analysand at that moment rightly refuses to abandon despite what may be the misguided efforts of the analyst to narrate the analysis along other lines. In this affirmative narration of resisting, the analyst may be an uncomprehending brute or an unwitting saboteur. One young woman's spontaneously defiant insistence on persistently excoriating her parents had to be retold analytically in two main ways: as a turning away from the unbearable horror of her imagined inner world and as a firm assertion on her part that the problem resided in the family as a system and not merely in her infantile fantasies and wishes. On the one hand, there was a crucial strategy of self-prevention implied in her apparent resisting: as she said at one point, "If I let myself appreciate myself and see what, against all odds, I've become, it would break my heart." On the other hand, there was the analysand's search for the self-affirming truth of parental madness. To have thought of her strident analytic activity simply as resisting would have been to start telling the wrong kind of psychoanalytic story about it.

A third way to retell the story of resisting radically questions the analysand's use of ability and inability words. It is developed along the following lines. "Resistance" seems to go against the analysand's wishes and resolutions. The analysand pleads inability: for example, "Something stops me from coming out with it," or "My inhibitions are too strong for me to make the first move," or "I can't associate anything with that dream." The narrative structure of inability in such respects is culturally so well established that it seems to be merely an objective expression of the natural order of things. Yet it may be counted as another aspect of the analysand as unconsciously unreliable narrator. In the first example (not coming out with it), the retelling might be developed along these lines: "You *don't* come out with it, and you *don't* yet understand why you *don't* act on your resolution to do so." In the third example (inability to associate), it might be developed like this: "You *don't* think of anything that seems to you to be relevant or acceptable, anything that meets your rules of coherence, good sense, or good manners, and you dismiss what you *do* think of."

In giving these examples, I am not presenting actual or recommended analytic interventions so much as I am making their logic plain. In practice, these interventions are typically developed in ways that are tactful, tentative, circuitous, and fragmentary. For a long time, perhaps, the "don't" element is only implied in order to limit the analysand's mishearing description as criticism and demand; *exhortation* has no place in the analyst's interventions. Nor am I suggesting that the analyst's initial descriptions are the decisive words on any important subject. They are only the first words on the subject in that they begin to establish the ground rules for another kind of story to be told and so of another kind of experience to construct. These are the rules of action language and the reclaiming of disclaimed action.

Choosing action as the suitable narrative language allows the analyst to begin to retell many inability narrations as disclaimings of action. In order to analyze resistance—now to be designated as resist-*ing*—one must take many narrations presented by analysands in terms of *can* and *can't* and retell them in terms of *do* and *don't* and sometimes *will* and *won't*. Usually, the analysand is disclaiming the action unconsciously. That this is so does not make the disclaiming (defense, resistance) any the less an action; nor does it make what is being disclaimed any the less an action. In analytic narration, one is not governed by the ordinary conventions that link action to conscious intent.

So often, the analyst, after first hearing "I can't tell you" or "I can't think about that," goes on to establish through close and sustained consideration of free associations the reasons why the analysand does not or will not tell or think about whatever it is that is troublesome. It may be that the action in question would be humiliating, frightening, or apparently incoherent and therefore too mad to be tolerated. It may be that unconsciously the not telling or not thinking is an act of anal retention or oedipal defiance that is being presented as innocent helplessness. It may be that an important connection between two events has never before been defined, so that the analysand, lacking a suitable narrative structure, simply does not take up the two in one consciously constructed context; connections and contexts might come into existence only through the analyst's interpretive activity. Interpretation may also give the reasons why the context and connections never have been developed. In all such instances, it is no longer ability that is in question; it is the proper designation of a ruled performance.

The same narrative treatments of action and inaction are common in daily life. One hears, "I couldn't control myself," "I can't concentrate on my studies," "I can't love him," and so on. Implicit in these narrations, as in the resisting narrations, is the disclaiming of the activity in what is being told. This disclaiming is accomplished by taking recourse to the terms of uncontrollable, impersonal forces. These accounts, too, may be retold analytically. For instance, after some analysis, "I can't concentrate on my studies" may become the following (synopsized) narrative: "I don't concentrate on what I resolve to work on. I think of other things instead. I think of girls, of my dead father, of all the failures of my life. These are the things that really matter to me, and I rebel against the idea that I should set them aside and just get through the reading like a machine. It's like shitting on demand. Additionally, by not working, I don't risk experiencing either frightening grandiose feelings if I succeed or the shame of mediocrity if I just pass. On top of which, really getting into the work is sexually exciting; it feels something like sexual peeping to read, as I must, between the lines, and it feels wrong to do that." Retold in this way, "I can't concentrate on my studies" becomes "I don't concentrate for certain reasons, some or all of which I did not dare to realize before now. I told myself I was trying to concentrate and couldn't when actually I was doing other things instead and doing them for other reasons." The narrative has changed from the consciously constructed one of helplessness and failure, designed to protect the consciously distressing status quo, to a narrative of unconsciously designed activity in another kind of reality. The new story, told now by a more reliable narrator, is a story of personal action, and as such it may serve as a basis for change.

Nothing in the immediately preceding account implies that for narrative purposes, *inability* words or, for that matter, *necessity* words are narratively ruled totally out of the analytic court. Rather, these words are now found to be useful and appropriate in far more restricted sets of circumstances than before. These sets of circumstances include unusual physical and mental ability and training and also one's inevitable confrontations with the forceful independent actions of others and with impersonal events in the world. Yet even these necessities become analytically relevant only in terms of how the analysand takes them. In any case, necessity (or happening) does not include mental forces and structures that reduce a person to impotence; much impotence is enacted rather than imposed (Schafer, 1978, lecture 5).

Thus the analyst may retell resisting to the analysand in two ways, as what the analysand *is not doing* and why and as what he or she *is doing* and why. It is a matter simply of how best to retell the actions in question. Both versions are technically useful in the analysis of resisting. Neither depends on a narration composed in terms of autonomous and antagonistic natural forces that are thwarting conscious and wholehearted resolve. Both may be encompassed in a narrative of action. In sharp disagreement with Ricouer (1977), I would assert that there is nothing in the analysis of resisting that necessarily leads beyond this narrative framework into the one structured in terms of psychic forces or other processes of desymbolization or dehumanization.[1]

REALITY TESTING

Traditionally, the official psychoanalytic conception of reality has been straightforwardly positivistic. Reality is "out there" or "in there" in the inner world, existing as a knowable, certifiable essence. At least for the analytic observer, the subject and object are clearly distinct. Reality is encountered and recognized innocently. In part it simply forces itself on one, in part it is discovered or uncovered by search and reason free of theory. Consequently, reality testing amounts simply to undertaking to establish what is, on the one hand, real, true, objective and, on the other hand, unreal, false, subjective. On this understanding, one may conclude, for example, that x is fantasy (psychical reality) and y is fact (external reality); that mother was not only loving as had always been thought but also hateful; that the situation is serious but not hopeless or vice versa; and so on.

But this positivistic telling is only one way of giving or arriving at an account of the subject in the world, and it is incoherent with respect to the epistemological assumptions inherent in psychoanalytic inquiry, that is, those assumptions that limit us always to dealing only with *versions* of reality. The account I am recommending necessarily limits one to constructing some version or some vision of the subject in the world. One defines situations and invests events with multiple meanings. These meanings are more or less adequately responsive to different questions that the narrator, who may be the subject or some-

---

1. Juergen Habermas, working within a purely hermeneutic orientation, has taken what is, from the present point of view, an intermediate position on this matter in his discussion of the contents of the unconscious as deformed, privatized, degrammaticized language. See his *Knowledge and Human Interests* (1971, chapters 10–12). My discussion owes much to Habermas's penetrating analysis of the linguistic and narrative aspects of psychoanalytic interpretation.

one else, wants to answer; they are also responsive to the rules of context that the narrator intends to follow and to the level of abstraction that he or she wishes to maintain. Sometimes, for example, an assertive action of a certain kind in a certain situation may with equal warrant be described as sadistic *and* masochistic, regressive *and* adaptive. In this account, reality is always mediated by narration. Far from being innocently encountered or discovered, it is created in a regulated fashion.

The rules regulating the creation of reality may be conventional, in which case no questions are likely to be raised about the world and how we know it; if needed, consensual validation will be readily obtained. But things can be otherwise. Once certain rules are defined, they may prove to violate convention in a way that is incoherent or at least not understandable at a given moment. In this case, the place of these rules requires further investigation and interpretation. Those rules that inform truly original ideas may necessitate revision of accepted ideas about the rules that "must" be followed and the kind of reality that it is desirable or interesting to construct. Freud showed his genius by developing his highly particularized "overdetermined" accounts of the idiosyncratic systems of rules followed in dreams, neuroses, perversions, psychoses, and normal sexual development.

One may say that *psychoanalytic interpretation tells about a second reality*. In this reality, events or phenomena are viewed from the standpoint of repetitive re-creation of infantile, family-centered situations bearing on sex, aggression, and other such matters. Only superficially does the analytic construction of this second reality seem to be crudely reductive; it is crudely reductive only when it is performed presumptuously or stupidly, as when the analyst says, "This is what you are *really* doing." The competent analyst says in effect, "Let me show you over the course of the analysis another reality, commonsensical elements of which are already, though incoherently and eclectically, included in what you now call reality. We shall be looking at you and others in your life, past and present, in a special light, and we shall come to understand our analytic project and our relationship in this light, too. This second reality is as real as any other. In many ways it is more coherent and inclusive and more open to your activity than the reality you now vouch for and try to make do with. On this basis, it also makes the possibility of change clearer and more or less realizable, and so it may open for you a way out of your present difficulties."

From the acceptance of this new account, there follows a systematic project of constructing a psychoanalytic reality in which one retells the past and the present, the infantile and the adult, the imagined and the so-called real, and the analytic relationship and all other significant relationships. One retells all this in terms that are increasingly focused and coordinated in psychoanalytic terms of action. One achieves a narrative redescription of reality. This retelling is adapted to the clinical context and relationship, the purpose of which is to understand anew the life and the problems in question. The analysand joins in the retelling (redescribing, reinterpreting, recontextualizing, and reducing) as the analysis progresses. The second reality becomes a joint enterprise and a joint experience. And if anyone emerges as a crude reductionist it is the analysand, viewed now as having unconsciously reduced too many events simply to infantile sexual and aggressive narratives.

At this point we may return once more to the question of the unreliable narrator, for it bears on the large question of validity of interpretation. To speak of the unreliable narrator, one must have some conception of a reliable narrator, that is, of validity; and yet the trend of my argument suggests that there is no single definitive account to be achieved. Validity, it seems, can only be achieved within a system that is viewed as such and that appears, after careful consideration, to have the virtues of coherence, consistency, comprehensiveness, and common sense. This is the system that establishes the second reality in psychoanalysis. The analysand is helped to become a reliable narrator in this second reality which is centered on transference and resisting. A point of view is maintained and employed that both establishes a maximum of reliability and intelligibility of the kind required and confirms, hermeneutically, that achievement. The increased possibility of change, of new and beneficial action in the world, is an essential aim of this project and an important criterion of its progress. It must be added at once that the appropriate conception of change excludes randomness or personally ahistorical or discontinuous consequences, such as abrupt and total reversals of values and behavior. The reallocation of activity and passivity is another important aim and criterion. Finally, the analytic accounts achieved may be judged more or less valid by their ability to withstand further tough and searching questions about the story that has now been told and retold from many different, psychologically noncontradictory though often conflictual perspectives and in relation to considerable evidence constituted and gathered up within the analytic dialogue.

Narration in the Psychoanalytic Dialogue

The Normative Life History

Psychoanalytic researchers have always aimed to develop a normative, continuous psychoanalytic life history that begins with day one, to be used by the psychoanalyst as a guide for participating in the analytic dialogue. Freud set this pattern by laying out the psychosexual stages and defining the instinctual vicissitudes, the stage of narcissism, phase-specific orientations and conflicts (oral, anal, etc.), the origins and consolidation of the ego and superego, and other such developmental periods, problems, and achievements. Yet it is safe to say that in the main, his life histories take shape around the time of the Oedipus complex, that is, the time between the ages of two and five. In his account, earlier times remain shadowy prehistory or surmised constitutional influences, not too accessible to subjective experience or verification.

Today the field of psychoanalysis is dominated by competing theories about these earlier, shadowy phases of mental development. These now include the phase of autism, symbiosis, and separation-individuation; the phase of basic trust and mistrust; the phase of pure narcissism, in which there are no objects which are not primarily part of the self; the mirror phase; and variations on the Kleinian paranoid-schizoid and depressive phases or "positions" of infancy. For the most part, these phases are defined and detailed by what are called constructions or reconstructions, that is, surmises based on memories, symbolic readings, and subjective phenomena encountered in the analysis of adults, though some direct observation of children has also been employed. These surmises concern the nature of the beginning of subjective experience and the formative impact of the environment on that experience, an impact which is estimated variously by different theorists. In all, a concerted attempt is being made to go back so far in the individual's subjective history as to eliminate its prehistory altogether.

These projects are, for the most part, conceived and presented as fact-finding. On the assumption that there is no other way to understand the present, it is considered essential to determine what in fact it was like way back when. Whatever its internal differences, this entire program is held to have heuristic as well as therapeutic value. It is not my present intention to dispute this claim. I do, however, think that from a methodological standpoint this program has been incorrectly conceived.

The claim that these normative life historical projects are simply fact-finding expeditions is, as I argued earlier, highly problematic. At the very outset, each such expedition is prepared for what is to be found: it has its maps and compasses, its conceptual supplies, and its probable destination. This preparedness (which contradicts the empiricists' pretensions of innocence) amounts to a narrative plan, form, or set of rules. The sequential life historical narration that is then developed is no more than a second-order retelling of clinical analysis. But this retelling confusingly deletes reference to the history of the analytic dialogue. It treats that dialogue as though—to change my metaphor—it is merely the shovel used to dig up history and so is of no account, except perhaps in manuals on the technique of digging up true chronologies. The theorists have therefore committed themselves to the narrative form of the case history, which is a simplified form of traditional biography.

Is there a narrative form that is methodologically more adequate to the psychoanalytic occasion? I believe there is. It is a story that begins in the middle, which is the present: the beginning is the beginning of the analysis. The present is not the autobiographical present, which at the outset comprises what are called the analysand's presenting problems or initial complaints together with some present account of the past; the reliability and usefulness of both of these constituents of the autobiographical present remain to be determined during the analysis. Once the analysis is under way, the autobiographical present is found to be no clear point in time at all. One does not even know how properly to conceive that present; more and more it seems to be both a repetitive, crisis-perpetuating misremembering of the past and a way of living defensively with respect to a future which is, in the most disruptive way, imagined fearfully and irrationally on the model of the past.

It soon becomes evident that, interpretively, one is working in a temporal circle. One works backward from what is told about the autobiographical present in order to define, refine, correct, organize, and complete an analytically coherent and useful account of the past, and one works forward from various tellings of the past to constitute that present and that anticipated future which are most important to explain. Under the provisional and dubious assumption that past, present, and future are separable, each segment of time is used to set up a series of questions about the others and to answer the questions addressed to it by the others. And all of these accounts keep changing as the analytic dialogue continues. Freud's major case studies follow this

Narration in the Psychoanalytic Dialogue

narrative form. His report on the Rat Man (1909b) is a good case in point; one has only to compare his notes on the case with his official report on it to see what different tales he told and could have told about this man, that is, *about his work with this man.*

I said that the analytic life history is a second-order history. The first-order history is that of the analytic dialogue. This history is more like a set of histories that have been told from multiple perspectives over the course of the analysis and that do not actually lend themselves to one seamless retelling; I shall refer to it as one history, nevertheless, inasmuch as analysts typically present it in that way. This history is situated in the present; it is always and necessarily a present account of the meanings and uses of the dialogue to date or, in other words, of transference and resisting. The account of the origins and transformations of the life being studied is shaped, extended, and limited by what it is narratively necessary to emphasize and to assume in order to explain the turns in this dialogue. The analysand's stories of early childhood, adolescence, and other critical periods of life get to be retold in a way that both summarizes and justifies what the analyst requires in order to do the kind of psychoanalytic work that is being done.

The primary narrative problem of the analyst is, then, not how to tell a normative chronological life history; rather, it is how to tell the several histories of each analysis. From this vantage point, the event with which to start the model analytic narration is not the first occasion of thought—Freud's wish-fulfilling hallucination of the absent breast; instead, one should start from a narrative account of the psychoanalyst's retelling of something told by an analysand and the analysand's response to that narrative transformation. In the narration of this moment of dialogue lies the structure of the analytic past, present, and future. It is from this beginning that the accounts of early infantile development are constructed. Those traditional developmental accounts, over which analysts have labored so hard, may now be seen in a new light: less as positivistic sets of factual findings about mental development and more as hermeneutically filled-in narrative structures. The narrative structures that have been adopted control the telling of the events of the analysis, including the many tellings and retellings of the analysand's life history. The time is always present. The event is always an ongoing dialogue.

15

Action and Narration in Psychoanalysis

Introduction

Psychoanalysts may be described as people who listen to the narrations of analysands and help them to transform these narrations into others that are more complete, coherent, convincing, and adaptively useful than those they have been accustomed to constructing. I emphasize that analysts *may* be described in this way, for they have been described in other ways, most notably, of course, by Freud, who described them or what they do in several other ways.

Today, however, there are many kinds of clinical work that are called psychoanalysis. Each kind satisfies one or another understanding of what it takes to meet the criteria of analyzing transference and resisting (in keeping with Freud's fundamental propositions in this respect). I shall be speaking of the modern Freudian analyst. But let me caution at the outset that there is considerable dispute among those who do their work under this banner as to what is modern, what is Freudian, and what is analysis. Notwithstanding these disputes, most of these analysts would agree that the work of today's clinician is different in some crucial respects from the picture of the work Freud presented or implied in his writings; they would also agree that critical examination of Freud's texts *alone*, such as that done by some of the French writers, however valuable it may prove to be, is arbitrarily ahistorical. Not only must one take into account advances beyond Freud in method, principles of interpretation, and general theory; one must also take into account that Freud has been shown to have presented many of his ideas and findings ambiguously and in some self-contradiction, and also to have misconceived crucial aspects of the discipline he founded. His major misconception was that psychoanalysis is a new natural science. On this basis, he would have rejected or at

240

least criticized as incomplete or pretheoretical my description of psychoanalysts as retellers of narrations. Consequently, when I refer in what follows to what Freud *demonstrated*, I shall be referring to my preferred modification and correction of his views on the matter. My version, in turn, takes into account the views of many analysts other than Freud, though in the interest of brevity I shall not develop a review of this literature.

In proceeding with this degree of independence, I am being no more presumptuous than a literary critic who dares to say what this or that poet or novelist was doing in a piece of writing, when this reading of the piece conflicts with the author's own explanations. It is not, after all, primarily the merit of the piece itself that is then in question; rather, it is the adequacy of the author's view of the piece, and to varying degrees that view may be incomplete if not confused or wrong. In principle, and without questioning Freud's genius as an interpreter of human action, anyone can claim to know better than Freud what the best conception of psychoanalysis is. More exactly, it would be a question of the best conception of psychoanalysis *for one or another purpose.*

Unfortunately, it has been traditional in Freudian scholarship to show that Freud knew it all or anticipated it all; at least it has been customary to invoke his authority about what psychoanalysis is or should be. For this reason, the remarkably innovative contributions of analysts as different as Melanie Klein, Heinz Hartmann, and Heinz Kohut can be shown to have been obscured and even diminished by their overconcern with the question of fidelity to Freud's judgments about his innovative precepts and practices. None of the foregoing implies, however, that Freud on Freud should not be listened to carefully. His conceptions, while not altogether privileged, retain considerable authority, and much of what follows stems directly from his writings. If it sounds at this point as though I am talking out of both sides of my mouth, it is because many issues remain to be defined, not to say decided, and so it is wise not to be absolute about these matters.

The Analysand's Disclaiming of Action

In my recent publications (1976, 1978), I have identified many of the locutions analysands use to disclaim their own actions. Examples are: "The impulse overwhelmed me" and "The thought of you slipped away." I have emphasized particularly the defensive or resistant value of disclaiming. What is being defensively disclaimed is the personal agency that would be plain if the analysand were to say instead: "I did the very thing that I consciously and urgently did not want to do" and "Unexpectedly, I stopped thinking of you." By attributing agency to impulses and thoughts rather than to oneself, the analysand disavows responsibility. Thereby the analysand attempts to preclude the experiencing of his or her actions in an anxious, guilty, ashamed, or otherwise disturbing manner. Through such disclaiming, one simply appears as the victim or witness of happenings whose origins and explanations lie entirely outside one's own sphere of influence—outside the "self," as some would say.

In using disclaimers, the analysand is constructing experience in a way that is different from acknowledging personal agency. Accordingly, any spontaneous restatement in action terms changes the mode of constructing experience. The two types of statement are not synonymous. The analysand's switching to action language, when it is not merely compliant, transforms experience rather than translates or paraphrases it.

I have also emphasized the rich store of disclaiming locutions in our common language. We learn to disclaim in learning to speak and think, which is to say in learning how to live in a human fashion. The art of disclaiming is a basic lesson in our socialization. This resource is useful in regulating emotional difficulties. As a rule, for example, it is more comfortable to say, "I couldn't get away from my thoughts of him" than it is to say, "I continued to think of him no matter how much I resolved to stop doing so," and the difference between the two is that in the former, disclaimed version, one is narrating thoughts as pursuing a single-minded, even if harried, self, whereas in the latter, action version, one is narrating that one has been performing contradictory actions and does not understand why one has been doing so. Ordinarily, it is the second narrative that is by far the more burdensome or threatening in that it throws into question one's ability to regulate and understand one's own conduct.

To continue with my review, I have emphasized that the origin of many of the disclaimers we use is to be found partly in the infantile "bodily ego" (Freud, 1923) or sensorimotor antecedents of thinking in words (Werner and Kaplan, 1963). What distinguishes this infantile mode is its concretized and animistic rendition of psychological activity, according to which it consists of the movements of substances and energies through physical space. "I don't know what's gotten into me" is one of the locutions that indicates the formative influence of the "bodily ego" on our ordinary notions of mind, personality, motivation, and action. As body-centered beings, we corporealize our mental actions from the first; the learning of ordinary figurative language facilitates and consolidates this apparently unavoidable way of constructing experience. In this connection Freud (1925b) referred to "spitting out" as the infantile prototype of negative judgments.

Among the instances of this corporealization that deserve special attention are the so-called mechanisms of defense (Schafer, 1968b). Each of these defensive actions has one or more bodily referents. For example, Freud (1926) pointed out that the mechanism of isolation commonly refers to preventing objects from touching dangerously. Similarly, projection is commonly taken to refer to physical expulsion of noxious emotion-substances. Another such instance of corporealization is the spatial narrative of mind in terms of internalization and the many variations and correlates of that word, such as inner world, internal objects, and external reality (Schafer, 1972).

Throughout these earlier writings I have indicated that people are fantasizing whenever they disclaim action. That is to say, they are imagining their selves or their minds as spatial entities existing in a split up and split off way. And I have also indicated, in connection with both the psychoanalytic life history and the multiple visions of reality, that it is more illuminating to approach these acts of imagining as narratives or tellings that constitute experience than as reports of some independently constituted, introspectible experience. Introspection— looking within the mind—is itself a spatial account of mental activity; this account is optional rather than mandatory. I want now to go on to show in more detail how disclaiming is a narrative action and how in each case the narrative being composed and the subjective world being constituted may be inferred from the analysand's language and its context.

In order to deal adequately with these topics, however, it will be necessary first to take up briefly the charge of literalism that has been directed against my proposal of action language as a new language for psychoanalysis (Meissner, 1979). It is an important charge in that it raises fundamental questions about what is conveyed by language in general and where the analyst stands in relation to language. According to this charge, as I understand it, in my critical use of action language I am ignoring the fact that people use metaphors knowingly when thinking and speaking, and I am making too much of conventional speech acts. For example, when a man says "I am crushed by this defeat," he knows, so the argument goes, that he is not literally crushed; he is merely using a manner of speaking. But, I would say in response, in one way or another people do act "crushed" when they say genuinely that that's how they feel; otherwise in most cases we would not know how to take their saying so. They slump physically, lower their voices, behave in a listless or dazed manner, etc. Certainly that man would confuse us or would appear to be dissembling or histrionic if, while saying he is crushed, he were to carry himself proudly and speak authoritatively. Suppose that this defeated man were to dream anxiously of a great stone falling on him; or suppose that he were to carry on in a curiously fragmented, uncoordinated way in both his physical and cognitive actions: given the expectable sorts of associations to these phenomena, an analyst might well surmise, as a partial explanation or retelling of them, that the analysand did indeed believe he had been crushed, which is to say that having been crushed was somehow psychically real for him. (In each case it would be desirable to elucidate the significance unconsciously attributed to being "crushed," such as having been punished for wanting to mix into the tangle of bodies in the primal scene.)

The point of my rejoinder, then, is this: the psychoanalytic listener must always listen literally in order to develop specifically psychoanalytic interpretations. Psychoanalysts say that, unconsciously, one always takes things literally, whether one has consciously decided to do so or not; in working as an analyst, however, one decides to do so deliberately. Freud's studies of dreams, free associations, errors, jokes, and symptoms amply established the heuristic benefits of this literalism, this listening as though there could be no purely figurative speech. Divorcing language from the concreteness of "the Unconscious" would be fatal to the psychoanalytic enterprise. At the same time, of course, the analyst must listen to the ordered, communicative, adaptive aspects of figurative language; in other words, he or she must take into account the relative autonomy and conventionalization of this language. There is no contradiction in saying that the analyst simultaneously listens in more than one way.

In the preceding chapter I introduced the concept of a second reality. I said that in the interest of developing specifically psychoanalytic accounts of action and thereby maximizing in this special way the intelligibility of otherwise puzzling or obscure phenomena, the psychoanalyst presupposes that there is a second reality. This is the reality of unconscious mental processes, and it is characterized by modes and contents of a special sort. To speak of this second reality is to restate the basic psychoanalytic assumption systematically set forth by Freud (1915b) in his paper "The Unconscious" and never questioned by him thereafter: that there is a concrete, magical, illogical mode of unconscious activity which plays a part, however variable, in all the ways that people constitute their lives. And to put this point yet another way, the distinction we draw between dream-thinking and thinking while awake is only relative; these two forms of thinking are not mutually exclusive. Described in the psychoanalytic way, we continue in part to dream while awake, so that our waking construction of experience can only be fully understood psychoanalytically by drawing on Freud's (1900) dream psychology.

Consequently, an analyst should welcome rather than reject the charge of literalism, for that charge may be taken as a statement that he or she is remaining psychoanalytic by taking this second reality seriously. In my own case, my attitude is equally welcoming when the charge of literalism is directed against my theoretical critique of Freud's metapsychological concepts. From the standpoint of action language, these concepts implement somatic-mechanistic-anthropomorphic narrative strategies which, far from satisfactorily explaining things psychoanalytically, themselves require psychoanalytic explanation. A structure, a mechanism, a mental apparatus, a discharge of energy, an automatization, or an internalization: these and other such metapsychological terms evidence the importing of blatantly corporealized fantasy content into psychoanalytic theory. Elsewhere I have tried to show how this is so, while at the same time recognizing and appreciating, as others have done, the historical-scientific grounds on which Freud usefully began, more than eighty years ago, to employ these narrative strategies to develop his account of psychoanalysis on the model of the laboratory sciences of his day (Schafer, 1972). In its being relatively demetaphorized, action language is beset by fewer of the problems that beset metapsychology in this regard and so may serve as a desirable systematic alternative to it.

It is not being advocated that action language be the enforced and exclusive or even pervasive language of the clinical dialogue. It would be fatal to clinical exploration and effectiveness to do clinical work in that way. A keen *recognition* of disclaimers is, however, technically useful, especially in analyzing resisting. And no matter what form the clinical dialogue has taken, any account of personal change and insight achieved through psychoanalysis must give a prominent place to an increase in the range and comfort of consciously acknowledged agency and responsibility on the part of the analysand.

Returning now to the fantasizing or narrative actions implicit in disclaiming, I shall first assemble and state one generalized disclaimer and then illustrate it with some of the more or less common locutions that convey and implement it.

The generalized disclaimer is this: *I inhabit a world of autonomously acting mental entities. These entities include thoughts, feelings, desires, attitudes, impulses, prohibitions, and judgments. They act on me or on one another, and these actions take place in me or around me in space. The actions of these entities are more evident at some times than others. They cause my suffering and my gratifications. At best they are only sometimes or partly subject to my influence or control.*

Examples:

I couldn't seem to shake off the sad feeling about my childhood.
The thought of revenge suggests itself.
My anticipation of today didn't let me go to sleep.
The sadistic fantasy came between me and my climax.
The dream stayed with me all day.
The idea of the hopelessness of our relationship washed away the good feeling about you.
The thought of the weekend took over.
Bad feelings about you came up suddenly.
The edge of a doubt began to intrude itself.
I can't escape the feeling that it won't work.

What sort of world is being made in these condensed narratives? Certainly it is very physical and animistic. It is full of surprises, many of them bewildering if not ominous. It is so densely populated that to be alone with one's thoughts is not to be alone at all. In these instances what Hamlet called "the pale cast of thought" does not adequately describe the experience of thinking. The world constructed through disclaiming of action is a hectic, often unmanageable world. This is so even when, as is often the case, the subjective self is portrayed either as a poised master of its fate or as a detached, passive witness of psychological events that are taking place. For whether they are mastered or merely witnessed, the events in question are being presented in ways appropriate to a tightly run ship, a bloody arena, a blooming garden, a fantastic theater, a turbulent or tranquil beach, or a raging battlefield. Viewed as narratives, these locutions do not seem to describe the personal life of a unitary, fully responsible agent.

246

Action and Narration in Psychoanalysis

How different the world seems when the mental actions just cited are being claimed by the analysand rather than disclaimed.

Examples (parallel to those given above):

I continued to review my situation sadly no matter how much I thought I wanted to conceive of it in other ways. (In this version there are no sad feelings to shake off.)

Just now I thought the word *revenge*, and I do not see its relevance to what I've been saying. (Alternatively:) I wish to take revenge! (In either case, there are no autonomous thoughts suggesting themselves.)

I kept on anticipating today so excitedly (apprehensively, eagerly) that I never did relax enough to go to sleep. (Now no independent power is being attributed to anticipations.)

I delayed and attenuated my climax by imagining sadistic situations. (No longer is there a rude intrusion by self-motivating fantasies.)

All day I continued to think about what I had dreamed. (Thoughts that stick or cling are not part of this narrative.)

I was thinking of you affectionately until I realized once again that I could not hope to have a relationship with you. (The account no longer depends on liquefaction of the modes of emotion.)

Once I began to think of the weekend, I thought of nothing else. (Personal authority is not now being usurped by thought-entities.)

Suddenly and surprisingly I do not like you, and I dread saying so directly. (Here buried thought-entities are not erupting.)

I am beginning to doubt the truth of what I just said. (The subject attributes no spatial extension and motion to thoughts.)

I continue to think that it won't work, and I wish I didn't think of it in that dismal way. (The speaker is not now beset by implicitly persecutory feelings.)

These action locutions (presented here only to clarify a narrative alternative and not as a standard to be imposed on the analysand) establish the analysand as a single or unitary and fully responsible, even if conflicted and puzzled, agent. Now the analysand is someone who is acting as a person in a world made up of other people who are also agents. Gone is the populous, animistic "inner world," and gone is the posture of either a commander or a detached, passive, helpless witness of dramatized psychological events. One might say that the analysand is more fully awake; alternatively, one might say that he or she is doing less dreaming while awake or at least is not emphasizing as much as before the dreamlike aspects of psychological activity or the second reality it implies. Now the analysand is not so much harassed by mental life as engaged in clarifying, extending, and communicating the complex, uncertain, distressed, or pleasurable aspects of his or her activity. In one way, not having fragmented and distributed himself or herself in an "inner world" narrative, the person as agent is more alone; in another way, having maintained personal agency, he or she is at least potentially involved in intersubjective or social relationships and communication.

In this connection it should be recalled that Freud (1921) emphasized the neurotic's retreat to fantasy, and that he called the neurotic asocial even if still, unlike the schizophrenic, fundamentally object (person)-related. Disclaimed action is asocial action in Freud's sense. Not that the use of disclaimers should be equated with neurosis; as I said, we all use this language and often use it adaptively. But in functioning neurotically, one is, among other things, likely to be depending excessively or desperately on the defensive use of disclaimers in critical life situations.

In other respects, such as presenting oneself grandiosely or as neurotically guilty, one is depending excessively on irrational *claiming* of action—but that is another whole chapter of psychoanalysis that I shall not review at this time.

Self-Reflexive Narrations

Constructing narratives in psychoanalysis is not limited to inventing or repeating disclaimers and excessive claims of action. It should not be going too far to assert that, for the analyst at least, it is profitable to regard any act of thinking and speaking as an instance of narration and, on the basis of this claim, to propose that one aspect of learning language is learning which tales to use in organizing action (knowing what you are doing) and which tales to tell about actions already performed or else encountered (knowing what one has done or what others are doing). Thereby, one learns not only how to compose and use these tales, but, more fatefully, how to act so as to be able to give a coherent and continuous account of everyone's activities. At least superficially, this account will be comprehensible and useful under one or another set of circumstances. One learns how to construct experience. In this view, language is a set of instructions for narratively constituting events, and the narrative constituting of these events is a uniquely and pervasively human form of action.

As narratives concerning the self make up a large portion of these analytic tales, and as the self figures ever more prominently in clinical and theoretical discourse, it should be useful to analyze further these self-narrations.

248

Action and Narration in Psychoanalysis

To begin with a clinical example: A male analysand is telling of having wanted to flirt with a married female colleague. He adds, "I didn't give in to myself." In this rendition he is giving a two-person narrative account of what, in action terms, could be presented as his having decided on a course of action that he did not altogether want to undertake. In his narrative, one person, with whom he consciously identifies, is insisting that he adhere to certain standards that he has set, while the other person is trying to overcome this opposition by insisting that the flirtatious course of action be undertaken. Although the analysand refers to the second person as "myself," he nevertheless maintains the vantage point of the first person, and he disapproves of this second or other self. In portraying the action as, in effect, going on between two people in opposition to one another, he is engaged in constructing experience on the basis of what some psychoanalysts have called "splitting" of the self-representation.

Another form of narrative splitting, in which disclaiming is still obvious, would go this way: "I overcame the impulse to flirt with her." Other such forms of disclaiming would be, "I controlled myself" and "I resisted the temptation." No splitting would be conveyed in a pure action statement of the following sort: "I wanted to flirt with her very much and was about to do so, but I decided it wouldn't be the right way to act and so I refrained from acting that way—reluctantly."

Of course, we do not ordinarily compose pure action narratives of any length (nor do I imply that we should). Sooner or later we are likely to introduce figurative and disclaiming language into any action-oriented narration; then, for example, we might say, "I told myself it wouldn't be the right way to act," "I made up my mind not to do it," "I wouldn't like myself for it," or, resorting to quantitative figures of speech, "I held off with all my might." But that we do resort to these locutions only shows how much we rely on disclaiming forms of narration. Potentially, one always has the option of employing other narrative modes.

In this respect, Nelson Goodman (1978) has spoken of "ways of worldmaking." The use of reflexive self-narratives is one way of worldmaking. An essential feature of analytic insight is the increasingly limited use of self-narrations of the sort that amount to flagrant disclaimers; at least this use is limited in critical situations, those which may have fateful consequences for the person, that is, the narrator.

There is a large stock of self-reflexive terms in which the person implicitly portrays himself or herself as subject and object simultaneously. In these instances, Freud said, the ego most obviously takes itself as object or perhaps is taken as object by the observing superego. These self-reflexive terms include self-control, self-love, self-hatred, self-indulgence, self-pity, self-searching, and self-destruction. (I discussed some of these at length in *Language and Insight* [1978].) Certainly one may simply take these terms in the way that has become traditional, that is, as representing a form of thought, namely the self-reflexive form; it should be noted, however, that this usage has become traditional only over the past few centuries. Or one may take the logical line that any notion of a self necessarily implies both self as subject and self as object. I am proposing that one may usefully take these terms differently, that is, as condensed narratives. One's warrant for doing so would be that in each instance it is possible to engage in and tell about the activity in question in some other way; for, as I indicated, there are nonreflexive ways in which to portray actions of this sort and thus to construct and communicate experience. One of these ways preceded the narrative language of the self by many centuries. In this way it is visitation by pagan or Christian deities, it is the god of War or Love, the protecting angel or tempting devil who is the other agent in the transaction rather than (or in addition to) the subject-self or the object-self. Except in unusual circumstances, these narrations are no longer widely used by educated persons.

My recommended alternative to the self-narrative approach is the utilization of action language. I recommend it for *theoretical* purposes. This approach is commonly used in an unsystematic or intermittent way in everyday discourse. One says, for example, "I wish I had thought of that" and "I regret my having yelled at him." But in order to clarify further the issues raised in this connection, let us consider one self-reflexive term, self-indulgence, and for the sake of clarity and specificity, let us refer only to the manifest form of self-indulgence usually called overeating. How might one tell of this activity in action terms rather than the reflexive terms of self-narration? One might say, "I ate excessively according to the standards I maintain regarding quantity, and I contemplate what I did regretfully and contemptuously." (The standards being referred to might just as well pertain to expense, occasion, manner of eating, etc., and the contemplating might be done guiltily or anxiously or in some other emotional way; however, as none of these variations of content would affect the form of the narrative, they may be ignored for present purposes.) In this action version of self-indulgence, rather than two selves being at odds with one another or at least interacting with one another, there is a single agent performing and considering certain of his or her actions in different, more or less incompatible ways, which is to say performing them, and perhaps consciously considering them, conflictedly.

By narrating self-indulgence in action language, one will confront the paradox that one is violating the very standards or ideals that he or she is applying at that very moment. What we call standards or ideals may be stated as actions. A standard or ideal refers to an agent's applying a set of criteria to an action; it has no force of its own. A standard or ideal is a way we use to measure performances against criteria of excellence or perfection. Contrary to Freud (1923), the tale of an Ego Ideal or Superego measuring the ego, judging it, and shaming or punishing it, as though it were another forceful person or another person's forceful will—this tale need not be told by a psychoanalyst in his or her theoretical formulations.

Finally, it must be emphasized that, according to the approach being developed here, self-reflexive narratives are not composed only subsequent to actions. Narration covers more than what has already been enacted. The actions come into being in narrative form or at least in narratable form, and that form is almost infinitely changeable. Clinically, the analyst may retell a significant action, such as overeating, in many ways before the analysis is considered reasonably thorough (for example, as nursing greedily, as retreating from heterosexuality, *and* as punishment of self and others).

Talking "about" Something as a Defensive and Controlling Action

If narration constitutes experience, then it, too, must always be regarded as a present action. Conventionally, however, narratives are thought to be "about" some actions or events other than themselves that have already taken place; they are said to refer to something else that is otherwise knowable. Narration has been defined "most minimally as verbal acts consisting of *someone telling someone else that something happened*" (Smith, 1980). For example, one may tell about one's last trip abroad or about a dream or memory. The story of narration is, however, more complex than this.

Analysands often raise the question, "What should I talk about?" or they demand, "Tell me what to talk about," or they announce, "I have nothing to talk about," or they come in with an agenda of "things to talk about," such as the events that took place over the weekend or a dream of the night before.

Talking "about" something may be regarded as a specialized form of telling. It is a present action by which one deliberately and explicitly encourages the listener to expect to hear just a story of some kind. By establishing this narrative atmosphere, one attempts to define and thus also to limit what will be experienced. One is giving instructions, much as authors do in the way they tell a story, if not in their explicit authorial pronouncements. For instance, the analysand may be establishing a detached position as chronicler of events; the analysand may be implicitly flouting the free-association rule; or he or she may be attempting to limit the analyst's attention to some presumably pure content whose only significant context exists outside the consulting room. Unconsciously or preconsciously, however, the analysand may be understood to be making such statements as these: "I am afraid to fall silent and thereby enrage you," "I am afraid to be alone with you," or "I am afraid that I will be shocked and mortified by what I unexpectedly think."

Although for technical reasons the analyst may decide not to intervene in this regard, he or she cannot listen to what is being told purely as story-content. The analyst's highest priority must be to attempt to understand *in a psychoanalytic fashion* the construction and communication of experience in the here and now of the analytic session. To achieve this understanding, the analyst must attend to the analysand's selection and arrangement of what to talk "about," the context and timing of this move in the discourse, the style or manner in which the telling is performed, the past and present subjective situations that may be inferred from this performance, and other such matters. Of course, the allegedly pure story-content may itself be treated as a valuable source of information about the here and now, as when what is being related is taken to be a piece of obvious acting out (the alternative to acknowledged remembering) or when an ostensible memory that just "came to mind" is taken to be a further elaboration of the current phase of the transference (for example, suddenly remembering how intrusive one's mother was just at the point when it seems that one dares not think consciously that this is how the analyst is being experienced).

Further, the analysand's account of what he or she is talking "about" must be regarded as merely one version of the story-content to which reference is being made. There are so many ways in which one can tell "about," say, a tennis match, an escapade, or an argument with one's spouse. Each account presents a more or less different event. There is no one, final, true, all-purpose account of that event. Synonymity exists only under very special circumstances. As an analyst, one wants to redescribe psychoanalytically the point of the specific story-content's having been introduced in the way that it was; in other words, one wants to formulate psychoanalytically the implicit question to which that story-content is an answer, the wishful and defensive course of action of which it is the compromised representative, the doubting it is intended to bring to an end, or the topic it is meant to exclude.

In daily life and for practical purposes, we accept paraphrases as referring to one and the same event; we proceed as though these paraphrases converge on one definitive account of the event in question, that is, as though synonymity is not to be questioned. Minor variations do not matter; we just know what is being told. Although in one's role as analyst one does often follow this practical course of action, too, one does so provisionally, that is, only so long as one detects no indications that the account being given by the analysand should be examined psychoanalytically as an account of a certain sort rather than as a transparent vehicle of the analysand's saying anything at all. The analysand's question, "What shall I talk about?" is an indication that transparency is not to be assumed. This is so because the rule of free association calls only for talking; essentially, it does not recognize talking "about."

In the ideal form of free-associating, one will say, "I think of what happened at work yesterday"; one will not say, "I'm going to talk about what happened at work yesterday," for in this latter case, one may be taken to be conveying a conscious plan, a deliberate selection, an imagined distancing of oneself from the content, and other messages of that sort mentioned earlier in this section. Analysands do not, of course, consistently free-associate in the way I just mentioned, but far from failing as analysands in this respect, they may be taken to be indicating where their problems lie and in what these problems consist. In the psychoanalytic retelling, there is no right and wrong in free-associating. It is in this sense that resisting is not fundamentally unanalytic or antianalytic; it is further material to be interpreted or retold analytically (for example, silence as an enactment of constipation or of triumph over the analyst's confidence, authority, phallus, or breast).

Insofar as telling "about" something deliberately, even if unconsciously, establishes a conventional narrative atmosphere, it tends to put the analyst in the role of audience or archivist and inactivates him or her (or so it is hoped) as analyst. It becomes plain that this is the intended effect when the analyst is made to feel hesitant to interrupt the account before it has been "ended" or when the analysand complains of having been interrupted or insists on getting to "the end" before (if ever) reporting thoughts and feelings that have "come to mind" during the narration. Further, even when the ostensible free-associating has been designed to be an uninterruptible narrative, it is anyway usually interrupted privately by the analysand, who will, for example, think things over while telling his or her tale or will notice but pass over emotional constituents of the telling. The analysand's insisting on going on with the narrative and deleting this allegedly extraneous material in the interest of remaining coherent, consecutive, and complete is, in this respect, usually a defensive action. Strictly speaking, free-associating cannot be said to be interrupted by analyst or analysand, for by definition it has no beginning or end. For the analyst, both the beginning and the ending of free-associating coincide with the beginning and ending of each analytic session.

Mention should be made here of Wittgenstein's (1942, p. 42) comment in this regard: he noted a self-contradiction in Freud's account of the free-association method in that, by definition and contrary to Freud, there is no way to determine the end of a chain of free-associations. I have tried to meet Wittgenstein's criticism elsewhere by putting the question of end points in the perspective of the complex circular and configurational ways in which analysts actually listen to and use the associations (Schafer, 1978, lecture 2).

Analysands do, of course, get to do productive, more or less freely associative work between analytic sessions, and then they may come to their session with analytic material to talk "about." The analyst, however, hears only those accounts of this continuing work that are given in subsequent sessions, and he or she takes them as narratives to be considered as actions that it might be fruitful to analyze further. These supplementary accounts may, for example, be more "revealing" than what was told within previous sessions; they may be presented in a self-effacing or competitive manner or in a way that is intended to prove that the analyst is not needed. None of which is to deny that this self-analytic work may not also advance the analysis appreciably.

As I mentioned, some analysands regularly come to their analytic sessions with an opening topic that they have selected to talk "about." It may be a report of the events of the day, a description of the mood they've been in, a rehearsed dream, etc. One defensive function served by this entrance is to avoid attending to the opening of the session itself—how it felt to come in and rejoin the analyst, how the analyst looked, what would just "come to mind." A similar function is served by silent or conspicuous preparation for the end of the session—for example, choosing not to say certain things because there is not enough time to talk "about" them. Often, entrances and exits of this sort may be viewed usefully as unconsciously contrived enactments. For example, they may be said to enact anal orderliness or omnipotent narcissistic control; for to flounder, blurt out things, or "be sent away abruptly" may signify to the analysand humiliating incontinence as well as angering rejection. Although it is often clinically appropriate to defer confronting the analysand with the apparent significance of this sort of talking or not talking "about," one may always approach it as a controlling action within the transference. Specifically, it may be taken to be a defensive escape from the transference and the as yet consciously unknown "self" who, one fears, might emerge if one were to engage the analyst more directly and spontaneously as a coagent in the here and now of the analysis.

The Second Reality

What has been presented here amounts to a hermeneutic version of psychoanalysis. In this version, psychoanalysis is an interpretive discipline rather than a natural science. It deals in language and equivalents of language. Interpretations are redescriptions or retellings of action along the lines peculiar to psychoanalytic interest. Action can only be named or described from one or another point of view, that is, on the basis of certain presuppositions and in keeping with certain aims. The analyst examines the presuppositions and aims of the analysand's narratives, which is to say, the rules the analysand is following in free-associating or resisting free-associating. But the analyst does not define these rules in a way that is theory-free and method-free. A simple positivistic conception of analytic work is inadequate, for there is no sharp split between subject and object. The facts are what the analyst makes them out to be; they are a function of the specifically psychoanalytic questions that guide this narrational project, and these questions implement the narrative strategies that are favored by the analyst's own presuppositions, however unsystematized these might be.

In saying there is no single knowable reality as a final test of truth, one establishes a basis for characterizing psychoanalysis as a narrative method for constructing a second reality. This second reality is organized largely in the terms of what Freud called unconscious mental processes, which he described as timeless, concrete, magical, tolerant of contradictions, etc. Analysts speak in this regard of psychical reality or unconscious fantasy. But so long as appropriate criteria of description are being applied systematically, this reality is as real as any other reality. Although this second reality sometimes overlaps the ordinary, conscious, rational, or pragmatic reality of everyday life, it need not do so, and in crucial respects it does not do so. In many ways, the second reality of psychoanalysis is more akin to the reality constructed in poetry, story, visual arts, and myth. It both supplements and competes with pragmatic conventionalized reality. Both kinds of reality are constructions. Each construction has its uses.

16
The Imprisoned Analysand

Far more people lead the lives of prisoners than are to be found in all the world's prisons. For anything may serve as a prison. As we learn from that eloquent authority on imprisoning love, Juliet Capulet, even a silk thread will do. A job, a marriage, a tradition, a vow of vengeance, a stain of dishonor, a dream of glory, a promise made or a promise broken, a tense body or a beautiful face, a small town or the whole wide world; every one of them and many more are potential prisons.

Psychoanalysts know that not one of these facts of existence operates in its own right as an imprisoning agency, nor need any one of them be primarily or solely experienced as confining. But unconsciously, people can make them into versions of being imprisoned and then endlessly spin out these versions in fantasy activity and play them out in their modes of relationship. People use these versions to build the stone walls, to dig the dungeons, to heap up the rock piles, and to forge the bars and chains of their imaginings and behavior. The prisons I am speaking of are constructed primarily in that second reality with which psychoanalysis is particularly concerned; that of psychical reality or the world of unconsciously developed meanings. In this world of unrecognized symbols, concretized metaphors, reductive allegories, or repressed storylines of childhood, each of these everyday realities may be repetitively reconstructed or retold as imprisonment. And through acting out by seducing others into the role of captors, this story of life as incarceration may be continuously confirmed.

Being imprisoned does lay down a powerful storyline in that its potential for multiple function and complex meaning is enormous. For example, imprisonment may serve not only to punish the guilty self; it may serve as well to indict the world and to torture the allegedly innocent through implied or stated masochistic incrimination and recrimination. The analyst as jailer is a familiar figure in the psychical reality of transference. And it is not unusual for the analyst to note the analysand's efforts to imprison him or her in the role of jailer—the prisoner can be imprisoning. But more about that later. For the moment what is to be emphasized is how readily one may work persons, places, times, feelings, substances, and the events of every sort into the prisoner's story. And as we know from world literature and drama as well as from the couch, a person can tell that story romantically or melodramatically, ironically or tragically, sometimes even with savagely parodistic or wry comic touches (Schafer, 1970). Each of these narrative modes itself serves multiple functions that call for interpretation at appropriate times.

It is easy to construct this kind of story, for there is nothing significant in a person's life that does not imply or entail some type and degree of limitation. And if one is so inclined—and everyone is at least a little so inclined—he or she may make of any limitation a prison. But it is when the inclination toward being victimized is pronounced that one may tell or retell one's entire past as a prison of some sort—for example, as Devil's Island, an insane asylum, being buried alive, a German concentration camp or POW camp, the world of Orwell's *Nineteen Eighty-Four*, or a smothering mother of early infancy. For example, one analysand who, unconsciously, had been living forever in a concentration camp, saw a successful analysis as culminating not only in the closing of the camp but in his death and the death of his mother, the two of them, in symbiotic union, being at one time or another the camp, the sadistic guards, and the hapless but surviving inmates. Paradoxically, his extermination camp was also a survival camp. It was both a death-in-life and a life-in-death.

Unlike psychoanalysts with their genetic approach, other therapists often tend to take at face value the patient's story of the past as simply some sort of prison with no exit. They do not hear it as a story which, whatever its face validity, also must be retold analytically through genetically oriented interpretation; that is to say, it must be retold in the terms of multiple function as a construction that serves a variety of cross-purposes. These other therapists do not see the story's usefulness for representing the necessity for renunciation, inhibition, defense, punishment, and compromise that enters into everyone's life. With this limited understanding they employ apparently supportive interventions that actually serve to consolidate implicitly paranoid and depressive positions. The wary psychoanalyst works against this unfortunate development.

The Imprisoned Analysand

Being imprisoned is only one of many storylines that get to be told, hinted at, filled in or unfolded, and endlessly varied in the course of any one analysis. Others commonly encountered include the trial, the phoenix, Cinderella, the exile, the odyssey, and the empty self. From among those fluid, fragmentary, elusive narratives, I have chosen that of imprisonment as my model. Not to be too bound by this model, however, I should like first to introduce some of my main points in connection with the odyssey, the journey, or travel in general.

The journey is one of the world's great storylines. This line is followed in *The Odyssey*, *The Canterbury Tales*, *The Divine Comedy*, *The Pilgrim's Progress*, *Gulliver's Travels*, *Ulysses*, and no end of modern thrillers and chillers. Also, when the journey is considered more broadly, it takes in the fateful crossroads of Oedipus Rex and the seducer's garden path; Sisyphus going up and down his existentially absurd hill; Huck Finn and Nigger Jim making their humanistic journey down the river; Hamlet's "to be or not to be" meditation on death and suicide; drug trips and ego trips; and so on and so forth. Alternatively, the journey may describe or allegorically imply, or be implied by, a trip through one's "past" or the development of one's "inner world." This is often the case in autobiographies (Olney, 1980).

We know that in the dreams of analysands all journeys are, among other things, trips through transference country. Analysts, taking account of both the dream's manifest content and the drift of the analysand's associations to it, study variations in the dream journey in order better to understand the analysis itself. Is it solo or are there companions? Who if anyone is driving, piloting, guiding, or blocking the way, and how well is that job being done? Is it up in the air, at sea, in the jungle, or in some dark and ratty basement? Is the route clear of snakes and pits? Has the way been lost? The station passed by? The train missed? Is the destination known? Is there light at the end of the tunnel? Having an array of analytic questions and expectations at our disposal, we know how to set up and to follow these dreamed and associatively elaborated stories of the journey through analysis. In this we show that we are competent storytellers and listeners. We belong to the same narrative community as the analysand.[1] Or, as Arlow put it in continuing the line of thought of Hanns Sachs (1942), we belong to the same daydream community (1969a) on which basis we may "dream along with our patients" (1969b, p. 49).

1. See in this regard Culler (1975) on interpretive competence and Fish (1980) on interpretive community. Cf. Sherwood (1969) and Ricouer (1977) on the narrativity of psychoanalytic life-historical interpretation. See also my essays on the analytic life history (1978b) and multiple life histories (chapter 13 herein).

Our narrative competence seems to stem from three main sources: from the language we have learned since childhood through example, instruction, and stories; from the daydreams we construct throughout our lives; and from our analytic training and experience which prepare us to anticipate, follow, and organize the narrative lines of psychical reality. It is the third of these that makes us specialists in a job that is performed more or less adequately by all analyzable members of the same culture, that is to say, all members of the same narrative community.

In the case of travel stories specifically, there is this additional source of narrative competence: infantile preoccupation with the innumerable and varied comings and goings of people and things, bodily substances, and subjective phenomena. Any one of those may become a prototype for travel (for example, in the child's spool play in "Beyond the Pleasure Principle" [Freud, 1920]). The analyst draws on all of these sources in competently recognizing fragments of travel stories (for example, a bus appears in a dream, or a path, or a traffic signal). The analyst is prepared to find more of this story in other material (for example, the analysand asks to borrow carfare, or takes the wrong exit off the highway to the analytic session, or stumbles on the way to the couch). The analyst is adept at then spinning the story out further. Similarly, the analyst will be alert to metaphors of travel in the analysand's language usage and will regard each such metaphor as an implied or potential storyline based on infantile prototypes.

Such was the case in connection with even so simple a comment as "I don't know where I'm going with this." The comment was made by an analysand who was disconcertedly reflecting on her associations. Once it had been charted by analytic exploration, her implied travel story was one of associating comfortably only when the destination was known, and so only giving the appearance of associating freely while in fact closely following a prearranged and confining agenda or travel plan; and in this strategy she was, as it turned out, preconsciously struggling against an identification with a scattered mother and also unconsciously enacting an abhorred identification with an overcontrolled and overcontrolling father. In a prototypical psychosexual account of her journey through free association that was arrived at later in the analysis, she was in one respect fearing to make an anal mess on the couch, and she was in a second respect indicating that she was a prisoner in her father's tight anus. Here, the analyst could recognize the simultaneous expression of two sides of a conflictual position, for travel and imprisonment coincided in one utterance. In what could be taken as another version of this woman's condensed, conflictual travel and prison stories, she presented herself as a severely trained dog—obedient, clean, protective, loyal, cowering at a harsh word and frisking at a kind one; thus, knowing where she was going in her associations was also being a good dog. A fine example of this aspect of interpretation will be found in Bertram Lewin's (1970) paper on the train ride in Freud's figurative language (see also Shengold, 1966). In that paper, however, as in Sharpe's (1940) classic paper on metaphor, the metaphor tends to be analyzed narrowly: it is taken as a symbol of a specific dynamic issue rather than being taken more broadly as a storyline that is open to varied and extensive elaboration and significance. In contrast, Arlow's papers on unconscious fantasies include some examples of storylines: for example, "Sleeping Beauty" (1969a) and the "pseudo-imbecilic 'detective'" (1969b). And although Arlow did not develop the idea of narration at length, he recognized its importance when he said, "the plot line of the (unconscious) fantasy remains the same although the characters and the situation may vary" (1969b, p. 47n).

The analyst does not expect there to be only one story of travel or confinement, only one binding archetype, only one strict allegorical code. The analyst does, however, encounter sets of told or implied stories which, because they share family resemblances, may be called conflictual narratives of movement in space and time. The analyst's competence in working out, working with, and working through all such narratives is a crucial constituent of his or her general competence in analytic interpretation. The properly selected analytic candidate shows some of this competence from the very beginning of training.

Being alerted now to the presupposition that analyst and analysand share narrative competence and community, even if they do so unequally, let us return to the wretched prisoner who, of course, isn't going anywhere. Even on an imagined death march through the analysis, the prisoner isn't going anywhere. In the prison narrative, time, place, and person stand still. In the timelessness of unconscious mental processes, the imprisoned analysand is always doing time or serving time. A success for the prisoner is at best a temporary reprieve. A break in the analytic schedule is not time lost but time off. Analysis ends not with a cure but a verdict. Those analytic candidates who unconsciously imprison themselves in their Institutes and their analyses are often attempting to do no more than just serve time in this way.

261

Imprisoned analysands develop distinctive versions of the common fear of being emotionally spontaneous. Emotion may drive one out of line and attract the hostile attention of the guard; or, if any emotion at all is permitted, it is limited to what is thought will suit the analyst-guard, though even then that emotion will have to be strictly controlled or, safer still, simulated, not really to please the guard, for the guard is beyond pleasing, but perhaps to lull or pacify him or to soften his next blow. To give voice to an independent thought or to engage confidently in a piece of reality testing are other ways of getting dangerously out of line, for prisoners dare not think or see for themselves; they must play dead. Nor dare they express needs by making requests; for them to ask for a change in the analytic schedule or a tissue is unthinkable. The imprisoned analysand certainly would never venture an interpretation or openly question one made by the analyst, for the guard is capricious, the prison rules of analytic conduct are complex, exacting, and ultimately unfathomable, and the punishment so certain to be severe that some propitiatory self-punishment may be one's only hope of survival. Propitiatory fits of stupidity, apathy, or depression frequently fill the bill. Sometimes, however, the analysand may stage the equivalent of a prison riot.

For the imprisoned analysand, the analyst is that sort of terrifying guard no matter how the analysis is being conducted. Even the analyst's apparent empathic interestedness may be understood as a ruse to get one to step out of line and into trouble, or if not that then it may be understood as an iron-clad directive to play with the guard at being trusting and intimate—or else!

On the basis of his or her narrative competence, the analyst is prepared for variations of this sort on the theme of imprisonment. The particular variations to be encountered in each case cannot be predicted with confidence, and the turns in the plot—the crime, the punishment, the implicit escapes from the confinement of analysis, and so on—may not be recognizable for some time. Nevertheless, the prepared analyst can anticipate that the imagined prison may prove to be shut up tighter than any real prison. And here we touch on what may prove to be one sort of limit on the analyzability of the prisoner fantasy and so of the analysand who has constructed it. As one analysand put it, "If I admit that I've changed for the better, I'll also be admitting that I was bad and don't deserve to be better."

Often enough, however, with interpretive progress in other areas of the analysis—for instance, in the defensively symbiotic aspects of the transference that are not totally pervaded by the prisoner fantasy—the imprisonment may seem to come to an end. One day the analysand says, "The camp has been closed for some time now." These words may announce that an important, beneficial change has been consolidated. But the analyst is well-advised not to be too confident that this is the case, for that which has been desperately fantasized over a lifetime may be "dutifully" rerepressed and a new "good" story may be ingratiatingly substituted for an old "bad" one. We are all familiar with the sad spectacle of compulsory freedom exhibited by certain incompletely analyzed persons. In them we see overidealized spontaneity and sincerity serving as prisons by reversal.

Another instance of false freedom is encountered when it is found analytically that even the greatest geographical mobility and bravado of a young wanderer has been based on a fundamental premise of aloneness. On this account the manifest wanderlust of one woman was interpreted as a version of solitary confinement. Here we have another instance in which travel and imprisonment coincided. If stone walls do not a prison make, neither do no walls establish true or total freedom. If there is escaping from freedom (Fromm, 1941), there is also consciously denying imprisonment. The storyline must be seen as inherently conflictual.

Denial and reversal: These defensive measures cannot be overemphasized in the present context, for there is a sense in which none of us ever does get out of prison. This sense of confinement is available to those who have narrative competence.[2] Great writers have always wrestled with this insight, and their readers, drawing on their own psychical reality, have responded intensely to the literary presentation of the struggle. I suggested earlier that limitation is inherent in being anything at all. To be something is to be different, to remain different reliably enough to be identified as who and what you are, to have an identity in the most general sense of that term. Identity is difference, and difference is limitation. Limitation is also inherent in family and group belongingness, in having any kind of definable past and values, and in undergoing any kind of development one way rather than another. In this respect, difference is cohesive.

But difference is also divisive. Difference entails opposition. Analysts know—it is part of their narrative competence to know—that unconsciously, if not preconsciously or consciously, what is different is dangerous, and what is dangerous is to be attacked. They are prepared

2. And *critical* competence, too; see, for example, Jameson's *The Prison-House of Language* (1972). Erich Fromm's (1941) analysis of the issues with which we are concerned does not do justice to them.

to interpret how active and passive threaten one another; how male and female threaten one another; how old and young threaten one another; how free and imprisoned threaten one another. Of these oppositions the stuff of tragedy is made, in life as in literature, and so the stuff of interpretation as well. The necessity to accept or stand for one identity, one value, one mode of being requires opposition to alternatives. Defensive measures are oppositions of this sort. Even one and the same value may embody such contradiction that it has been called a tragic knot (Scheler, 1954). Truthfulness, for example, may be simultaneously moral, self-affirmative, and self-destructive. I would say that in Hans Loewald's view (1979), the waning of the Oedipus complex is a tragic knot in that at the same time as it is parricidal, it permanently and lovingly instills parental authority in the conduct of one's life.

This tragic knot has also been discussed rather more ironically as the happy prison, for example, not long ago, by the literary scholar Victor Brombert (1973; see also Carnochan, 1977). We have now arrived in our journey at the gates of the happy prison and, as will be immediately evident, we are much closer to the multiple functions and the meaningful prototypes of the prisoner fantasy. But first, what is the happy prison? One version of it is provided by King Lear when, near the end of the play, he and Cordelia have fallen into the hands of Edmund, and he speaks these lines to Cordelia:

> LEAR.　　　　　　　　Come, let's away to prison;
> We two alone will sing like birds i' the cage:
> When thou dost ask me blessing, I'll kneel down,
> And ask of thee forgiveness. So we'll live,
> And pray, and sing, and tell old tales, and laugh
> At gilded butterflies, and hear poor rogues
> Talk of court news; and we'll talk with them too,
> Who loses and who wins; who's in, who's out;
> And take upon 's the mystery of things,
> As if we were God's spies; and we'll wear out,
> In a wall'd prison, packs and sects of great ones
> That ebb and flow by the moon.
> EDMUND.　　　　　　　Take them away.
> LEAR. Upon such sacrifices, my Cordelia,
> The gods themselves throw incense.
>
> —Act V, scene 3

From Brombert's review of the varied appearances of the happy prison in Romantic literature, I select some outstanding features; for example, the prison is a place of safety, a retreat from the unpredictable and traumatic causality of civilization, and a withdrawal from apparently hopeless relationships into onanistic solitude, aloof self-sufficiency, and omnipotent self-possession. Thus, in analysis as in literature, the grandiose aspect of the happy prison may be that of a triumphant crucifixion that validates a latent identification with Christ. The happy prison also stands for potential revolt and escape and so is implicitly hopeful and assertive. These celebrations of imprisonment exist in ironic tension with the everpresent tragic or pathetic sense of imprisonment as loss, defeat, punishment, and the like. Brombert aptly cites Bertram Lewin's (1950) proposition that closed spaces serve as places of safety through their allowing one to be in hiding. Most generally this Romantic narrative of imprisonment implies or states the achievement of secret victory. One might say that the convict has the courage of his conviction. Obviously, the story is laden with ambivalence. All of these ironies or paradoxes may now be carried over into a consideration of the multiple function and significance of the prisoner's story in analysis.

As a general rule, the analyst will see every imprisonment in psychical reality as being unconsciously a version of the happy prison. That is to say, the analyst will see it and retell it as a construction that combines different types and degrees of sensual and hostile gratification, defensive security, guilt-relieving punishment, and perhaps some vestiges of adaptation to what were experienced early in life as traumatizing experiences. The analyst will draw on "multiple function," "overdetermination," "compromise formation," "synthetic function," and other such concepts in order to develop what the noted anthropologist Clifford Geertz (1973) has elaborated in terms of "thick description" (in this, following the lead of the philosopher, Gilbert Ryle), what we analysts have called complete or worked through interpretations, and what I am now presenting in other terms as suitably complex narrative revisions.

As the story of the imprisoned analysand is intermittently encountered and constructed over the course of an analysis, it will be retold by the analyst in the terms of our well-established psychoanalytic variables. These I need not review here. As with dream symbols, however, no one variable or set of variables can be taken for granted in working out this retelling. Analysts should be neither imprisoning by insisting on a fixed line of interpretation, nor imprisoned themselves within one interpretation of the story of imprisonment, for that story figures prominently only in certain cases and then only at certain times and frequently in different ways. The danger is always with us of making

265

of our interpretations the kind of prison known as the Procrustean bed. It may well be, for example, that in a given case the prison story will be most usefully interpreted or retold as, in essence, a superego story, but it need not be developed in that way, and in principle it cannot be developed only in that way. Instead of or in addition to the superego story, imprisonment may be, to mention only a few possibilities, a preoedipal sadomasochistic story or a breast or bowel story. It should therefore be useful at this point to review some of the obvious interpretive possibilities under a number of familiar, conceptually overlapping headings.

Symptomatically, imprisonment may be a cover story for an agoraphobic orientation; that is to say, it may be in large part a flight from the libidinal and aggressive temptations of the world and the primal scene. Alternatively, imprisonment may elaborate a sexually perverse or a hypochondriacal position in relation to actual or imagined defect. And it may stand for an obsessionally isolated, depressively depleted, narcissistically aloof, or paranoiacally persecuted life as a whole. Thus, the prison story may put the analyst on the track of undisclosed or uncrystallized symptoms, character traits, or fantasies.

Within the perspective of the *stages of infantile psychosexuality*, imprisonment may be oral (imprisoned in the breast), anal (in the bowel), or phallic-oedipal (in the vagina or womb, between the parents in sexual "combat," or in one's own castratedness); most likely it will be some combination and permutation of these themes.

With respect to the *type of infantile wish-fulfillment*, imprisonment may be predominantly libidinal or aggressive or more likely, some configuration of these types. This configuration may be in the form of bondage to a love object or identification-figure, homosexual subjugation, repetitively being raped in fantasy, or vengeful or accusatory withdrawal and abandonment. Among the manifest narrative variations on these id themes is the all-purpose one of the overwhelming impulse from which there is no escape. This last theme is one of the most common, consciously developed rationalizations of activity which, with the help of repression or other defense, the analysand does not acknowledge and endorse as personal desire or personally devised compromise.

With this mention of id themes and the previous mention of superego themes, I have touched on the set of designations that may be called *structural* narrative categories. As I mentioned, psychical imprisonment often represents an attempt at complete domination of infantile psychosexuality and aggression by archaic superego morality and the rigid defensiveness which this morality entails. Imprisonment may, however, refer primarily to the arrest (bondage) of certain aspects of early ego development in a symbiotic tie to the mother and the minimal separation-individuation attainable under that condition (Mahler, Pine and Bergman, 1975). Sometimes, that symbiotic tie appears as a haven, a holding environment (Winnicott, 1971) that protects against traumatic impingement and provides one with some sense of having boundaries and privacy; at other times, however, it appears as subjugation by a hostile introject or other primary process presence (Schafer, 1968a). Structurally, therefore, it is not only archaic superego activity that is in question; it is also archaic aspects of id and ego activity. But with respect to superego interpretation, it must be said that, despite all conscious pleas of innocence to the contrary, the imprisoned analysand is also unconsciously acknowledging guilt for wishing to engage in or believing that he or she has engaged in parricidal, incestuous, devouring, soiling, and other such forbidden actions. As Freud never let us forget: unconsciously, the prisoner is after all a real criminal.

I would emphasize that in its most general structural aspect, being imprisoned may be taken to refer to conflictedness itself as a steady state of existence; however, it is not that the psychic structures express themselves through fantasy activity (which would be the reifying way to put the matter); rather it is that structural concepts are among our preferred ways to classify the constituents or implications of fantasy activity.

Continuing now with our survey of multiple function and meanings of the prison story, we should not overlook *activity and passivity*. Manifestly, being imprisoned appears to reverse activity to passivity. Upon further analysis, however, it is likely to prove more useful to view being imprisoned as also intensely active. Among other things, it is likely to involve accusation, omnipotent repudiation of any form of being controlled, and a demonstration that one is successfully walled off from the influence of persecutory authorities. Much of the analysis of this complex and influential storyline will depend on the clarification of the activity it denies and the explanation of this denial.

With regard to *developmental factors* I have not been able to establish specific factors common to the childhoods of severely imprisoned analysands. There might be a documented or constructed history of severe and premature habit-training; of early and severe pain or physical immobilization owing to birth defect or illness; of a sadistic father who enforced overt submission and unconscious identification with

267

the aggressor; of a depressive and symbiotically inclined mother or a psychically fragile, destructible father who had to be protected by the child's adopting a role of weakness; or of emotional deprivation and persecution that promoted the triad of omnipotent fantasy, depressive fixation on feelings of helplessness in meeting grandiose ideals (cf. Bibring, 1953), and convictions of one's own inherent worthlessness and badness. But as no one of these factors has invariably been central in the cases I have studied, and as any one of them has been central in other cases which have not featured imprisonedness, I think it best to leave open the question of origins. It is, however, always worth considering whether the extensive development of the narrative of being imprisoned may be one kind of expression of the "deformation of the ego" that Freud took so seriously in his final review of the limits of analysis (1937a).

Because it is a tenet of our theory of interpretation that all experience is constructed, each analyst must regard his or her own clinical experience as itself being a construction. What follows is an overview of the clinical-technical experience I have constructed in relation to the story of the imprisoned analysand. First of all, to neglect this story or to brush it aside as a mere derivative of basic conflictedness is to risk leaving unanalyzed many factors that make up transference, resisting, and other significant activity; for, as I mentioned, these factors are embodied in storylines, and in that form they are the basis for the relatively more abstract designations of conflictedness that we use to summarize the concrete phenomena. Considering all the ways in which the analysand must unconsciously experience the analytic situation as reproducing life's limitations, it is no surprise that metaphors of incarceration abound in free associations. By neglecting the implied storyline, the analyst runs the danger of ending up either with an analysand—implicitly sullen, masochistic, and castrated—accepting formulaic interpretations and making sterile efforts to corroborate them, or with an analysand—unconsciously rebellious, sadistic, and parricidal—dismissing the interpretations. Most likely, one will end up with an analysand utilizing both of these strategies. It is under these mechanical or impatient and therefore unanalytic conditions that the analysand will be encouraged to go on enacting the prison story in the way he or she produces material and responds to interventions.

With respect to *resisting*, it is especially important to realize that the story of being imprisoned amounts to an insistent paranoid denial of

The Imprisoned Analysand

the analyst's neutrality, and as such it may provide a firm and relief-giving rationale for the analysand's remaining manifestly affectless, immobile, aloof, and justifiably suspicious of every one of the analyst's interventions. Then, the analyst's interventions may be taken as seductive tricks, traps, and cruelty or as undependable or condescending leniency or reprieve. And with respect to the interpretation of *transference* (already much mentioned in this discussion), being imprisoned amounts to reinstating unconsciously and ambivalently every kind of confinement, deprivation, humiliation, and punishment that has been experienced, dreaded, and longed for throughout the analysand's development.

With regard to technical difficulties, however, it is worth spending a little more of our time on the analyst's *countertransference* responses to the imprisoned analysand. The analyst may come to feel that conducting an orderly analysis is imposing on the analysand a regime of bread and water, humiliation, and castrating powerlessness. By an orderly analysis I refer not only to matters of schedule and fees, the use of the couch and free association, judicious abstinence and reliance on words, all of which this kind of analysand takes as strict prison rules. I refer as well and more importantly to the sustained neutrality and open-mindedness that characterize the analytic attitude and that are forever under attack by the analysand. The analyst may be led to want to let the analysand out of jail through extraordinary modifications of technique. But to want to do so is likely to signify only that, irrationally, the analyst has accepted the part of judge or jailer in the analysand's transference story, and in turn the acceptance of that part in the story signifies that the analyst feels unduly imprisoned within the requirements of disciplined technique or basic clinical theory. There exists then imprisonment-in-common, that is, a neurotic identification with the imprisoned analysand. This identification may perhaps be a self-imprisoning remnant of unanalyzed negative transference from the analyst's own personal analysis. When I speak of the analyst's feeling *unduly* imprisoned, it is in recognition of what I mentioned earlier, that in psychical reality any form of constraint, no matter how adaptive or sublimated, has its incarcerative aspects—is a happy prison and in favorable cases, as in the case of our clinical theory, a very happy one!

If this countertransference is more common than we would like to recognize, so is its counterpart, that ever-increasing rigidity of attitude we observe, for example, in punishingly prolonged analytic silences that are retaliatory responses to the analysand's acting out of the pris-

269

oner's hunger strike or of attempted escapes from the analytic prison. Refraining from making timely interpretations of resisting and transference—of, for instance, the fact and meaning of violations of the fundamental rule or of signs of rage or homosexual feeling—may also be imprisoning and thereby conducive to further and futile strikes and escapes. Through rigidity or through being dilatory, the analyst may indeed put the analysand into solitary confinement and thus be joining in the prison story rather than analyzing it. In this case, too, there is a version of imprisonment-in-common. It may require some delicate and patient judgment, perhaps preferably with the help of a consultant, in order to decide whether or to what extent it is first of all the analyst rather than the analysand who is in need of some parole through insight.

Although there is no guaranteed way to modify the story of imprisonment so as to open up the analysis to new and more beneficial perspectives, the most promising way to start is to trace and fill in many of the story's endless variations. Thereby one may hope to reduce the isolation of its elements that culminates in affect-blocking, relationship-blocking, and overt activity-blocking. For in making that integrative effort the analyst may be able to define the ground on which the analysand will take a stand in defense of the storyline and at the same time begin consciously to experience its harshness, its rewards, and its terrible poignancy. At this point the analysand will emerge as someone who has a stake in sticking to the storyline. The tale will be seen and felt more clearly to be an old strategy that has been used to construct emotionally charged experience of certain kinds and to block experience of any other kind; it will be exposed as a species of unconsciously gratifying and protective self-fulfilling prophecy.

For the analysand, the stake in this story is indeed high, for any and all of the danger situations Freud (1926) outlined may be involved in it. In this light, imprisonment appears as a form of protective custody or preventive detention. In analysis, the analysand retreats into deprivation, humiliation, asceticism, and self-castration. As a prisoner, he or she remains a child, does not have to grow up to face the problems of renunciation, separation, gender identity, oedipal rivalry, social assertiveness, the end of infantile omnipotence, and death. The prisoner insists on his or her helplessness, hopelessness, and apathy, meanwhile continuing unconsciously to construct beating fantasies and biting fantasies and soiling fantasies. More than construct these fantasies, the analysand constructs actual situations which, psychically, verify and justify imprisonment; this may be done by consistently provoking the domineering and brutalizing tendencies of others. These tendencies are part of what the analysand hopes to provoke in the analyst.

In the role of prisoner, the analysand need not confront explicitly the limits on control, perfection, self-sufficiency, and blamelessness. These are limits that are essential aspects of any socialized or object-related existence and mature love. Implied in the prisoner's conviction that, really, the analytic verdict—Guilty as charged!—is already in, is an unconscious refusal to acknowledge parental law and care in the form of ego and superego identifications; one denies both that one is reliving a past and that that past can be reexamined and revised in order to shape a better future. In these denials we witness a refusal of life history and self-reflexiveness.

What point can there be then in being in analysis? The analysand's negative answer to this question—No point at all!—steadily corrodes, erodes, and compromises the always vulnerable rational objective of getting better through analysis. Against this self-limiting and analytically self-defeating strategy, the analyst's interventions may be powerless, and an analytic stalemate may be the result. Consequently the analyst cannot give too much thought to the well-developed imprisonment story or some equivalently stultifying or nullifying story.

Not that the analytic work is to be confined to tracing the storylines of fantasy activity. To stop there would be to settle for incomplete interpretation and thereby to facilitate the development of substitute forms of neurosis, perversion, or whatever. This undesirable development would take place along the lines described by Glover (1931) in his essay on the therapeutic effects of inexact interpretation. The analyst must go on to take each storyline as a derivative or compromise formation which itself requires further analysis. But as well as its being itself open to interpretation as a derivative or compromise formation, a storyline is an indispensible means of producing, integrating, and reinforcing derivatives and compromises. What we call a derivative or compromise comes into being in the terms of, and by virtue of, a narrative strategy. The analysand uses the storyline to develop ever new opportunities for repeating and perpetuating unconsciously maintained infantile psychosexual dilemmas and dangers. And these prototypes are themselves narrativized, so that *the progression in interpretation is toward ever more archaic storylines or fantasies.*

If it is accepted that every important psychoanalytic variable is inherently narrativized, it follows that our working conceptions of termination of analysis should be related to the interpretive storylines that have guided the analytic work. Thus, the analyst must give thought to how, in order to be consistent in interpretation, he or she should envisage termination in relation to the guiding stories of the analysis. With respect to the prisoner's story, termination should not be just getting out of prison or out of solitary confinement, although these themes may be developed during the termination period and give it a particular shape. Nor ideally should termination just be based on the analysand's settling for a prison that is happy only within narrow limits or declaring that the prison no longer exists, although these turns in the story may also figure in the work of termination. What is perhaps most important and realistic is that the following three criteria be met more or less. The analysand no longer shows a predominant reliance on repeating and acting out the prison story, especially when under stress or in critical life situations; the analysand's sense of life, of his or her adaptive regulation of action, can be shown and told to the analyst spontaneously, unanxiously, and convincingly in terms other than those of imprisonment—for example, in not repetitively victimizing oneself by bringing out the worst in others, and in not taking actual abuse by others as conclusive evidence of what after all life is really about; and finally, these changes can be demonstrated to the analyst without the analysand's denying the old appeal of the prison story itself and without the analysand's ignoring the ways in which that story, however much it may have been discredited, will continue to figure in psychical reality as a subordinate tale. The tale itself must be regarded as an inevitable residue of analysis; this persistence follows from both the analysand's previous investment in the storyline and the amount of constraint required to live effectively in civilization. Briefly, the imprisonment story will no longer be used by the analysand to block more adaptive alternatives and yet will not be altogether dismissed through the adoption of a manic posture of untrammeled freedom and sincerity. This, I think, is as Freud would wish in these cases. The acid test of this change will be the extent to which, and the consistency with which, the analysand gets to want the analysis to be just that—an analysis.

The topic of termination brings us to the final section of this account of the narrative strategies inherent in psychoanalytic interpretation. I want to end by returning to Freud. ("Back to Freud!" as we are fond of saying.) I do so in order to clarify some points in our theory of interpretation. But it is central to my thesis to recognize that one can only get back to Freud by following one or another route. That is to say, when one goes back to Freud, one necessarily engages in a reading of Freud that tends to conform to the account of Freud's work that one is already committed to elaborating, at least preconsciously. At the present stage of the development of psychoanalysis, we are aware as never before that the reader is always engaged in a selective, specialized approach to Freud. This specialization is required not only because Freud's restless genius led him to present his ideas in many different and not always coordinated ways; it is required also because any reading of Freud's texts, as of all texts, is necessarily an interpretive reading and so is also a retelling of Freud for one or another purpose.[3]

On this account no one of us may rightly claim to have achieved *the* definitive reading, an authorization for our work that is now and will forever remain beyond question or revision. We deal only in competing accounts of Freud. There are, however, limits of credibility, coherence, and usefulness on these alternative versions. Even though these limits are not altogether beyond dispute, it is, I think, safe to say that one cannot persuasively retell Freud in any way at all. At a given time and for a given purpose, one reading of Freud may be far more exact and authoritative than another. It is just that each reading will have to be assessed as to its consistency within the Freudian tradition, its limits, its heuristic potential, and the new gaps, errors, and contradictions which it substitutes for the old. As these remarks merely summarize the history of Freudian scholarship, they are devoid of radical implications.

In another phase of my theoretical endeavors, the yield of which I have used here as the foundation for the present chapter, I tried to show that what I call action language has always been the native tongue of clinical psychoanalysis (1976, 1978). In that project I was engaged in a specialized reading of Freud and of those who have followed in his footsteps. I claimed to find much in these writings to support this reading, and I went on to try in various ways to show how this reading is consistent with and illuminates the traditional practice of psychoanalysis. Regarded by some as a departure from Freud, it has been for me and for some others a return to Freud with fresh eyes. But like every other return, it is a specialized project.

On this understanding, let us consider a few discussions in which Freud may be said to have more or less recognized the narrativity of psychoanalytic interpretation.

Without slighting earlier work, such as his essay on the family romance (1909c), I would suggest that it was not until his essay, "Some

3. Thus, for example, Schneiderman (1980) presents a set of Lacanian essays under the title *Returning to Freud*.

Character-Types Met with in Psycho-Analytic Work" (1916), that Freud fully established the uses of the storyline in developing psychoanalytic interpretations. There, he did not use the technical psychosexual and diagnostic labels that were featured earlier in "Character and Anal Erotism" (1908) and later in "Libidinal Types" (1931). *The Exceptions, Those Wrecked by Success, Criminals from a Sense of Guilt:* the brilliance of these literary captions has not faded with time. In the present context I should prefer to say that there is something peculiarly liberating in these captions in that they encourage the imaginative narrativizing of lives. Although Freud organized these impressions in terms of character-type rather than storyline, the literariness of his characterology cannot be denied, and there are those (for example, Bergler [1948] with his "injustice collectors") who have successfully followed Freud's lead. Moreover, to describe a type is in effect to specify the kinds of things one may safely go on to say about the subject thus designated (see chapter 9). In this respect, the type, like the metaphor, is not a static idea; it is a center of narrative possibility, a folded-up story waiting to be unfolded on suitable occasions and in expectable ways. To have someone typed is to be able to read that person like an open book, as the saying goes; and in that saying, it should be noted, dynamic interpretation is implicitly identified with narrativity.

It is therefore probably no coincidence that in this study of character-types Freud drew so heavily on literary texts for his illustrations; character-typing and analytic interpretation of literature became one and the same in this bold essay. Richard III, Lord and Lady Macbeth, Rebecca West: conflict-ridden character, plot, and action defining one another and so forming finally a dramatic narrative unity.[4] In the present discussion on imprisonment, storyline has referred to this narrative unification of conflictedness. Although I have mentioned a number of other characterologically slanted storylines, most particularly the storyline of the prisoner, I have not aimed to reinvigorate literary characterology; indeed not every one of the storylines mentioned here need refer to character (for example, The Journey). Rather, I have used the idea of storyline to shed some light on the nature and technique of psychoanalytic interpretion; perhaps between the lines I have also lit up a bit the art of empathizing.

4. To what Freud said about Richard III, it might be added that Richard made out of his being deformed and humiliated not only a basis for claims against an unjust world and a justification for devious strategies and ruthless ambitions, but also an instrument of sexual seduction and kingly presence—thus, a malignant phallus by which he attempted to undo his psychic castratedness. We see (reconstruct) this genitalization of deformity or defect in many forms in the course of our clinical work.

The Imprisoned Analysand

I turn next to Freud's (1909a) boast (as he put it) to Little Hans. Freud said to Hans that he knew the story of his life before he was born. The life story in question was only an abbreviated version of the oedipal story, but Freud presented it to Hans as the life story it was important to tell. In what sense did Freud know that story in advance? To say that he knew it as a norm or a law of development is only to begin answering this question. What is needed to complete the answer is an account of how the individual life story gets to be seen as normative or as an instantiation of a developmental law. So many highly particularized, even seemingly opposite life stories get to be retold convincingly as the familiar oedipal story. How does this come about?

On my reading of it, what Freud's "boast" amounted to was that he could plausibly expand and then reduce the particular story of Hans to the prototypic oedipal story; schematically, he could elicit and encompass selected prominent life details within a unified and unifying story of an oedipal little boy afraid of castration; he could richly and succinctly narrativize the boy's life to his satisfaction and to Hans's therapeutic benefit.

In his having done the same with enough initially varied life stories provided by other analysands, Freud established a psychoanalytic norm or law of development. It is a norm or law not so much subject to disproof as it is vulnerable to narrative strain in particular cases. *It is a norm or law of interpretation*, a narrative and therapeutic strategy, and as such it can be misapplied, overdone, or underdone. One might therefore want to regard evidence of narrative strain as the kind of disproof to which psychoanalytic interpretation is vulnerable. Crude reductionism is one of the many types of strain I have in mind.

The oedipal story is always the product of psychoanalytic retelling, for it may be taken as a rule that it is never encountered as a clear, unified, and fully told or transparently enacted version of a life. The psychoanalyst is bound to mistrust apparent exceptions to this rule and to view them as pseudoneurotic or defensive screens for developmental disturbances of another sort. And this mistrust is warranted because ready-made oedipal self-presentations as well as facile oedipal interpretations are self-contradictory. By definition, the unfolding of the story should be the product of much reflective work and thematic transformation. In this perspective, one may go on to say of the Oedipus complex that it is a superb storyline, a brilliant narrative strategy for selectively elaborating and unifying, and creatively and therapeutically retelling, the heterogenous, obscure, and even seemingly contradictory major developmental details of individual lives.

To judge by all of his case reports, beginning with those in "Studies in Hysteria" (Breuer and Freud, 1893–95) and peaking perhaps in the Rat Man (1909b) with all its intricate rat tales, Freud knew a good story when he saw one. But, I ask, what does it mean to say that? It can only mean that Freud saw the makings of a story that remained to be told *in his terms,* a story he could work out *in his inimitable way,* a story that more and more he organized around *what he called* the nuclear complex of the neuroses, that is, what was *for him* and remains *for us* the most adaptable, trustworthy, inclusive, supportable, and helpful storyline of them all: the Oedipus complex in all its complexity and with all its surprises.

My emphasis on stories may have suggested that, in my view, the Oedipus complex does not refer to anything real. But in the realm of modern epistemological and narrative theory, to speak of stories or fictions is not to deny reality to what is being told (see, for example, Kermode, 1966). It is merely to emphasize that what we call reality can only be presented from one or another point of view, and on this account it is necessarily a reality of a certain kind in a certain context which has been established and told for certain purposes. It is a kind of worldmaking (Goodman, 1978).

In every case, reality has to be told. Related but different versions of reality cannot present exactly the same set of facts. In our daily lives we can for the most part afford to ignore the principle that all facts are mediated by some kind of narration. This is so because pragmatic conventionalization has rendered many facts too "factual" and many aspects of reality too "certain" to question usefully or meaningfully. But in conducting an open-minded psychoanalysis, one questions the so-called facts or certainties all the time. Nothing need be taken for granted. Thus, some of the facts in life histories prove to have been only imagined while others are open to constant revision, both gross and subtle, as the work of interpretation and reconstruction proceeds. For example, just what the analysand is doing in ostensibly coming for analysis is a bottomless bag of surprises. Consequently, one may say that the modern narrative view of factuality and reality has always been inherent in psychoanalytic interpretation.

And where the analyst stops questioning the facts is, as we see from the heterogeneity in our field, always a function of the analyst's pre-established theoretical commitments as well as of each analysand's tolerance in the clinical situation. In narrational terms, explanatory closure is a function of both the basic storylines that guide and regulate the analyst's interpretations and what is bearable by the analysand.

The Imprisoned Analysand

Today, for example, the separation-individuation storyline (Mahler, Pine, and Bergman, 1975) and the cohesive self storyline (Kohut, 1971) require additional questions, if not alternative questions, to those typically posed by Freud; and analytic closure or "the sense of an ending" (Kermode, 1966) of interpretation is affected accordingly. There do seem to be certain analysands whose tolerances are such that they benefit especially from a full development of these alternative storylines. The analyst's own sensitivity, tolerance, and imaginativeness also play a part in the selection and accentuation of certain storylines and in his or her sense of when the analytic questioning may stop, that is, when it is too late to introduce significant revisions of the storylines already used.

Personal factors aside, however, the truth of a psychoanalytic fact resides ultimately in the way it fits into the system of interpretation within which it and its significance have been defined. Disputes as to the facts and the significance of the facts are not disputes between theory-free observers; they are disputes between analysts who have adopted different systems of interpretation and used different methods prescribed or legitimized by these systems and who have perhaps also attracted different types of analysands into their practices. The idea of a theory-free and method-free observer may be regarded as an instance of denial of imprisonment, in this case confinement within a system that is the basis of whatever orderly work one is doing (Schafer, 1980a, 1980b). Those who follow Freud's leads in more or less the same way can agree readily on many, even if not all, of the facts of an individual analysis. Working within the same tradition and predominantly with neurotic and character-disordered analysands, they hold the same things to be true, and they do it in so conventionalized and fruitful a manner that they may safely consider themselves to be simply objective observers who need not bother with epistemological puzzles. So long as they remain within the bounds of their system and their analytic population, they are not wrong to think this way. The epistemology is important in understanding what a system of knowledge is, how it works, and what its limits are, and so it is important in understanding the history of dissension within psychoanalysis—but what a history that is!

In presenting this relativistic point of view, it has not been my purpose to say that every analyst is simply and automatically entitled to his or her perspective, or that reality is unknowable, or that psychoanalytic interpretation is mythmaking in the pejorative sense of that term. Quite the opposite is the case. It is just that I have wanted to make it clear that, for psychoanalysis, what is factual or what is real is available only through systematic narratives which retell in analytic terms familiar life stories and the "events" of the analytic situation.

Back again to Freud who spoke to this point of facticity in another place in his report on Little Hans. There he said:

It is true that during the analysis Hans had to be told many things that he could not say himself, that he had to be presented with thoughts which he had so far shown no signs of possessing, and that his attention had to be turned in the direction from which his father was expecting something to come. This detracts from the evidential value of the analysis; but the procedure is the same in every case. . . . In a psychoanalysis the physician always gives his patient (sometimes to a greater and sometimes to a less extent) the conscious *anticipatory ideas* with the help of which he is put in a position to recognize and to grasp the unconscious material. . . . It is true that a child, on account of the small development of his intellectual systems, requires especially energetic assistance. But, after all, the information which the physician gives his patient is itself derived in its turn from analytic experience; and indeed it is sufficiently convincing if, at the cost of this intervention by the physician, we are enabled to discover the structure of the pathogenic material and simultaneously to dissipate it (1909a, pp. 104–105, emphasis added).

In my terms, Freud was saying that the analyst always works from his theory-based storylines. Inherently circular (in hermeneutic fashion), these storylines are based on observation which itself has been influenced by expectations. This is the sense I make of what Freud had to say about the "anticipatory idea." We are confronted here by the question of evidence, and to deal with it further let us consider the still imprisoned analysand one last time.

The evidential or factual status of the prisoner story cannot be decided simply. Sometimes the prison story has been forcibly suggested by the analysand's recurrent use of prison metaphors, in which case it seems to be simply encountered or uncovered and followed as an unconscious fantasy already constructed. Sometimes, however, it is the analyst who has introduced the storyline explicitly after having noted varied and often only implicit references to confinement, surveillance, and harsh authority; and at these times the manifest story has been introduced by the analyst as what Freud called an "anticipatory idea," an organizing theme, a narrative device that had begun an interpretation and facilitated further interpretation. Most of the time, however, it seems in retrospect to be the fairest account to say that analyst and analysand have developed the story jointly. By this I do not mean that they have developed it in a happy collaboration; I mean rather that each has made a contribution, often of different sorts, at different times, and with different degrees of awareness, reflectiveness, and conflictedness. The story seemed to recommend itself, and once it had been mentioned, and by whomever, it caught on and got to be co-authored (cf. Reider [1972] on metaphoric interpretation). For this reason it is likely to be inaccurate to say that major storylines are simply uncovered as tales already fully told unconsciously; similarly, it is likely to be inaccurate to say that they are simply and regularly imposed by the analyst.

The evidence emerges in full or incipient story form, and the analyst has had a hand in developing that form. For example, a dream of being in prison may follow a remark by the analyst that the analysand is defensively playing the part of a poor, disadvantaged wretch, whereupon being imprisoned may begin to become an organizing theme. There then develops an analytic story, filled with dreams, memories, perceptions, etc., of something that is true and important in psychical reality; then, the imprisoned analysand really exists. But that same analysand will really exist in a number of other psychoanalytic narratives as well, for being imprisoned is but one version, and an incomplete one, of the psychical realities and the analytic life histories that will be developed over the course of the analysis. Because the analysand's individualized and variable use of it forecloses rather than opens up the possibility of personal change and change in others, it is essential that sooner or later the prison story be called into question by the analyst's clarifications and interpretations. Given enough interest, patience, tact, and narrative competence, and some help by the analysand, this questioning may have notable success. In the end, the psychical fact of being imprisoned may be put in its analytic place. Far from being imprisoning (as it is so often depicted by those who fear it), psychoanalysis will prove to be the key to the prison.

But as I have tried to show in my account of the imprisoned analysand, analysis is a special kind of key. It opens up our understanding of the origins, the functions, and the fantastic and conflictual aspects of the narrative of imprisonment. Thereby it is the key to transforming the static, timeless prison into a setting of personal and beneficial change. This narrative redevelopment of the case, which cannot take place without much emotional distress and experimentation on the part of the analysand, both within and outside the transference, amounts in one respect to liberation from unconsciously held, characterological convictions that are pathologically confining in their fixedness and narrowness. The new freedom, such as it is, will be that of a readiness to entertain multiple and less acutely conflictual possibilities of understanding and, along with these, multiple possibilities of feeling, revaluation, and action in the world. But in another and equally important respect, the narrative redevelopment of the case leads to the analysand's seeing the prison in a new and happier light, that is, seeing it also as one of the expectable, unconsciously developed narratives of committing oneself steadfastly to personal aims, values, and human relationships.

17

On Becoming a Psychoanalyst of One Persuasion or Another

I plan here to survey once again the constituents of the analytic attitude, this time, however, from the standpoint of some of the important tensions in the professional life of the contemporary psychoanalyst. I recognize that in one form or another these tensions have existed for analysts almost from the beginning of the development of psychoanalysis. I recognize, too, that in some places at least I may be speaking from a purely personal point of view.

The question of what an analyst is may be approached by way of what analysands say we are. They say, for instance, that we are shrinks. Shrink is a terrible misnomer for a psychoanalyst in that it suggests that the analyst transforms passive people by diminishing them, whereas the truth is that our work proceeds in the opposite direction, that is, it helps people transform themselves in a way that expands and enhances their lives. We hear other things from analysands—that we are, to give another example, their fix. One of my analysands used to say, "I've come here today for my fix," anticipating each day that by the time he left he would be feeling a little better, a little soothed. He was, of course, seeming to reduce the analysis to the satisfaction of an addictive craving, and he was unconsciously likening the analyst to a good breast. Other analysands portray us as toilet trainers, enema givers, or garbage collectors. Still others call us whores who sell our interest and affection for limited periods of time. In dreams we often appear as bus drivers or other transporters taking passive people to some definite destination that we have in mind. And, as I mentioned in the preceding chapter, some regard us as prosecutors, judges, or jailers.

In contriving these fantasies, analysands assume implicitly or explicitly that being an analyst is being a finished and fixed product, as though there is an end point to one's becoming an analyst. What they do not recognize and what they neurotically fear is one of the things I want to emphasize particularly; namely, that one is, in fact, always becoming an analyst, and that graduating from an analytic institute is only reaching a way station on what is an endless journey. It is a journey with no last stop. For each of us, every ending turns into another beginning. In other words, because being an analyst ideally entails continuous development and change, it always contains within it many tensions. By tensions I refer not just to the varying degrees of anxious uncertainty one experiences in doing any kind of clinical work. I certainly do not have to dwell on these experiences.

The first of the tensions I want to mention pervades anyone's working as an analyst. It arises from the fact that there are schools of psychoanalysis. What makes each school a school is its having a substantial body of literature and eminent members who make persuasive claims as to their special vision of the psychoanalytic truth and the results to be obtained by those who share this vision. The existence of schools raises the problem of comparative psychoanalysis which, in my view, is a virtually undeveloped intellectual pursuit. Efforts to establish a discipline of comparative analysis have been made—for instance, some years ago the notable effort by Ruth Munroe, *Schools of Psychoanalytic Thought* (1955)—but I think in every case the result has been no more than a first approximation of the necessary form and content of this endeavor.

Why is comparative psychoanalysis so undeveloped? It seems to me that the problem of analyzing the structure of thought within any one school is so formidable that even analysts who belong to that school cannot agree altogether on which basic assumptions have to be made, on the mutual interrelations of the various key propositions of that school, on what constitutes evidence, and on what the relation of evidence is to the particular analytic methods that are practiced. All such matters are up for debate within each school, and this unsettledness adds to the school's intellectual vigor and clinical development. All the more, therefore, will this be the case when radically different points of view prevail, that is, when it comes to comparing the assumptions and the claims of different schools. The formidable problems are epistemological as well as methodological in that comparative psychoanalysis must deal with questions concerning not only *what* we know but *how* we know what we know, how we establish that something is certain, how we argue from one proposition to another, and so forth.

That there are schools of psychoanalysis establishes the relevance of ideas that have been of much concern to literary critics and historians. There is, for example, Frank Kermode's (1966) discussion in *The Sense of an Ending*. There he works with the distinction between fictions and myths. Fictions, a term used with no pejorative implication, refers to an organized set of beliefs and a corresponding way of defining facts. A fiction amounts to a structuring principle or a shared vision of reality which can be shown to have some significance and usefulness but which is recognized to be an approach to reality, an organized set of storylines, rather than a picture of reality plain and simple. Unfortunately, when analysts belonging to different schools make their competing claims, they very often lose sight of the fact, not only that there are different schools, but that the beliefs within any one school are heterogeneous and have been undergoing evolution. The truth is that once a school has been in existence for a while, propositions that once were accepted unqualifiedly as *the* truths of that school have been progressively and substantially modified in various ways. The storylines change.

When it is forgotten that any one school of thought is a loosely integrated and changing body of fictions, the fictions become myths. As myths they are ultimate, unchangeable assertions about reality pure and simple. Like primitive religious beliefs, they claim direct access to one and only one clearly ascertainable world. Then they are beyond comparative analysis; other conceptions of the order of things are discredited. A simple positivist orientation prevails.

As soon as one pays genuine attention to the claims made by analysts of other persuasions, one realizes how unsatisfactory it is to ask the naively empirical question, "Well, what are the facts?" Each school marshals its facts in a plausible fashion. On the basis of certain leading assumptions and the influence these exert on the methods that are used to do analysis, that is, the types and range of interventions, the analysts of each school elicit and highlight somewhat different analytic phenomena. These phenomena are consistent with, and more or less confirmatory of, fixed assumptions and the methods they define. Consequently, in belonging to a school of analysis, one is working within a more or less closed system. This system is very much like a culture or a certain period of history in that one is locked into it, in large part unconsciously. I shall return to this point when I discuss the second in the series of tensions that pervade analytic work.

Insofar as the fictions of a school are taken as myths, other schools tend to look wrong, simple-minded, perverse, old-fashioned, and dangerous, and they are subjected to considerable scorn and mockery. Even within schools, it is not uncommon, when someone presents a case report of analytic work, for some colleagues to say, "I wouldn't call that analysis." This response, by the way, is one of the great deterrents to presenting case reports at the meetings of psychoanalytic societies. This being the case, members of other schools are even more likely to say of one's own work, "I wouldn't call that analysis." The judgment is usually arbitrary; it simply does not recognize the fact that we are far from having a well-developed comparative psychoanalysis on the basis of which to make such absolute judgments.

Other factors help create myths. For instance, each school tends to be organized around one or several dominant personalities, analysts such as Karen Horney, Harry Stack Sullivan, Melanie Klein, and, of course, Freud. These are the people who established the school or were early leaders within it. There are also some analysts who, even though they have not been identified with an organized school, have developed a very special point of view that has had a great impact on others. I'm thinking of people like Erik Erikson and D. W. Winnicott. These leaders or leading thinkers have an enormous formative influence on others. When I first began to study, and fortunately to have supervisory contact with Erik Erikson, I was absolutely enamored of his way of thinking, his way of integrating social psychological, biological, and anthropological material with psychoanalytic material. I then found myself in a position of a kind that I think is not rare among young analysts. I was imitating my hero, thinking and talking like him. It was only when I tried writing like him that I became aware that it was as though I was trying to be Erikson himself. Helpful at first, it got to be more and more ridiculous. There is a very strong personal element in the influence exerted by the vision of analysts of this high quality. Consequently, one of the problems facing every analyst is to come to terms with these influences, to respect them without overidentifying with them and thus becoming a party to mythmaking. For me there was another period in which I felt Winnicott's influence in the same way. I would have given anything to be able to think, feel, and analyze in the way it seemed to me that Winnicott did. I had to learn that I couldn't be Winnicott and for all kinds of reasons, including my growing up Jewish in the Bronx. Yet, both theoretically and clinically, I learned a great deal from the writings of this gifted analyst.

On Becoming a Psychoanalyst of One Persuasion or Another

These dominant personalities introduce us to different kinds of life histories and different dominant images of analysands to guide our analytic work. For instance, Freud mostly envisions the phallic boy, and usually he treats the other facets or phases of development, however important, as variations on this theme. Winnicott seems mostly to envision a baby with the mother of primary maternal preoccupation; he paints a portrait of an early phase of development. The picture painted by the separation-individuation concepts of Margaret Mahler emphasize a somewhat later phase of development. I am simplifying things here, but one does inevitably simplify the rich thought of leading contributors. As there are altogether too many things to note about analysands, we are inclined to fall back on one or another of these schematized images in order to give shape and consistency to the way we think about and analyze wide sectors of each analysand's life history.

Yet, although it is important to try to pay open-minded attention to what the different schools propose in order to protect fictions against becoming myths, one does need a firm base, a consistent orientation, a defined culture of one's own in which to work. Here I move on to the second in the series of analytic tensions. It is a tension inherent in working within one particular tradition. In this connection you find, particularly around the time of graduation or shortly thereafter, that you have developed many ties to the people who have been central to your training and to the decisive events of that training, including your own analyst, your impressive teachers and supervisors, and also the analysands you first worked with and the ways you learned to work with them. All these people and experiences exert a kind of imprinting effect. This effect is constituted of feelings of gratitude, loyalty, identification, gratification, competence, and idealization.

Useful as these ties are in helping you along in your acculturation in that school, ultimately they also begin to feel confining in certain respects at least. Particularly is this the case when the ties involve more transference of a positive and negative sort than is really good for one's personal life and one's analytic work. Perhaps most of all it is the negative transference which may not have been adequately dealt with in one's training. To give only one example, the result can be— and I remember this from some of my own early work—a determination to be not as austere, more responsive, nice, and more present than one's analyst. In my case I had to a significant extent continued to hate my analyst for having been, as I experienced it, remote and ungiving; that aspect of my negative transference had simply not been dealt

285

with adequately in that analysis. I got some good work done on it in my second analysis. I also worked through more of it in my continuing work with my own analysands, who sooner or later let me know when I was paying more attention to my needs than theirs.

I do not have to describe at length all the integrative advantages of respecting and building on the positive ties I mentioned. I will only point to the sense of continuity and collegiality, the kind of confirmation one gets from one's peers, and the needed confidence one develops on this basis. In working and developing within a tradition, one is not left with the impossible job of making oneself up totally. There is a sense of authenticity that comes from working within a form, a form that is a set of constraints as well as opportunities. You would be engaged in living out a rather simple-minded, romantically individualistic fantasy to think that you could simply make yourself up from moment to moment; you would be disregarding the necessarily interpersonal matrix of learning and adaptation.

Nevertheless, with all of the advantages of working within your school wholeheartedly, there are also advantages to questioning the traditions within which you work. As times goes on, you inevitably become aware that there are gaps and contradictions. There are important things you begin to see in your work that your teachers told you were not there or were not important; or else they never led you to expect to see them and so, when you do see them, they startle and dismay you. Kuhn's (1970) discussion of scientific revolutions may be recalled in this connection. As your eyes open to these new sights, you may for a time simply try to explain them away. At some point, however, you may face them directly and begin to raise some serious constructive questions about the tradition within which you work or the fictions you have assimilated and begun to make into myths.

In addition to what you see for yourself in your own work, you discover a lot of heterogeneity within your school. When you consider your different teachers and colleagues carefully, you find them understanding basic concepts in many different ways and utilizing markedly different versions of the approach that you all say you share in common. You may feel confused and dissatisfied in recognizing the existence of uncritical eclecticism within your own tradition. The individual differences I am referring to stem in large part from the fact that each group of analysts includes people of many different kinds. But even after allowing for personality differences, there remain different ways of understanding basic concepts and carrying out basic methods. Within each school, inevitable and unresolvable ambiguities result in heterogeneity. The components of any one system are not that binding, really. You identify yourself with what seems to be a unified tradition of thought and practice, and you find that you have committed yourself to what is partly an illusion.

One of the ways in which one confronts this heterogeneity is filled with personal significance. The time is likely to come when you ask yourself, "To whom would I refer someone I love?" or "To whom would I go for a second analysis?" All too often, these are not easy questions to answer. You may well wonder then what your uncertainty implies about the extent of your confidence in the official point of view and the methods of your school. How much is actually shared in practice by the members of one group?

These considerations of individual variation lead into the next few tensions I want to mention. The first of these is variations within your own experience in working as an analyst. Experience is a tricky factor to consider. I think it was Sartre who said somewhere that experience usually consists of somebody's repeating the same errors over a long enough period to feel entitled to claim some absolute authority for doing things in that faulty way. Sometimes when one looks at one or another senior colleague, one can't help thinking that there must be a lot of truth in what Sartre said. Nevertheless, you must rely on a large part of what you consider your own experience. Reviewing your work with previous analysands, you assess how things went, what you've learned from each undertaking, and progressively you build some kind of integrated point of view. From this point of view, you look for what is familiar and what you have learned to deal with effectively within some range of variations. Developing self-consistency in this way is fine up to a point; it can, however, end in rigidity. Then you will be creating personal myths rather than working with provisional fictions, and you will interrupt the process of becoming an analyst. The tension is one that exists between organizing your experience and becoming a slave to it.

Even within your work with one analysand you may develop a rigidity that is equivalent to a cultural lag. After you have worked with someone for some time and have usefully analyzed certain prominent disturbances of feeling and have worked through their many different manifest forms, you may discover at some point that the analysand is now on significantly different ground and that you have been unprepared to recognize this change. I think of one analysis in which we worked for several years on difficulties created by the infantile experience of a tempestuous, difficult and in some ways brutal father, a man who was also overstimulating and seductive. Many and varied disturbances of a masochistic and bisexual sort had been analyzed. These disturbances had shown themselves prominently in the transference in the form of seeking certain kinds of negative and inverted oedipal gratification through efforts at provoking fights and seeming to suffer the consequences. On the whole it had been quite useful to trace the many ways in which the experience of that father-son relationship had been a destructive influence. One day, however, I began to realize that for a while this analysand had been reemphasizing material pertaining to an impoverishing, depressing, annihilating kind of experience with his mother; the point of this reemphasis was to show that relative to his experience with her, his relationship to his father had represented life, vitality, emotion, doing something in the world. The father then emerged as also a significant source of strength, as someone who had become so important to his son not just because of the embattled oedipal entanglement but because it was only through that difficult man that he could escape from the "bad" mother and become something himself. None of which canceled out the previous analytic work; what was required was a review of many things from this added point of view and an acknowledgment on my part that I had developed a cultural lag in my work with this young man. For a time I had been rigidly narrowing my experience of him. A second life-historical narrative was now called for.

Tensions of a similar sort arise in connection with what we regard as our successes and failures, that is, the work we are satisfied with or dissatisfied with. I believe that there is a not uncommon tendency to begin to use technical terminology to derogate analysands who don't work out well. Terms begin to be used really as invectives. Too quickly and arbitrarily these analysands are said to be too manipulative or passive-aggressive or narcissistic, to be really borderline or psychotic and in any case unanalyzable. Too often these characterizations are attempts to rationalize ununderstood major difficulties rather than admit that something has either happened or not happened that one simply doesn't understand. Sitting in the analyst's chair, it can be very difficult to acknowledge that one just doesn't understand. One of the common sources of negative countertransference is the analysand's persistently presenting material that is difficult to grasp. But if the analysis reaches an impasse and is given up or broken off, how far is it possible and safe to explain this state of affairs or to undertake to explain it at all, seeing that it has remained so obscure?

With regard to what we take to be our successes, we often generalize

On Becoming a Psychoanalyst of One Persuasion or Another

from them to all such analysands or indeed to all people, and we are tempted to explain everything in their terms. In my view, such generalizations are particularly apparent in the literature on the treatment of schizophrenia and borderline conditions. There are many different and authoritatively stated views of what is the right way to treat such problems, but in many instances these views are based only a single case report of a treatment that seems to have gone well. Furthermore, if you read these reports closely, many of them tell of people who are still in treatment after ten or twelve years and who, although apparently significantly better, do not seem to have passed beyond the danger of major regressions. One must grant that overeagerly generalizing from success is as much a problem as the temptation to derogate analysands with whom one is unable to get anywhere.

Yet another source of tension invades our work in connection with "success." It is difficult to be certain just what you did that made that much difference in the analysis, and often it is equally difficult to be sure just how much it is what you did that mattered versus what use the analysand made of you. One of the things that makes it difficult to form these judgments is what Heinz Hartmann, in "Technical Implications of Ego Psychology" (1951), called the multiple appeal of interpretations. The idea here is that in making an interpretation along a certain line, you cannot help but be introducing one factor into the complex dynamic field of the patient's unconscious mental functioning. On this basis the analysand can make various uses of your intervention, bring it into relation with various other ideas and feelings and memories, and produce effects that you neither intended nor anticipated and the origin of which you cannot pinpoint. You may, for example, make an interpersonal interpretation that the analysand will seem to use in an old-fashioned Freudian way and vice versa. You mention low self-esteem and the analysand responds in terms of small penis; you mention oedipal guilt and the analysand responds in terms of failure of empathy; etc. Thus, the language that is the currency of the analysis may not reflect clearly or consistently enough just how the crucial changes take place. Still, we wish to speak authoritatively on such matters and to deny the limits of our perception and understanding.

I go on next to an issue that has to do with somewhat more private and individual aspects of being an analyst. It is well known and accepted that your own personality is your instrument in doing psychoanalytic work. Inevitably your personality is evident to the analysand, even if, as is also inevitable, it is significantly misperceived *in certain respects.* And there is every reason to believe that the effects of your personality are considerable even if difficult to trace. Adopting the much caricatured incognito of the Freudian analyst is methodologically naive because whatever method you use is going to play a part in shaping the phenomena you will then observe. Unfortunately, many Freudian analysts still seem to consider the extreme incognito, the impassive formality and strictly maintained reserve, as always the right way to act in order not to contaminate the field of analytic observation. It is, however, a misguided striving toward neutrality and objectivity to try absolutely to screen yourself out of the analytic interaction. The thing is to be as clear as possible about the kind of interaction you are establishing.

At the same time, analytic work does call for significant subordination of the analyst's personality to the analytic work. The sense in which your personality is your instrument is not that of simply offering the analysand a good personal relationship or corrective emotional experience, however you define it or however you and the analysand jointly define it. Fundamentally, a social relationship, however "understanding" it may be, is not what the analysand has come for; nor is it consistent with any school of psychoanalytic thought to act as though it were, for to some extent every school recognizes the key role of interpreting unconsciously distorting repetition within the transference and resisting. Simply offering corrective emotional experience, as though there were no major unconsciously maintained impediments to its acceptance, is not the same as doing analysis.

On the one hand, you don't want to be exactly the same for all analysands; that is the way of rigidity. On the other hand, you don't want to try to be altogether different for each analysand, for then, in addition to lacking authenticity, you will not develop any baseline for comparing analysands with one another or comparing one analysand with himself or herself from one time to another. As in other respects, the tension consists in finding and continuously refinding a balance between remaining the same and yet changing appropriately. The problem is to calibrate yourself as an analyst.

One difficult aspect of calibrating yourself will stem from your being narcissistically concerned over facing your limits as an analyst. Nobody can analyze every type of analysand; at least one cannot do so equally well in all instances. It is a recognition difficult to achieve, especially during one's earlier years of development as an analyst. This is so because one does not yet have enough experience in having persisted long enough with enough different types of analysands and having done so with some assurance that one was analyzing reasonably well. The temptation then is great to blame either the analysand or yourself, but either way you are only putting off the recognition that there are certain types of empathizing and certain types of situations that are simply not your cup of tea. No one is to be blamed, really. Clinical experience itself is not necessarily instructive in this respect; it must be accompanied by relatively neutral and constructive critical self-observation. When it is not accompanied this way, you get the kind of analyst who develops a self-infatuation as the years go on, a sense that he or she can really do anything. For a time one may envy these analysts, but only for a time.

Because inevitably one is working with one's personality, even after one has achieved the desirable subordination of personality, one must confront the question of what sense it makes to speak of psychoanalytic *technique*. Is doing analysis a question of technique, and does the idea of technique somehow distort or spoil what is the more truly human aspect of psychoanalytic work? There is something to be said on both sides of this question. It does have to be recognized that analysis does not work well unless it is carried out under some constraints that define it as a method and that transcend questions of personality; the definition of and means of abiding by these constraints fall under the heading of technique. One might speak of guidelines rather than constraints. But I want to emphasize another set of considerations in this connection. In our best work as analysts we are not quite the same as we are in our ordinary social lives or personal relations. In fact, we are often much better people in our work in the sense that we show a greater range of empathizing in an accepting, affirmative, and goal-directed fashion. This observation suggests that there is a kind of second self which we develop, something comparable to that of the narrative author. Robert Fliess (1942) has called this second self or at least certain aspects of it the analyst's work ego. This second self is not and cannot be discontinuous with one's ordinary personality; yet, it is a special form of it, a form that integrates one's own personality into the constraints required to develop an analytic situation. It is within this form that one expresses his or her humanity analytically. On this basis a special kind of empathic intimacy, strength, appreciation, and love can develop in relation to an analysand which it would be a mistake to identify with disruptive countertransference. Admittedly, the distinction between this kind of closeness and disruptive countertransference is not always an easy one to draw, and it is not absolute, but I think that it is a distinction that can be made; indeed it must be made in the interest of developing and maintaining the analytic attitude.

Perhaps in this respect it would be more correct to put the matter this way. Within the interaction between analyst and analysand, there develops a mutual construction of two analytic second selves. The self of the person in analysis also is not identical with what it is in the outer world. It is within this mutual construction that personal experience can become possible that will at times transcend in richness and intensity what is ordinarily possible even in the most intimate of daily relationships.

I go on now to another tension involved in being an analyst. The question always hangs over analysis as to how much to emphasize the "inner world" and how much to emphasize the "outer world." How much do you talk about real interactions and how much do you talk about the analysand's fantasizing, particularly the unconscious infantile aspects of what is fantasized? It is my impression that this question weighs more heavily these days owing to our increasing interest in the earliest phases of ego development and the matrix of object relations during these phases.

There are, of course, a number of object-relations theories. The source of object-relations theories is the work of Melanie Klein. In her work, as set forth both in her own writings and those by members of her school, there is a virtually total disregard of the external world. Everything is discussed in terms of infantile fantasies that express instinctual tendencies, especially those connected with frightening destructiveness. In Otto Kernberg's work, by virtue of his emphasis on ego psychology, we find what is largely a softened version of Melanie Klein. The same is true of Winnicott and Guntrip in certain ways. In Winnicott's writings, for instance, it is not unusual to find him describing the mother of a schizophrenic patient in a gentlemanly English manner: she comes across as an ordinary devoted mother. I have never seen the mother of a schizophrenic patient who has met that description, and when I ask other colleagues, I find that they haven't either. Here it is not primarily a matter of whether or not one is a courteous Englishman; it is a matter of how carefully one attends to the external world. Guntrip makes equivalent statements about the spouses of very disturbed people, as though he has no sense that in relationships of this sort, even though there is no melodramatic villain, the significant disturbances and provocations under consideration must have been defined jointly. It is not really claiming much to

292

say this. One may recall in this connection studies of the families of schizophrenic patients, studies which have turned up many interesting observations along these lines. For these reasons I would say that Guntrip and Winnicott show how much they are of the Kleinian School of object-relations theory. Within the fictions of this school, real events and personalities are obscured by what are often extraordinarily illuminating interpretations of fantasy life as expressed in transferences particularly.

In contrast to these object relations approaches, we have the opposite extreme of almost purely sociological psychoanalytic approaches. In recent years, for example, this extreme has been evident in connection with discussions of student protest and revolution, racism, and feminism. We are pressured to take an all-or-none position in these respects. But one does not have to take an all-or-none position, for the problem is that of finding the right balance, and this too is not an easy problem to solve. When do you acknowledge, in the course of doing analysis, the way things are or were in the world or in the analytic relationship, and when do you continue to press your questions concerning the content of the unconscious fantasies and its projection onto "external" reality, as in the transference? Significant variations exist not only among analysts of the same persuasion but within one's work with the same analysand. Serious questions about reality testing and shared responsibility arise in this connection.

I will mention just one more tension before concluding this discussion. This tension stems from the problem of maintaining an affirmative attitude within one's analytic work. Necessarily, the analyst always remains alert to the irrational, the destructive, the pathological, or, if one does not want to use a medical model, the deeply conflictual and archaic aspects of the analysand's productions. These aspects are often presented in a smooth, well-rationalized manner or else they are carefully concealed or minimized. It is poor practice not to pay attention of the strictest kind to these features. It is the analyst's responsibility always to protect and enhance the analytic work. At the same time, however, it seems to me to be an intrinsic aspect of effective analytic work to remain always on the lookout for what is affirmative in the analysand's productions. Affirmations may be found even in the most troubled and troubling aspects of what the analysand is presenting.

I think in this regard of one of my analysands who has a terrible fear of any kind of affect and so is a frozen person. It has already become clear that she has a terrifying fantasy that if she begins to get well, that is, if she begins to have feelings and to express them, she will die. We don't yet understand the origin of this conviction. If one became impatient with her, one might be tempted to think that she is just being rigid, hypersensitive, obsessional, and narcissistic. These terms, if they are not being used pejoratively, do apply in this case, but they do not convey that she is trying to maintain and use what integration she has laboriously achieved and to save herself from something worse. Here we are in the realm of the danger situations that Freud emphasized when he developed his second theory of anxiety. Unconsciously, our analysands are living in dread; they are trying to cope in the best way they can with infantile danger situations which have been carried forward into the present. They show us that this is so by the problems they present in the analysis.

The analyst's job, then, is to find something of value even in the most destructive features of a case; as Freud pointed out in his papers on technique, there is something there that can be built on. Analysands on their part, while they long for this affirmative approach, in various subtle ways constantly attack us and try to undermine our affirmative orientation. One of the great problems in doing analytic work is to withstand this battering or seduction and not to abandon this fundamentally empathic stance. But it is not just a matter of empathizing that springs from our own good natures or out of our own basic humanity; to think that it is, is to be involved in a naively romantic view of what it is to be an analyst. What we work with is a structured form of empathizing. It is empathizing based on and guided by some organized fiction; we bring to bear some set of ideas about how people develop and how they are organized, where their difficulties might come from, what risks and pain may be entailed by changing. Within this form or fiction, we are able to empathize in a sustained and balanced psychoanalytic way so far as that is possible. In this we must draw on our ordinary everyday empathic responsiveness, but we must transform this responsiveness through the second self we develop as analysts, for ordinary empathizing is not yet analytic empathizing and as such it cannot be conducive to fundamental change.

Well, contrary to what the reader might be thinking by now, my review of these various tensions has not been leading to the conclusion or question, Who would want to be an analyst, given all these things to juggle and balance, all these perplexing uncertainties about tested knowledge, all these fine and fluid discriminations? Speaking at least for those who are interested in human development and relationships, the question really is, Who wouldn't want to be an analyst?

On Becoming a Psychoanalyst of One Persuasion or Another

There's so much about being an analyst that it is challenging, interesting, exciting, and rewarding, and as I mentioned there are certain experiences whose marvelousness one doesn't quite encounter in any other relationship. Not, of course, that other relationships do not provide marvelous experiences of their own, but that there is something distinctive about those that occur in the course of doing analytic work. Recognizing the tensions I've described should not lead to obsessional uncertainty and doubt; rather, it leads to the same destination that exploration in analysis does, that is, it leads through knowledge of how emotionally complicated and often painful things are, to a greater and well-founded sense of freedom. It only sounds paradoxical to say both that in doing analysis we help people realize that things are a lot more complicated than they ever dreamed and that there is something liberating about realizing that this is so. This realization is liberating even if the analysand does not have everything very neatly, consciously, and verbally synthesized at the end of analysis; in fact, one would have some reason to mistrust too great a sense of order at that time. In reflecting on the unending effort involved in becoming an analyst, one can only empathize more keenly with the analysand who is also interminably undergoing change and facing ever more directly the uncertainties, the hazards, and the opportunities of existence.

References

Abraham, K. (1924), A Short History of the Development of the Libido, Viewed in the Light of Mental Disorders. In *Selected Papers of Karl Abraham*, ed. E. Jones. New York: Basic Books, 1953.

Arlow, J. (1969a), Unconscious Fantasy and Disturbances of Conscious Experience. *Psychoanalytic Quarterly*, 38:1–27.

————. (1969b), Fantasy, Memory and Reality Testing. *Psychoanalytic Quarterly* 38:28–51.

————. and Beres, D. (1974), Fantasy and Identification in Empathy. *Psychoanalytic Quarterly* 43:4–25.

Bergler, E. (1948), *The Battle of the Conscience*. Washington, D.C.: Washington Institute of Medicine.

Bibring, E. (1953), The Mechanism of Depression. In *Affective Disorders*, ed. P. Greenacre. New York: International Universities Press, pp. 13–48.

Blos, P. (1968), Character Formation in Adolescence. *The Psychoanalytic Study of the Child* 23:245–263. New York: International Universities Press.

Blum, H. P. (1971), On the Conception and Development of the Transference Neurosis. *Journal of the American Psychoanalytic Association* 19:41–53.

Bollas, C. (1974), Character: The Language of Self. *International Journal of Psychoanalytic Psychotherapy* 3(4):397–418.

Booth, W. (1961), *The Rhetoric of Fiction*. Chicago: University of Chicago Press.

Brenner, C. (1976), *Psychoanalytic Technique and Psychic Conflict*. New York: International Universities Press.

Breuer, J. and Freud S. (1893–95), *Studies on Hysteria*. *Standard Edition*, 2. London: Hogarth Press, 1955.

Brombert, V. (1973), The Happy Prison: A Recurring Romantic Metaphor. In *Romanticism: Vistas, Instances, Continuities*, eds. D. Thorburn and G. Hartmann. Ithaca, N.Y. and London: Cornell University Press, pp. 62–79.

Carnochan, W. B. (1977), *Confinement and Flight: An Essay on English Literature of the Eighteenth Century*. Berkeley: University of California Press.

Cooper, A. M. (1982), Discussion–Problems of Technique in Character Analysis. *Bulletin of the Association for Psychoanalytic Medicine* 21:110–118.

Culler, J. (1975), *Structuralist Poetics: Structuralism, Linguistics, and the Study of Literature*. Ithaca, N.Y.: Cornell University Press.

Easser, B. R. (1974), Empathic Inhibition and Psychoanalytic Technique. *Psychoanalytic Quarterly* 43:557–580.

Eissler, K. (1953), The Effect of the Structure of the Ego on Psychoanalytic Technique. *Journal of the American Psychoanalytic Association* 1:104–143.

Eliot, T. S. (1933), *The Use of Poetry and the Use of Criticism*. New York: Barnes & Noble, 1970.

Fenichel, O. (1941), *Problems of Psychoanalytic Technique*. New York: Psychoanalytic Quarterly.

————. (1945), *The Psychoanalytic Theory of Neuroses*. New York: W. W. Norton.

Fingarette, H. (1963), *The Self in Transformation*. New York: Basic Books.

Fish, S. (1980), *Is There a Text in This Class? The Authority of Interpretive Communities*. Cambridge, Mass., and London: Harvard University Press.

Fliess, R. (1942), The Metapsychology of the Analyst. *Psychoanalytic Quarterly* 11:211–227.

Freud, A. (1936), *The Ego and the Mechanisms of Defense*. New York: International Universities Press, 1946.

Freud, S. (1899), Screen Memories. *Standard Edition* 3:299–322. London: Hogarth Press, 1962.

———. (1900), The Interpretation of Dreams. *Standard Edition* 4 & 5. London: Hogarth Press, 1953.

———. (1905a), Three Essays on the Theory of Sexuality. *Standard Edition* 7:125–243. London: Hogarth Press, 1953.

———. (1905b), Jokes and their Relation to the Unconscious. *Standard Edition* 8. London: Hogarth Press, 1960.

———. (1908), Character and Anal Erotism. *Standard Edition* 9:169–175. London: Hogarth Press, 1959.

———. (1909a), Analysis of a Phobia in a Five-Year-Old Boy. *Standard Edition* 10:5–149. London: Hogarth Press, 1955.

———. (1909b), Notes Upon a Case of Obsessional Neurosis. *Standard Edition* 10:153–318. London: Hogarth Press, 1955.

———. (1909c), Family Romances. *Standard Edition* 9:235–241. London: Hogarth Press, 1959.

———. (1910a), The Future Prospects of Psycho-Analysis. *Standard Edition* 11:139–151. London: Hogarth Press, 1957.

———. (1910b), A Special Type of Object Choice Made by Men. *Standard Edition* 11:163–176. London: Hogarth Press, 1957.

———. (1911), The Handling of Dream Interpretation in Psycho-Analysis. *Standard Edition* 12:91–96. London: Hogarth Press, 1958.

———. (1912a), On the Universal Tendency to Debasement in the Sphere of Love. *Standard Edition* 11:177–190. London: Hogarth Press, 1957.

———. (1912b), The Dynamics of Transference. *Standard Edition* 12:97–108. London: Hogarth Press, 1958.

———. (1912c), Recommendations to Physicians Practising Psycho-Analysis. *Standard Edition* 12:111–120. London: Hogarth Press, 1958.

———. (1913), On Beginning the Treatment (Further Recommendation on the Technique of Psycho-Analysis). *Standard Edition* 12:123–144. London: Hogarth Press, 1958.

———. (1914a), Remembering, Repeating and Working-Through (Further Recommendations on the Technique of Psycho-Analysis II). *Standard Edition* 12:147–156. London: Hogarth Press, 1958.

———. (1914b), On Narcissism: An Introduction. *Standard Edition* 14:73–102. London: Hogarth Press, 1957.

———. (1915a), Observations on Transference-Love (Further Recommendations on the Technique of Psycho-Analysis III). *Standard Edition* 12:159–171. London: Hogarth Press, 1958.

———. (1915b), The Unconscious. *Standard Edition* 14:161–215. London: Hogarth Press, 1957.

———. (1916), Some Character-Types Met with in Psycho-Analytic Work. *Standard Edition* 14:309–333. London: Hogarth Press, 1957.

———. (1917), Mourning and Melancholia. *Standard Edition* 14:237–258. London: Hogarth Press, 1957.

———. (1919), Lines of Advance in Psycho-Analytic Therapy. *Standard Edition* 17:157–168. London: Hogarth Press, 1955.

———. (1920), Beyond the Pleasure Principle. *Standard Edition* 18:1–64. London: Hogarth Press, 1955.

———. (1921), Group Psychology and the Analysis of the Ego. *Standard Edition* 18:67–143. London: Hogarth Press, 1955.

———. (1922), Some Neurotic Mechanisms in Jealousy, Paranoia and Homosexuality. *Standard Edition* 18:221–232. London: Hogarth Press, 1955.

References

————. (1923), The Ego and the Id. *Standard Edition* 19:3–66. London: Hogarth Press, 1961.

————. (1925a), Some Additional Notes on Dream-Interpretation as a Whole. *Standard Edition* 19:125–138. London: Hogarth Press, 1961.

————. (1925b), Negation. *Standard Edition* 19:235–239. London: Hogarth Press, 1961.

————. (1926), Inhibitions, Symptoms and Anxiety. *Standard Edition* 20:77–175. London: Hogarth Press, 1959.

————. (1931), Libidinal Types. *Standard Edition* 21:217–220. London: Hogarth Press, 1961.

————. (1933), New Introductory Lectures on Psycho-Analysis. *Standard Edition* 22:1–182. London: Hogarth Press, 1964.

————. (1937a), Analysis Terminable and Interminable. *Standard Edition* 23:216–253. London: Hogarth Press, 1964.

————. (1937b), Constructions in Analysis. *Standard Edition* 23:257–269. London: Hogarth Press, 1964.

————. (1940), An Outline of Psycho-Analysis. *Standard Edition* 23:139–207. London: Hogarth Press, 1964.

Fromm, E. (1941), *Escape from Freedom*. New York: Farrar & Rinehart.

Geertz, C. (1973), *The Interpretation of Cultures: Selected Essays.* New York: Basic Books.

Gill, M. M. (1976), Metapsychology Is Not Psychology. In *Psychology Versus Metapsychology: Psychoanalytic Essays in Memory of George S. Klein*, eds. M. M. Gill & P. S. Holzman. *Psychological Issues, Monograph* 36:71–105. New York: International Universities Press.

Glover, E. (1931), The Therapeutic Effect of Inexact Interpretation: A Contribution to the Theory of Suggestion. In E. Glover, *The Technique of Psychoanalysis*. New York: International Universities Press, 1955, pp. 353–366.

————. (1955), *The Technique of Psychoanalysis*. New York: International Universities Press.

Goldberg, A., ed. (1978), *The Psychology of the Self: A Casebook*. New York: International Universities Press.

Goodman, N. (1978), *Ways of Worldmaking*. Indianapolis: Hackett.

Gray, P. (1973), Psychoanalytic Technique and the Ego's Capacity for Viewing Intrapsychic Activity. *Journal of the American Psychoanalytic Association* 21:474–495.

Green, A. (1975), The Analyst, Symbolization and Absence in the Analytic Setting (On Changes in Analytic Practice and Analytic Experience). *International Journal of Psycho-Analysis* 56:1–22.

Greenson, R. R. (1954), The Struggle Against Identification. *Journal of the American Psychoanalytic Association* 2:200–217.

————. (1960), Empathy and its Vicissitudes. *International Journal of Psycho-Analysis* 41:418–424.

————. (1967), *The Technique and Practice of Psychoanalysis*, Vol. 1. New York: International Universities Press.

Grossman, W. I. (1967), Reflections on the Relationships of Introspection and Psycho-Analysis. *International Journal of Psycho-Analysis* 48:16–31.

————, and Simon, B. (1969), Anthropomorphism: Motive, Meaning, and Causality in Psychoanalytic Theory. *The Psychoanalytic Study of the Child* 24:78–114. New York: International Universities Press.

Habermas, J. (1971), *Knowledge and Human Interests*, trans. J. J. Shapiro. Boston: Beacon Press.

Harding, D. W. (1963), *Experience Into Words: Essays on Poetry*. London: Chatto & Windus.

Hartmann, H. (1939), *Ego Psychology and the Problem of Adaptation*. New York: International Universities Press, 1958.

————. (1950), Comments on the Psychoanalytic Theory of the Ego. In *Essays on Ego Psychology*. New York: International Universities Press, 1964, pp. 37–68.

————. (1951), Technical Implications of Ego Psychology. In *Essays on Ego Psychology*. New York: International Universities Press, 1964, pp. 142–154.

Holt, R. R. (1976), Drive or Wish? A Reconsideration of the Psychoanalytic Theory of

Motivation. In *Psychology Versus Metapsychology: Psychoanalytic Essays in Memory of George S. Klein*, eds. M. M. Gill & P. S. Holzman. *Psychological Issues, Monograph* 36:159–197. New York: International Universities Press.

Jacobson, E. (1964), *The Self and the Object World*. New York: International Universities Press.

Jameson, F. (1972), *The Prison-House of Language: A Critical Account of Structuralism and Russian Formalism*. Princeton, N.J.: Princeton University Press.

Kermode, F. (1966), *The Sense of an Ending: Studies in the Theory of Fiction*. London, Oxford, and New York: Oxford University Press.

Kernberg, O. (1975), *Borderline Conditions and Pathological Narcissism*. New York: Jason Aronson.

Klein, G. S. (1975), *Psychoanalytic Theory: An Exploration of Essentials*. New York: International Universities Press.

Klein, M. (1948), *Contributions to Psycho-Analysis 1921–1945: Developments in Child and Adult Psycho-Analysis*. New York: McGraw-Hill, 1964.

Knight, R. P. (1940), Introjection, Projection and Identification. *Psychoanalytic Quarterly* 9:334–341.

Kohut, H. (1971), *The Analysis of the Self: A Systematic Approach to the Psychoanalytic Treatment of Narcissistic Personality Disorders*. New York: International Universities Press.

———. (1977), *The Restoration of the Self*. New York: International Universities Press.

✓ ———. (1979), The Two Analyses of Mr. Z. *International Journal of Psycho-Analysis* 60:3–27.

Kris, E. (1952), *Psychoanalytic Explorations in Art*. New York: International Universities Press.

———. (1956a), The Recovery of Childhood Memories in Psychoanalysis. *The Psychoanalytic Study of the Child* 11:54–88. New York: International Universities Press.

———. (1956b), The Personal Myth: A Problem in Psychoanalytic Technique. *Journal of the American Psychoanalytic Association* 4:653–681.

Kuhn, T. S. (1970), *The Structure of Scientific Revolutions*, 2nd ed. Chicago: University of Chicago Press.

Laplanche, J. and Pontalis, J. B. (1973), *The Language of Psycho-Analysis*. New York: W. W. Norton.

Leavy, S. (1973), Psychoanalytic Interpretation. *The Psychoanalytic Study of the Child* 28:305–330. New Haven, Conn.: Yale University Press.

Levin, F. M. (1980), Metaphor, Affect, and Arousal: How Interpretations Might Work. *Annual of Psychoanalysis* 8:231–245.

Lewin, B. D. (1950), *The Psychoanalysis of Elation*. New York: W. W. Norton.

———. (1970), The Train Ride: A Study of One of Freud's Figures of Speech. *Psychoanalytic Quarterly* 39:71–89.

Lewis, C. S. (1946), *The Allegory of Love: A Study in Medieval Tradition*. Oxford: Clarendon Press.

Lipton, S. (1977), The Advantages of Freud's Technique as Shown in his Analysis of the Rat Man. *International Journal of Psycho-Analysis* 58:255–274.

Loewald, H. (1960), On the Therapeutic Action of Psycho-Analysis. *International Journal of Psycho-Analysis* 41:16–33.

———. (1971), The Transference Neurosis: Comments on the Concept and the Phenomenon. *Journal of the American Psychoanalytic Association* 19:16–33.

———. (1979), The Waning of the Oedipus Complex. *Journal of the American Psychoanalytic Association* 27:751–775.

Loewenstein, R. M. (1957), A Contribution to the Psychoanalytic Theory of Masochism. *Journal of the American Psychoanalytic Association* 5:197–234.

Mahler, M. S., Pine, F., and Bergman, A. (1975), *The Psychological Birth of the Human Infant: Symbiosis and Individuation*. New York: Basic Books.

Mann, T. (1913), Death in Venice. In *Stories of a Lifetime*, Vol. 2. London: Secker & Warburg, 1961.

References

Meissner, W. W. (1979), Critique of Concepts and Therapy in the Action Language Approach to Psycho-Analysis. *International Journal of Psycho-Analysis* 60:291–310.

Menninger, K. A. (1958), *Theory of Psychoanalytic Technique.* New York: Basic Books.

Moore, B. E. and Fine, B. D. (1968), *A Glossary of Psychoanalytic Terms and Concepts,* 2d ed. New York: American Psychoanalytic Association.

Morawetz, T. (1978), *The Importance of On Certainty.* Amherst, Mass.: University of Massachusetts Press.

Munroe, R. (1955), *Schools of Psychoanalytic Thought: An Exposition, Critique, and Attempted Integration.* New York: Dryden Press.

Olney, J., ed. (1980), *Autobiography: Essays Theoretical and Critical.* Princeton, N.J.: Princeton University Press.

Rado, S. (1954), Hedonic Control, Action-Self, and the Depressive Spell. In *Psychoanalysis of Behavior: The Collected Papers of Sandor Rado,* Vol. 1. New York: Grune & Stratton, 1956, pp. 286–311.

Reich, W. (1933–34), *Character Analysis.* New York: Touchstone Books, 1974.

Reider, N. (1972), Metaphor as Interpretation. *International Journal of Psycho-Analysis* 53:463–469.

Ricouer, P. (1977), The Question of Proof in Psychoanalysis. *Journal of the American Psychoanalytic Association* 25:835–872.

Rycroft, C. (1958), An Enquiry into the Function of Words in the Psycho-Analytical Situation. *International Journal of Psycho-Analysis* 39:408–415.

———. (1968), *A Critical Dictionary of Psychoanalysis.* New York: Basic Books.

Ryle, G. (1943), *The Concept of Mind.* New York: Barnes & Noble, 1965.

Sachs, H. (1942), *The Creative Unconscious.* Cambridge, Mass.: Sci-Art Publishers.

Schafer, R. (1959), Generative Empathy in the Treatment Situation. *Psychoanalytic Quarterly* 28:347–373.

———. (1964), The Clinical Analysis of Affects. *Journal of the American Psychoanalytic Association* 12:275–299.

———. (1967), Ideals, the Ego Ideal and the Ideal Self. In *Contributions to a Psychoanalytic Theory of Behavior: Essays in Honor of David Rapaport,* ed. R. R. Holt. New York: International Universities Press.

———. (1968a), *Aspects of Internalization.* New York: International Universities Press.

———. (1968b), The Mechanisms of Defense. *International Journal of Psycho-Analysis* 49:49–62.

———. (1970), The Psychoanalytic Vision of Reality. In *A New Language for Psychoanalysis.* New Haven, Conn., and London: Yale University Press, 1976, pp. 22–56.

———. (1972), Internalization: Process or Fantasy? In *A New Language for Psychoanalysis.* New Haven, Conn., and London: Yale University Press, 1976, pp. 155–178.

———. (1973), The Idea of Resistance. In *A New Language for Psychoanalysis.* New Haven, Conn., and London: Yale University Press, 1976, pp. 212–263.

———. (1976), *A New Language for Psychoanalysis.* New Haven, Conn., and London: Yale University Press.

———. (1977), Psychoanalysis and Common Sense. *The Listener* 10 November 1977, pp. 609–610.

———. (1978), *Language and Insight: The Sigmund Freud Memorial Lectures 1975–1976, University College London.* New Haven, Conn., and London: Yale University Press.

———. (1980a), Action Language and the Psychology of the Self. *Annual of Psychoanalysis* 8:83–92.

———. (1980b), *Narrative Actions in Psychoanalysis: Heinz Werner Lecture Series, 14.* Worcester, Mass.: Clark University Press, 1981.

Scheler, M. (1954), On the Tragic. In *Tragedy: Modern Essays in Criticism,* eds. L. Michel and R. B. Sewall. Englewood Cliffs, N.J.: Prentice-Hall, 1963, pp. 27–44.

Schimek, J. (1975), The Interpretations of the Past: Childhood Trauma, Psychical Reality, and Historical Truth. *Journal of the American Psychoanalytic Association* 23:845–865.

Schneiderman, S., ed. (1980), *Returning to Freud: Clinical Psychoanalysis in the School of Lacan.* New Haven, Conn., and London: Yale University Press.

Segal, H. (1964), *Introduction to the Work of Melanie Klein*. New York: Basic Books.

Shapiro, D. (1965), *Neurotic Styles*. New York: Basic Books.

Sharpe, E. F. (1940), Psycho-Physical Processes Revealed in Language: An Examination of Metaphor. *International Journal of Psycho-Analysis* 21:201-213.

Shengold, L. (1966), The Metaphor of the Journey in *The Interpretation of Dreams*. *American Imago* 23:316-331.

Sherwood, M. (1969), *The Logic of Explanation in Psychoanalysis*. New York: Academic Press.

Smith, B. H. (1980), Narrative Versions, Narrative Theories. *Critical Inquiry* 7 (2):213-236.

Snell, B. (1953), *The Discovery of the Mind: The Greek Origins of European Thought*. Oxford: Blackwell.

Stone, L. (1961), *The Psychoanalytic Situation*. New York: International Universities Press.

———. (1967), The Psychoanalytic Situation and Transference: Postscript to an Earlier Communication. *Journal of the American Psychoanalytic Association* 15:3–58.

———. (1973), On Resistance to the Psychoanalytic Process: Some Thoughts on its Nature and Motivations. *Psychoanalysis and Contemporary Science* 2:42-76.

Strachey, J. (1934), The Nature of the Therapeutic Action of Psycho-Analysis. *International Journal of Psycho-Analysis* 15:127-159.

Waelder, R. (1930), The Principle of Multiple Function. *Psychoanalytic Quarterly* 15:45-62, 1936.

Werner, H. & Kaplan, B. (1963), *Symbol Formation*. New York: John Wiley.

Wilde, O. (1889), The Priority of Art. In *The Modern Tradition*, R. Ellman & C. Feidelson, eds. New York: Oxford University Press, 1965, pp. 17-24.

Winnicott, D. W. (1958), The Capacity to be Alone. *International Journal of Psycho-Analysis* 39:416-420.

———. (1971), *Playing and Reality*. New York: Basic Books and London: Tavistock Publications.

Wittgenstein, L. (1942), *Lectures and Conversations on Aesthetics, Psychology and Religious Belief*, ed. C. Barrett. Berkeley and Los Angeles: University of California Press, 1972.

———. (1969), *On Certainty*. New York: Harper & Row.

Zetzel, E. R. (1965), The Theory of Therapy in Relation to a Developmental Model of the Psychic Apparatus. *International Journal of Psycho-Analysis* 46:39-52.

Index

Ability words, 231
Abraham, Karl, 3, 74
Abreaction, 97
Abstinence, 23
Abstraction, levels of, 85, 160, 235
Accident, 31, 100, 107
Acting out, 5, 88, 134, 164, 252; remembering in, 27, 222–23; resisting through, 73
Action, 83–84, 98, 212, 247; affect as, 89, 101–3; archaic modes of, 223; asocial, 248; changes in, 157, 159; character as, 109–10, 140–44; continuity, coherence, and consistency of, 139; disguised, 224; displaced, 224; goal-directed, 60; multiple designation of, 85–86, 101; narrative, 209, 218, 240–41; new, 86–87, 130, 133; nonspatial description of, 87–88; patterning of, 45; as set of possibilities, 86; psychoanalytic terms of, 236; repertoire and modes of, 65; symptoms as, 108; *see also* Agency
Action language, *x*, 34, 65, 96, 98, 101, 143–44, 162, 273; in clinical dialogue, 245; conflict in, 92; for diagnosis and therapy, 112; and dream work, 61; impulse in, 105–6; literalism charge against, 143–45; multiple descriptions in, 160; personal agency in, 141, 190; rules of, 232; second self and, 52–53; synopsis of, 83–91
Activity, 113; attributions of, 226; and imprisonment, 267; and introspection narrative, 225; reallocation of, 236; reversing passivity to, 179; theoretical assumptions on, 135
Adaptation, 45, 136, 197; and disclaimed action, 143
Adaptive ego, 144
Addiction, 217
Adultomorphism, 189
Adverbs, 85, 103, 138
Adversarial approach, 73, 148; to resisting, 165–71
Aesthetics, 55

Affect, 136; as action, 89, 101–3, 128–29n; isolation of, 145; paucity of, 48, 73
Affirmative approach, 12, 293; to character analysis, 148, 152–56; and second self, 45–46; to resisting, 19, 162, 164–65, 168–71
Affirmative self-presentation, 60
Agency, 62, 63, 107, 110, 128–29n, 139, 141, 142, 190–93; consciously acknowledge, 246; disclaiming, 190–91; excessive claiming of, 190–91; narratives of, 226; regulatory, 138; *see also* Action
Aggression, 99; and conflict, 91, 187; and imprisonment, 266; in life history, 204; as mode of action, 223–24, 226
Agoraphobia, 266
Allegories, 261; reductive, 257
Ambivalence, 8, 145, 265; in depression, 102; expectations of, 12; splitting of, 120
Anality, 23, 99, 110–11, 146, 170, 171, 198, 232, 239, 255, 260; of "good patients," 68; of imprisonment, 266; in resistance, 230
Anal-sadism, 118, 141, 145, 170, 177, 180
Analysts-in-training, *see* Training, analytic
Analytic attitude, *ix*, 96, 156, 182n, 281; abandonment of, 73; analyzing in, 8–11; appreciation in, 65; attempts to delineate, 58; and attention to conflict, 82; avoidance of either-or thinking in, 7–8; contributions on, 3–4; empathy in, 34; Freud on, 3; helpfulness in, 11–13; modifications of, 14; neutrality in, 5–7; problem of formulation of, 4–5; toward resisting, 165, 167–71, 181; in transference interpretations, 126
Analytic process, 95, 209; active, 69; development of, 67; history of, 206, 209; significance of resisting in, 171; theory of, 164, 166n
Analytic relationship, 113, 123; archaic versions of, 100; collaborative, 126, 148, 189, 222; coordinated histories of, 207; emptiness in, 210; fictive aspect of, 42, 52–54; healing powers of, 117; here and now context of, 185, 188

303

Index

Analyzing, 8–11
Anamnestic data, 21
Anatomical differences between the sexes, 100, 192
Anger, 90; *see also* Aggression
Animism, 242
Anthropomorphism, 82; of affect, 102; of ego, 138; of resistance, 230
Anticipation, 48, 51; of traumatic situation, 97
"Anticipatory idea," 278
Anxiety, 96–105, 154, 224; catastrophic, 70; and conflict, 93; empathizing with, 47; experiential theory of, 97; infantile, 17; neurotic, 106; primal, 46; in resistance, 19; signal, 103
Appreciation, 58–65
Archaic experience, 293; openness to, 44
Arlow, Jacob, 3, 37, 259, 261
Art, 132; and emotions, 128*n*
Asceticism, 50
Associations: withholding, 164, 169, 171; *see also* Free association
Attention, evenly suspended, 21
Autism, 237
Autobiographical stories, 219, 259
Automatization, 245
Autonomous mental functions, 138
Autonomy, secondary, 134

Beast, child as, 213, 215
Becoming an analyst, 281–95
"Being alone together," 124
Beliefs, fundamental system of, 145
Beres, D., 37
Bergler, E., 274
Bergman, Annie, 267, 277
Bibring, E., 268
Biography, analytically illuminated, 207, 208; as independent material, 211
Biological-adaptational terms, 137
Birth, 224; of siblings, 30; trauma of, 97
Bisexuality, 149, 288
Blos, P., 136
"Bodily ego," 242–43
Bodily experiences, 99–100; formative, 41; of individuating baby, 122
Bodily happening, 84
Bodily zones, 224
Bollas, C., 140*n*
Booth, W., 53, 222
Borderline conditions, 14, 22, 73, 146–47, 288, 289
Brenner, Charles, 3, 62
Breuer, J., 276

Brombert, Victor, 264
Brute organism model, 88, 215, 227

Carnochan, W. B., 264
Case history, narrative form of, 238
Castration, 32, 46, 68–70, 101, 126, 150, 180, 268; analysis of resisting as, 81, 123; of analyst, 72; through defensive pseudostupidity, 175; enactments of, 108; and father, 118, 201; oedipal fear of, 275; self-, 178, 183
Category mistakes, 136
Cathartic method, 75
Causality, 90, 91, 131; tautological, 93
Censorship, 170; in dreams, 229
Certainty, 214, 276; and construction of experience, 145; unconscious, 125–27, 130
Change, 236, 294; appropriate, 290; character, 153, 156–61; complexity and ambiguity of, 20–23; dangerous, context of, 51; difficulties in way of, 17–20; fear of, 12, 70; of function, 189; and model of analysand, 42; and personal agency, 190, 191; and retelling, 227, 233; safety of, 122; structural, 14, 66, 77; through understanding, 11
Character, *ix*, *x*, 134–36, 274; as action, 140–44; change, 156–61; as dispositional concept, 141; and ego-syntonicity, 144–48; "good," 39; literary designation of, 141; metapsychological view of, 136–40; and narrative possibility, 274; predictive aspect of, 141; remembering through, 27; resistances, 72
Character analysis, 67; affirmative approach to, 152–56; and borderline personality, 147; and identification, 148–52
Character traits, 109–10; gratification through, 29; and imprisonment, 266; integrative value of, 153; multiple function of, 62; relation of symptoms to, 109; in transference, 116
Child analysis, 129
Circularity, 220, 254, 278; in interpretations, 208–9; in reconstructions, 196, 201, 203; temporal, 238
Clarifications, 9, 187
Cognitive elements: in empathizing, 36–37, 55; maturity of, 100
Coherence, 236; rules of, 206; thematic, 227
Colloquial sayings, 214
Collusion, analytic, 181, 221
Common sense, 213–14, 218, 236; in rules for listening, 228

Index

Comparative psychoanalysis, x, 42, 282–83

Complementarity, principle of, 217

Compromise formation, x, 8, 13, 226, 258, 265, 271; fostering of, 21; in identification, 152; neurotic, 62

Compulsions, 109

Concretization, 242

Condensation: in dreams, 61; in narratives, 250

Confidence of analyst, 26–28

Confidences, sharing of, 24

Conflict, 8, 134, 140, 161, 187, 267, 293; affirmative approach to, 46; experienced in analytic session, 76; id-ego, 106; infantile, 19, 22; intrapsychic, 88; and neutrality of analyst, 6; as paradoxical action, 91–95; parents', 224; phase-specific, 237; and resisting, 162; unconscious, 63, 78, 82, 113

Confrontation, 9, 75, 156, 166, 187

Confrontational therapists, 14

Conscious actions and processes, 5, 98; and action language, 86; appreciation and, 63; conflict in, 92; in reconstruction, 202

Consciousness, 89, 98; as narrative standpoint, 221

Constipation, 109, 118

Constitutional factors, 112, 190

Construction of experience, 89, 99, 123, 186, 194, 232; action mode of, 242; in analytic situation, 268; change in, 159; defensive, 146; and ego-syntonicity, 144–46; in here and now, 252; of infantile past, 27; in learning of language, 248; mutual, 292; by observers, 141; and transference neurosis, 20; unconscious actions in, 161

Content: change of, 158–60; and form, 131, 135; switch to process from, 180, 181

Context: narrative, 223; remembering as function of, 204; rules of, 235

Continuity of analysis, disrupting, 164

Contradiction: in analysand's activity, 148, 169; among identifications, 152; tolerance of, 8

Control, 93, 255

Convention, rules violating, 235

Conventionalization, 254, 276, 277

Convictions, 124–26; of imprisoned analysand, 279; infantile, ix; and resisting, 153; about self, 71

Corporealization, 242–43, 245

Corrective emotional experience, 290

Countercathectic energy, 97

Counterphobic actions, 178

Counterresisting, 170, 179

Countertransference, 6, 53, 56, 123, 156, 181, 187, 221, 228, 291; approaches manifesting, 11; and empathizing, 35, 50; to father-transference, 118; identification in, 58; and imprisonment, 269–70; narcissistic, 74, 81; negative, 12, 50, 288; and resisting, 170–71, 179, 180; self-analysis of, 32; unawareness of, 12

Creative writers, 44

Criticism, intervention taken as, 169

Crying, 75–76

Culler, J., 49, 259n

"Cure," as narrative choice, 221; as personal transformation, 112

Damage, archaic ideas of, 118

Danger situation, 17, 19, 32, 46, 69–70, 96–112, 149, 187, 196, 201, 294; analysis as, 94; and anxiety, 97–105; and character, 140; and imprisonment, 270–71; and inhibition, 105–8; interpretation of, 190

Darwinism, 213, 225

Data of psychoanalysis, 212–13, 217

Daydream community, 259

Daydreams, 260

Death, 198, 200; fear of, 70

Death wishes, 200, 201

Defense mechanisms, 243; analysis of, 162

Defenses, 75–76, 93, 110–11, 113, 134, 136, 224, 258; as actions, 83, 137; analysis of, 19, 67, 70, 187, 188; compromises and, 62; conflict between drives and, 82; and disclaimed action, 143, 242; flux of, 109; in imprisonment, 265; intensification of, 21; and life history, 204; modification of, 14; motive for, 97; relaxation of, 44

Deficits, presentation of, 211

Deformity, genitalization of, 274

Degradation, of love object, 115

Dehumanization, 234

Delay, 93, 106

Denial: in countertransference, 171; of imprisonment, 263–64; manic, 90

Depletion, 176

Depressiveness, 5, 102, 131, 154, 158, 198, 217, 224; analyst's, 181; empathizing with, 47; helplessness, 46; and insatiability, 74; as resistant strategy, 71

Depressive position, 237, 258

Deprivation, 10; analyst's, 181; childhood experiences of, 176n

Derivatives, 271

Derogation of analysand, 58, 59, 288

Description, 187; see also Redescription

Descriptive-explanatory language, 138

Destructive trends, 59

Desymbolization, 234

Index

Explanations, closure of, 276; complexity and novelty of, 21
Expressive movements, 222
Expressiveness, models of, 56
Externalization, 225
External reality, 234
Extra-analytic relationships, 79–80

Fact-finding projects, 238, 239
Facts, 255, 276; drives as, 225; and fictions, 283; psychoanalytic, 188–89, 194, 277
Failures, analytic, 288
Falling in love, 114
Family, 188; as system, 231
Family drama, 30, 224
Family romance, 273
Fantasizing (fantasy), x, 84, 243; by analyst, 187; archaic, 271; change in, 160; corporealized, 245; and defense mechanisms, 162; and imprisonment, 266; infantile, ix, x, 45, 70, 217; omnipotent, 190; shared, 36; unconscious, 31, 52, 72, 100, 111, 113, 183, 192, 217, 261
Fate, 131; fear of, 70
Fate neuroses, 190
Father, defiance of, 29; transference, 118, 178, 199
Father imago, see Imagos, parental
Femininity, 150
Feminism, 293
Fenichel, Otto, 3, 55, 111, 136, 163, 166, 180, 190
Ferenczi, Sandor, 3
Fictions, 283, 294
Fictive aspect of analytic relationship, 42, 52–54
Figurative language, 187, 191, 243, 244, 249
Finding out, attitude of, 20–23
Fine, B. D., 136, 138, 144, 165
Fingarette, H., 133
Fish, S., 259n
Fixation, 110, 150; decreased power of, 159
Flexibility, 26, 54
Fliess, Robert, 34, 37, 44, 58, 291
Flight into health, 67
Flux, 148; of defenses, 109; of identifications, 151–52
Folk wisdom, 214
Form and content, 131, 135
Fragmentation, 64; of self, 46, 70
Free association, 80, 178, 185, 244; evasive use of, 164; interrupting, 254; metaphors of incarceration in, 268; and narratives, 226–29; rule of, 253

Freedom, 279–80; false, 263; manic posture of, 272; sense of, 295
Frequency of analytic sessions, 21
Freud, Anna, 3, 5, 74, 163, 168
Freud, Sigmund, 11, 12, 45, 47, 56, 57, 101, 121, 202, 222, 237, 240–41, 244, 248, 260, 261, 284, 285; on "bodily ego," 242–43; case histories of, 238–39; on character, 141, 149, 150; on danger situations, 46, 69–72, 96–99, 182n, 190, 270; on dreams, 61–62; on empathizing, 54–55; on imprisonment, 267, 268; on interpretation, 129–30, 133, 139, 185, 186, 194, 207, 272–78; metapsychology of, 82, 136, 216, 245; on mourning and melancholia, 102–3; narrative structures used by, 212–18; on overdetermination, 8, 235; on phase-specificity, 100; on resistance, 67, 74, 76, 163, 164, 166–68, 170, 174, 181, 207, 229; on safety, 14–33; self-reflexive terms used by, 250; structural theory of, 103, 106; on technique, 3, 14–33, 58; topography of, 89; on transference, 114–17, 124, 166, 196, 207; on transference neurosis, 43; on unconscious fantasizing, 110–11; on unconscious mental processes, 256
Freudian models, 40–41
Fromm, Erich, 263
Fundamental rule, 12, 21, 80, 169, 185, 227, 229; agency and, 227; violations of, 270

Game of analysis, 125
Gastric distress, 109
Geertz, Clifford, 265
Gender differences, 224
Gender identity, 149
Gender of self, 230
Genetic constructions, 181, 258
"Genetic fallacy," 189
Genitality, 190
Genital meanings, 99
Getting well, 271; fear of, 70, 168
Gill, Merton M., 3, 82
Gitelson, 58
Glover, Edward, 3, 163, 165, 271
Goldberg, A., 171
Goodman, Nelson, 249, 275
"Good patients," 68, 228–29
Grandiosity, 144, 179, 223, 248; analyst's experiences of, 181; in fantasies, 70, 160, 175, 217
Gratification: in defeating analyst, 72; in analytic work, 10; in imprisonment, 265; infantile, 77; oedipal, 288; in suffering, 71–72; unconscious, 19
Gratitude, 50

Index

Gray, Paul, 75, 180, 182*n*
Greediness, 175, 176
Green, A., 124
Greenson, Ralph R., 3, 37, 58, 163, 165–66
Grief, fear of, 79
Grossman, William I., 12*n*, 82, 123, 138
Growing up, meaning of, 200–201
Guilt, 50, 154, 224; criminals from sense of, 274; neurotic, 190, 248; unconscious, 72, 226; *see also* Superego
Guntrip, Harry, 292, 293

Habermas, Juergen, 234*n*
Hallucination, wish-fulfilling, 239
Happenings, 131, 233; affects as, 128–29*n*
Happy prison, 264, 269
Harding, D. W., 127
Hartmann, Heinz, 4, 45, 138, 167, 177, 241, 289
Hatred: of analyst, 155; fantasy of analyst's, 176
Headaches, 109
Helpfulness of analyst, 11–13
Helplessness, 7, 70, 97, 99, 268; fantasy of, 160; infantile, 46; strategies of, 47
Here and now of analysis, 195, 196, 202, 203, 206, 207, 220; construction of experience in, 252
Hermeneutic orientation, 131, 234*n*, 236, 239, 255, 278
Heterogeneity among analysts, 286–87
Heterosexuality, 181
Hierarchic mental functions, 138
Higher-order concepts, 137
Holding environment, 267
Holding relationship, 58, 119–20
Hold, R. R., 82
Homosexual: love, 94, 178, 200; rape, 175; seduction, 81
Homosexuality, 170; identification in, 115; passive, 145; in transference, 25, 181, 270
Horney, Karen, 284
Humanism, 216
Hypersexuality, 74, 150
Hypochondria, 217, 266

Id, 5, 8, 61, 72, 82, 104, 108, 137, 142, 159, 213, 217, 266; and childhood identifications, 149; conflict of ego and, 106, 214; description of action in terms of, 160; neutralization of energies from, 216
Idealization, 175–76; of analysand, 59; and

ego-syntonicity, 144; resisting through, 69; of second self, 53; in transference, 56
Ideals: analytic psychology of, 35; violation of, 251
Ideal self, 36, 176, 188; syntonic modes of action with, 152; *see also* Ego ideal
Identification, 188; abhorred, 260; with aggressor, 267–68; and character analysis, 148–52; in countertransference, 58, 269; cross-sex, 149, 150; depressive, 199; and empathy, 35, 47, 56, 64; in homosexuality, 115; incomplete, 221; with parents, 72, 118, 179, 271; same-sex, 149; in transference, 122
Identity, 263, 264; actions and, 103; defensive, 175; diffusion of, 48
Ideology, 53
Illnesses, physical, 224
Imagos, parental, 119–20; sexualized, 150, 155
Imitating, 54–56
Impersonality of analyst, 11
Impersonalization, 69
Implied author, 44
Impotence, 235
Impregnation, anal, 200
Imprisonment, 257–73; countertransference, 269–70; and danger situations, 270–71; denial of, 263–64; and resisting, 268–69; storyline of, 257–59, 261, 268, 271, 278
Impulses, 92, 93, 105–6, 143, 266
Inability words, 231, 233
Inactivity: legitimation of, 20–21; *see also* Passivity
Incest, 92; symbolic, 154
Incoherence, analytic, 228
Indebtedness, feelings of, 49
Industrial Revolution, 216
Inertia, principle of, 139, 215
Infantile psychosis, 217
Informed consent, 23–24
Inhibition, 93, 105–8, 258; in transference, 116
Injured third party, 115
Injustice collectors, 274
"Inner world," 247, 292
Insatiability, 74
Insight, 113, 129, 143, 196; and character change, 157; fear of, 12; in life histories, 204, 208; mutative, 66; routes to, 22
Inspiration, 45
Instinctual point of view, 99, 141, 213, 215, 237
Integrative measures, 77
Intellectualization, 68, 73
Intelligence: and anticipation, 48–49; sexualization of, 184

308

Index

Intelligibility, 28, 139, 143, 171, 186, 188, 189, 213, 236; assumption of, 47; and common sense, 214; through interpretive simplification, 122; of symptoms, 108, 109
Internalization, 225, 243, 245
Interpersonal transactions, 151
Interpretation, 183–92, 213, 255; of actions, 224; as code, 212; coherence, comprehensiveness, consistency of, 206, 236; creation of meaning in, 87; and developmental law, 275; disagreements over, 85–86; of emotional overtures of analysand, 9; filling in by, 194; of identifications, 150–51; inexact, 271; too insistent, 22; multiple, 31; multiple appeal of, 289; mutative effect of, 35; and new experience, 128–31; particularity of, 8; personal, 89; and personal agency, 190–93; as primary responsibility of analyst, 38; as redescription, 90–91; relativistic point of view on, 193; second effort in, 172, 182; specifically psychoanalytic, 91, 95; synthesizing in, 143; theory of, ix, 272; of transference, 30–31, 113, 121–24, 207; and transference neurosis, 20; transformational effect of, 30, 56, 146, 208, 209, 279; validity in, 206, 222, 236
Interpretive competence, 49
Interpretive discipline, psychoanalysis as, 212, 216, 255
Interpretive heterogeneity, 40, 286–87
Interrupting, 254
Interventions, 10; action language in, 85; corroboration of, 68; provisional, 172; provocative, 165; taken as criticism, 166, 169; timing of, 172
Intimacy: analytic, 37; fear of, 79, 153
Introjection, 149; in depression, 102; in empathy, 36
Introjects, 221, 267; good, analyst as, 125
Introspection, 89, 123, 143, 243; narrative of, 225, 226
Introspective-empathic method, 139
Ironic vision of reality, 59, 216
Irritability, 199
Irritation, 76
Isolation, 110, 243

Jacobson, Edith, 3
Jokes, 214, 244; multiple function of, 62
Jones, Ernest, 58
Journey storyline, 259–61
Jungian models, 41

Kaplan, B., 242
Kermode, F., 277, 283
Kernberg, Otto, 147n, 292
Klein, G. S., 82
Klein, Melanie, 3, 111, 163, 217, 218, 237, 241, 284, 292
Knight, R. P., 37
Knowing, principles of, 125
Kohut, Heinz, 3, 37, 41–42, 45, 46, 58, 68, 78–79, 121, 139, 147n, 166n, 171, 217–18, 230, 241, 277
Kris, Ernst, 3, 37, 44, 45, 54
Kuhn, T. S., 286

Language, 260; acquisition of, 143, 248; equivalents of, 255; see also Action language; Figurative language
Laplanche, Jean, 140n
Lapses of analytic attitude, 32
Learning, interpersonal matrix of, 286
Lewin, Bertram, 261, 265
Lewis, C. S., 127
Libido, 97; and imprisonment, 266
Life histories, 27, 59, 61, 72, 87, 96, 191, 213; multiple, 140, 194, 204–11; normative, 237–39; psychoanalytic, 190, 194, 203–5, 208, 243, 279; stories of, 219; and transference repetition, 122
Liking, 39, 58
Limitation, as imprisonment, 258
Limits of analysis, 19, 156, 262
Listening, 10; focused on action of telling, 228; Freud on, 28; literal, 244; ordinary, 227–28
Literalism, 243–45
Literary studies, 53, 127, 241, 264–65
Literature, 214
Little Hans, 101, 275, 278
Loewald, Hans, 4, 57, 58, 264
Loewenstein, Rudolph, 3, 16, 58–60, 169
Loneliness, 181
Loss, 224; danger of, 32, 33, 46, 69–70; and depression, 102; fear of, 79
Love: alienating form of, 230; analytic type of, 58; conviction of being undeserving of, 145; loss of, 32, 46, 70; mature, 271; in transference, 15–16, 56
Loving: and character change, 161; conditions for, 114–17, 124

Mahler, Margaret, 267, 277, 285
Manic modes of action, 158; in denial, 90;

Index

Index

Refraining, 92–93, 108, 224; and taboos, 106

Regression, 38, 60, 164, 196; analytic, 197; from oedipal danger, 110; reduced rate of, 159; in service of ego, 37, 44; tradition in analyst's, 44–45; in transference, 113, 220; in transference neuroses, 132

Regressive self-experience, 16

Regularity of analytic sessions, 21

Reich, Annie, 3

Reich, Wilhelm, 3, 72–73, 79, 136, 153, 163, 165, 166, 170, 171, 180

Reider, N., 279

Reification: of ego, 138; of theoretical assumptions, 61

Reik, Theodore, 3

Reinterpretation, 187

Rejection: fear of, 73; self-blame for, 199

Relationships: commitment to, 280; protection of, 176; revisions of, 154–55; see also Analytic relationship

Relativistic point of view, 277

Reliable narrator, 222, 233, 236

Remembering, 129, 194, 223, 252; acting out as, 222–23; forms of, 27; repetition versus, 117; resisting, 18, 67

Renunciation, 258

Reparation, 50, 198, 200, 201

Repeating (repetition), 156, 164, 176; compulsive, 95; disclaimed, 230; gratification through, 30; and interpretation, 189; and resisting, 18, 67, 180; in transference, 57, 113, 116, 121–24

Repression, 5, 110, 217; and borderline personality, 147

Rescue fantasy, 115

Resisting (resistance), ix, x, 66–81, 99, 109, 162–82, 185, 206–8, 245; adversarial approach to, 165–71; affirmative narration of, 231; analysis of, 19, 180–82; analyst's reinforcement of, 11; "attacking" the, 73; in character analysis, 153; in collaborative attitude, 12, 170; defiance of father in, 29; disclaiming, 28–30, 242; in emotional overtures of analysand, 9; and empathizing, 69–81; expectations of, 12; Freud on, 17–20; and imprisonment, 268–69; in manifest behavior, 164; multiple function in, 62; narrative of, 220, 229–34; in nonanalytic relationships, 54; obsessional, 71; oedipal aspects of, 232; as problematic conception, 164–65; reinforced by metapsychological thinking, 64; schizoid, 71; and self-presentation, 42; strategies of, 66–69; technical suggestions on, 171–80, 234; theoretical presuppositions on, 40; traumatic anxiety and, 46; uncovering, 76–77, 167, 173–74, 180

Respect, attitude of, 58

Responsibility, 112; consciously acknowledged, 246; for dreams, 62; frightening sense of, 30; inappropriately assumed, 191; and introspection narrative, 225

"Resultant" of forces, 86

Retelling, 187, 194, 218, 219, 251, 255; through acting out, 223; analytic, 227, 233; archaic ideas of, 118; of resisting, 233–34; second-order, 238; and second reality, 236

Reversal, 263, 267; of generations, 120

Revolution, 293

Ricouer, P., 234, 259n

Rigidity of attitude, 269, 287

Riviere, Joan, 115

Romantic narrative of imprisonment, 264–65

Rules: analysand's, 185, 255; of context, 235; governing narration, 218; of normative life history, 238; unintentional violations of, 228; see also Fundamental rule

Rycroft, Charles, 117n, 140n

Ryle, Gilbert, 225, 265

Sachs, Hanns, 259

Sadism, 171, 196, 268; reaction formation against, 187

Sado-masochism, 5, 158, 160; and imprisonment, 266

Safety, atmosphere of, 9, 14–33, 122; in character analysis, 153, 155, development of self in, 71; remembering in, 194

Sartre, Jean-Paul, 287

Scheler, M., 264

Schizophrenia, 248, 289, 293

Schneiderman, S., 273n

Schools of psychoanalysis, 282, 293

Scientific revolutions, 286

Screen memories, 27, 130

Second analysis, 287

Secondary process, 197

Second reality, x, 235–36, 244–45, 255–57

Second self, 24, 42–51, 291–92, 294; analysand's response to, 56–57; and action language, 52–53; presentation of, 42

Security measures: against infantile dangers, 46; resisting as, 77

Seduction, 16, 68, 294; into adversarial relationship, 168; of aggressor, 16, 59–60, 169; anxious, 197; away from hostile activity, 78–79; by disclosure, 77–78, 172; homosexual, 81; impacts of, delayed, 100; interventions regarded as, 126;

313

Index